GOOD DAY BY DAY

D0589566

FOLLOWING THE WEEKDAY LECTIONARY

VOLUME TWO

ORDINARY TIME:

※ MATTHEW ※

※ COMMENTARY ON THE TEXTS ※

SPIRITUAL REFLECTIONS ※ SUGGESTED PRAYERS

</br>

MARCEL BASTIN · GHISLAIN PINCKERS · MICHEL TEHEUX
TRANSLATED BY MATTHEW O'CONNELL

Paulist Press ● New York/New Jersey

Library of Congress
Catalog Card Number: 84-60391

ISBN: 0-8091-2643-5

Published by Paulist Press
545 Island Road, Ramsey, New Jersey 07446

Printed and bound in the United States of America

CONTENTS

PRESENTATION

This volume is the second in a series that covers the entire weekday lectionary. There have been many books of commentary, suggestions and prayers for the Sundays of the three-year cycle. There was still a need, however, of a similar aid for the days of the corresponding weeks; this need has been met here.

The structure and organization of each volume is simple. The order of the weekdays has been followed, with groupings according to the liturgical seasons or to other coherent units, each of which opens with an introductory statement.

For each day there are three sections:

1. A short commentary on the readings and psalm. Here a professional Scripture scholar derives a substantial, clear and coherent message from the sacred texts.

2. Spiritual reflections for use in personal meditation, homily preparation, or other individual and collective purposes outside of Mass.

3. Suggested prayers, offered as ways of prolonging meditation through (for example) thanksgiving or for use during the day. These prayers are characterized by biblical language.

The commentaries, suggestions and prayers are not meant, of course, to replace the texts and prayers of the liturgy itself. On the contrary, by helping to prepare for the liturgy and to prolong it outside of Mass, they aim to be at the service of the liturgical action proper. The following pages, springing as they do from the eucharistic liturgy, have for their purpose the sanctification of each day, and to this end they offer a message that will bring to light the spiritual benefits of that privileged liturgical action.

The Publisher

N.B. These volumes are based on the ministry and experience of the parish of Saint-Denis in Liège. A very large congregation comes daily to this church that is located in a section of the city devoted exclusively to trade, administration and leisure-time activities. A constantly shifting community has thus been formed. This is another face of the Church that may be glimpsed in the following pages.

INTRODUCTION

The aims and possible uses of this work have already been explained in the first volume (Lent and the Easter Season).

This second volume covers Weeks 10–21 of Ordinary Time in both uneven and even years. The division we have chosen for Ordinary Time is based on the reading of the three Synoptic Gospels. Volume 2, therefore, covers the weeks in which the Gospel According to Matthew is read.

The exegesis of the Gospel (which is read every year) is given under the heading of "Uneven Years." For the even years we simply refer the reader back to the correct page in the uneven years.

In the uneven years a good deal of space is given to the Book of Exodus and the other biblical books connected with it. For this reason we have provided a rather full commentary on these books, which are essential for an understanding of the biblical faith.

We have nonetheless remained faithful to the general principle that governs the entire work: to set the two readings side by side and use each to shed light on the other, at least whenever this is possible.

A reader who prefers to link his daily reflection to a continuous commentary on the Gospel will find at the end of the book a table enabling him to do this and referring him now to the uneven year, now to the even, now to both.

UNEVEN YEARS

ORDINARY TIME
WEEKS 10–21

Gospel According to St. Matthew
Second Letter to the Corinthians
Genesis 12–50: The Patriarchs
Striking of the covenant: Exodus, Numbers, Deuteronomy, Joshua, Judges
First Letter to the Thessalonians

The First Gospel is quite definitely ecclesial in its orientation. In it the Church is given the norms needed for its life and activity; by listening to Jesus and experiencing his presence among men it learns to be the place of this presence and word.

A comparison of the Gospel with the Letters of Paul is instructive in this regard. The apostle reminds both the Thessalonians and the Corinthians of the power inherent in the good news and claims freedom for an apostolate that owes its origin to the Spirit of Christ. In both Gospel and Letters alike it is the face of a living Church that is shown to us.

There is, of course, a change of climate when we turn to the story of the patriarchs or the Exodus. On the other hand, if it is indeed true that the Church is the people of God, how can we fail to seek in these accounts of the first covenant the guiding thread for the history of the Church among men?

From Abraham and Moses to Jesus it is one and the same people that receives the covenant and with it a responsibility for the world. And because this covenant is always an unmerited act of God, the Church learns from it the truth that is at the heart of its own existence: the Church is the sacrament of the Father's love for the human race.

3

The Sermon on the Mount (Chapters 5—7)

Tradition assigns the composition of the First Gospel, at least in its original form, to the tax collector of Capernaum, whose Hebrew name, Mattatyahu, means "gift of God"; the final redaction, on the other hand, is dated in the 80's. This Gospel is addressed primarily to the Jewish-Christian communities of northern Palestine and Syria, and it reflects the confrontation of these communities with orthodox Judaism after 70. We cannot but be struck by the harsh tone the evangelist adopts toward the "scribes and Pharisees." We know, however, that Judaism survived the destruction of the temple only because of the extraordinary effort made by the rabbinical schools, which had taken over the role of the priests.

The exegetes of every age have endeavored to extract an outline of the Gospel that will clarify its structure. Even today exegetes are not in full agreement, but they still call attention to the existence of five major discourses, each ending with the stereotyped formula: "When Jesus had finished . . . ." Each discourse is also linked to a section of narrative. But while many commentators link each discourse to the narrative section preceding it, J. Radermakers[1] proposes an original solution in which each discourse is linked to the narrative section following upon it; the final stage of the narrative—the death and resurrection of Jesus—is thus connected with the eschatological discourse, while the infancy "narrative" is regarded as an Old Testament "discourse" on the person of the Messiah.

The first unit (Chapters 5—9) is made up of a first discourse, the Sermon on the Mount, and a section of miracle stories. The purpose of these two stages is to show the authority that emanated from the person of Jesus through his preaching and actions. Jesus indeed showed himself "a great prophet by the things he said and did (en ergô kai logô)," as Luke too is pleased to emphasize (24:19).

The Beatitudes form the introduction to the Sermon on the Mount. In Jesus Christ the Kingdom has drawn nigh to the poor, that is, to all those who look to God alone for their salvation. The body of the discourse emphasizes the point that the gift of God must be matched by a way of life which is based on a "new justice," a justice which must go beyond that of the scribes (5:21–48) and the Pharisees (6:1–18). Some concluding pericopes stress the necessity of making a practical decision. The verb "do" is repeated several times therein.

FROM MONDAY OF THE 10TH WEEK
TO THURSDAY OF THE 12TH WEEK

The Revolution of Faith

The first discourse of Jesus in Matthew begins with Chapter 5. The words of the man from Nazareth cause a radical upheaval, for he preaches with the authority of God and yet speaks in his own name: "But I say this to you." Jesus proclaims a new order of things, and, in keeping with this, the evangelist proposes a real revolution in the life of the community.

There is a great deal of moral teaching in these early chapters. It is a demanding morality. The face which Jesus shows here is sharply etched: the face of a new Moses who calls men and women to a radical commitment. Nonetheless, the morality is really secondary; it flows from an event that has changed the course of history. The real issue is to realize the stupendous change represented by the death and resurrection of the Messiah, and then to draw conclusions from it. We are now living in the last times; the urgency of the situation will not allow any half-measures. To preach a morality that is not radical would be to disavow God's victory on the cross; on the other hand, to preach a radical morality but without reference to grace would be to overwhelm human beings with their own helplessness. The Beatitudes bear witness that the world has been turned inside out; on his cross the poor man of God has shown that the foolishness of God is wiser than the wisdom of men.

When coupled with the beginning of the Second Letter to the Corinthians, the beginning of this first discourse in Matthew takes us to the very sources of Christian behavior, to an art of living in times of revolutionary urgency.

5

The Church is not founded upon a cult nor upon a peculiar organization of its own, but on a profession of faith in Jesus Christ. It has no other reason for existing except to be the Church of Jesus Christ. Its task will always be to serve the cause of Jesus, to make this cause prevail, and to promote it within human society. Chapters 4 and 5 of 2 Corinthians not only ask us to reflect on the ministry of the word in the Church; they also lead us to discover the ministry of the Church in human history.

Nor is the Church founded on a law. Jesus was not a legislator, even if he never preached anarchic disorder. Rather he called first and foremost for obedience to God the Father—a simple, crystal-clear, liberating call.

To be a Christian means to hear and heed a call which draws the human person out of himself. Abraham was told: "Leave your country and your father's house." The Gospel sets man directly in the presence of God and will not allow him to take refuge behind the merits he may claim for observance of the law. The reign of God and the good news of it stand in the perspective of what is definitive, and they expect human beings to undergo a radical change: "Abraham set out, and this was counted as justifying him."

MONDAY OF THE 10TH WEEK

HAPPY THE FORGIVEN!

2 Corinthians 1:1–7. "Blessed be the God of all consolation!" The "comfort" in question here has nothing to do with assistance of any kind or with trite condolences; it means the "consolation" of which Second Isaiah speaks when he tells the city of Jerusalem that its sins are forgiven ("Console my people, console them"). The prophet's message is of the end of the exile and the restoration of the Jewish nation or, in short, of the salvation of God. For Paul, as for the New Testament as a whole, "consolation" means "the joy and strength brought by the good news and by the Spirit."

Finally, the word "consolation" also evokes an idea that runs throughout the Letter, namely, the sharing of situations by Christ and Christians that

6

results from the paschal mystery: "As the sufferings of Christ overflow to us, so, through Christ, does our consolation overflow." Later on, the Apostle will also make the point that "for our sake God made the sinless one into sin, so that in him we might become the goodness of God" (5:21; cf. 8:9 and 13:4–5).

Psalm 34, which is an alphabetical psalm, belongs to the genre of individual thanksgivings. It contains formulas of a hymnic kind along with a reminder of the prayer which the believer addresses to Yahweh.

Matthew 5:1–12. The Beatitudes serve as the introduction to the first discourse; according to J. Radermakers, "the program of Christian life begins with a call to happiness that is repeated eight times (the number eight symbolizes the completion of human history). The Beatitudes bid us discover a new fullness in situations that, viewed externally, are the least promising." Three of the Beatitudes, which may be part of a primitive nucleus, call attention to the gift of God and suggest that this gift is Jesus Christ. They pick up themes from Isaiah 61:1–2 and Psalm 106:9 and show that Jesus fulfills the expectation of Israel. In this view, Jesus, after having received the Spirit at his baptism, proclaims the good news of the kingdom:

How happy are the poor; theirs is the kingdom of heaven.
Happy those who mourn: they shall be comforted (Is 61).
Happy those who hunger: they shall be satisfied (Ps 106).

In so doing, Jesus would be breaking with a certain Jewish tradition that connected eschatological happiness with the restoration of the earthly Israel. In fidelity to the prophets "he would be presenting himself as the Messiah sent to the poor, God's favored ones, those who enjoy no advantages on this earth and depend on God alone."

But the introduction of the macarisms in vv. 7–10 shifts the perspective. The point is no longer to assure the poor of God's predilection for them but to exhort the disciples to a specific kind of behavior (to be merciful, upright, peaceable). Matthew thus gives his Beatitudes the character of a program to be carried out in order to attain to evangelical "justice" (virtue). Finally, the macarism in vv. 11–12 is addressed to preachers, who will be persecuted because of their message. "Rejoice and be glad": such had already been the message of the prophet Zephaniah to the messianic Jerusalem. When the persecuted man trusts in God and is willing to receive his happiness from him alone, he becomes salt for the earth and a light for the world.

■

"Blessed be the God of all consolation!" Long live God! He has pronounced his decree of grace; in his Beloved he has concluded with us an eternal covenant that is life-giving and filled with tender love. "The spirit of the Lord has been given to me, for he has anointed me. He has sent me to bring the good news to the poor, to proclaim liberty to captives and to the blind new sight, to set the downtrodden free, to proclaim the Lord's year of favor" (Lk 4:18–19). Jesus has spoken. In a message that expresses what has filled God's heart since creation, he announces the truth about our world and our history: Happy are you, because God has decreed his year of favor! Jesus cures, because the word of God does what it says. Human beings disfigured by sin and enchained by inhuman forces are restored to their original beauty. "I came to do your will; I have given them the gift of your word." When Jesus proclaims the Beatitudes, he makes use of his people's secret code; he announces an event that had been awaited for centuries and sets in motion the beginning that had been so greatly desired.

The Gospel is a good news of grace, a proclamation of liberation. From one end to the other it sings the refrain of God's mercy: "Happy you who have seen," and the Church repeats age after age: "We tell you this that your joy may be full." Happy the disciple, for he is a man of hope; he knows that he is called to salvation. Just as there is something that precedes the Beatitudes and the Sermon on the Mount, so Christian life supposes the proclamation of salvation. Happy the disciple, for now that God has intervened in history, man is born no longer into a hostile world but into a world permeated with a promise. Happy they who discover the hidden face of the world; in his Son God has turned our certitudes and evidences upside down. We used to think we had to make the best we could of life, no matter what the cost; now we have been told that life is given to us in superabundance. We used to think ourselves obliged to capitalize on our merits and good works; now we must recognize rather that "grace is even greater."

"Blessed be the God of all consolation!" We are familiar with the

8

world's tragedies, its anxieties, its searchings, its failure, its confrontations. But happy are we, because we know that across the warp of these painful childbirths God is weaving the fabric of his grace. Our lifetime is already part of an eternity that is in God's hands. Happy the present moment in which we are living: it is a groping but decisive inauguration of eternity; it is the transition between promise and complete fulfillment. Blessed the foolish ones of God who are willing to stand the world on its head and make the Beatitudes a force for change!

■

Lord, our Father,
God of all consolation,
blessed are you:
   in Jesus your Beloved
   you have shown us your favor.
Let your Church be ever sustained by your tender love:
May it live in love, peace and justice
   and lead the world
   to eternal happiness.

■

We bless you,
   God, whose only happiness
   is to make us happy.
We thank you
   for the favor you have heaped upon us.
You have sent forth your Word
   to renew the face of the earth,
   and our world finds itself transfigured
   when it learns of your tender love for us.
We know your kindly plan
   in revealing the secret of life to us;
in your Beloved, the first of the poor,
   you unveil your Kingdom of happiness;
through him, gentlest of the children of men,
   we are already winning the promised land.

We ask you:
   Sustain the courage of those persecuted for what is right
   and the hope of those who are calumniated.
Gladden with your light
   all peacemakers.
Let your mercy support our stumbling steps
   and may you be happy
   to welcome us someday into your Kingdom.

TUESDAY OF THE 10TH WEEK

GIVING A TASTE

2 Corinthians 1:18–22. Paul's relations with the Corinthian community
were marked by some stormy episodes, due both to the activity of the
Apostle's enemies and to the lack of depth in the Christians of the
community. Exchanges of letters and plans for journeys to Corinth
alternated, but Paul finally had to abandon the visit he had been planning.
He was then accused of inconstancy, a charge he hastened to rebut
because such a reproach could well hinder him in his apostolic work.

How could he be suspected of inconstancy when he preached the God
"with whom it is always Yes"? In a splendid sequence of ideas Paul's
thought ascends from the Gospel to him who totally embodies this Gospel
in his person, since the life and death of Jesus bear witness to his
unqualified adherence to the Father's will. This constancy is now the
pledge of the stability of the Gospel message, just as it is the source of
fidelity in Christians.

Psalm 119. This strophe expresses the fidelity of the psalmist to the
demands made by God.

Matthew 5:13–16. These three sayings of Jesus have a literary history
which it is difficult to retrace, but at bottom all three say the same thing:
they give clear expression to the disciples' responsibility toward the world.
Salt? This gives flavor to food while also helping to preserve it; in Palestine
it is also mixed with dung in fertilizing the soil. Following the rabbinical
tradition, salt in the present context stands for the practical wisdom about

life which Jesus passes on to his disciples in order that they in turn may bring "spiritual help" to the world. This comparison enables us to gauge the full importance that Matthew assigns to the life of the Church: if believers neglect their responsibilities, they are like salt which has become tasteless and which a housewife would discard in the refuse-bin.

The other parables make the same point. When the lamp is lit (the reference here is to the receptivity of the disciples to the source of light, which is Christ), it should not be hidden. The "city" gives a further ecclesial impress to the discourse of Jesus: it symbolizes the new Jerusalem that is to shine upon all the nations and reveal the true law of God (cf. Is 2).

■

Jesus has just laid down his programatic law. The Beatitudes are the signal agreed upon between God and the people of the covenant. The new world is underway, and God's "disembarkment" calls for a decision that is equal to the situation. "Repent, and believe the good news." The crisis has begun; the time for procrastination is past; urgent measures are needed. A man must either cast himself into the water or else fall back on positions that now belong to the former world. Matthew the evangelist has seen all this clearly. He offers the Beatitudes as a charter of Christian life; he repeats the words of Jesus and does not hesitate to amplify them, so that they may bear fruit in Christian life.

"You are the salt of the earth." On the final evening of his life, Jesus will pray for those whom he has sent into the world. The word exists only if it is shared, exchanged. If a person holds it back and hoards it, it becomes empty and barren; it no longer exists. For the peoples of antiquity salt was a condiment and a fertilizer as well. "You are the salt of the earth." There, formulated once and for all, is the Church's program. The psalmist had already sung: "The just man will shine in the darkness." Now Jesus says: "You are the light of the world." The light dawns, pierces the darkness, and removes the veil that covers things. What an astonishing parallel between what Jesus says of himself: "I am the light of the world," and what he says of his disciples: "You are the light of the world."

"Be the salt of the earth!" Unhappy the Church that is distrustful of the salt: it has already lost its taste for God! Unhappy the Church that is satisfied with an insipid bread, that takes pleasure in compromises and half-measures! Unhappy the Church that protects its children and distrusts words that burn the lips like a hot pepper!

God grant that the Church may share not only bread with us but salt as well, for that is the sole reason for the Church's existence: to give men a taste for God!

■

God, our Father and the Lord of light.
  we ask you:
By the power of your Spirit
  renew your people,
that they may proclaim
  the wonderful deeds you do
  in your Son, Jesus Christ.
Then every human being will be able to taste
  your words of tender love.

WEDNESDAY OF THE 10TH WEEK

A NEW LAW

2 Corinthians 3:4–11. In response to attacks on his apostolic function Paul appeals to his consciousness of mission. This impels him to explain his mission more fully, with its two special characteristics: his ministry comes from God, and it is in the service of a new covenant. The first of these two themes recurs in most of the Letters, especially in the addresses, in which Paul never wearies of calling himself an Apostle by the will of God and Christ.

A series of antitheses initiates the development of the second theme. A ministry of death and condemnation is set over against the ministry of the Spirit and justification. The first of these is temporary, the second permanent. The ministries are those of Moses and Paul respectively, of the

12

first and the new covenants. Behind this contrast there is evidently Paul's conviction of the failure of the Mosaic law. Because the law could not be fulfilled in its every detail, it was incapable of bestowing life. It enabled human beings to discover their own shortcomings but provided no remedy for correcting these. The ministry of Moses was therefore indeed a ministry of condemnation. On the other hand, it had but a transitory role, for through his own obedience Christ brought the work of salvation to its completion.

Psalm 99 was used at the enthronement of the ark of the covenant. The liturgy has kept the second strophe, which is preceded and followed by an exhortation to prostration before God.

Matthew 5:17–19. These three verses are an introduction to the body of the discourse; the entire discourse is bounded by the major inclusion in 5:17 and 7:12: "the law and/or the prophets." The interpretation of these three verses is difficult because the words of Jesus seem to have been reread both by the early communities and by the various redactors of the Gospel. The difficulty in interpretation focuses on the question: Did Jesus abolish the Jewish law or bring it to its completion?

In this connection, the accusation brought against Stephen is very enlightening (cf. Acts 6:14). His enemies accuse him of saying that "Jesus the Nazarene is going to destroy this place [the temple] and alter the traditions that Moses handed down to us." Jesus certainly presented himself as a critic of the law, but criticism was not his main purpose. His emphasis was on conversion (Mt 4:17) rather than on interpretation of the law. In any case, as the Church of Matthew saw it, Jesus had not substituted a new law for the old; he had not come to fulfill but, in a sense, to radicalize. As a matter of fact, it was by giving first place to the commandment of love that Jesus brought the law to completion.

■

"All our qualifications come from God. He is the one who has given us the qualifications to be the administrators of this new covenant." Blessed be the Church that in the truthfulness of its faith realizes how it was born! The Church was born at the foot of the cross, when water and blood ran from the pierced side of the crucified Jesus. In Mary who received the body that had been slain for having loved too much the Church sees itself as entrusted with the body of the Lord. "We have not chosen God, but he has chosen us."

"Before God, we are confident of this through Christ: not that we are qualified in ourselves to claim anything as our own work." Jesus did not choose his disciples after the manner of a master who tests his servants to see how efficient they are. Rather he enveloped them in that current of love and gratuitousness that comes to him from the Father. Neither fear nor enslavement has ever given birth to love. The disciples must experience the emptiness of the cross in order that they may finally discover true love and learn that such love exists purely for the sake of loving and nothing else. Here, then, the new order of things can be seen: God reveals himself no longer in the lightning and thunder of Sinai but in the mockery heaped on a torn body. Human beings no longer receive a law that is forced upon them; instead, under the movement of the Spirit, they hear the word that brings them a new birth: "You are my Son, for on you I have set all my love." Happy the Church that is scorched in the fire of love; the only witness it need give is to proclaim the grace out of which it has been born.

Human beings were trying desperately to find God. They gave proof of heroism in this passionate quest as they looked for support to sacrifices and laws. The Sermon on the Mount inverts the order human beings thought proper to religion: it tells them that God is in quest of man! Happy the Church whose only religion consists in adhering to this revolution! God must make his sheer madness resonate in us until we awaken to the joy of being chosen: the joy of being chosen without any merits on our part and without dependence on some program or other; the joy of rebirth. God has shown his favor to us; how can we fail to thank him for this goodness?

■

Lord, you are our God,
*   and yet you call us your friends.*
Help us to observe your law
for you command only
*   that we love you ever more fully.*

YOU MUST NOT KILL

2 Corinthians 3:15—4:1, 3–6. Is the difference between the two convenants due to a veil? We will recall that, according to the Book of Exodus, after meeting God Moses had to hide the unbearable brightness of his face behind a mask. But in Paul's time, the rabbis claimed that what the veil really concealed was the transitoriness of that brightness. The Apostle proclaims that Christians, on the contrary, radiate a permanent brightness.

It is also possible that the mention of Moses' veil is an allusion to the prayer shawl which the reader wore on his head in the synagogue. The reference serves Paul as a basis for arguing that a veil hides the deeper meaning of the Scriptures from the Jews: "The veil is over their minds." Jesus, on the other hand, has made this meaning fully clear. In his death he has revealed God's love and has replaced the rule of law with the rule of grace. Thus, just as at the beginning of the world God made light shine in the midst of darkness, so Christ has made the glory of God shine in the midst of men; he is the image of God. In turn, those who follow Christ, and whose minds have not been darkened by the god of this world, contemplate and reflect the glory which transfigures Jesus Christ. This is because the covenant of which they are the beneficiaries is a definitive covenant.

Psalm 85. The liturgy keeps only the last part of the psalm, that is, a response intercalated between the public prayer (vv. 2–8) and the oracle uttered in the temple.

Matthew 5:20–26. The term "justice" (literal translation of the Greek word) expresses an attitude, namely, one "that undergirds and sustains a communion covenant between two parties" (X. Léon-Dufour).[2] The Bible tells us that Abraham's persevering faith brought him justification (Gen 15:6): God declared him just because his attitude strengthened their communion. According to Matthew, the disciples of Christ should likewise live in a way that expresses and maintains the covenant with God; this way is the new "justice" or virtue that flows quite naturally from the gift which God has given to men in Jesus Christ. This new way of life has been made possible by the interpretation of the law which Jesus gives.

Was his interpretation a new one? As a matter of fact, Matthew contrasts

15

the exegesis of Jesus with that of the scribes, less because Jesus proposes a new law than because he brings out all the exigencies that are contained virtually in the Mosaic precepts.

Jesus penetrates down to the very root of the law. When the law prohibits murder, it really has in view interhuman relations. Consequently, Jesus condemns not only what we think of as "blows and wounds," but also the source of these offenses, namely, discord, quarrels, insults. He makes it clear that the deterioration of human relations presupposes the deterioration of relations with God. A man must therefore be reconciled with his brother or sister, even if the latter be at fault, before he brings his offering to the altar; for he who goes to court at odds with his brother risks being condemned by God himself.

■

"Your light must shine in the sight of men, so that, seeing your good works, they may give praise to your Father in heaven." Here we have the motive and source of the new law: Christ has not substituted one law for another, but has removed the veil from the very foundation of the law. "God . . . has shone in our minds to radiate the light of the knowledge of God's glory, the glory on the face of Christ." It is from this depth that the behavior of Christians arises. We have come to see the love with which we are loved and the love which has been grafted onto our hearts. The situation has been reversed: human beings were trying to love God by observing his law; now they have discovered that God first loved them. "You have learned . . . . But I say this to you." Jesus is inaugurating a new order that is based solely on his own example. To those whose minds have not been darkened by the spirit of the world he is the very image of God, and his manner of acting is the "developing agent" (like the "developer" in photography) of the new covenant.

"You have learned . . . . But I say this to you." The light that has sprung up in the bosom of the darkness acts to turn over the subsoil of the heart and to flush out the shadowy recesses hitherto unexposed. "But I say this to you: anyone who is angry with his brother will answer for it before the court." This amounts to saying that a person with hatred in his heart has already, in his thoughts, "killed" the one he hates. The crime takes place in the heart. The person who actually kills is not the only criminal; also guilty is the one who indulges in spite, jealousy and scandal-mongering and thus no longer opens his heart as he should to the other. When a man excommunicates his brother, he has already, even if unwittingly, shown God the door.

"You have learned . . . . But I say this to you." The career of Jesus will lead him to the cross. On Golgotha the darkness, unable to put up with the light that exposes its evil power, seems to be once again victorious. Hatred is unleashed, Love is crucified; false witness has been given, Truth has been reduced to silence. But in the night that once again spreads over the whole earth the voice of the Word is raised in a final gasp of love: "Father, forgive them; they do not know what they are doing." A message of forgiveness—words that launch a renewal instead of retreating still further within the circle of malediction, resentment and hatred. Easter morning is already dawning on the horizon of Golgotha.

"You have learned . . . . But I say to you." You are still subject to the spirit of the world; nations use armed violence to settle their conflicts, and we ourselves engage in the noiseless violence of slanderous hints and backbiting remarks to get rid of someone who might hinder our interests. "But I say to you: Happy the gentle!" Not the spineless, the people without character, and not those who are resigned to anything and everything, but the persevering and the patient: those who even in the midst of confrontations preserve a passionate concern for peace. The Light is already making to shine in their hearts that love of God that radiates from the face of Christ.

■

God of all human beings,
Father of lights,
  you cause your word of tender love
  to radiate in our darkness.
Father of all love,
  your Son died from an excess of love,
  but death was unable to ban from our world
  his fiery words.

Blessed be you
  who still teach us
  the heart's words.
Rescue us from our rash judgments,
  flush out the evil
  that disfigures our feelings,
and enable us to follow your Beloved
  even in love irretrievably given.
On the face of your Christ,
  O God of eternal brightness,
  your splendor shines forth.
Grant us so to contemplate him
  that we will be transformed
  by this light,
in the freedom of that Spirit
  whose name is love,
  joy and peace.

FRIDAY OF THE 10TH WEEK

PROPHET OF HAPPINESS

2 Corinthians 4:7–15. What ought we admire the more: the Apostle's confidence or God's power? The human body is a thing of clay, yet it is given life by the breath of God; the vase containing the rose is fragile, but the flower is brilliant in its beauty. "Man, poor man, skinny toad swollen with self-importance," sing the poets of our day; but it is precisely for man so described that God gave his life. This is the man who reflects the divine glory, the same glory that radiated from the face of Christ!

The whole glory of the ministry is revealed here. Paul compares the ministry to a gladiatorial bout. A missionary can be in difficulties on all sides, harried, driven into blind alleys, even laid low, and his body may be filled with incomprehensible agony; what difference does all that make, if he bears within him the power of the resurrection? But why such a savage struggle? In order that the glory of Christ may be revealed in the life of the Apostle, and in order that the community may grow through the influx of new converts.

Psalm 116, together with Psalm 115, is a song of thanksgiving. In it the psalmist recalls his own fidelity.

Matthew 5:27–32. "From the heart come evil intentions: murder, adultery, fornication . . . ." The Jewish law forbade adultery, but Jesus condemns even the look that usurps the wife of another. The integrity of the married couple is something so sacred that if the situation arises it must take precedence over physical integrity. If a man's eye or hand, indispensable though these are, becomes a snare for him, it is better that he remove it. The hyperbole shows how serious the law is; but do we not move into an even higher sphere of seriousness when we consider that conjugal love is an image of the love of God?

We leave aside here the words about divorce, as well as the "Matthean exceptive clause"; they will come up again in Mt 19:9 (Friday of the 19th Week).

■

Brothers and sisters, we have naught else to say to you except that God first loved us! We repeat ourselves, but how can we remain silent? God is Love and, like all lovers, he does foolish things when words of tenderness rise in his heart!

But how can we make this treasure known when we are so attached to ridiculous values? Like you, we let ourselves be attracted by tinselly wealth; like you, we prefer our certainties and habits; we are convinced that the law of the stronger is in fact the best law. In our innermost depths we have not reached the point of wagering everything on the word of this man who said: "You have learned . . . . But I say to you."

How can we pass this treasure on to you, when we have so failed to make it our own inheritance? Nonetheless we are filled with a certainty: "However great the number of sins committed, grace was even greater . . . . The grace that he gave me has not been fruitless." Yes, we carry our treasure in earthen vessels, but we dare say to you, with all the power our hope gives us, that God is a loving God!

You too carry this treasure in weak vessels. Your faith is not your own possession; rather you bear witness in the midst of the world that God is still at work. Words doubtless stumble when we try to express mysteries by means of them; but when transfigured by the Spirit of God, they overcome our clumsiness and reach the very heart of God.

Our hearts, though they love justice and tenderness, are condemned to bruise themselves against the dullness of words and the inertia of selfishness. But let the power of the Spirit enter into us, and our hearts will share in the very movement that is the life of Jesus! Let our hearts lay hold of God's promise, and they already have a presentiment of his reign becoming a reality! When we turn again to the words which Jesus has left us, our hope turns into prayer and our labors already cause the brightness of the Kingdom to dawn upon the world.

Yes, if we dare speak today, it is because we have believed.

■

Let us pray for preachers and pastors
  that they may listen in silence
  to the word it is their mission to proclaim;
  that they may live in tender love
  the reality it is their vocation to promote.

Let us pray for all who teach
  that they may serve the truth.
Let us pray for poets and thinkers
  that they may show their fellow human beings
  new paths.

Let us pray for all the Church:
  that they may carry on,
  in poverty and without pretension,
  their ministry of the word;
  that they may reflect the Gospel
  and inspire faith in men and women!

IN TUNE

2 Corinthians 5:14–21. Paul compares life to two things that are indispensable for living: housing and clothing. Man's earthly life is like a garment which he must remove if he is to put on the heavenly garment. If, then, a man is to enter heavenly life he must strip himself and expose himself, naked and defenseless; in short, he must die, and this is a terrible testing for man, since he has no more bitter enemy than death and would prefer therefore to put the one garment on over the other. Only the promise which possession of the Spirit gives him enables man to overcome his fear and await inevitable death and the judgment that will set him naked before God. But did he not in fact already die on the day when he put off the old self in baptism?

What is this confidence that the Spirit gives? Paul reminds the Corinthians of a recent event in their history. When the city was being rebuilt, Caesar brought in settlers from Greece and all parts of the empire; they were people with shady pasts, and the consul was offering them another chance. God acts in the same manner: he too calls upon all human beings to build the new Jerusalem, and Christ has come as an ambassador for a ministry of reconciliation. But will anyone dare say openly the price exacted by this embassy? "For our sake God made the sinless one into sin, so that in him we might become the goodness of God."

Psalm 103 blesses Yahweh for the goodness he has showered on his people.

Matthew 5:33–37. The disciple of Jesus should not have recourse to oaths; his word itself should be enough. It would seem that the tradition has altered this saying of Jesus. A first adaptation would have taken the form of giving this saying the same structure as the preceding verses, so as to contrast the Gospel with the Jewish law. For, while the law forbade false witness, the Gospel condemns any and every oath. In a further step, Matthew would have added vv. 34b–36 in order to counter the craze, inherited from the Jews, for swearing without rhyme or reason, and in particular for swearing "by heaven and earth," which were substitutes for the name of God. The universe belongs to God, and human beings should not swear by it, since God is not at their service. Finally, it is more a way of speaking that is at issue in these various specific warnings: truth is not comfortable with excessive verbiage.

■

"Be reconciled to God!" We are urged to let the Spirit "torment" us in his desire to reconcile us to God and establish agreement between us and God.

Agreement is a very suggestive word. It calls to mind the harmony that exists among instruments when their sounds and rhythms obey the same laws and form part of a single movement. It also calls to mind the shared impulse that focuses the hearts of many on a single goal. "Agreement" also smacks of laborious efforts; agreement is reached only beyond disagreement that is first acknowledged and then resolved by the power and patience of the heart. It suggests painful dissonances but also the confident power of hope.

"Let yourselves be brought into agreement with God." We may try to hide the dissonances between God and ourselves, but we must have the courage to bring them out into the open. The need is not so much to inventory and weigh what we call sins as to recognize the inertia that prevents us from making our own the tone and rhythm of God. To let ourselves be reconciled means first of all to recognize that we are not "in harmony." When musicians tune their instruments before a concert they listen to one another, but they listen first to a note they carry within themselves, a note that sings within them, in order that they may echo and amplify it.

"Be reconciled to God." Our need to is allow the note which the Spirit gives us to be heard within us. If we listen to this note which no noise can distort, we will be able to listen to one another and allow each player to sound the single note in a manner that accords with the character of his instrument. Then there will rise up from the universe a melody in which all the harmonics will sing the victory of God!

■

God our Father,

what shall we expect from you
  except love?
What do you expect from us
  except love?

Blessed be you!
In your beloved Son
  you enter into a covenant with us
  which nothing can dissolve.

Blessed be your name!
In Jesus we have come to know you
  and we thank you
  because he is our blessing
  for all eternity.

MONDAY OF THE 11TH WEEK

REASONS FOR HOPE

2 Corinthians 6:1–10. "We beg you not to neglect the grace of God that you have received." We might be tempted to add: How foolish that would be! In Jesus Christ God has uttered his word of forgiveness, and the Apostle has been commissioned to a ministry of reconciliation. Let human beings therefore abandon their narrow views and stupid quarrels and immerse themselves in God's love.

"Happy the man for whom I am not a stumbling block." Paul is aware of the revolutionary character of his preaching; he is therefore all the more careful to keep his ministry beyond reproach, for he does not want to scandalize any of these entrusted to his care. But do people really understand the deeper reality of this ministry? In a list that strikes a lyrical note the Apostle emphasizes once again the fire that burns in him and drives him on.

Psalm 98, which takes the literary form of a hymn, is an invitation to praise of God.

Matthew 5:38–42. "Eye for eye and tooth for tooth": the law of talion cannot but shock a Christian; nonetheless it must first be put into its proper context. We need to bear in mind that this law was an effort to channel man's tendency to take the law into his own hands; what it did, in effect, was to introduce the rule of law into a situation of anarchy and to prohibit the infliction of punishment that was out of proportion to the offense. In addition, we must be aware that the Old Testament made in fact only symbolic applications of this law (for example, the obligation of freeing a slave who had been blinded or had lost his teeth as a result of ill treatment); this represented considerable progress in relation to the customs of Israel's neighbors, who applied the law of talion in all its harshness.

Jesus nevertheless moves beyond this law and establishes the principle of non-violence. He urges us not to stand up to an aggressor, either by returning blow for blow or by counter-attacking in court. The need, as Paul will say later, is not to let ourselves be overcome by evil but rather to overcome evil by good. The principle is illustrated concretely by the example of a loan. In Jewish law a person lending money could take his debtor's cloak as a pledge during the daytime hours (Ex 22:25); on the other hand, to demand the man's tunic, which was an indispensable garment, would have been exorbitant. Jesus, however, says that you should yield both tunic and cloak.

■

"Now is the favorable time." And like an echo we hear the prophet Isaiah saying: "Behold, I am making a new world; even now it is coming to light, do you not see it?" But we are wrapped in the same darkness as Isaiah's addressees long ago, and we are subject to the same weakness: it is difficult for us to recognize the decisive turning point in our own personal or collective history. "Now is the favorable time." How are we to recognize it? Twenty centuries have wrought so little change in the face of the earth.

Nonetheless, brothers and sisters, do not let God's gift in you remain fruitless! A believer will always have to resist the seeming facts and the wisdom of this world. He will always be called upon to discern, in the intertwining forces that tear man apart, the tapestry of God's plan. In the wild growth of a history that thrusts in every direction the believer's vocation is to discover those growths that will turn into spring flowers. When others go around saying that everything is going to the dogs, we persevere in saying: "Now is the favorable time!"

Some years back a newspaper supported its subscription campaign with this advertisement: "Others see the dark side of everything; we see reasons for hope." The world may declare the violent to be justified and may claim to resolve conflicts by force; we shall continue to believe that the future belongs to those who form brotherhood around them. The world may continue to build itself on exploitation of others; we shall keep as our rule of life a hunger for justice and a transparency of heart.

They will treat us like fools, but we rely on the word of God and know that hope will have the final say.

■

God, you deserve our trust,
  and we bless you because of Jesus:
while in the world he kept the word
  that cannot be kept;
he lifted the veil
  from the truth about our world,
  and spoke the word that is a folly
  wiser than our certainties.

God, who are the promise of life,
  praised be you for your blessing:
  today the favorable time is at hand.
Your word accomplishes what it promises:
  today the time of salvation is at hand.

Listen to the Spirit who speaks within us
  the words of life,
  inexhaustible words
  and grace ever given.
And let this word that comes from you
  rise back up to you,
  more certain than our failing faith.

THE MEASURE OF LOVE

2 Corinthians 8:1–9. In Chapter 8 Paul begins a new subject. But though new, his emphasis on the collection for Jerusalem fits quite naturally into his deeper vision of the Church. Paul is the champion of an open Church; in his view, the death of Christ has inaugurated the new age announced by the prophet Isaiah. From now on, Jews and Gentiles form but a single people, and a concern for the poorest should give evidence of the unity of the Church.

It seems, however, that the practice of sharing possessions, to which was added a famine (Acts 11:28), had impoverished the mother church of Jerusalem. Paul saw in this situation an occasion for testing the solidarity of the churches, and therefore he immediately subscribed to the Corinthian idea of a collection to help Jerusalem. But it was a long step from words to actions. The Corinthians got the idea of a collection, but they left it to others to carry it out, while they themselves had to be coaxed into action. The Apostle reminded them of their duty, and also, not without a smile, of the great share of "faith, eloquence and understanding" which the Corinthians had received. Now it was up to them to prove that they could be generous as well.

Psalm 146. Like all hymns of this type, Psalm 146 combines congratulations with hymnic formulas that apply to individuals.

Matthew 5:43–48. Is this discourse directed to the scribes or to the churches? When a Pharisee asked him about the greatest Commandment, Jesus answered: "You must love your neighbor as yourself." He saw in this precept (from Leviticus 19:18) the fulfillment of the Decalogue and did not hesitate to connect it with the Commandment of love. But was there not a need to go beyond this law? Did not the Sermon on the Mount water down the thought of Jesus?

The answer is to be found in Leviticus 19:18 itself. This is how the full text of that passage reads: "You must not exact vengeance, nor must you bear a grudge against *the children of your people.* You must love your neighbor as yourself." But who is my neighbor?

What about the encouragement to hate one's enemies? True enough, there

26

is no explicit trace of this in the law, but hatred of enemies was nonetheless a reality in the Old Testament. This enemy is the "fool" of the Psalms, the person who rejects the covenant. At Qumran the "enemy" is the adversary of the community; for Matthew, or rather for the Jewish-Christian Church, it is the scribe or Pharisee, the abhorred Jew, the persecutor.

Who is my neighbor? "Love your enemies and pray for those who persecute you," Jesus answers. Then you will be perfect, with a perfection like that of the Father who "causes his sun to rise on bad men as well as good, and his rain to fall on honest and dishonest men alike."

■

"The measure of love is to love without measure" (St. Bernard). See what trust God has in us: he bids us love as he loves. "You must therefore be perfect just as your heavenly Father is perfect." This is the incentive at work in evangelical morality. We are living in a time of "crisis" that calls for pressing measures: we must decide for the Kingdom, and there is no room for compromisers. The only model for this new kind of life is the action of God himself. "Just as": *that* is the basis of a life according to the Gospel. To be "like" God: nothing more, nothing less.

Christians are not heroes, marvels of virtue. When they love their enemies, they nonetheless feel the sting of that enmity; when they make no claim against one who steals from them, everything in them nonetheless cries out for justice. On the other hand, neither is the Christian just "an ordinary, decent chap"; he hopes that love will change the face of the earth, and he pays the price for this conviction. If he wishes good to those who curse him it is because he believes in the power of the divine blessing; he believes more in patience than in violence. If he judges no one, the reason is that he has an unflagging hope of his brother's conversion.

He believes in the power of grace. "If you love those who love you, what right have you to claim any credit?" If the life of a disciple entailed only the development of human potentialities, what would be the point of the Spirit of God? Love is a wager, an act of trust, a commitment to live like God, with no other security than the Spirit of God; to live without expecting anything in return, whether from men or from God, except for grace that is given without measure. It is to want nothing but to reflect the God who gives everything, without measure and without calculation.

Happy those who dare dream of a new world and are ready to surrender everything in order that their dream may become a reality in the lives of men and women. The Kingdom of God is already in the hands of such as these.

■

Who are we, Lord,
*   that we should do good*
*   to those who strike us?*
But, then, who are you
*   that you should make your sun shine*
*   on the good and the wicked?*
Make us like you,
*   that we may become*
*   the reflection of your matchless love.*

WEDNESDAY OF THE 11TH WEEK

TRUTH

2 Corinthians 9:6–11. This short note, which originally was probably an independent communication, was addressed by Paul either to the Christians of Corinth or to all of the Greek churches. Its subject is still the collection for the poor of Jerusalem. The Apostle tells these Christians of his approaching visit and asks them to get their gifts ready with the help of the emissaries he has sent. Once again he exhorts the addressees of the note to show themselves worthy of the generosity that God himself has always shown to them. It is also out of self-interest that they should be generous: "Do not forget: thin sowing means thin reaping."

Psalm 112 is an alphabetical psalm. Its opening verses have led to its being listed among the psalms of congratulation that were addressed to pilgrims on their reaching the temple.

Matthew 6:1–6, 16–18. "When you give alms . . . . When you pray . . . . When you fast . . . ." There is here a nice parallelism that would be appreciated by educated Jews; the three sentences put Christians on guard—while serving as a threat to pious Jews—against the danger of self-display. Fasting, praying and giving alms in order to be seen by others were characteristic failings of the Pharisees; they could also be seen trying to get the first places at banquets and in the synagogues.

Jesus repeatedly calls the Pharisees "hypocrites," but if they merited this reproach, it was less because their actions did not correspond to their words than because they turned these actions aside from their proper goal. Almsgiving, prayer and fasting are, after all, religious practices which have God for their object and achieve their purpose when God sees them. There is no need of their being seen by men; when they are done to be thus seen, God is deprived of his due place in them. As the Aramaic language suggests, the "hypocrite" is almost the same as the "evildoer." Once again, the intention is the important thing.

■

What is Jesus trying to do? He claims to speak in the name of God, and yet he turns everything topsy-turvy. The structure patiently erected by religious men in order to secure respect for the law of God is abused and even overturned. The evangelists have good reason for noting on more than one occasion that Jesus' hearers were disturbed because he taught a different doctrine than the scribes: "They are changing our religion."

What, then, was Jesus trying to do? The answer is now clear. He was trying to defend the cause of God. "Your will be done": that is the source from which Jesus draws his life, even to the point of accepting the cross. The important thing is not to respect a law, however admirable, nor even to be "religious" ("they say their prayers standing in the synagogue for people to see them"); the important thing is that what God wants should come to pass. Jesus knows of no other rule of life, and the same will be true of his disciples: "Anyone who does the will of my Father in heaven, he is my brother and sister and mother" (Mt 12:50).

Jesus sets human beings in the presence of God. There, in this face to face encounter, the truth of their lives becomes clear. The human

person no longer stands before God in a juridical relationship that is determined by a code of law; rather he is confronted, without possibility of evasion, with his Lord and Master. The human person is responsible for himself before God. He will share in the promises of the Kingdom only if he does God's will, resolutely and without turning back. But God's liberating requirements are radical. He lays claim not simply to man's external behavior but to the interior attitude that is not subject to verification from without; in short, he lays claim to the human heart. He wants not only good fruit but a good tree (Mt 7:16–18), not only the action but the being, not something of mine but me myself, and the whole of me.

Matthew will often call the Pharisees "hypocrites." Hypocrisy is a fact of our lives too: in all the false appearances, in all the defense systems we erect around ourselves in order not to be confronted with the only summons that matters—to do the will of God. Happy the man who does the truth, for the reign of God has already entered into him.

■

As we stand before you, Lord,
our prayer is a sign of our watchfulness.
Put your Spirit into our hearts
    that he may do your truth in us.
Induce us to do your will,
and let the day come
    when, truly set free,
    we will belong to you forever.

THURSDAY OF THE 11TH WEEK

BETROTHAL

2 Corinthians 11:1–11. Some critics think that the end of this letter must be regarded as an independent entity. Paul does indeed engage once more in a brilliant defense of his apostolate, but his tone now is clearly more passionate than it had been in the early chapters. In addition, the Apostle's enemies seem to be different now. At the beginning of the letter, he was dealing with Gnostics, and in particular with a member of the community who had seriously offended Paul; here, however, Paul is attacking some Jewish Christians.

Paul claims that his rights to the apostolate are as good as those of his opponents. Moreover, the church of Corinth is one of the jewels in his crown; it is his "letter" of recommendation to men (3:2), because while begotten amid privation and suffering, it is born of the breath of the Spirit. In any case, there cannot be two Gospels. Either the Corinthians will persevere in the Gospel which Paul preached to them, or they will deny Christ.

Psalm 111. Is it Paul or the Corinthians who are giving thanks? Psalm 112, which is alphabetic, can be classified as a hymn.

Matthew 6:7–15. Prayer in secret is less a matter of withdrawing from the crowd than of praying in "the secrecy of God," the place where the Spirit dwells within us, the place where we come to realize our true needs, which are known to the Father even before we can formulate them. Pray in secret: not in order to overcome the divine resistance by wearying God out with endless prayers, but in order to place ourselves in the truth. Pray to our Father, our heavenly Father, the wholly Other who has drawn near to human beings.

The Our Father, while expressing Christian hope, is a realistic prayer. Even the opening petitions, though turned to the future, spring from everyday reality. On the one hand, they acknowledge that the world is corroded by evil; on the other, they proclaim that in Jesus Christ the reign of God is at hand. They already announce the final victory, when earth will be like heaven and the name of God will be acknowledged by all. "In the Lord's Prayer . . . a congregation is praying which knows that the turning point has already come, because God has already begun his saving work."[3] For this reason if no other, the Our Father is a school of prayer.

The fourth petition takes us into a more familiar world: human sustenance, life in society, evil. Scholars will have to debate a long time yet in order to decide whether "daily bread" is the bread we put on our tables or the eucharistic bread, but as a matter of fact Jesus has connected these two. The final petition is a very radical one; it refers not so much to the temptations of everyday life as to the test which can topple a man into the camp of the tempter. Finally, it is impossible to exaggerate the emphasis with which Matthew links the bestowal of divine forgiveness to our readiness to be merciful.

"I only wish you were able to tolerate a little foolishness from me." My friends, I have to tell you that we must propose a marriage to you—surprising proposal, because a risky one: the spouses will have trouble getting along. I hesitate, then, to submit the proposal to you. God is asking for you in marriage. I agree with you: he doesn't realize how foolish he is being, but I can assure you that it is really love that inspires him. Love has reasons of which reason is ignorant.

God—we babble about him as the pagans do, and faith no longer makes our hearts beat faster. And yet to be a Christian means entering into the madness of God. When you say "God," do not repeat what everyone one else says, but let the words of God himself permeate you; he himself will teach you his name. The Our Father is more an art of living than a formula to be recited.

"Father, may your name be held holy, your kingdom come," for you alone are God. The spouse cries: "Maranatha, come, show yourself as God!" From its very opening words, this prayer passes judgment on us, for the spouse lives only through her Beloved for whom her entire being calls. To be a Christian means giving ourselves up, body and soul, to the reign of God. "Your will be done!"

"Give us this day our daily bread." Everything in us cries out our hunger and desire. The husband misses his wife, the wife her husband. Prayer evangelizes us, teaching us that we miss God as much as God misses us. "Give us this day our daily bread." We do not need God in order to fill up our lacunae; he is indispensable to us because husband and wife cannot live without one another. "Give us our bread": otherwise how shall we continue to exist?

"Forgive us our debts, as we have forgiven those who are in debt to us." Make us live according to the same rhythm as you do. "He has overridden the law, and cancelled every record of the debt that we had to pay; he has done away with it by nailing it to the cross." It is at the foot of the cross that we ought to say the Our Father, and say it with the wind of the resurrection blowing on us. Then we could not help forgiving and cancelling our debtors' debts.

"And do not put us to the test." Do we grasp the fact that encounter with the living God is a test, a "temptation"? Anyone who touches love gets burned. Let God tempt you! Faith is not something hackneyed; it is alternately seduction and rebellion, and it subjects us to the greatest possible testing. In prayer, we who have already been burned by the tender love revealed to us call upon God: "If it please you, keep us in faith; be both our test and our fortress."

Brothers and sisters, we have to be a bit mad to say the Our Father. We have to be mad to respond to God's proposal and tell him: "I pledge you my fidelity in marriage: for better or for worse!"

■

Father, let your reign come,
*   give us your Spirit who is fire and peace,*
*   strong wind and soft interior breath,*
that our lives may be surrendered to love.

With your Son who came to do your will
*   we dare call you our Father.*
Keep us faithful amid the testing of faith,
*   and do not subject us to the temptation of infidelity.*
Give us today the bread of life
*   so that our longing may find fulfillment in you.*

Your love is an overflowing love;
*   the time of forgiveness and peace has come.*
You do not remember our former sins against us:
*   may we forgive others as you forgive us.*

■

For your holy Church
*   we pray to you:*
she is your spouse and your gracious gift.
Let her not lose the simplicity
*   of her first love;*
let the world's seductions
*   not tarnish her wedding dress.*

Let her not heed the voices of strangers,
   for you alone can speak to her of love
   while asking naught of her
   but to return you grace for grace.

Let your truth be her pride,
   and your word her only joy.

FRIDAY OF THE 11TH WEEK

TREASURE

2 Corinthians 11:18, 21b–30. There is passion but also anger in Paul's diatribe. It is the anger of a man who sees the success of his work endangered by the stupidity of men and the ill-will of his enemies. The community of Corinth, despite its reputation for intelligence, has lent a willing ear to the claims of the Jews; it has accepted the accusations leveled against Paul and is perhaps making ready to let itself be sucked down in the bogs of the law. Can human beings be really so stupid? But why should we in our day be surprised? Are not the applications of Vatican II meeting with the same kind of resistance?

The only purpose Paul has in listing his justifications and sufferings is to make the community aware of the soil from which it is sprung. This is one of the great pages in Paul's writings, and it is hard to know which to admire more: the Apostle's zeal or the power of the Gospel. In the final analysis the one bears witness to the other. "My anxiety for all the churches": Paul's anger is that of a missionary, yes, but also that of a loving man, passionately concerned for his people.

Psalm 34 is an alphabetical psalm, usually listed among the thanksgivings.

Matthew 6:19–23. A higher justice than that of the scribes and Pharisees . . . . How are we to describe the justice of the Kingdom, to which Christians are called? To begin with, what does this justice presuppose? What are the foundations on which it is to be built?

It presupposes a radical choice and radical commitment. The Christian's eye must be "sound"; his yes must be a straightforward, uncompromising

34

yes. He cannot simultaneously serve two masters; then he would be a divided person, and his eye would be diseased. To what values is his heart attached? The ancients liked to say that the "fear of God" is the beginning of wisdom. What were they saying if not that apart from God human beings cannot build anything substantial and lasting? Inflation is not a danger for heavenly treasures.

■

"Where your treasure is, there will your heart be also." "Happy the poor, for the Kingdom is theirs." "The hungry he has filled with good things, the rich he has sent empty away."

I, who am so poor in strength, so lacking in virtue, I who am incapable of ensuring my own salvation and constantly fall back into the same mistakes and sins—I am pursued by divine mercy. God loves me as I am. He has faith in me; he hopes that my heart will gradually return to him; he believes that I can indeed cling to salvation, and he dreams of my presence in this Kingdom in which my life will correspond to his desires for me. That is where our treasure is! Faith means simply to discover this anew each day. There, too, is the source of transformation for our hearts. If we allow ourselves to develop a sense of wonder at the treasure God offers us, we provide ourselves with a possibility of change which no moral code can bring about.

"Where your treasure is, there will your heart be also." The promise of God's own treasure astounds us. But it puts us in a state of tension too, for there are also other "treasures" offered to us. We are drawn by a message that makes freedom available to us, but we are also still attached to our old slavery. We are heirs of a promise, but we still return to our old loves. Here is where faith comes in; we take the risk of selling everything in order to buy the field in which the pearl of great price is buried, and of responding to the tender love that draws us beyond ourselves. Your treasure will have only the value that you have had to pay for acquiring it. "Where your heart is, there will your treasure be also."

■

We bless you, Father of tender love,

35

through Jesus Christ, your Beloved.
He is the pearl of your beauty,
  the treasure of your love.
He is the incomparable joy
  of those who seek him without wearying
  and find him present in the depths of themselves.
To those who have risked everything to find him
  this world holds no other treasure,
  for he alone can make their hopes come true.

May your Church, her heart pierced by your love,
  live in constant desire
to know the priceless pearl
  she must reveal to men.
Let your Spirit take possession of her,
  for where her heart is there will her treasure be.

SATURDAY OF THE 11TH WEEK

MONEY OR LIFE

2 Corinthians 12:1–10. Paul does not practice a false humility. He knows what he is and what he is worth, and he proclaims this loudly and clearly when the welfare of the Church is at stake. But he is also conscious of the fact that it is in human weakness and in the ambiguities of life that God's power is most clearly manifested.

The Apostle had extraordinary mystical experiences, but he had also known illness. What was this illness? We do not know, and we must respect Paul's reserve. The important thing is that he prayed to be delivered from this evil and for the strength to work more effectively. But God did not grant his prayer, and the Apostle regards the matter as settled. He has come to understand that in God's hands he himself was but an instrument and that the power of the Spirit would shine out more brightly if the instrument were imperfect.

Psalm 34 uses a sapiential vocabulary to express trust in God.

36

Matthew 6:24–34. Has any page of Scripture been more misused than this one? It has been taken as rewarding a lack of concern and as a challenge to insurance companies. But behind this misunderstanding, is there not the almost instinctive human refusal to trust in God?

There is a Christian peace which is worth as much as all insurance policies together: the peace of the tax collector when he asks God to have mercy on him. It is the peace of a heart that has discovered the limitless love of God for us and has measured the depths of the divine mercy. This peace springs from the cross, where human beings can judge from a sample how far the tender love of God extends.

Love and do what you want! For serenity is not resignation; on the contrary, it spurs to commitment; it becomes a good news to be proclaimed, a peace to be shared, a solidarity to be put into practice each day. Serenity repeats the Our Father; it knows that the Kingdom of God is at hand, but at the same time it takes the measure of human realities. It urges the person to work, but it is not anxious; it keeps telling itself that each day has enough trouble of its own. Serenity leads to balance. The birds sing as they build their nests for the hatching; the flowers exert their magical influence as they sway in the breeze. God takes care of them; he will not leave the disciples of his Son in the lurch.

■

The word of God has turned everything upside down. What seems evident is challenged; shares high priced until now come tumbling.

Money runs the world. Everyone is aware of its power: it installs and topples governments, it is the lifeblood of our consumer societies. Those who have it possess an envied power; those who do not have enough of it yearn for more. Money is life, says the world.

"Why the wind," says the poet, "if it does not sow at random? Why time, if it only makes things pass away? Why the bird, if he does not enchant the trees? And why man?" Why lock the harvest in the barn since grain is meant for bread and for the future harvests that will begin the hymn to life anew each year? Avarice is absurd, since money is only a means of exchange and asks only to be spent and shared. Life is made for rebirth, discovery, germination. Money tends to make men prisoners; it is an enticing bait and more treacherous than a snake.

Set your hearts on his Kingdom first, and on his righteousness. Jesus does not urge us to resignation. How is it possible that he should have been turned into a defender of property and guarantor of an unjust order that oppresses the poor? How can men have so betrayed the Gospel and turned the Church into a propertied class? Jesus speaks in parables, and an economist will find no tricks of his trade in the Gospel. The Gospel offers us a fresh air cure! "Set your hearts on his Kingdom first!" Neither labor nor capital has the final word to say about man, for both are mute in the face of death and of the mystery of life. "Set your hearts on his Kingdom first!" Live, and let everything else take a back seat! God has turned everything upside down; what he wants is your happiness and your life.

■

"Seek the Kingdom and its righteousness."
  God made the eternal Son poor
  for our justification.
  Happy those who are poor in possessions and virtue:
  the Kingdom is their inheritance.
"Do not worry about life,"
  Do not remain earthbound
  when Christ would lead you onward
  to the fountains of life.
"Each day has enough trouble of its own."
  God has taken great pains
  to rescue you from your enslavements.
  Take hold of life with open arms,
  and lift your hearts on high.

The Patriarchs and History

The patriarchal "sagas" are dominated by the figures of Abraham and Jacob. But while modern research has shown the historical basis of these traditions, it has also reduced the personages that fill them to proper size. Abraham, Isaac and Jacob were the ancestors only of small and originally independent clans, and the direct line of descent that is depicted as uniting them was the result of a fusion of the traditions which each of these clans carried with them from one grazing ground to another, until these successive migrations finally brought them together. The Yahwist, Elohist and Priestly traditions are thus themselves the result of a long process of assimilation which, when the nomads settled down for good in Palestine, produced a common genealogical tree that expressed the unity of the twelve tribes and their kinship with the Aramaean people as a whole.

As soon as we begin to compare the traditions of the various clans, certain constants quickly make their appearance. We see, for example, that all of them attest the existence of a promise—of a fertile land or a posterity—that had been made to the ancestor of the clan by the divinity that was protector of the group. Such a belief was very widespread in the second millennium. In other areas we find perceptible differences between the religious ideas of nomads and those of settled peoples. In general, the gods of settled populations were associated with fixed sanctuaries, while those of the nomads were associated with the names of individuals and especially with the ancestor of the clan. Thus the clan of Isaac adored "the Kinsman of Isaac" (Gen 31:42); that of Jacob adored "the Mighty One of Jacob" (Gen 49:24). On the other hand, the sanctuaries of Mamre, Beer-sheba, Bethel and Shechem were dedicated to El, the supreme divinity of the Canaanites, who was invoked in these temples under different patronal names which the nomads gradually took for their own use in the course of their migrations. We may therefore conclude that the patriarchal traditions grew out of the encounter of cultic traditions with the "historical" patrimony of the various nomadic clans.

What, then, can be said about the history of these clans? The traditions concerning Abraham locate his group in the area of Mamre in southern Palestine, where there was a sanctuary dedicated to El Shaddai. A legend, one that is also found among other peoples, told that at Mamre three mysterious beings had appeared to a prominent man of the area and promised him that a son would be born to him. While, therefore, the adoption of the legend by the clan of Abraham contributed to turning Isaac into Abraham's son, we must bear in mind the fact that the direct descent described really expresses only the existence of ties between the different clans. The same applies to the traditions of the Moabites and Ammonites who had preserved the memory of a man from Mamre intervening in behalf of their ancestor, Lot (Gen 18:16ff); when these traditions were fused with those of the clan of Abraham, Abraham quite naturally became Lot's uncle.

Our information is more fragmentary as far as concerns Lot, whose clan lived its nomadic life much further south. Before uniting with the groups of Abraham and Jacob, it had adopted the sacral legends connected with the sanctuary of Beer-sheba, dedicated to El Olam (the Eternal God). We have no detailed knowledge of these legends, except that they are perhaps to be connected with the sacrifice of Isaac. Good neighborly relations between the clan of Isaac and the nomads in the far south of Palestine seem better attested; Isaac shared with these Ishmaelites the well of Lahai Roi, where there was another sanctuary of the god El. Evidently no closer tie than this was needed in order to turn Isaac and Ishmael into half-brothers.

The Bible is better documented with regard to Jacob. First of all, the traditions make him an important person, since they show him active in central Palestine as well as in Jordan. But whereas the Jordan legends connect the patriarch with the sanctuary of Penuel, where a hero had distinguished himself by winning a victory over the local god (Gen 32:33ff), the Palestine traditions center around the sanctuary of Bethel. Also to be considered are the legends developed around Jacob and Laban; these have for their purpose to account for the kinship existing between Israelites and Arameans.

What of Jacob-Israel? The change of name from Jacob to Israel (which appears in Genesis 32) probably bears witness to the fusion of two neighboring clans. For the traditions regarding Israel also locate his group in central Palestine and in particular at Shechem where the god El was worshiped under the name of El-berith (El of the covenant). We may therefore think that just as the clan of Jacob had adopted the cultic legend of the sanctuary of Bethel, so the clan of Israel had adopted that of Shechem. Moreover, the name "Jacob" refers also and above all to the twelve tribes, that is, to the concrete fulfillment of the promise of a fertile land that had been given to the different patriarchs. But it is at Shechem that Joshua 24 places the meeting between the Mosaic group, recently arrived from Egypt under the leadership of Joshua, with tribes which scholars increasingly recognize as not having experienced the events of the exodus.

MY FATHER WAS A WANDERER

Genesis 12:1–9. By the time the story of the tower of Babel ends the atmosphere is one of depression. All the people of the world were in confusion; no light pierced the darkness that covered the future. Would God continue to be angry at his human creatures? No, he took the initiative again and singled out of the masses that made up the nations an individual with whom he could renew relations.

"Leave your country!" The order is vague, and the destination unspecified. Abraham is launched upon an adventure after having broken all inherited ties. Here he is, alone on the road, journeying to a country of which he knows nothing except that God will show it to him. Abraham's history extends beyond him in every direction: the real concern is not with Bethel or the Negeb, but with a blessing intended for all the families of the earth.

In the person of Abraham God opens up a new road: the road to be traveled by all those who, after Abraham and like him, abandon everything because they have believed in love. Abraham's destiny is matched by that of Israel, which finds itself removed from the community of nations, never fully at home, completely dependent on him who alone knows the route and the destination.

Psalm 33 is a hymn. The macarism, or beatitude, in v. 12 is meant for the community; it declares happy those who choose to serve the Lord.

Matthew 7:1–5. "You shall love the Lord your God . . . ." "You shall love your neighbor . . . ." Choose God, but choose man as well. Our relations with others are a good sign of the truthfulness of our relations with God.

"Do not judge," Jesus commands us. He is doubtless referring to "condemnation" rather than "judgment," but when we "judge" do we do so for any other reason than to nail someone to the cross? There are two reasons for not condemning. First, we too shall come to judgment; God will be the judge, and he will apply to us the standard we have habitually used in judging others. Second, we have our faults just as others do, and even greater faults. Who, then, are we to judge?

■

41

"Abraham, leave your father's house." Leave behind you your past, your heritage and your roots. Depart without asking the road, because God's country is one where you will have to sow the seed of your own faith. The land is promised to you, and with it a posterity more numerous than the sands on the seashore, but the coming life will have to take flesh in the suffering your hope endures, because God's plan is to renew everything that is in you.

"Abram went as Yahweh told him." The verb "leave" is resonant with the joy of traveling, the hope vacation brings, the hope of discovery. "Somewhere else" is a key idea in advertising, since people seem to work for eleven months in order to be able really to live in the twelfth. The attraction of the exotic is undoubtedly a distinctive element in the mentality of the late twentieth century. "Leave"—the word smacks of the sun, life, rebirth. The child leaves the mother's womb; the adolescent leaves childhood behind.

Life is a series of beginnings. "Leave" is a word filled with hope: the hope of a new life for those who go away because "life is impossible now"; the hope of discovery for those who are looking for "something different."

But "leaving" also brings the musty smell of ashes. Everyone knows the pain of separation, the tears at departures, the fears that partings bring. "Leaving" suggests a vanished sense of security, and reassuring traditions and habits that must be forgotten. "Leaving" carries the echo of tears and uncertainty, weakness and vulnerability. To leave is always to die a little.

Abraham went. The believer is a nomad. For faith, like life, is a constant beginning. A faith that has settled down is a faith taken back and already unfaithful. "Go, leave your family." Abandon the easy securities. Forget your old certainties about God: they are perhaps only another image of yourself. "Go, leave your father's house." God is not to be found in the past; he appears ahead of you. Let go of your last crutches; go forward without your illusory supports, drawing your strength solely from a faith that is a gift to you. Rise up, for in the desert to stop is to die.

"So Abram went as Yahweh told him . . . . Then Abram made his way stage by stage to the Negeb [a country of desert and drought]." To be a Christian is to enter upon this long pilgrimage of radical poverty. In the solitude of the desert Abraham will come to know the face of the Eternal One; in the poverty of his body, which is stamped with sterility, he will learn that God is life. Faith sometimes has the taste of ashes. There is no faith without separation, no hope without uncertainty. To follow in the footsteps of Jesus is synonymous with accepting discomfort, surprises and conversion. But if faith is always a leaving, an exodus, this is because it leads us to another land, the country of God. The great departures are often dreams that turn into reality.

■

Leave . . .
Abandon . . .
Go . . .
  strong words,
  words that make a man rise up.
Leave . . .
Abandon . . .
  the securities one leaves behind,
  the certainties one forgets,
  the habits one reverses.

God of Abraham and God of Jesus Christ,
  God of the promise
take us from our barren ground,
lead us to freedom,
for you are our hope; you make our lives fruitful.

■

Lead, Kindly Light; amid the encircling gloom
  Lead Thou me on!
The night is dark, and I am far from home—
  Lead Thou me on!
Keep Thou my feet; I do not ask to see
The distant scene—one step enough for me.

I was not ever thus, nor prayed that Thou
  Shouldst lead me on.

I loved to choose and see my path, but now
  Lead Thou me on.
(J.H. Newman⁴)

TOWARD MAMRE

Genesis 13:2, 5–18. Yahweh had said to Abraham: "I will bless you and make your name famous." That was what the people at Babel had been dreaming of: to make a name for themselves, to have a posterity, to possess a land. It was the dream of the gardener in Genesis when God gave him a garden to cultivate. It is the dream of human beings in every age as they wage war on the forces that would reduce the world to primeval chaos. The eyes of Lot gleamed with desire when from the heights of Bethel he surveyed the entire Jordan valley, as fertile as rich Egypt.

When his nephew went off to Sodom, drawn as though by an irresistible force, Abraham found himself alone with God. What the accursed tower had not been able to accomplish, and what Lot was to seek in vain in the depraved city, Yahweh bestowed upon the man of his choice. Abraham settled at the oak of Mamre, at Hebron. According to tradition, the patriarch was later buried in this spot which would become a much frequented place of pilgrimage for all peoples.

Psalm 15 was used in liturgies of entrance into the temple. It served as a kind of memorandum that listed the requirements for anyone wanting to present himself before Yahweh.

Matthew 7:6, 12–14. Because the passage on prayer of petition (vv. 7–11) has been read on Thursday of the first week of Lent, the lectionary here combines vv. 6 and 12–14. In doing so it evidently ignores the important law of inclusions which, in the literature of antiquity, define the boundaries of logical units. The inclusion in v. 12 (the law and the prophets) is to be linked with 5:17; it serves to define the boundaries of the main theme of the discourse, namely, the "new righteousness" which is contrasted with that of the scribes and Pharisees. As a result, vv. 13–14 form one of the concluding pericopes.

44

Let us proceed in an orderly manner. Discernment is urged in v. 6. We must respect the pace at which people advance, that is, we must accept the seeming slowness of divine grace. If "dogs" is a reference to the pagans and if "pearls" means the Gospel or even the Eucharist (cf. *Didache* 9:5; 10:6), then the sense is that "holy things" must not be given to those who do not grasp their meaning. What a lesson for sacramental pastoral practice when today so many baptized persons live in bad faith!

The "golden rule" (v. 12) was already familiar to Judaism, which expressed it, however, in a negative form. The Targum linked the golden rule with the commandment of love of neighbor, while Rabbi Hillel claimed that it summed up the whole of the law. Jesus renews this rule of moral action: for him, it is not enough simply to avoid what harms your neighbor; you must also take the initiative in doing good.

■

Abraham went. From camp to camp he advanced toward the Negeb. He advanced toward the wilderness, and kept pitching his tent on a pilgrimage whose route he did not know. "Abraham believed in God." He set out without knowing where he was going. But that was to advance in the best possible direction, St. Augustine would later comment. The eyes of Lot gleamed with desire when from the heights of Bethel he surveyed the entire Jordan valley, as fertile as rich Egypt. Abraham for his part would remain a man of the wilderness; he takes the road again and keeps shifting camp until he reaches the oak of Mamre. Moved by an interior inspiration, he advances without any other purpose than to carry out the message that fills his heart.

Abraham, father of our faith! God reveals himself at the heart of the desire that lays hold of the person, and this revelation is extended and deepened only in the measure of faith's entire surrender. Faith has nothing to purify it but itself!

Abraham, father of our faith—but, even more, father of our hope! Yet faith and hope are inseparable. We have turned God too much into an idea without a context, an unproblematic certainty. We talk of God as if he were right here in front of us, as if we had seen and heard him. Abraham, on the other hand, rose up and departed in response to a simple word that emerged from the depths of his heart. Our God is the God of Abraham, the God of the wilderness. He is the God who

45

speaks in the empty space created by human desire, for it is there that his promise echoes: "Look all round . . . . I will make your descendants like the dust on the ground . . . . Come, travel through the length and breadth of the land."

God is present every time a human being hears the call of a new infinity, but he disappears as soon as the person believes himself to be in possession of a horizon that is in fact always further off. Adam immediately wanted to be like God; he took the fruit and lost himself. Abraham, for his part, undertakes the long journey through the wilderness in order that he may come to know something of God. "And this was counted as making Abraham justified." There you have the authentic human being who allows hope to rise up in him, and does everything he can to make this hope come true. At Mamre Abraham will soon receive a visit from the three angels who will confirm the promise made to him.

Abraham was a man of God. He "sensed" God. What he sensed was undoubtedly his own life crying out for its fountainhead. But the real fountains leap up in the desert, and authentic human beings will always have something of the nomad in them—nomads in quest of God!

■

God, Father of our faith,
you have put thirst and desire
*   into the human heart,*
and your Spirit gives this heart a share
in the life that streams from you.
Happy those who believe and hope in your word;
happy those who go out into the desert
*   to hear the word that speaks to them in solitude;*
happy those who follow your Son,
*   the light that shines for a moment on their paths of doubt!*

Let your grace sustain our hope;
grant us to walk without wearying
*   to the fountain of life,*
*   to the place of meeting*
*   where you will confirm your promise to us forever.*

■

You promise us a land of streams,
* a land of happiness and peace.*
You give us your Son,
* as promise of life and an infinite beyond.*
Lord, teach us to conquer doubt;
* let your word be our bread*
* and the joy that matches our hope.*

■

Who will dwell in your house,
* O God of pilgrims,*
* who calls us ever forward?*

The man who takes the truth
* to heart*
and sets out with no other purpose
* than to bear witness.*

The man who walks with his brethren
* and does not cause the poor man to stumble*
* at the turns in the road.*

The man who carries neither gold nor silver,
* who puts his trust in your word*
and mistreats no one
* for his own profit.*

Lead us, God our Father,
* to your dwelling*
* where all is peace,*
* all is joy.*

PROMISE

Genesis 15:1–12, 17–18a. Abraham travels alone; fate has proved cruel to this old man who has cut all family ties and is now advancing toward death without an heir. But God is with him, repeating his promise, and the heavens are filled with stars.

God commits himself; God makes a promise. Abraham readies the sacrifice, but only a divine fire burns the pieces of animal flesh. According to ancient notions of the laws governing covenants, this means that God alone will incur a curse in case of infidelity; he takes the entire burden on himself. During this incident Abraham sleeps—the sleep of the just, it may be said; the sleep of one who has taken seriously the plans of the God in whom he has put his trust. But what are the birds of prey doing? What misfortune do they portend? Is the covenant already threatened?

Psalm 105. "Give thanks to the Lord!" This psalm sings of the mighty deeds of God.

Matthew 7:15–20. According to popular wisdom, a tree is known by its fruits. As the eye is the lamp of the body, so the fruit bears witness to the heart. If the heart is sound, a man will produce tasty fruits; otherwise, his fruits are spoiled. The same has been true of Israel: the Lord expected good grapes from his vine, but he received only sour ones (Is 5). In the Church, too, there can be false prophets who speak only lies and deceit; they will be condemned at the judgment. We must therefore produce fruit; the final words of the passage are an exhortation not to be satisfied with words but to commit ourselves to deeds.

■

"The word of Yahweh was spoken to Abram in a vision." Chapter 15 of Genesis is neither history nor legend. Rather it transmits the faith of Israel's believers; from one end to the other the text speaks of God and it speaks of man in the act of believing. The real heroes of the story are not Yahweh and a distant ancestor but Yahweh and the Israelite people.

Israel recognized itself in this Abraham who had no posterity and no country, this man who had left Mesopotamia in search of a country of his own. In the presence of this same text we too recognize our own questions and fears, our hopes and desires. This text speaks of God to us.

Abraham faced the experience of death in its most primordial form: his body, grown old, was sterile. In Abraham's experience Israel recognized its own: filled with doubt by the failures of its history and filled with fear in the face of a problematical future, it asked itself whether its God who had called it from a far-off country in order to settle it in the land of the covenant was indeed the God of the promise. We have the same experience; we are confronted with our own "sterility" in the form of anguished sin, concealed distress, fatalism. Death is experienced in its most primordial form when human beings can no longer do anything but cling to the immediately given and let themselves be limed in a history that is "without child" and without promise. Lacking past and future, we ask with the Israelite writer: "I go childless . . . . How am I to know that I shall inherit this land?"

It is by the action of the eternal God that Abraham comes forth from the prison of his sterility and exile. It is in hearing once again the voice of a God who acts gratuitously and freely that the people of the Old Testament recover the meaning of the covenant, which is a promise of fruitfulness. And for us, too, a new future is available. Despite the contrasting experience of so many actions that bore no fruit, Abraham believed that from his body with its sterility a child of his old age could emerge. Despite so many betrayals on its part, Israel believed that out of its ceaselessly repeated "yes" a faithful response to its benevolent God could spring. Despite the contrary experience of so much barrenness we surprise ourselves by keeping hope alive within us.

The tree bears fruit in the measure of its vigor. The tree in turn remains alive only due to the sap that carries its life-giving power to the very ends of the branches. It is there that the buds emerge which bear within them tomorrow's flower. Into the ancient trunk of the human race God has cut the name of Jesus, and so beautiful is this name that the tree has flowered again. Lift up your head, Abraham! Your descendants will be as many as the stars! Despite his old age

Abraham believed, and "this was counted as making Abraham justified."

■

We are your people
  and the posterity of your Beloved.
Father, do not forget your promise.
If you do not sustain our hope
  how are we to know
  that we possess
  the land you have given to us,
  a new land
  where tears and death are no more?
God of the covenant,
  for the honor of your name
  hear our prayer!

THURSDAY OF THE 12TH WEEK

ON ROCK

Genesis 16:1–12, 15–16. Is the covenant being threatened? The people at Babel had wanted to make a name for themselves, and God had scattered them over the earth. Lot had trusted only in himself in his efforts to find a country of his own, and God had sent him among the Sodomites. Will Abraham follow the same path? Because the fulfillment of the promise is delayed, his wife finds it smarter to thrust another woman into his arms. Her laughter will become forced when it is announced that a child is on the way!

"Your slave-girl is at your disposal. Treat her as you think fit." The leader of the tribe is pulled between the two women. The slave-girl flees and takes refuge in the wilderness, where God is waiting for her. He deals with the past and with the future. As for the past, Hagar must return to Abraham, because it is not right that a servant should leave the house of her masters.

50

As for the future, that, as always, resides in the child that is to be born. This child, conceived due to bravado and a lack of faith, cannot inherit the promise, but he will be the ancestor of a free people, the bedouin whom Israel so greatly admired because they had never known a master. The child will be named Ishmael, which means "God hears." Does the name commemorate Yahweh's compassion for the child's mother? For Hagar, too, the wilderness has yielded tender blossoms.

Psalm 106. The child had been conceived in unbelief. Psalm 106, which is a confession by the entire nation, develops the theme of the people who are unfaithful despite the blessings given them by God.

Matthew 7:21–29. The end of the Sermon on the Mount is Deuteronomic in tone: "See, today I set before you life and prosperity, death and disaster" (Dt 30:15). Two paths are open to man. Happy he who hears the words of Christ and puts them into practice: he builds his life on solid rock. On the day of judgment, when the human person must face the whole truth about himself, he will be asked only one question: Did you, or did you not, do the will of your heavenly Father? It will be useless then to cry "Lord, Lord," useless to point to all he has done. It will be too late. The words are stern ones, but they tell us how serious a matter life is. The evangelist emphasizes the fact that the crowd was deeply impressed. Jesus had not been content to explain the traditions of the elders; instead he had spoken with authority: the authority of a new Moses, an authority which originated in God, as the deeds of power which Christ did will show (Chapters 8–9).

■

"Who will be saved? Those who do the Father's will." "As we see it," says Paul, "a man is justified by faith and not by doing something the law tells him to do" (Rom 3:28). These were revolutionary words which the Church, unfortunately, has too often forgotten. What saves a human being is, first and foremost, not obedience to a law, even a law promulgated by God, but faith. "Abraham put his faith in Yahweh, who counted this as making him justified." It was this faith that made him a "just" man. We are not saved because we can present ourselves before God with hands that are filled with merits; we are saved because God wishes to save us.

That is precisely the good news of Jesus Christ. We are saved because

Jesus, in obedience to the Father, went even to Golgotha in order to tell human beings what God had "on his mind." And what fills God's mind is a passionate love!

"The Father's will must be done." There is no way around this; we must decide to follow this road even if it leads us into the wilderness. Only there can the fountain of life spring up.

To believe in God is to cast ourselves upon the words in which he stubbornly insists: "I am giving you this land as your inheritance." To believe is to be carefully attentive to the route the word has traced out for us. The Bible likes to keep reminding us that our God is a jealous God. Love begets love. When God stoops to us as a father to a child, he expects us to respond as children do. "To do the Father's will" means to choose with determination the way of love.

Those who act in this way build on rock. The rain and the torrents will beat upon us, and the powers of evil will not spare us. But we will be strong because the word and the promise are our bastion.

Who will be saved? Not those who cry God's name and talk everlastingly about him, but those who take the road with no baggage save their hope. "Our father was a wanderer!"

■

Your word, O Lord, is a promise,
  and your fidelity is our rampart.
If you yourself do not build the house,
  our hope will be empty and ridiculous.
Your word is a sword;
  it will judge us.
Let your Word lay hold of us;
  in him is our calling and our salvation.

The section of miracles divides into three groups ten actions of Jesus which demonstrate the efficacy of his word; each group is separated from the next by a kind of interlude which explains the meaning of the group. First come three "sayings of healing" spoken in behalf of a Jewish leper, a Roman centurion, and a person from the circle of the disciples themselves (Peter's mother-in-law). These three healings are interpreted in light of the songs about the servant who takes our sicknesses away and carries our diseases for us (Is 53:4), that is, performs a saving work, since among the Jews illness, like every kind of disorder, was assimilated to sin. By curing these illnesses Jesus restores creation to its original state of integrity. But the citation from Isaiah also sheds light on the way Jesus brings salvation: the cures point ahead to the resurrection, which will crown the servant's obedience. His word is effective because it is the final word God has to say regarding the world. Jesus therefore urges his disciples to commit themselves: their following of him is a matter of life and death.

The power of Jesus over sin is illustrated by three "sayings of authority" that are addressed successively to the sea, the spirits and a paralytic. We should note the nice progression: first the sea, which is regarded as the refuge of the evil spirits; then the spirits themselves; finally sin, which has the spirits as its agents. The interlude for this group points to the source of forgiveness for sin: the heart of God, who prefers mercy to sacrifices (Hos 6:6). In the person of Jesus God celebrates his covenant with the human race, a new and everlasting covenant. This is not the time for fasting, but a day will come for the spouse to be taken from the disciples when, on the cross, he shows the face of the servant.

The final four sayings, which have been called "sayings of life," repeat the lesson of the preceding sayings, while also revealing the definitive shape of the project of Jesus. He awakens human beings to grace and forms a community. His word has, therefore, the same efficacy as that of Yahweh at the first creation. Out of the chaos of illness and sin the word of Jesus brings a community that already shares in the power of the resurrection. The harvest is ripening; all that is needed is workers to bring it in. Jesus will entrust these workers with his own authority.

A Covenant That Is a Promise

Throughout the narrative of the doings of Abraham, Isaac and Jacob, a people is questioning itself, expressing its faith and bearing witness to this faith. These "stories," the groping expressions of a faith that is ceaselessly on the alert and always threatened with erosion, were transmitted from generation to generation by a people in search of God and its own identity, and as such they still awaken today a profound echo in the hearts of believers. Who are we, when all is said and done? Are we still a people, when our Church seems to be splintering in every direction? Has not God's promise lost its credibility in our day?

The answer to the believer's question will not take the form of a miraculous intervention that suddenly changes the course of history. The answer takes the form rather of a few words: "I will bless you." The world may laugh at our naiveté, but we in fact believe that God is caught in the snare of his own word: another name for his covenant is promise. From our ancient earth will spring the pledge of what we hope for. That pledge is a child who will give expression to the foolishness of our faith by showing the limitlessness of grace. This people that is born of the faith of Abraham and the patriarchs will, throughout the long battle that is its history, retain an indelible mark, the sign of its election.

■

God of the long promise,
God of the covenant never withdrawn,
  we turn to you.
Are you not our Father
  who begot us for freedom
  and for hope?
The earth is still a place of slavery for us
  unless your Spirit comes to renew all things.
Our life remains barren
  unless your Breath dwells in it to raise it up.
Blessed be you

54

for the long history of your people
in whom your covenant became a reality,
when a single hope lifted the eyes of men
to the horizon of a promised new future.
What would we be without you?
Condemned by our mediocrity,
paralyzed by our fears?
But your voice made itself heard
and your hand laid hold of us:
our sins were canceled
and our existence was shored up,
when the light of a new covenant dawned.
God, source of blessing,
let your peace descend upon us.

FRIDAY OF THE 12TH WEEK

LAUGHTER

Genesis 17:1, 9–10, 15–22. Abraham bowed to the ground and began to laugh: a father at the age of a hundred! There was something mournful about this laughter, for it was the laughter of a faith permeated by doubt. Enough of this jesting! It was time to attend to Ishmael, since the boy was now grown and, as the proverb says, a bird in the hand is worth two in the bush. However God does not get upset: "No, but your wife Sarah shall bear you a son whom you are to name Isaac. With him I will establish my covenant." God will also take care of Ishmael, and he shall be a great people.

While waiting for the birth, God and Abraham agree on a sign of the covenant: the sign will be circumcision. This rite in fact antedated the patriarchs and was practiced outside of Palestine. It had originally been a rite of initiation to marriage and of incorporation into the clan. During the exile it will be interpreted in the latter of these two senses: it will become the sign par excellence of membership in the people of God.

Psalm 128 is a psalm of blessing. It served as a memorandum for the

55

priests in charge of welcoming pilgrims. Happy they who walk in the presence of the Lord!

Matthew 8:1–4. "His teaching made a deep impression on the people because he taught them with authority." Now these same crowds come down from the mountain with him, and Jesus performs ten miracles for them—ten signs for the men and women whom he has just told that the Kingdom of God is at hand, the Kingdom that is meant for the poor, the afflicted and the hungry.

Ten acts of power, like the ten fingers of the hand which express man's power over his history. In the Old Testament God has already revealed himself through his action in history; now the actions of Jesus save human beings by reintegrating them into their own history.

But who is Jesus? A new Moses? Doubtless, but something more. To the Church of Matthew he is the risen Jesus of Easter morning, the Jesus who is the meaning and center of history, and his miracles proclaim the presence of this same resurrection in the midst of everyday life. The first beneficiary of these miracles is a Jew, a leper whom the law declared unclean. He approaches Jesus, though such an approach was forbidden, and Jesus touches him, an action which caused him to contract a legal uncleanness. Jesus touches him and heals him. Let the man now give evidence to the priest and the lawyer—evidence, really, of another time and place, since the old laws are now null and void.

■

"Abraham bowed to the ground, and he laughed." Just think, a father at the age of a hundred! Well, God can have his dreams, but we live in an everyday world; it's not right to make fun of serious things. Abraham began to laugh: the world can have its dreams too, but too much is too much! "Shout without fear; say . . . 'Here is your God' " (Is 40:9). Yes, we believe we have a mission and a conviction to communicate to the world: Here is your God; he is coming with power and renewing the earth. Yes, in the name of God we continue to claim that the land's name is no longer "Abandoned" but "My Delight"; that love will have the final word; that truth will gain the victory over deceit, and mercy over illusory merits.

How could the world fail to break out into loud laughter? Everyday experience surely offers reason enough: international politics and personal relationships are controlled by the interplay of forces and by power; deceit pays off; appearances alone have value. In order to believe that the ancient carcass of humankind could give birth to something new, and to hope to see barrenness turn into generous fruitfulness, one would certainly have to have a touch of madness. Faith and realism have never gotten along well together. Yes, the world likes to dream, but while illusions are sometimes pleasant, life forces us to shrug our shoulders and toss the illusions aside.

Yet God repeats: "No, but your wife Sarah will bear you a son!" We who are the children of the modern world have accepted its hopes and passions, we have exhausted its illusions. Nevertheless we persist in hearing and heeding the promise that is so foolish. "You will have a son!" There is a new atmosphere about the elderly Abraham; he is still a hundred years old, but he now has a new name that has the resonance of hope in it; fresh air fills his lungs.

The Spirit gives himself and enlivens us from within. With this fresh air inside us, why should we not try to escape from our false realism and begin to love the fruitfulness given to us, the incredible newness, to love life, and to want life to be less inhuman for the human race? This dream can become a reality, and the laughter which once expressed only disbelief, can turn into an enraptured wonder in the presence of the unexpected child.

■

I believe in the promise:
  our God has but a single word,
  and he is mindful of his people.
What long ago he promised
  he is now fulfilling for those
  who put their trust in him.

HOSPITALITY

Genesis 18:1–15. It was midday, and the heat was making man and beast drowsy. Suddenly, a surprise: three men stand before Abraham as he rests in the shade of the oak of Mamre. Like any good Easterner, the old man shows them an exquisite hospitality. He has water brought for them to wash in, bids his wife prepare loaves, and hastens to the flocks in order to pick out a fine tender calf which his wife will serve with milk and cheese. Good for you, Abraham! You have passed the test. "You have found favor" in the eyes of the strangers.

But do you know who these people are? Later on it will be said that the Trinity in person paid a visit that day, and Rublev will immortalize the scene in the most marvelous of all icons. Modern exegesis, however, is more critical, for other countries have numerous legends about visits by gods in the guise of strangers from afar. It is therefore possible that Israel took this story from the peoples who had preceded it in the land of Canaan. But we may leave aside these scientific considerations and observe only the element of incognito associated with Yahweh's visit. This element takes on its full significance when we note that Yahweh reveals himself to Abraham but hides behind the two messengers in punishing Sodom.

"Next year your wife will have a son." Sarah, who is listening behind the door, bursts out laughing. It is an unseemly laughter, and matches the coarse language the old woman uses toward her guests. Frankly, she would have done better to remain in her kitchen in the tent and to think twice before speaking. "Is anything impossible for God?" Doubtless not, but it has been so long since he gave his promise. Yes, but Mary will not laugh when Gabriel tells her of her approaching motherhood.

Luke 1. A child! It is a child who is bearer of the promise to the nations, and Mary agrees to carry him in her womb.

Matthew 8:5–17. After the Jewish leper comes a foreigner, a sensitive man who anticipates Jesus' hesitation and suggests that Jesus heal his servant from afar. Moreover, this soldier is enthusiastic about his host; in return, Jesus praises his faith. The centurion's little address is helpful in determining the precise object of this reciprocal admiration. This man has a sense of authority; it is from this that his faith springs. For, just as he himself commands in the name of Caesar, so he senses that Jesus represents an Other than himself.

The final cure involves the entourage of the disciples themselves. Once more we see Jesus exercising his authority: it is he who enters Peter's house, sees the sick woman and touches her (cf. Mk 1:29–31). The crowd repeats together the words of the prophet: "He took our sicknesses away and carried our diseases for us." The allusion to the suffering servant, himself a leper, is quite clear. This servant whom the hand of Yahweh will take hold of and raise up is Jesus who accepts all human weaknesses as his own in order to turn them into a force for salvation.

■

God comes from elsewhere! Three men from nowhere present themselves at the camp of the man of the desert; once again God shares the table of men. He invites himself; he does not care whether he finds a king's banquet or an improvised meal. "Look, I am standing at the door, knocking. If one of you hears me calling and opens the door, I will come in to share his meal, side by side with him" (Rev 3:20). What an overwhelming encounter! "I shall visit you again next year without fail, and your wife will then have a son." This encounter is both covenant and promise.

God comes from elsewhere. We expect him to come in one way, and he comes in another. We look for him in great things, and he is present in very little things. We expect to be dazzled by light, and we find him in the shade of a nomad's tent. We expect him at the great turning points of our lives, at the crossroads, and he invites himself to an everyday camp, amid the lowliness of everyday things. We look for him afar off, and he is very near.

God invites himself. Covenants among human beings are often based on self-interest, and even love itself has spiteful dreams of monopolizing the other. The partners promise each other wonderful things, but each keeps a jealous watch in order to profit by the contract. The promise was "until death," but time has eaten away at everything. They wanted to share everything, but then both partners enter their own separate tent, enter their own cave and their own selfishness.

God invites himself, and at the improvised meal man discovers once more the fresh and simple joys of an unexpected covenant, an impromptu visit, a renewed love, and extraordinary proposal. God invites himself, and the course of life is changed. Let Sarah laugh! Tomorrow her womb will quiver with unexpected life.

Man establishes programs and gives commands: "Go and do this!" But life makes its appearances when God says: "I will come myself and cure him." Man may indeed be surprised and shocked: "I am not worthy to have you under my roof." God, who comes from elsewhere, invites himself: "It is with you that I shall dwell." Sarah is surprised; tomorrow another woman, this one at Nazareth, will be filled with wonder at the visit of a man of God. Emmanuel will pitch his tent among men.

■

Who are you, then, our God,
  that you take your place at our table?
And who are we
  that you should stay in our tent?
Here is the bread in which we must believe,
  living bread, the flesh of your Beloved.
Here is the bread which we must share,
  bread broken to become your dwelling,
  your Church in this world.
Invite us to your house:
  let your Promise be born!

■

He knocked at my door, my passing guest.
He pushed the door open, this Face I did not expect.
He spoke.
As he spoke, he reviewed my life,
and the barrenness of my joys and sorrows
  turned to fruitfulness:
  with him, something new occurred at my table.
When he departed
  and told me: "Until next year!"

I was no longer the same person,
and I surprised myself by saying:
"Return quickly, my Love!"

■

I believe in the joy of childbirth,
  for our God is life,
    and from our earth springs the Beloved,
    Emmanuel, God-with-us.
The children of men may fall to laughing,
  but the dream has already become reality,
  and Love has made itself fruitful.

I believe in the foolishness of hope,
  for the wisdom of God is realistic.
The Spirit of God transforms our world:
  our earth will bring forth its fruit;
  justice and peace shall kiss,
  love and truth shall embrace,
  and the new heavens shall appear.

MONDAY OF THE 13TH WEEK

CAUGHT IN THE SNARE

Genesis 18:16–33. This passage, which acts as a transition between the divine visit and the punishment of Sodom, is a very bold one, and it is all the more interesting in that it makes known to us the heart of the Yahwist's thought. The passage is marked by great psychological insight, from the thoughtfulness of Yahweh who does not want Abraham to learn from anyone else of the threat weighing upon the city, to the increasing boldness of the patriarch as he derives encouragement from the divine good will.

We find ourselves on the heights overlooking the valley where Sodom lies. The city is dozing in the oppressive heat of the sun, and Abraham asks a question. What is the problem that disturbs him? Are we confronted here, as has been somewhat hastily suggested, by an individualistic soul who is in rebellion against the herd mentality of his time? Not quite that. Abraham does not pray that a few innocent people may be spared, since the fate of the city is already determined. Rather he dares ask about the criteria according to which judgment has been passed. Was the deciding factor the wickedness of the great majority or the innocence of a few? In the eyes of Abraham, bearer of a promise that is universal in scope, a small number of innocent people should be enough to win the acquittal of the guilty. In God too the will to save wins out over the will to punish. A single person, therefore, can save the many.

Psalm 103. In the form of a hymn by an individual, Psalm 103 calls us to praise: "God does not deal with us according to our sins."

Matthew 8:18–22. A scribe steps forward from the crowd and tells Jesus of his intention of following him wherever he goes. It is time for Matthew to give an idea of what is entailed in the "following" of him who came to make his own the weaknesses and illnesses of human beings in order to bring life out of them (v. 17). First of all, daring is required, for at the moment when the scribe steps forward, Jesus is giving the order to row over to the other shore of the lake, that is, to go among the pagans. Secondly, a person must be ready for anything: the disciple of Jesus will have no fixed dwelling and must be prepared to set out at a moment's notice. "Leave the dead to bury their dead." In its harshness this saying makes clear the urgency of the mission. One who has found the Lord of life must not look back again!

■

A shrewd bit of haggling! God offers discounts! God is caught in his own snare. "All the tribes of the earth shall bless themselves by you": such is the covenant promise. Now Abraham takes his role seriously and intercedes for the condemned city. God is caught in the snare of the covenant, for love does not exist unless it has already given everything. God is the victim of his own fidelity, for he has but a single word. His honor is at stake! The psalmist will one day drive God into a corner: "We are the laughing-stock of our enemies; for the honor of your name, save us!"

Thirty, twenty, ten . . . Why not continue the bargaining? "If there is even a single just man, will you destroy the city?" "No," God will say, "I will not destroy it." This just man on whom the life of the entire city depends has a name, and the name is Jesus. Because of him who proved himself obedient unto death, even death on a cross, God will be unable to destroy the city of perdition, the fallen and prostituted human race. "If it is certain that death reigned over everyone as the consequence of one man's fall, it is even more certain that one man, Jesus Christ, will cause everyone to reign in life who receives the free gift that he does not deserve, of being made righteous" (Rom 5:17). God will never be able to forget the appeal of his Son: "Father, I want those you have given me to be with me where I am" (Jn 17:24).

The promise is no longer simply a possibility, a problematical possibility; in Jesus it has become a reality. Our prayer turns into an appeal: "God, remember what you did through your Beloved. How could you forget your own work and the passover of your Son?" When we commemorate the Son, our prayer becomes fervent intercession: "Let your Kingdom come among us!" But even our "remembering" is already a hearing of our prayer, for there is no doubt that God remembers. Thirty, twenty, ten . . . God is no longer to be bought; once and for all, he has lost everything. In his Beloved he has sold all he had in order to acquire the precious pearl. God has paid the price beyond what had been agreed on. The laws of supply and demand are no longer valid; how then can we fail to enter the only order of things that God acknowledges: the order of gratuitousness and grace?

■

God of the faithful promise,
  we stand before you.
In our words the cry of human beings arises to you,
  and their distress and their goodness.
Awakened by your word
  and impelled by your Spirit,
  here we are, on the watch for your dawn.
Open our hearts to the fullness of life,
  keep us alert for the hour of your coming,
  expand our prayer to embrace the world.

May your grace in us be superabundant
and may the moment come
when you shall complete your work.

TUESDAY OF THE 13TH WEEK

PACIFICATION

Genesis 19:15–29. Yahweh enters Sodom incognito. This precaution suggests perhaps that the divine holiness cannot come in contact with sin. In any case, the youthful beauty of the two companions soon rouses the lust of the Sodomites, and Lot is hard put to beat off the nocturnal attacks of these depraved individuals. As a matter of fact Abraham's nephew is quite indecisive. Were it not for God's insistence on saving him, he would still be in the condemned city.

Dawn has not revealed the presence of any innocent persons in Sodom. Lot is urged to flee to Zoar, on the other side of the Dead Sea, while oil and brimstone rain down upon the area. Oddly enough, Lot's wife is changed into a statue of salt; this occurrence is probably an allusion to some rocky formation caused by erosion, but it also suggests that the divine judgment does not accept any kind of delay. When full daylight has come Abraham can see only a column of smoke where the city had been. Sodom has had its day; it will remain in the memory of men only as the city that had been punished. But Lot is saved, and with him his clan, the future Moabites and Ammonites. Thus the universal blessing entrusted to Abraham is already at work.

Psalm 26 is the complaint of an innocent person who does not hesitate to recite his own praises to God. If the people of Sodom had repented . . .

Matthew 8:23–27. "Whatever kind of man is this? Even the winds and the sea obey him." While Israel's neighbors made divinities out of natural phenomena, Israel itself contributed greatly to the demythologization of such things. Genesis had already stated that the heavenly bodies are only creatures and are meant for the service of man; the marine monsters of Mesopotamian legend were simply the products of Yahweh's sense of humor, and the Israelites, who were not good sailors, had assigned them the sea for their dwelling. God alone could control them. Consequently, when Jesus calms the troubled sea, there is more than a simple miracle; there is also the assertion of an equality with Yahweh.

May it not be possible to overcome death? In light of the significance which Matthew gives the sign of Jonah (cf. 12:42), it is of interest to observe that a verb associated with the resurrection is used in the present passage: Jesus "stood up [= arose] and rebuked the winds and the sea." Just as Jonah had saved from the storm the sailors of the boat on which he had embarked, so Jesus, *sleeping and then waking* (= dying and rising), saved his followers from definitive death. This is something to be kept in mind in times of doubt and hesitation.

■

The ship was being thrown about, the wind was increasing, the fear of the disciples was intensifying . . . . The prophets of doom are multiplying, disaster films follow in rapid succession, people grow ever more apprehensive . . . . The Church itself is no longer able to steer its ship.

In the Bible the sea symbolizes the obscure forces that assail human beings and endanger their lives. We have no need of imaginary terrors! We human beings are not fully at home in the world we think we have mastered. We can keep on reassuring ourselves and defending our sources of security, but in fact our lives are still marked by a desolating frailty. In vain do we keep our fears hidden below the ship's water line, for storms are the inescapable companions of the human voyage! We panic at the prospect of our own future and we cry out: "Save us, Lord!"

"Jesus rebuked the winds and the sea; and all was calm again." The purpose of the Gospel is not to intensify our feelings of fear. Though Jesus did not strip the world of its mystery or provide answers for the difficult adjustments of life, he did lift his eyes to God with quiet confidence and murmur the name "Father." He invited his disciples, not to return to solid land but rather to continue the adventure of life in a spirit of faith.

We know, too, that a passenger has boarded our ship. His presence is hidden from many, but he has taken the tiller and will lead the human race to a safe harbor!

■

Lord, save us!
If you do not make our cause your own,
    how can we abide?
If you were to forget us,
    the abyss would close over us.
Arise in our defense!
O Lord of time,
    take the tiller of our history
    and guide us to a safe harbor.

WEDNESDAY OF THE 13TH WEEK

A CHILD OF OLD AGE

Genesis 21:3, 8–21. Isaac: "May God smile on the child!" Ishmael: "God has answered!" An attentive ear, a benevolent smile! Isaac and Ishmael are the children of the future, for God himself watches over them. The entire narrative is concerned with the future. First, there is Sarah, who is wholly preoccupied with the future of Isaac. At the very moment of rejoicing over the weaning of her child, she takes offense at the affection shown by Abraham to the servant woman and to the child born of their union. Sarah cannot forget that Ishmael is the elder, even though he is still at the age of innocent play. Therefore she has the child sent away, and Yahweh approves, because it is Isaac who is the child of the promise.

But what is to be the future of Ishmael, this little boy whom his mother sets down under a bush, this little boy who is dying of thirst and exposed to the hungry gaze of the buzzards? What future is there for Hagar and Ishmael over whom the shadow of death is already hovering? Why, quite simply, the future God has in store! The child is destined not to die in the wilderness of Beer-sheba but to become the father of a great people which, like Israel, will be nomadic—but not after the manner of Israel. Ishmael is the man of the steppe, living by his wits and by pillage; he is the bedouin. And when he marries an Egyptian woman, he will have moved even a bit further away from the people of the covenant.

Psalm 34 is classified among the thanksgivings. It serves to describe the protection which God has promised to the son of the servant woman.

Matthew 8:28–34. After having tracked down the powers of death in their marine lair, Jesus lands on pagan soil. He is once again confronted by uncleanness: the tombs in which the demoniacs live, and the presence of a herd of swine. Once again he will get the better of them, and the swine will end by joining the evil spirits in the sea.

In addition, the incident of the demoniacs locates this narrative in the line of the preceding. For the expression "before the time" is an allusion to the final judgment at which all demons will be reduced to impotence. Here, then, as in the episode of the calming of the storm, there is an anticipation of Jesus' victory over death. It is to be noted that the pagans are not yet ready to accept Jesus. For the moment, the only important thing to them is the loss of the swine. But they do feel challenged in their innermost depths.

■

Abraham and Sarah had become resigned. They had even made the necessary provisions: Sarah had, according to custom, given her servant girl to her husband in order that he might have some posterity. They still dreamed at times, but they knew the dream was an impossible one. Their faces had grown wrinkled with the years, and there came a point when life was simply a matter of living on.

They were on their way, resigned, to death. But one day three visitors had said: "We shall visit you again next year without fail, and your wife will then have a son." Sarah, who was quite familiar with the laws governing life, had had a good laugh. But then the unexpected child had come! They had to improvise a cradle in which the child began to sleep and cry and soon to smile as well. The promise had sounded utopian, but it became more real than reality; the child of the free woman astonished the entire household.

Earth too had become resigned: the only posterity it would know

would be that of the slave woman. It was necessary to choose the lesser of the two evils: to remain barren or to give the slave woman to the husband. The earth had adopted the fruit of this compromise: mistreated love, justice of a barely minimal kind, brotherhood constantly undermined. One dictatorship succeeds another, each more refined than its predecessor. Self-interest, individual or collective, is the norm of behavior in human relations. Intolerance wins out over mutual respect. Earth had to settle for having children through a slave woman.

Then one day the wife had a child. With his coming the whole flavor of the human changes, for after his astonishing arrival he is henceforth new beginning, life, light, salt, leaven in the human mass, the blood of God at the heart of light, Emmanuel, God-with-us, the Son of the promise and of freedom. The children of the compromise, the children of the slave woman, grow anxious: "What do you want with us, Son of God?" They no longer belong to the household, and their inheritance is threatened. The Child of the promise is born despite all indications to the contrary. As a result of his actions and words a new existence lays hold of us, and the horizon opens up to infinity. "To all who did accept him he gave power to become children of God." What a dizzying prospect is now offered to everyone: to be born of God! Now we are the children of the free woman, for ever since the day when the legitimate Child rose alive from the tomb, the children of darkness have been expelled from the house of Abraham. Peace, justice, truth, love are no longer a laughable promise, but can be born and become real. Earth can then rejoice over the child she holds on her knees and can claim her rights as a free woman.

■

Faithful God, our Father,
most holy God, who loves us,
blessed be you:
   for you keep your promise
   and your Spirit makes the earth fruitful.
You place in our bodies the seed of happiness
and rescue us from our sad necessities:

mediocrity and sin
are no longer our gift to our descendants.
Your Spirit brings us to birth
as men and women of the promise,
as children of freedom,
as heirs of grace.
Those who believe in your only Son
bear names that come from you;
they belong to your household
and can say
what only a legitimate child may say:
"Father!"
Through your Spirit, come again
and make our old age fruitful;
then our wrinkles will radiate
the joy of the new-born.

■

God, you open the future to us:
blessed be your name!
Reveal to those who laugh at such folly
the joy of a heart that finds itself loved.
Grant to the satisfied
the desire of new departures
and the grace of new discoveries.
Point out to those who have deserted you
the path to your ever-open arms.
Blessed be you, Father,
for calling us!
Grant us to advance without halting
until the day when we shall exist in you,
united in your covenant,
begotten by your gracious love.

LIMITLESSNESS

Genesis 22:1–13, 15–19. "Take your son, your only child Isaac, whom you love." Is it even possible to imagine such a thing as having to slay the child of the promise? What is this new test God is imposing on Abraham? The man has already had to break with his past; must he also destroy his future on an altar of stone? A deathly silence hovers over the patriarch's journey. A three day trek, its silence broken only by a question from the child: "Where is the lamb for the burnt offering?" A three day trek during which Abraham meditates on the impenetrability of God.

"Abraham saw a ram caught by its horns in a bush." He offered this to God in Isaac's place, and everyone was all smiles again. Yahweh smiled at the child, and the child smiled at his father. The covenant was now definitively sealed—sealed by a smile, the smile of grace. Isaac is indeed the fruit of the divine good will; he owes his entire existence to God, just as Ishmael did. Later on, when Jesus sends his disciples to prepare for Passover, they find a room all made ready (Mk 14:15). They say to one another: "Where is the lamb for the burnt offering?" and they see Jesus stretched out on the wood. On that day, again by pure grace, the covenant will be sealed in the blood of the Son.

Psalm 115. The verses chosen are part of a hymn of thanksgiving. They tell of the distress in which the psalmist had found himself.

Matthew 9:1–8. If we want to understand the point being made by Matthew in this passage, it is worthwhile to trace its literary development as well as to compare it with the same pericope in the other Synoptics (especially Mk 2:1–12). The pericope must originally have told only of the cure of the paralytic; at a later point the section on the forgiveness of sins was introduced. Due to this addition the miracle became a sign, enduing him who commanded the sea and the demons with the power to forgive sins as well.

In point of fact, there really is an investiture here in Matthew. He who forgives sins is the Son of Man. This title obviously recalls the enthronement scene in Daniel 7, during which the Ancient of Days bestows an eternal sovereignty upon the Son of Man. In Matthew's view, then, Jesus has not usurped the authority he claims; on the contrary, God himself has conferred it on him by raising him from the dead so that he in turn may "awaken" (= raise up) paralytics and all human beings who are the prey of the powers of darkness.

The ending of Matthew's pericope is no less noteworthy, since it records the admiration felt by the crowd for the God who "gives such power to men." There is no longer question solely of the Son of Man, but of "men." According to the evangelist of the Church the power to forgive sins has been entrusted not only to the Son of Man but to the entire Church, which is the depository of this power.

■

"Abraham named the son born to him Isaac, the son to whom Sarah had given birth . . . .'Take your son,' God said, 'your only child Isaac whom you love, and go to the land of Moriah.' "

Why give the child at all if he must be immolated on the altar of sacrifice? Why the promise, if the child must be destroyed under the knife? Why? The question is never answered. When Abraham raises the knife, no one is there to echo aloud the questions that weigh down his heart. No one is there to be troubled by the distress of this lonely man who has left his native land and his possessions simply because God told him to. Has Abraham, then, lost everything—his past and now his future in the person of the child who kneels on the wood? What kind of God is this? Is the promise to remain forever an unfulfillable dream? Just when it seems to have been fulfilled, it is once more removed far from man! Is God truly the Lord of the covenant?

The Israelite people always saw itself in young Isaac. The child of sacrifice was the chosen people, a people dedicated to God. When Abraham raises his knife, God shows him the ram; God thus saves the boy's life and restores life to his people as well. As a people saved by God, Israel knows itself to be the child of the divine good will, the child of grace. "Take your son, your only child Isaac, whom you love, and go to . . . a mountain I shall make known to you." A day will come when God himself climbs the hill, leading his only Son to the sacrifice. On Mount Moriah God will once again show that he is Promise; the cross erected on Golgotha will make it clear that for God the covenant is not an empty, hollow word, for it costs him life itself. Jesus, the Son of the Promise, climbed that other mountain. He did so out of love, in order to restore their original beauty to human beings and the world. In order to raise up human beings who are crushed by too much wretchedness and paralyzed by inhuman forces, Jesus stretched himself out on the wood. The cross raised over the world is the irradicable sign that God makes peace with human beings: "Your sins are forgiven."—"With God on our side who can be against us? . . . God did not spare his own Son" (Rom 8:31–32).

Brothers and sisters, your faith involves you in the world of the limitless. God will ask you what is closest to your heart, what is truly the "only" thing for you. You will have to strip yourself of what is useless and offer in sacrifice that to which your heart clings and even that which God has given you in fulfillment of his promise. But in its place you will find a limitless love that embraces even the foolishness of the cross! "I swear to you," God says, "that I will load you down with blessings!"

■

Brethren, if God is for us, who will be against us?
Who will accuse us,
  now that Jesus Christ has died and risen?
May God remove our sins from us
and raise us up by his grace;
  then, standing erect, we will sing
  of his covenant and his promise.

■

You know well, O God, what it costs to see
  one's beloved die.
You make Easter morning dawn
  over the darkness of Golgotha.
Allow us not to cherish life
  without realizing the price paid for it
  and without abandoning it into your hands.

■

It is good for us to give thanks to you,
  God of Abraham and God of Jesus Christ,
  God of the new and everlasting covenant!
It is good for you to praise you
  through your beloved Son, Jesus Christ!
He offered himself to you
  on the hill of Calvary
  and you raised him up to the light of Easter.
He calls us to join him on the mountain,
  and his light forecasts
  the land promised to all our exoduses.
May the Church rejoice in his word!
May human beings have joy,
  enlightened by his love!
May earth and heaven rejoice
  as they sing of you without ceasing!

FRIDAY OF THE 13TH WEEK

FATHERS OF THE CHURCH

Genesis 23:1–4, 19; 24:1–8, 62–67. Abraham grew very old, but he remained a stranger in the land of Canaan. Was he to die without having seen the divine promises fulfilled? No, for Sarah had just died, and her husband negotiated the purchase of a cave to be used for the family burial place. In death the patriarchs were finally to become citizens of the land which God had never ceased to promise to them.

But before joining Sarah in the cave of Mach-pelah, Abraham still had to arrange the marriage of his son. Only then could he rest peacefully, for then there would again be a wife to ensure the family line. The servant's journey constitutes one of the finest pages in the epic of Abraham, but unfortunately the lectionary has mutilated the story to a large extent by retaining only the servant's oath and the various instructions given by Abraham. The steward is to betake himself to the patriarch's tribe and bring back a wife for Isaac. In no case, however, is he to take the young man off with him to his cousins, and if the young woman refuses to

73

accompany the servant, the latter is released from his oath. The mission expresses both the acknowledgment of a kinship of the Israelite tribes with the Arameans and a formal determination not to return whence they had come, not to turn back. The promises of God are concerned with the future, not with the past.

Psalm 106. The verses chosen would not suggest that this is a national confession, which in fact it is. Vv. 1–2 make an antiphon for a hymn, while v. 3 has the general form of a macarism or beatitude.

Matthew 9:9–13. These few verses reveal the care with which the Gospel was written. A citation had concluded the portrait sketched by the three cure sayings in 8:2–15; it pointed to Jesus as the suffering servant who took upon himself the burden of human weaknesses. This citation was then followed by a listing of the qualities that anyone wishing to become a disciple of Christ must have (vv. 18–22).

The authority sayings (8:23—9:8), which have already been the subject of comment, are now succeeded by Jesus' call to Matthew the tax collector: Jesus has come to save not the just but sinners. Moreover, an attachment to rituals, however creditable, must never be allowed to frustrate the higher commandment of mercy.

Finally, by means of this citation from Hosea, Matthew, perhaps with some excessively rigoristic Christians in mind, makes clear the true nature of the Church: the Church is not a sect of the perfect but a family of sinners, from among whom Jesus does not hesitate to choose his disciples.

■

Happy Abraham! He arose and departed because of the trust he placed in a word, and God blessed him, giving him a child as pledge to encourage his hope. Holy Abraham, father of our faith! Happy he who arises and sets out with the grace of the Lord as his sole baggage. Happy the poor! The call that came down from the hills of Galilee was truly revolutionary! The Chosen One of God traversed the land in search of the poor whom nothing would cause to turn back. Happy Matthew, who recognized the one bestowing a favor on him! Saint Matthew, father of our faith and spokesman of him who has the words of grace!

A seedy official, a customs inspector whose only thought was to fill

his own pockets and who taxed each individual as he felt like it in order to recover the money he had to pay out to the occupation authorities for a tax booth: such is the man Jesus calls to arise and follow him. In addition, it is with such people as this that he begins to sit at table. And this among Orientals who, if anyone, have a feeling for meals and what they signify! It is with the unimportant people that Jesus shares his food! Happy the poor! Those whom men have judged unworthy of the covenant are called to the table of God. Those whom "good" people considered to be outcasts from the Kingdom have become citizens of heaven.

Happy the "outcast" Church! Like Abraham, it will be a people of journeyers. A nomad people, a people of the desert where to stop is to die and where a little water is a fountain of life. A people of the promise: from its old age the child of hope will be born. And when the hour of final encounter arrives, God will give it a field as foretaste of the promised land. Happy the Church of Abraham!

Happy the band that accompanies Jesus, the Church of tax collectors, women, sinners and children, the Church of unimportant people and those excluded from the religious systems. Happy the Church of Matthew, a festive table to which God invites himself!

God had taken a man away from his own country; he had promised an old man that all the nations of the earth would bless themselves by him. What foolishness in the eyes of men! Jesus called the tax collector; he hobnobbed with a bunch of people that were not "very Catholic"; he wanted to bring everyone on board so that they might change their manner of life. What a scandal to the orthodox and the "upright"!

Happy the Church born of that foolishness: the covenant is its life!

Happy the Church that preaches this scandal: the word is its reason for existing!

■

The Kingdom is grace and superabundant tender love!
The word that calls,
a Communion table.
"Come, follow me": the invitations are out:

will there be a crowd at God's banquet?

O Word of grace that cares not
  for the proprieties,
  Lord, have mercy!
O covenant Word that opens a new future,
  Christ, have mercy!
O Word of God and Gospel of the Church,
  Lord, have mercy!

■

Lord, you give
  your light and your word
  to those who seek them.
Your Kingdom belongs to the poor and the sinner.
Do not send us away empty-handed,
  but sit yourself at our table
  and fill us in Jesus Christ,
  who is your Word of grace for all times.

■

For Rebekah

A man came to you
out in the fields,
a man before whom you hid your face!
In his tent he looked at you;
in the empty place within himself
he loved you!
For twenty years your love
was barren
and you became acquainted with the infinite delays
of the God of the living.
Crafty woman,
mother of Jacob the beloved,
a wife like other wives,
mother of a persecuted people:
are you not our mother too?

Mother of Jacob
and mother of Israel.
Crafty woman,
veiled woman.

SATURDAY OF THE 13TH WEEK

INTOXICATION

Genesis 27:1–5, 15–29. We see here a family that has no sympathetic qualities left; its members watch one another, are jealous of one another, lie to one another. Esau's physical appearance is unattractive; the lies of Rebekah and Jacob border on blasphemy (v. 20b). It is not surprising therefore that the story ends with the scattering of the family, as Jacob is obliged to go to Mesopotamia to escape his older brother.

This story has a bit of everything: the social and the political, the cosmic and the religious, even the magical. The social, because Esau inevitably suggests the woodsman, and Jacob the more refined sedentary man. The cosmic, because the brutal woodsman suggests the threat which the forces of chaos always hold over man's head, while the townsman suggests the creative effort of civilization on the march. The magical, finally, is indicated by the good meal the old man must enjoy in order to transmit his paternal blessing under the proper conditions, and also by the idea that Rebekah can take upon herself the curse which her younger son may incur (v. 13). The religious element is also present because despite the powers of magic, human intrigues and the laws of succession, God's freedom remains intact. He gives his blessing to whom he wishes. The promise of a land is accompanied by a promise of hegemony, because in the time of David the priority of the younger over the elder will justify the supremacy of the Jewish monarchy over the Edomites, who are the descendants of Esau. In like manner, the efforts of Rebekah call to mind the struggle of Bathsheba to ensure that Solomon will inherit the throne of his father David.

Psalm 135 urges thanksgiving for the great deeds of God who has chosen the twelve tribes of Jacob.

Matthew 9:14–17. Authority sayings! New sayings! Who is this Jesus that

77

he forgives the paralytic his sins? He is the physician who attends to the illnesses of human beings, the servant who will overcome death by means of the cross. In order to express its idea of God the Bible also uses the allegory of marriage.

In Jesus God has definitively espoused the human race; henceforth nothing will be as it was before. But have you ever seen people weep at a wedding, except for joy? Yet the disciples will someday experience affliction, because Jesus will have shed his blood as the price to be paid for the purification of the Church.

There are new sayings here, and a kind of language that is unsettling. There is no doubt that the meals Jesus took with tax collectors must have set the tongues of "proper folk" wagging. Is it possible that this Jesus has come from God when he does things like this? Doesn't he see that these people are sinners? Is it right that he should cultivate their company? These meals of Jesus, which were gestures of welcome and reconciliation, are no less challenging than the Beatitudes.

■

Your teacher is a glutton!

As we follow the trail of Jesus through the Gospels we move from meal to meal. So much attention has been paid to the Supper on Holy Thursday that we sometimes forget this lengthy series of encounters around a table. These meals of Jesus give rise to surprise and scandal in those around him. He eats with anyone at all, and even with those whom society rejects! There is something here that deserves sharp rebuke from religious people.

Even the disciples of John the Baptist protest. Their master has just been put to death, and they are in mourning. They are shocked by the festive spirit that surrounds the One sent as he frequents the village squares and the meals of tax collectors.

Brothers and sisters, I know, as you do, the burden that weighs down the world. It seems to give us the right to wear perpetual mourning. And yet Jesus answers John's disciples by saying: "Surely the bridegroom's attendants would never think of mourning as long as the bridegroom is still with them?" Our world is dying of asphyxiation; its childless old age has become a morbid condition.

What is the point of patching an old garment with new material? There is only one solution: turn the world inside out. We must learn once again to dance to the crazy rhythm of our God.

We who are sinners yet are loved to the point of folly, we who are guests at a wedding that is our own: we have the future of the world in our hands! It is a future in which only meditation on the impossible and the display of tender love will lift us beyond the world of our death masks. It is of no importance that people will look upon us as simple-minded. It is not new wine that sets us dreaming; it is the fervor of the Spirit that sets our heads spinning!

"The time will come for the bridegroom to be taken away from them, and then they will fast." Yes, we fast today, but we do not do so because we contemn life; our real reason is that we love life too much! We fast because the vast desire that excites us will never be satisfied. We fast because tenderness and love are still too besmirched. We fast because our reason for living is not something everyone finds obvious: that hope is still a risk and a wager. We fast, but we do so because Christ has been taken from us, and the world keeps on crucifying him. We fast, but we fast in faith, and nothing will keep the dance from casting its spell on our hearts, because our bridegroom is continually speaking words of grace and salvation to us.

■

New wine, new bottles!
Brothers and sisters, how can we continue mourning
when God tells us his good news?
How can we not succumb
to the rhythms of festive joy
when God invites us to his table?

■

Lord, our wine has failed
*   and our hearts are dried up.*
*   Have mercy on us!*

We have listened too much to the prophets of doom,

and we are sad enough to die.
Have mercy on us!

Your love is limitless,
and we fear to be intoxicated by your Spirit.
Have mercy on us!

■

You have laid hold of us, Lord;
you lead us to a new world.
Let not our past imprison us,
for you came out alive from the tomb,
and you give us the breath of the Spirit
who makes all things new.

■

You invite us to your banquet;
fill us with your Spirit,
that our cup may overflow with new wine
and our lives may sing of your eternal covenant.

MONDAY OF THE 14TH WEEK

CHURCHING

Genesis 28:10–22a. What a distance has been traveled since the moment when Joseph decided to stop for the night at a place chosen quite arbitrarily and when this very spot was then promised the status of a national sanctuary. At the period when the Elohist writer is editing the story (vv. 13–16 and 19 are Yahwist and repeat, with application now to Jacob, the promises made to Abraham and Isaac), the temple at Bethel is regarded in the northern kingdom as an important center of pilgrimage. It possesses its letter patent of nobility because it was founded by Jacob the patriarch.

That, at least, is what can be claimed once history has been rewritten! Genesis 28 is, in fact, a good example of the fusing of traditions some of which are connected with a sanctuary, others with a nomadic tribe. In his time Jacob must have been an important man, since there are traditions locating him in east Jordan as well as in central Palestine (Bethel). It is probable that a westward migration connected the clan of Jacob with the legend about the foundation of Bethel, a legend piously kept alive by the priests in charge of the sanctuary.

This legend told how the god El had appeared in a dream to a distant ancestor who saw him descend the steps of what sounds like a ziggurat; this accounts for the temple, the function of which is precisely to be the place of meeting between heaven and earth and thus the gate of heaven and "house of God" (Beth-El). When the clan of Jacob occupied central Palestine, it simply identified the god El with its own divine protector (the "Mighty One of Jacob") and attributed the foundation of the existing sanctuary to the patriarch. Jesus will apply the Bethel tradition to himself and thus reveal himself to be the sole gate leading to heaven (Jn 1:51).

Psalm 91 expresses in the form of an oracle the protection God bestows on his friends. It fits in quite well here at the point when Jacob is leaving his own country to escape the anger of Esau.

Matthew 9:18–26. Who is this man, and what is new about him? Yahweh, as we know, commands the sea and the winds; moreover he is the enamored husband who forgives the infidelity of Israel. But in Jesus he has also drawn close to human beings and has even himself become a man in order to establish a definitive covenant, a covenant of life, with the human race.

For Jesus is life, bringing as he does the forgiveness of God. He "awakens" the little girl who had been given over to death. He also saves the woman whom life was gradually leaving. This twofold cure serves as a parable, a manifestation of the Kingdom through deeds. On the one hand there is a woman who has been hemorrhaging for twelve years and is slowly approaching death, especially since her infirmity excludes her from society. On the other hand there is a young girl who was just beginning to taste life to the full and then suddenly died. For both Jesus has life-giving words.

■

Death in any form seems absurd. How much more so that of a young girl! Her father has come running: "My daughter has just died!" Is there anything that more clearly shows the absurdity of life than to bring a child into the world, raise it, and then see it die? How intolerably scandalous that a body should die just at the moment when it becomes capable of engendering further life! "My daughter has just died": this statement, which does nothing to avert the inevitable, expresses the entire drama of human existence.

We have engendered life and then given the best of ourselves to our children. We have tried to give love a concrete form in our everyday actions. We have attempted to build justice and peace by sharing, forgiving, supporting. Yes, all of us are zealous fathers of life; we stand astonished before what has been accomplished by our hands and our desires, our pursuits and our passions. But then we are confronted with what cannot be remedied; death in all its forms seems to have the final word. They can talk to us of new wine, but nothing can silence such a claim more quickly than the rebellious cry: "My daughter has just died!"

The covenant, which is a promise, does not magically turn the drama of existence in a new direction. In the presence of our dead children God has but one answer to give: he takes his creatures by the hand and raises them up. In the ongoing process of life our only recourse, in the final analysis, is to lift ourselves up, begin again to love, recover communion, and keep on struggling for justice and freedom. The covenant challenges us not to close our eyes but to hope and go on living despite everything.

■

God of the living,
your Child gave his life without reserve,
  knowing no measure but your passionate love.
Renew our hope;
teach us to live in the freedom of the Spirit
  until the moment when we enter
  into the endless banquet.

82

AT THE FORD OF THE JABBOK

Genesis 32:23–32. A mysterious struggle and a no less complex history of names. Let us first unravel the skein of names, since, for the ancients, "to know someone's name was to have access to the mystery of his being and even to control him to some extent."[5] Thus when Jacob tells the unknown adversary his name, he is as it were naked and defenseless before him; and when, suspecting the other's divine origin, he asks him to reveal his name as well, he wants to learn the other's nature and intentions so as to have a hold on him. This mutual exchange and acknowledgment, says G. von Rad, is "a type of that which Israel experienced from time to time with God. Israel has here presented its entire history with God almost prophetically as such a struggle until the breaking of the day."[6]

This daybreak also brings entry into the promised land, for the crossing of the Jabbok opened up Palestine to all who were with the patriarch and, in particular, to his children, who would be the ancestors of the twelve tribes. Thus in Jacob's wake all of Israel left the dark woods of Gilead for civilization. Because Jacob the trickster allows God to overcome him in Peniel, he will henceforth be Jacob-Israel.

Psalm 17, which is an individual lament, contains cries for help, protestations of innocence and expressions of trust, and thus gives a good picture of the feelings of divided man. Let the divine oracle be favorable to him and so lead him in peace!

Matthew 9:32–38. The leper, the centurion's servant, Peter's mother-in-law, the demoniacs, the paralytic, the woman with a hemorrhage, and the daughter of Jairus: a real display of miracles! But does it not accurately tell us what the Church really is, with its countless forgiven sinners? Preceded by Matthew himself, men and women have stood up and followed Jesus; a community that seeks to answer the call of the Beatitudes is on the march.

These men and women have been set free in heart and in flesh, and their sickness now shows its true face. It represents in each case an obstacle to the Kingdom, but one which the cross of Jesus has overcome. The human race can henceforth "awaken" to the life of grace. Yes, out of the initial chaos there emerges a community that grows quickly like a harvest ripening. That is precisely what the Church is: the fruit of a creative act of

God. Now men must pray to the Father, for "the harvest is rich, but the laborers are few." Jesus must hasten to give the Twelve the authority that will enable them to bring in the harvest.

■

God did not remain heartless in the face of human tragedy. Jesus rises up and accepts the challenge: he journeys through towns and villages proclaiming the good news. The covenant and the tender love it embodies will be engaged in a bitter struggle against all that diminishes human beings. From the day at the ford of the Jordan when the Eternal One had said: "This is my Son, the Beloved . . . . Listen to him," until the day when the Chosen One is taken up to heaven, God will be struggling with man, and he will not withdraw from this struggle without being forever marked by it. He will suffer forever from the wound opened in the side of his Son. God will not abandon the struggle until the day when he departs with the blessing of man who will thank him for so much tender love. The covenant is not simply an external action of God; it touches the very depths of his being.

"I beg you, tell me your name." We shall leave off the struggle only on condition that God reveal his face to us. The covenant is this struggle from which we shall not exit unscathed.

Brothers and sisters, have you crossed the ford of the Jabbok? If you have not struggled all night with the hand that seized you by the shoulder, then you have not yet found the Kingdom. The other is strange and a stranger, and yet he seems familiar to you. You can overcome him only if you are broken by him; you cannot meet him without being marked in life and in death. If this unwearying battler can overcome you only by wounding you, may not the reason be that he has first been wounded by you?

Have you crossed the ford of the Jabbok? The Kingdom is indeed at hand for you if you have struggled all night in order to learn the stranger's name at any cost. You have entered into the covenant if you have experienced in your flesh the wound of desire and the fervor of the kiss given to you, you know not how. In the depth of your being you carry the indelible mark, the blessing upon you, of him who has overcome you by his weakness.

Brothers and sisters, continue the struggle to learn the name of him who bears within himself the wound you have inflicted. Someday the covenant will take the form of an eternal communion, when at dawn you cross to the other bank and see at Peniel the face of him who today wishes to be conquered.

■

Who could possibly know you
*   if you do not reveal your name?*
Who could possibly love you
*   if you do not stir our desire?*
Lord,
*   life will not be long enough*
*   to lift the veil from your mystery.*
A lifetime will be needed
*   for you to find the place*
*   wherein to wound us.*
Burn us with your fire,
*   awaken our passionate desire,*
*   that we may experience our Easter morning.*
And when we cross to the other bank,
*   place on our finger the ring of tender love,*
that we may discover the beauty of your face
*   and the grace of your covenant.*

■

All night long
*   your Son struggled*
*   on the banks of the river*
*   where death held him captive;*
All night long,
*   until the dawn*
*   of a new land*
*   in which life is resplendent.*
Wounded to the very soul,
*   he arose*
*   on Easter morning,*

leading after him
  the long train of pilgrims
  who conquered with him in the night.
Your blessing marked his body,
  and from his opened side,
  the fountains of the future
  still flow for us.
God of the living,
  God of our struggles against hell,
  grant us victory!
God, lead us
  to the pastures of life!
Let our struggle not cease
  until the day when, in your Son,
  we shall know
  the promised land of eternal happiness.

Joseph and the Twelve Tribes

There is no doubt that to a large extent the story of Joseph reflects the concerns of the sages who made their appearance at the royal court of David and Solomon as they had at the royal court of Egypt. The story of Joseph is that of a young man who is "well bred and finely educated, steadfast in faith and versed in the ways of the world" as the masters of wisdom described it for the young in their sayings.[7] The emphasis on the importance of oratorical skill in a courtly milieu, as well as the story of Potiphar with its picture of the danger represented by foreign women, is evidence enough of this. Joseph is the very prototype of the man who "fears God."

It is also quite obvious that God plays hardly any part in this book. We find few traces of the sacral legends that proliferate in the other patriarchal traditions. In fact, when Joseph speaks of God, he does so only for a pedagogical purpose. We hear him saying on two occasions that God carries on a salutary activity in the history of human beings (45:5–7; 50:20). Von Rad thinks that these passages are an interpretation by the Yahwist to whom (in this view) we owe the introduction of the detailed story of Joseph into the great body of patriarchal traditions, the insertion having for its purpose precisely to call attention to the action of God. The Yahwist would thus share the concern of the Deuteronomistic historian, for the latter too, especially in his account of the succession to David's throne, shows the importance of the human heart as the privileged place of God's action.

But the story of Joseph and, through it, the story of the sons of Jacob is also the story of the tribes whose ancestors these men are said to be. We know, however, that the merging of the tribes was not completed until the reign of David. It follows that all the clues given both in the patriarchal traditions and in the accounts of the exodus and the conquest of Canaan shed light on the gradual integration of these tribes and on the commingling of traditions which this integration brought with it. The story of Joseph is especially suggestive inasmuch as it is concerned with the establishment of the two great blocs which later became the northern and southern kingdoms.

In its remote origin the story of Joseph is not Israelite. Scholars generally refer us to two ancient stories: the story of a set of brothers (this is found in other cultures as well), and an Egyptian story which sounds like a legend connected with a local shrine (perhaps the sanctuary of Heliopolis?). As far as the Joseph of history is concerned, he, like Jacob, is to be located near Shechem. What do we know about him—or, rather, what do we know about the tribes descended from the sons of Joseph? The patriarchal traditions link these tribes with the children born of Jacob's union with his two Mesopotamian wives, Leah and Rachel, and with two serving girls, Bilhah and Zilpah. Leah's sons are Reuben, Simeon, Levi and Judah; to these Issachar and Zebulun are later added. Reuben is the eldest, which explains the preponderant place he has in the story of Joseph. However he is often replaced by Judah; this seems to reflect the fact that the tribe of Judah gradually absorbed all its neighbors, to the point of later being simply identified with the kingdom of David. In addition, Judah is not the name of a person but of a mountain in Palestine that gave its name to the human beings settled on its lands.

Theories about the settlement of the tribes in Palestine have been radically revised after de Vaux's demonstration of the possibility of there having been two exoduses: an exodus-expulsion and an exodus-flight. His theory is that around 1550 there was a first exodus, the result of a rebellion of Egyptian princes against pharaohs of Semitic origin, the Hyksos, who had occupied the country for two hundred years. The exodus-flight, which was the exodus of Moses, would have occurred only around 1250, in the time of Rameses II. The tribes descended from some of Leah's sons (Reuben, Simeon, Levi and Judah) would have formed at the time of the exodus-expulsion and would have gradually penetrated southern Palestine as far as Hebron where their advance would have been halted by the barrier formed by the Canaanite cities (for example, Jerusalem). The tribes of Issachar and Zebulun, on the other hand, would not have come down from Egypt at all. They were located in Lower Galilee, and their expansion would have been checked by another Canaanite barrier, located this time in the northern part of the country. Issachar would have hired out its services to those Egyptians who owned rich farming estates in the plain of Jezreel; and in fact Genesis 49 treats this clan with a certain degree of contempt, describing it as a "strong ass" suited to be "a slave to forced labor." As for the tribes of Gad, Asher, Dan and Naphtali, which were descended from Jacob's sons by the two serving girls, their servile origin would (according to this theory) bear witness to a more or less sizable infiltration of Canaanites into their ranks. They too, being located in the north (Dan as a result of migration), would have had no experience of Egypt.

This leaves Joseph and Benjamin, the sons of Rachel. But it also leaves tribes such as Ephraim and Manasseh, descended from the sons Joseph had from his marriage with an Egyptian woman. It leaves, finally, the surprising adoptions of which we are told in Genesis 48 and 50: the adoption of the sons of Joseph by Jacob the patriarch, and that of the great-grandsons of Joseph (the sons of Machir, son of Manasseh). The first thing to be said here is that all these tribes—the tribes making up the "house of Joseph"—are those that fled Egypt under the leadership of Moses and Joshua. After their long exodus they reached central Palestine from the east by crossing the Jordan at Gilgal. Three clans must be taken into account: Ephraim, Benjamin and Manasseh. The first of these chose to settle in the northern part of central Palestine; like Judah in the south, it adopted the name of the local mountain, Mount Ephrain (Joshua, Moses' successor, was an Ephraimite). Other immigrants settled in the southern part of central Palestine; they were called "Benjaminites," the "sons of the south." As for the tribe of Manasseh, it was part of Ephraim, but broke off from the mother-tribe and settled further north.

What of Joseph? It has been proposed by de Vaux that the Joseph of history belonged to the Machirite clan, which had settled near Shechem. Now the name Machir could mean "hired out" (somewhat like Issachar);

this suggests that the clan was made up of mercenaries. After the exodus, the Machirites (according to the theory) were absorbed by the tribe of Manasseh, which would then have adopted the Josephite traditions. The memory of this absorption would be seen in the story of the adoption of the sons of Machir, son of Manasseh, by Joseph (Gen 50), and the adoption of Manasseh, son of Joseph, by Jacob. But Genesis 48 also notes the adoption of Ephraim, the other son of Joseph, by Jacob. We would here have a remembrance of the dominant place of this mighty tribe: like Judah in the south, Ephraim would have gradually absorbed its neighbors. It is clear that there would very quickly have been left only the tribes of Judah and Ephraim, which became the nuclei of the future kingdoms of Jerusalem and Samaria. Judah was a son of Leah, and Ephraim a grandson of Rachel. These two women each claimed a share of the heart of Joseph, Israel's ancestor, and the rivalry between the two women served to express the antagonism of the tribes located in northern and southern Palestine respectively.

Reading and Understanding Matthew

The Missionary Discourse (Chapter 10)

The harvest is ready for gathering and needs workers. Jesus calls the Twelve and gives them his own authority over evil spirits. To these disciples, now become "Apostles" (this is the only time Matthew gives them this name), Jesus imparts instructions, which are here gathered into a single discourse called "the missionary discourse."

What do these instructions say? They say essentially that "the disciple is not superior to his teacher" and that the apostolate consists primarily in revealing Jesus Christ, the Father's authentic Word. But this conformity of the disciple to the teacher here takes on a very precise character, since the word of Jesus (as the New Testament abundantly testifies) is as sharp as a sword. It makes its way into the smallest recesses of human hearts and forces men and women to take up a position with regard to it. It is not surprising, therefore, that after defining the place of the disciples, Jesus should think it advisable to add: "If they have called the master of the house Beelzebul, what will they not say of his household?"

The following chapters show that the word and salvific work of Jesus will be challenged; both John the Baptist and the Pharisees will be scandalized by his behavior (cf. Chapters 11—12). Thus after describing the manifestations of authority by Jesus, Matthew goes on to describe their impact as well: Jesus will be as it were an occasion of downfall for the men and women who must come to some decision about him. Consequently, no one will be surprised if the Apostles, who are essentially messengers of peace, may expect to see this peace returning to them, since men and women are no more ready to listen to them than the lake towns had been to be converted. They will therefore be persecuted.

FROM WEDNESDAY TO SATURDAY OF THE 14TH WEEK

Ministry of the Covenant

The words of the call are harsh; they have the burning sharpness of high summer about them. "The one who disowns me in the presence of men, I will disown in the presence of my Father in heaven." The Gospel will not tolerate half-measures. But then is it not true that there are days when love must set out without looking back, and this under pain of shriveling up and dying? We have often thrown cold water on what seemed mere enthusiasm and foolishness. Perhaps it would be better not to read the Gospel if it were impossible for us to see it as the source of a free, joyous, passionate call.

"I am sending you out like sheep among wolves." The witness dies of loving too much, for his fellows cannot bear the fire of his passionate concern. How can we, as bringers of the mad proclamation of God's gratuitous love, fail to show the same gratuitousness? How could the scandal of the message fail to attach to us ourselves? We bear witness to a tender love whereas everything in the world is based on force and power. We fight for justice whereas the world worships the idol of money. The Witness to the covenant paid the price for his preaching. How, then, can the disciple escape trial by fire?

■

As Witness of the word
and Word made flesh,
   Jesus lived your covenant to the end;
   he let the Spirit lead him
   to the supreme gift that cannot be recalled.
May his breath today
   quicken the prayer of your Church.

Yes, Father, let your reign come!
Clothe us in Jesus Christ,
   that we may set out with no baggage
   save his fiery word and peaceful gaze.
Burn us with his fire
   when we are tempted to turn back;
strengthen our hope
   when the pressure of mockery discourages us.

The harvest is abundant;
   do you yourself gather what you have sown
   when we have labored until evening.
The peace you give is limitless;
   may it be our joy
   when we have carried it to the ends of the earth.

WEDNESDAY OF THE 14TH WEEK

SERVANTS OF THE WORD

Genesis 41:55–57; 42:5–7a, 17–24a. Imagine Joseph in the presence of his brothers! What a long road had been traveled since the day when the young man had been sold by his older brothers, who were jealous of the special affection their father had for him. Joseph, who possesses all the qualities looked for in the courts of Egypt and Jerusalem, is now grand vizier; he controls the grain reserves that have been stored up to deal with the famine he had foreseen.

His concern at the moment is to find out whether his brothers have changed. He subjects them to a test: they must return to Palestine and bring back with them their youngest brother, Benjamin, the son of Jacob and Rachel; meanwhile he will retain Simeon. Thus the brothers will find themselves in the same position they had been in long ago when, heads high, they had gone back to their father after ridding themselves of Joseph. But whereas at that time their hearts had been filled with hatred, they are now burdened with pain. They have therefore changed, and Joseph will be able to rejoice with them at this alteration. As formerly, so now Reuben's voice is heard; it is the voice of conscience, the same one that had tried to defend Joseph.

Psalm 33. Would we have expected to find a hymn in this context? Yet that is what Psalm 33 is. It rejoices in advance at the happy ending of the story of Joseph and his brothers.

Matthew 10:1–7. "Ask the Lord of the harvest to send laborers to his harvest." Jesus has come on the scene as a shepherd who is anxious to gather the long-scattered sheep. He now needs fellow workers who in their turn will exercise their master's authority. Nonetheless, Jesus goes off by himself "to teach and preach in their towns" (11:1). According to Matthew, who differs on this point from Mark and Luke, it is only after the resurrection that the disciples will likewise go out.

Meanwhile, who are these disciples, who are called here, for the first and only time, the "twelve Apostles"? They are "the Twelve," that is, those who embody the consciousness Christians very quickly acquired of being the true Israel. It is along this same line that we may understand the strange instruction of Jesus that they are not to go to the pagans or the Samaritans but rather "to the lost sheep of the house of Israel." There was doubtless a development in the thinking of Jesus and of the Church with regard to mission, but the recommendation seems to envisage the eschatological Israel, that is, the Church. The "lost sheep of the house of Israel" would then designate all those who have rejected the Kingdom. "Pagan territory" and "any Samaritan town" would symbolize "a manner of life and a kind of social existence" that are opposed to Jesus. The point of this instruction would therefore be to avoid all behavior that is opposed to Jesus and to go out to all those who have rejected the Kingdom.

∎

He called twelve of them and sent them on a mission. The entire dynamics of the covenant is summed up in these two words: call and send. Down through the centuries this twofold movement will characterize the Church. "Proclaim that the Kingdom of heaven is close at hand!" Here we are, the Church of God, constituted as the servants of the word of grace for the sake of the covenant. Jesus devoted his whole life to this service; his words and actions had for their sole purpose to create such fraternal ties between human beings that the Spirit can then consecrate these men and women and thus bring the Kingdom to birth. To serve the covenant means to establish between human beings bonds which life constantly loosens. The excluded are restored to communion; sinners are raised up, and forgiveness is able to forge a new body; even strangers receive a share in the family inheritance and belong henceforth to the house of God.

Jesus devoted himself unreservedly to this service of the covenant, to the point of gathering everything up in himself on the cross. On this day he chooses twelve disciples and founds the new Israel. The word is fulfilled and the covenant sealed. Down the centuries the Church will be for the world a sign that already fulfills the promise, for it is the pledge of the covenant between God and the human race.

■

God of peace,
  your Spirit reveals your plan;
you wish to enter upon
  a new covenant with men!
Grant that we may prepare the ways of the Kingdom;
  send us forth as spokesmen of your promise.

THURSDAY OF THE 14TH WEEK

THE WORD FOR BAGGAGE
Genesis 44:18–21, 23b–29; 45:1–5. Joseph had wanted it believed that

young Benjamin had stolen his cup. The supposed theft was not in itself a very serious crime, but it was complicated by the fact that the cup was used in divination. Throughout this entire story Benjamin's neck is at stake.

In this way the clever vizier gradually cuts Benjamin off from his half-brothers. What are the latter to do? Shall they abandon the boy to his fate in order to save their own lives? The answer is given in Judah's plea, which focuses entirely on the recollection of his lost brother. It describes the perplexity of the brothers and the distress of Jacob at the thought of allowing the second of Rachel's sons to depart for Egypt. The speech also makes it clear how much the hearts of the brothers have changed, for Judah quite spontaneously offers to take Benjamin's place. All's well that ends well, and nothing remains but to celebrate the reunion of Joseph and his elderly father. But before this takes place Joseph must emphasize the divine action: it is Yahweh who has pulled the strings of this history, which has been a history of salvation, since it led the guilty brothers to the light and to reconciliation.

Psalm 105 is a fine example of a hymn celebrating the great deeds of God in the history of the Jewish people. The verses used here tell the story of Joseph down to the point of his elevation to office in Egypt.

Matthew 10:7–15. The first instructions given to the Apostles may be summed up in two attitudes: be conformed and be available. The Apostle is to be like the one who sent him; like the latter he will proclaim the breakthrough of the Kingdom into human history. He will do this both by preaching and by performing the deeds of power that accompany the preaching.

The Apostle is also to be available. This availability or readiness finds clear expression in the Greek text when Jesus bids his disciples ask the master of the harvest to send laborers into his harvest. The Greek verb used for send in 9:38 means literally "to throw out, cast out," as if the sending out on a mission required a kind of forcible uprooting in order to set the envoy moving in the right direction. The verb thus underscores the divine initiative. The apostolate is not a right to be claimed but a gift to be received without antecedent merit.

This readiness will also mark those towns upon which the peace proclaimed by the Apostles remains. For only those towns that welcome the disciples as messengers of God will be judged worthy of them. The

94

others will receive a more severe judgment than that which fell on Sodom and Gomorrah.

■

We would have planned some formation weekends, written a summary of all the things to be kept in mind, and reviewed the strategies to be applied; then at the moment of departure we would have run after the disciples like overly protective mothers: "Have you forgotten anything? Remember, I've put a box of biscuits in your knapsack, just in case."

But there is none of that here! Jesus tells his friends to set out without taking anything with them: no bread, no knapsack, no money in their belts. No short book of instructions, no advice. Nothing but a staff to support them when tired, and sandals so that they can keep going. Jesus tells them, first and last, to rely on hospitality. In short, he makes them dependent on those they are to evangelize. Utter poverty!

They must set out with nothing but the word, the message, the good news, the breath of the Spirit that keeps the messenger going. The important thing is not oratorical skill or strategy or pedagogy but the Spirit of fire, the Life that goes in quest of life. The messenger is burdened only by the word which he brings and the word to which he will give birth.

They are to speak unwearyingly of their master without fully understanding their own message, for they will be tossed about between unbelief and faith. "There is in your midst one whom you do not know, whom we do not know!" The more they spoke about the Lord, the more they came to understand that with his coming a new age had begun: "Believe in the good news; the Kingdom of God is at hand!"

Brothers and sisters, that is indeed what faith is like. It begins to take shape in witness and in sharing. Faith awakens where, without preliminaries and without external help, it takes the risk of relying on a word, a life. Faith is not a nicely corded piece of luggage to be transmitted as such; rather it is discovered, deepened and put on a sure footing by being shared. It is by traveling the road with the Lord that we believe in him.

Jesus sent them on a mission. Happy the Church that has only the journey to strengthen its faith!

■

You call us, Lord,
  to follow your Son
  and travel the road of the Kingdom.
Through your Spirit set our hearts free
  and keep our eyes fixed on the goal,
  with no baggage save your promise,
  with no certainty save your word.

FRIDAY OF THE 14TH WEEK

SERVING TO THE END

Genesis 46:1–7, 28–30. The mingling of traditions makes this chapter somewhat blurry. According to the Yahwist tradition, Jacob-Israel decides to leave Hebron for Beer-sheba where he offers a sacrifice to the God of his father Isaac. According to the Elohist Jacob decides to go to Egypt only after a nocturnal vision. The difference in the vantage points of the two redactors is thus emphasized. The Yahwist stresses more the free will of human beings, while the Elohist makes Jacob's decision rest on the divine word. The Elohist thus enlarges the perspective in which the journey of Jacob and his family is viewed. The patriarch does not see this as an ordinary journey; instead he is leaving the land promised to his ancestors and thus embarking on a new adventure in God's company.

Psalm 37 is alphabetical and contains disparate pieces. It greets the faithful of the Lord and gives expression to the feelings that grip travelers at the moment when they leave their beloved homeland.

Matthew 10:16–23. "Hand over": the term recalls the wording of the predictions of the passion and emphasizes once again the similarity between the mission of Jesus and that of the disciples. It is he who has chosen them; it is his word they are to proclaim openly; it is his fate they are to share. Like Jesus again, they will profit by the testimony of the Spirit, who is the Father's gift to them. The Apostles will thus be indebted to God for the strength they show in time of persecution; the apostolate is in its entirety a freely given gift.

But the person and word of Jesus are at the center of this discourse. To this extent there are analogies between the sending on mission and the Galilean controversies as reported by Mark. In Galilee the word breaks through into human history in order to challenge this history and be challenged by it, but the word continues to do the same today in the person of the Apostles. They too learn from experience that the family home is not necessarily the same as the believing community. On the contrary, the dividing line cuts right through the group of the disciples, and brothers will hand brothers over to death.

We may end with a remark about the final verse: "You will not have gone the round of the towns of Israel before the Son of Man comes." There is no doubt that the verse envisages an imminent "coming"; but in light of the eschatological meaning of the word "Israel" we may also see in this verse an allusion to the universality of the mission: there will always be human beings to whom the word and peace must be proclaimed.

■

"I am sending you like sheep among wolves." The words of the call are harsh; they have the burning sharpness of high summer about them. The Gospel of Jesus Christ is not a palaver, still less an essay! One is either for the Gospel or against it. "Follow me" means "immediately and directly," and the sending on mission that is connected with faith is a sure promise of opposition in store.

The moment of call is a trial by fire. The call has the fierceness of an emergency; it is as radical as judgment. Perhaps we are missing something when we read the Gospel. Twenty centuries of familiarity have taken away our sense of "the end of time," the sense of urgency and of the violent reign of God among men. In the circles in which we move the opposition nowadays is often polite; indifference and ignorance are more destructive than open opposition. The lukewarmness of the disciples is itself a sign that the salt has lost its savor.

97

The disciples will truly be "followers" of Jesus only when they have traveled the entire road, to the point of meeting opposition, to the point of ascending Golgotha. They must still be baptized in fire, they must still drink the cup, if they are to be able to bear witness in truth. The Church will be born of Pentecostal fire. If the disciples are to become the community of those who have been called, they must live the paradoxical life of the Son who is a servant and has come not to reign but to serve. The day will come when the community will bear witness with its blood and will go forward to martyrdom, but between now and then it must learn from the master a total detachment. The disciple who has acknowledged the Lord has committed himself to an exodus in which each step forward strips him of his securities so that he is ready for new departures.

■

In his passionate resolve to do your will,
  Lord, our God,
  your Son resolutely took the road to the cross.
May he rekindle our burning desire to follow him.
May the Spirit be your Church's strength.
  Then it will accept the risk of witnessing
  and will be like its Lord
  who came to serve your word.

SATURDAY OF THE 14TH WEEK

TO DARE TO WITNESS

Genesis 49:29–33; 50:15–24. Despite Joseph's assurances, his brothers remain uneasy, and the death of Jacob revives their fears. They again ask the vizier's forgiveness; this must have reminded the latter of his dreams in the distant past, when he saw the sheaves of his brothers bowing down to his own. They base their request on the common faith that binds them all together; Joseph is urged to be gracious to "the servants of your father's God." In replying that he does not wish to take the place of God, Joseph once again points to him who, from the outset, was bringing together the invisible threads of what seemed on the surface to be only a family history. God was there; he kept his promise. Neither Sarah's disbelief nor Rebekah's trickery nor the hatred of Jacob's sons could destroy the covenant God had entered into with Abraham. No, Joseph will not take the place of God; he has no wish to punish when Yahweh himself has pardoned.

But the story of Joseph is also the story of the tribes that will one day make up Israel. Today's pericope gives a hint of this when it relates how Joseph took on his lap (a gesture equivalent to adoption) certain of his great-grandchildren, namely the sons of Machir, who himself was a son of Manasseh. This adoption echoes a fusion of tribal traditions, which in turn was caused by the integration of various clans which had successively settled in central Palestine. The name Manasseh designates a part of the great tribe of Ephraim, which had absorbed the Machirites, the group to which the Joseph of history belonged. The mingling of traditions caused the latter to be shared by the clans of Machir and Manasseh; Manasseh then came to be regarded as the first-born of Joseph, and the latter adopted the sons of Machir. Later on, when Ephraim in its turn absorbed all the other tribes, it took as its own the tradition regarding Joseph, and people began to speak of a "house of Joseph" which included Machir-Manasseh and Ephraim, all of whose members were then called "sons of Joseph."

Psalm 105. The beginning of this psalm is read in the liturgy. All who share the faith of the reconciled sons of Jacob are urged to thank the God who guides the course of history.

Matthew 10:24–33. Here again we may refer to the Gospel of Mark and, in particular, to what is usually called "the day of parables." The reader will recall that the parable of the sower, in which three of the four soils on which the seed falls are unsatisfactory, might well leave an impression of failure. But Jesus immediately went on to parables inspiring confidence, such as the parable of the mustard seed. The tone is rather similar here in Matthew. After envisaging the possibility of a bad reception and describing the persecutions that the Apostles must expect, Jesus wants to reassure his followers. On the one hand, we must bear in mind the power of God's word, which never returns to him without having borne fruit; like seed, God's word contains an irresistible dynamism that enables it to overcome all obstacles, and the Apostle must therefore hope firmly that "everything that is now covered will be uncovered, and everything now hidden will be made clear." Moreover, it is not human beings who are to be feared, but "him rather who can destroy body and soul in hell."

Thus the discourse gradually reveals its eschatological character. The Apostle must be aware that what he proclaims is not his own word but a word that comes from elsewhere. It is the Kingdom to which he is bearing witness, and if he reaches the point of denying Christ, it is to the Kingdom that he proves to be an obstacle. As for those who refuse to accept the Apostle, they are quite simply rejecting the word which the disciple brings. The missionary discourse determines the responsibility of each party; it states the price which the divine word exacts, but also the power it exerts, and therefore the unimaginable future to which it is called.

■

Nowadays Christians are accused of keeping silent. They hardly ever speak the name of God; they hide their Christian life within their hearts and restrict religion to the private sphere. Will not this generation incur the reproach of Jesus: "The one who disowns me in the presence of men, I will disown in the presence of my Father in heaven"?

After the tragic disappointment of Good Friday the disciples locked themselves in the upper room; they thought they could bolt the doors and windows and find contentment, come what might, in memories. They thought it much too dangerous to risk speaking out for Christ. But the Spirit pushed them out of doors so that the word might ring out with the good news of salvation: "What I say to you in the dark, tell in the daylight."

The word of God, like every living word, cannot exist in a germ-free environment; the word exists only if it is spoken and thereby subjected to risk. The word of God must take its chances in the words and conduct of human beings. We thought we could preserve the word by locking it up, and now we are told that we must sow it freely or else we will deny it. We thought we could remain satisfied with formulas which the centuries had drained of vitality, but instead we must come up with new words that express God, and we must go out and bear witness to our fellows under penalty of rendering barren our own profession of faith. Because human lifestyles change, we must find fresh words with which to speak of God. A life according to the Gospel cannot let itself get bogged down in inherited ways; such a life exists only in the form of an unwearying search for an existence that incarnates the truth.

"Do not be afraid of those who kill the body." Men thought they could throttle the Word by nailing it to a gallows of shame; now, they thought, they could once more go on saying what people had always said and could be content with the age-old ways. They thought that by killing the Word they would be able to return peacefully to their books and their customs. But "do not be afraid of those who . . . cannot kill the soul!" On Easter morning the Word was raised from the tomb, and from that point on it has taken its chances in the words and lives of those human beings who dare give witness to its continual newness!

■

To whom shall we go, Lord?
You have the words of eternal life for us.
  Have mercy on us!

Deliver us from our old refrains
  and make known what is still hidden.
  Have mercy on us!

Be our help and our strength;
  let us not be ashamed of you.
  Have mercy on us!

"What I say to you in the dark,
  tell in the daylight."
That is the Lord's command to his Church.
In prayer
  let the words which speak God to us
  rise up within us.

Speak your word about the world,
and let your kindness, Lord,
  be made known in the daylight!
Speak out in our behalf
  and make our words firm,

that you may not be ashamed of us
at the hour of judgment.

The Book of Exodus

A Book in Which Everything Begins in Pairs

The Book of Exodus is perhaps the most difficult book of the Bible to
interpret. Not only does it contain historical traditions and theological
rereadings of these, but it is also very difficult to locate these traditions in
history. It is possible indeed, here as elsewhere in the Pentateuch, to
distinguish a Yahwist source, an Elohist source, a Deuteronomistic source
and a Priestly document, but even this distinction, valuable though it is,
does not account fully for the complexity of the book. To understand this,
we must also realize that the Yahwist and Elohist sources—to mention
only these two—are the vehicle for memories peculiar to individual tribes.
As far as Moses is concerned, we have reason to think that a good deal of
the information comes from the tribes of central Palestine, since they were
the ones that experienced the exodus-flight and the journey through the
wilderness before entering Israel across the eastern border. But the
problem is complicated by the fact that on the far side of the Jordan these
tribes had come in contact with the tribe of Dan which not only had its own
traditions but had also preserved divergent recollections with regard to the
death of Moses in its territory. In addition, when the tribe of Dan migrated
to the north it had taken with it a descendant of the son of Moses who was
to minister at a local sanctuary; here too traditions were preserved. These
two examples will be enough to show the complexity of the traditions
which a writer like the Elohist brought together in about the eighth
century B.C.

In the south the Mosaic tradition was doubtless less important. We may
think, nonetheless, that in the tenth century B.C. the Yahwist writer
inherited various sagas of the tribes that had settled in the southern part of
Palestine and had finally merged to form the house of Judah. But the

102

traditions of this group were focused on the oasis of Kadesh, a place which is of interest for the epic of Moses, inasmuch as scholars like Cazelles and de Vaux no longer hesitate today to defend a stay of Moses in this area.

Mention has already been made of the hypothesis regarding the existence of two separate exoduses. We must return to it here and recall that the exodus-expulsion, which (it is claimed) took place around 1550 B.C., involved the tribes of the south. These tribes (the Leah group) departed by the northern route—the sea-road, later called "the way of the Philistines"—and made their way to the oasis of Kadesh before entering Palestine from the south. On the other hand, the exodus-flight, which took place three centuries later, is the exodus of Moses; his group (the Rachel group) took a southeastern course in order to avoid the Egyptian frontier posts.

The accounts in the Book of Exodus bear profound marks of this duality. It might be thought, on a priori grounds, that the Elohist source has preserved the memory of the Hebrew flight and that the tradition of the exodus-expulsion is to be found in the Yahwist source. In fact, this view of things is too simplistic and does not take into account the influence which the traditions exerted on each other, an influence which indeed may have already been at work in Kadesh when the group led by Moses encountered there various clans that had kept the memory of their ancestors' expulsion from Egypt three centuries earlier. But if we accept two exoduses, the question inevitably arises: With which of the two is the miracle of the sea to be connected? In a very thought-provoking book, Cazelles has shown that according to the Elohist Moses passed directly into the desert with the help of a bank of fog that hid him from the eyes of the Egyptians. According to the Yahwist, on the other hand, a wind from the east dried up the sea which lies in the northern part of the Sinai peninsula near Baal-Zephon, thus allowing the Hebrews to pass. As heir to the traditions of the south, the Yahwist was thus connecting the miracle of the sea with the exodus-expulsion; he would thus be in agreement with the often renewed hypothesis of a drying up of a strip of land between the Mediterranean and the lagoon of Sirbonis.

But de Vaux, who is more critical of the localizations proposed to account for the stages of the journey in the wilderness, connects the miracle of the sea with the exodus-flight, while admitting that in the texts as we have them this miracle is depicted in two forms. According to the one, Moses splits the sea in two in order to allow his companions to pass dry-shod through it; according to the other, it is not Moses but Yahweh in person who comes to the aid of the fugitives by using wind, fire and cloud. In addition, nowhere in this second account is anything said about the Israelites passing through the sea; it is said only that the Egyptians are destroyed in the sea. This point is an important one, because this version resembles closely the ancient canticle of Miriam: "Yahweh I sing: he has covered himself in glory, horse and rider he has thrown into the sea" (Ex 15:1). In any case, the two presentations cannot be harmonized, and the hypothesis of the destruction of the Egyptian army seems the best founded of the two.

It is also quite significant that we find this same basic duality in other details, having to do this time with the journey in the wilderness. Take, for example, the miracles of the manna and the quail, each of which is told twice. The phenomenon of the manna is connected with central Sinai (the geographical area containing insects which secrete the "manna" on the tamarisk in the springtime), while the phenomenon of the quail could only have taken place along the coast, and then only in autumn when the migrating birds alight on the sand, exhausted after their crossing. Once again, the quail would have to be connected with the exodus-expulsion, and the manna with the exodus-flight—unless the manna of central Sinai (Num 11:7–9), which was yellow and tasted like honey, is not the same as that of Exodus 16, which was white.

If the explanation of the miracle of the sea requires answers to some hard questions, the localization of the mountain of God raises seemingly insoluble problems. Is the mountain in question Mount Sinai? Are Sinai and Horeb one and the same? Was Moses trying to get back to Midian where he had received the revelation of the divine name and where some scholars see Yahwism as originating? Once again, we come a step closer to a solution when we realize that the two answers given depend on two ways of envisaging the traditions about the exodus and Sinai. If one separates these two traditions, one also distinguishes the mountain of God from Sinai; if, on the other hand, one accepts that these two traditions were welded into a single whole before the entrance into Canaan, one will identify Sinai with the mountain of God.

One thing is sure: the truth of the tradition regarding Moses' sojourn and marriage in Midian. Facts such as these could not have been invented but must have been historical, given the growing enmity between Israel and Midian. As for the supposition that Yahwism originated in Midian, de Vaux regards this as an unprovable hypothesis. We must, however, certainly keep in mind the importance of the region around the Gulf of Aqabah, which de Buit calls a "land of revelation." It is in Midian that the highlands of Edom are located, as are the highlands of Seir which are connected with the name of Yahweh (Jgs 5:4); there the Edomites and the Midianites came together, as did the descendants of Cain; it was there, finally, near the oasis of Kadesh, that the Ephraimite group of Moses met the tribes of southern Palestine.

What of Sinai? De Vaux, who devoted careful study to the question of localizations, admits his preference for the traditional view, but he also grants that the mountain could have been closer to Egypt than is usually thought. He even asks whether "Sinai" might not have been the name for a whole area, as, for example, a wilderness or desert, within which stood the mountain of God, the proper name of which was "Horeb." Cazelles, who uses archeological findings as a means of shedding light on the epic of Moses, has suggested that the first halt on the journey may have been at Serabit el-Khadem, in the western part of central Sinai, where there were mines but also a temple of the goddess Hathor, alongside which was a sanctuary of the god Sopdou, who has been identified with the El of the Semites. The conditions required for entrance into the holy place could have provided the content of the tablets of the law. From here the group would have advanced to the Gulf of Aqabah from the northeast.

The literary analysis of the story of the burning bush also deserves attention, because it brings to light elements belonging to both the Yahwist and the Elohist sources. The two sources agree in locating in the wilderness both the revelation of the divine name and the theophany that accompanied the revelation. But whereas the Elohist source has preserved the memory of the revelation of the divine name and of Moses' mission, the Yahwist source relates the theophany as well. In addition, the Yahwist uses for "bush" the word *seneh* which is rare in the Old Testament and evidently echoes the word "Sinai." Thus if we compare Deuteronomy 33:16 with the ancient canticle of Deborah (Jgs 5:5) we find that Yahweh is both he "who dwells in the bush" and "the One of Sinai" (Jgs 5:5). The next step is to ask whether the Yahwist has not identified the manifestation of God in the sacred bush with his manifestation on the holy mountain, especially since it seems natural to connect the fire in the bush with the fire on Sinai.

But the theophany on Sinai is itself not easy to interpret. The critics agree that two traditions are represented, but they disagree on the attribution of verses. Thus, according to de Vaux Exodus 19:16 belongs to the Elohist stratum, but according to Cazelles it belongs to the Yahwist. However, while not taking an a priori position on the influence of the liturgy on the redaction of the text, scholars are generally in agreement that the phenomena accompanying the divine manifestation are of two kinds: storm phenomena and volcanic phenomena. According to de Vaux the Elohist tradition with its storm is the older; it obviously has in mind the Canaanite god of rain who was often represented brandishing the thunderbolt. It is therefore interesting to see the same Elohist in 1 Kings 19 removing from Yahweh the attributes of Baal; his concern is clearly to purify the idea of God. Telluric phenomena, on the other hand, are assigned to the Yahwist source; these might (I am still following de Vaux) be borrowings that would reflect the interest of Solomon's contemporaries in natural phenomena that were unknown in Israel but occurred frequently in Midianite country.

A book in which everything begins in pairs: such is the impression given by the Book of Exodus; it must be noted, however, that the number two quickly proved inadequate.

FROM MONDAY OF THE 15TH WEEK
TO WEDNESDAY OF THE 16TH WEEK

Set Free
The Book of Exodus was in Israel's mind *the* book within the Book and the core of Scripture, since it testified to the origin of Israel's history and the basis of its obedience to God the liberator. Passover was to be the annual commemoration of this liberation. Perpetual forced labor, servitude, non-existence: such was the enslavement from which the sons of Israel were to be rescued; the birth of this people took the form of a "going out," an exodus. In the wilderness they would experience freedom and would henceforth stand erect instead of bowing under Pharaoh's yoke. They would be gathered into a people instead of being torn from one another. They would learn the name of their Savior instead of clinging to alien gods.

The God of the Bible will forever be "he who delivered us from the hands of the Egyptians." The God of Moses is, of course, master and Lord; in the story of the exodus he "shows his power" abundantly. But the exodus shows above all that God is God because he delivers or sets free. His name creates history, and his action composes an epic of liberation. God has seen the wretched state of his people and he intervenes in their behalf. "He came among his own": the extraordinary exodus of a God who suffers at the sufferings of a people he calls his own! "I am the Lord" could be the revelation of any God whatever: a God who does not set free but reduces to serfdom, an all-powerful God who is Lord and master. But the God of the Bible, the God of the exodus, says: "I am the Lord *your God*." God is henceforth involved, and the history of human beings becomes his own history. This is a God who makes himself into a neighbor, a God who says: "I have decided to make you my concern." This God rescues human beings from the oppression that enslaves them, and year after year the night of Passover will be a night of hope. The God of the exodus reveals his name by acting. "I am who I will be": his revelation will reach its completion when human beings begin standing erect and are free.

God raises up, God saves, God establishes a people. But it is not easy to be free men and women. The children of Israel learn this lesson on the morrow of their departure. The Chinese lanterns have been extinguished, the feast is over. The exultant accents of the canticle of Moses are succeeded by complaints and murmurings. Israel is no longer sure of anything, and it is already hankering for the concentration-camp world of Pharaoh and the fleshpots of Egypt. Forty years of wandering in the wilderness will not be long enough for the children of Israel to accomplish their real pass-over and to learn authentic liberation. For the true exodus occurs when human beings no longer say: "Our salvation is the work of our own hands." The Israelites must come to understand the new relations which God established with them when he revealed himself as "the Lord your God."

Is the Book of Exodus just an ancient epic tale? But what if it were our own story in which God is leading us to the discovery that he has become "our neighbor"? What if this "old story" made us aware of the ever new story of our own liberation? of the journey constantly to be undertaken in order that we may to some extent rise above the determinisms that form a prison for our lives? of the passage from the "death" that inclines us to give up, to the life that is to be attained by risking an existence in the wilderness? The exodus is in fact our own setting out and our own Passover, as unity is created in us despite all the forces of death and disintegration ("Moses set out to visit his countrymen"), as freedom rises superior to all the determinisms that attack it from within and from without ("Who am I to go to Pharaoh?"; "The king of Egypt will not let you go unless he is forced"), and as solidarity and love gain the upper hand over inertia and hatred (Moses "saw an Egyptian strike a Hebrew"; "This is the bread the Lord gives you to eat").

"In every generation one must look upon himself as if he personally had come out of Egypt, as the Bible says: 'And thou shalt tell thy son on that day, saying, it is because of that which the Eternal did for me when I went forth from Egypt.' "[8]

■

Blessed be the Eternal One
  who brought us out of the land of slavery,
  the God who bestows freedom
  and is concerned about his people.
Blessed be you, God of Jesus Christ,
  the Father who leads us to the promised land,
  the God who begets us for the freedom of the Spirit!
In the depths of the darkness
  you take our side:
  you strike death down
  and denounce what imprisons us.
The seal of your victory is already on our lives,
  for in the morning, with your risen Son,
  you will bring us forth from our graves.
May the fervor of your Spirit
  stir us from our lethargy,
  and may we cross to the other shore
  and the wilderness of encounter.

OPPRESSION

Exodus 1:8–14, 22. The two cities of Pithom and Rameses tell us that we are in the land of Goshen, which was located in the eastern part of the Nile delta. The region had always known Semites, from the Hyksos who ruled Egypt for a century and a half to the many nomads seeking water for their flocks. The sons of Jacob had settled there, while the Shasu, a small tribe from south of the Dead Sea, led a nomadic existence between the delta and the Arabah.

"Then there came to power in Egypt a new king who knew nothing of Joseph." This king is identified as Rameses II. Not only was this pharaoh the successor to those who had expelled the Hyksos invaders, but he was relentless in his efforts to win back various districts in northeastern Egypt. He was therefore distrustful of the Semites, who might prove to be dangerous enemies should a war or rebellion break out; he therefore employed them in building the garrison cities of Pithom and Pi-Rameses. The work was not particularly difficult, but the proud nomads felt it to be a form of servitude and therefore humiliating.

It is from this servitude that the God of Moses will deliver his people. With a sense of joy the writer emphasizes the uselessness of Pharaoh's efforts. The more the Hebrews are oppressed, the more they multiply. Even the order to kill all the newborn males fails of its purpose, since Moses survives. This passage already gives us a glimpse of the power of Yahweh, whose wisdom will supplant that of Egypt.

Psalm 124, one of the "songs of ascents," was meant to be sung by a group; it follows the model of the thanksgiving psalms. The formula "let Israel repeat it" has turned it into a national psalm, but the verses recalling past distress are well suited to express the humiliation of the Hebrews in Egypt.

Matthew 10:34—11:1. Because the Church is the place of witness, its reason for existence is to be found not in itself but in the message which it proclaims and which is greater than it in every way. In this sense, the welcome given to the disciples is more than a gesture of hospitality; it is an acceptance of the Kingdom of God.

The fact that everything is at stake where the Kingdom is involved explains the power of the Gospel message to challenge human beings. Peace or the sword. But what is this peace which the disciples proclaim and which is able to return to them if the house to which it is offered is not worthy? The peace of the Kingdom is by its nature disruptive; it is rich in divine blessings but in turn it requires a choice and divides families. Jesus is this peace; he is this sword, for he is the sharp-edged word that rends the daughter of Zion. He is the obstacle across the path, the light which searches the hearts of men and women. One is either for him or against him, but who is worthy of him? What house is worthy to receive the peace of God, except for the house that is not ashamed of him before men?

■

From servitude to covenant: we may sum up thus the journey of an entire people. It arises, leaves the land of slavery and enters again into the land of its fathers; it returns from a foreign land because it discovers the name of its God. In the exodus of Israel a people passes from fear to freedom. On this long journey a people that had not been a people but had been imprisoned in the ghettos of Egypt thrills as it recalls the story which it recognizes as its own; through the generations it passes on the tradition of its founding.

Brothers and sisters, we have entered upon the same journey. What then will be the quality of our faith if it is not as deeply rooted as that of Israel? God has set us free; we have been rescued from slavery and from our fears, and have been brought together to form a free people.

"The Egyptians forced the sons of Israel into slavery." The children of Israel became aliens in the country they had adopted. We too were oppressed and enslaved. What is our slavery? It is that our land is never entirely our own. Alienated from ourselves, we cannot truly understand ourselves and are aware of unknown countries within us— to say nothing of the servitude of the senses and feelings. Who can claim to be master of himself?

We are strangers each to the other and can enjoy true life only if we open ourselves to others and are accepted by others. Yet by force of circumstance or the ill-will of human beings or our own interior confusions we are rejected, passed over, reduced to nonentities.

Think of all the human beings who are immured in a meaningless life and who begin to desire death as a deliverance rather than a misfortune! If pictures of war can seem like anticipations of the end of the world, this is not primarily because they remind us of a "rain of brimstone and fire," but because we see in them the faces of human beings tearing at one another.

Strangers to ourselves, strangers to others, strangers to our world! Who of us does not feel overwhelmed by events, enslaved by crushing economic, political and social forces, and made the plaything of a machine which no one can really control?

We are exiled in a foreign land and tested by our fellows or by events; we cry out for justice and goodness but do not find them. We feel tragically forced to think that no eye will ever look upon us with tender love and that the mysterious, incomprehensible Other who can be glimpsed behind the riddles of the universe casts the disquieting shadow of a monster. Yes, we are subjected to a harsh slavery. There are around us too many musty odors of death and mourning. It is time for God to rise up in our behalf.

■

Lord, we so often hear it said
  that you are not a stranger to us,
  that you are not far from those who invoke you.
Look on our wretched state,
  hear the cry that arises from the inhuman earth;
  break through the ghetto of our fears,
  rescue us from our isolation,
  deliver us from the death that lurks everywhere.
Rise up in our behalf,
  and be our liberator.

■

For the men and women oppressed
  under the whips of forced labor,
and for all who are condemned
  to inhuman tasks:

God, hear our prayer!

For rejected minorities,
for those of whom others are afraid;
for the immigrants
looked upon with fear and scorn:
God, hear our prayer!
That we may not weigh down our fellows
beneath the yoke
of a burden we refuse
to carry ourselves:
God, hear our prayer!

Hear us, God of freedom;
put into us a heart
that is just and compassionate;
give us the courage to struggle
for our brothers and sisters
with the fervor of faith
and a will inspired by your love.

Reading and Understanding Matthew

Jesus, a Sign That Is To Be Rejected (Chapters 11—12)

The Sermon on the Mount and the account of the acts of power have manifested the authority with which Jesus was invested at his baptism and which he passed on to his disciples. The missionary discourse, moreover, has given a glimpse of the way in which this authority was accepted during the lifetime of Jesus, for throughout this discourse he warns the Apostles of the difficulties that await them. Thus we can see the connection between Chapter 10 and Chapters 11—12: the prediction of possible persecutions is now seen in the light of the reception given to Jesus himself and to his works.

As a result, we also gain a better grasp of the role of the miracles reported in Chapters 8 and 9: the purpose of these acts of power was to reveal the deeper reality of him who performed them. On the other hand, they were viewed as provocations by those who saw them. Finally, they served as tests, for by bearing witness to the Kingdom, they confronted the onlookers with a judgment. Those who welcomed the Kingdom which these acts of power made known were worthy of that Kingdom; those who understood these acts as the acts of the Christ, the Messiah, were saved. But many of Jesus' contemporaries challenged the message conveyed by his actions. The resulting balance-sheet is very clear: on the one side, there are the wise; on the other, the ignorant. A day will come when Jesus will thank the Father for having revealed "these things" to the ignorant and having hidden them from the learned and clever.

In Matthew, however, we must never lose sight of the Church. Just as the missionary discourse warned the disciples in advance of the persecutions that would come, Chapters 11 and 12 give an account of the Church of Matthew. There are still, for example, disciples of John the Baptist who continue to contrast their master with Jesus; Matthew refers them to the saying Jesus had intended for John when the latter, in prison, found Jesus preaching a message of tenderness and goodness, whereas he himself had spoken of a fearsome judge: "Happy is the man who does not lose faith in me." Then there are the rabbis who, after the year 70, had taken the place of the scribes and were attacking newborn Christianity. The evangelist is forced to remind them that the kinsfolk of Jesus are those who do the Father's will. Finally, there is the Church of every age, whose words and deeds will always be challenged.

TUESDAY OF THE 15TH WEEK

HE CAME TO HIS OWN DOMAIN

Exodus 2:1–15a. Here again the point of the story can be easily seen: it is to be found in the explanation of the name "Moses." In Hebrew, Moses is *Moshe.* What could be more obvious, then, than to connect the name with the verb *masha,* meaning "to pull out," and to take it as referring to the intervention not only of Pharaoh's daughter but also, and above all, of God? The history of the child pulled from the water is already the history of the people saved from the sea.

In fact, however, the name Moses is derived from the Egyptian *mesu*, which means "born from, son of" and is found as a component of names like Rameses (son of Ra). The name Moses therefore recalls the child's adoption by the Egyptian princess and reminds scholars of other stories of children abandoned and picked up, as, for example, the story of Sargon in the twenty-fifth century B.C. The intention was to place the founder of the Jewish people on the same footing as the great men of history.

Finally, whose son is Moses? Other texts attempt to provide him with a birth certificate, but when all is said and done, is it not preferable to return to the popular explanation? Like Noah in his ark, Moses in his basket (the word is the same) was saved by God, and both men gave birth to a new race. Before performing this great deed, Moses must have left Egypt and gone to the wilderness of Midian, east of the Gulf of Aqabah. There he met the God of his fathers. In his exile the future adventures of the Jewish people can already be glimpsed.

Psalm 69. Whereas the story of Moses' birth is oriented entirely to the future, Psalm 69 is an individual lament in which the writer describes his precarious situation, while at the same time expressing his hope of soon being able to give thanks.

Matthew 11:20–24. The works of Jesus bore witness to the Kingdom he was proclaiming, yet many disputed his message. Many—there are still such today—rejected the God he revealed. Chorazin, Bethsaida and Capernaum were three towns that played a part in the "Galilean springtime"; they were also three towns that rejected Jesus. More was given to them than to Tyre and Sidon, which were pagan cities; therefore they, too, have earned a harsher judgment. They shall go down to the dwelling place of the dead along with proud Babylon (Is 14:15). These are stern words that tell us a great deal about how God suffers at the unbelief of human beings.

■

"Save me, God! The water is already up to my neck!"

Lengthy indeed is the lament that rises up from the land of slavery.

Among these cries of horror can be heard the weeping of an infant. Just when despair seems to be winning out over life, a newborn child becomes the light at the end of the tunnel. Its gleam is still a wavering one, and the wickedness of men may yet extinguish it; but God does not allow death to extend its sway without causing the hope of spring to make its appearance somewhere or other. The child has still to grow up; he does not know as yet that the future of an entire people will rest on his shoulders.

The history of Israel will be transformed when this man, outwardly like the Egyptian oppressors, arises and goes to his brothers and sisters. What an astonishing and momentous going out! In a world made up of mud, sweat and blood Moses becomes a Jew again. He returns to his own, and his return means a rebirth for an entire people. "Moses saw what a hard life they were having." In the presence of the injustice and degradation suffered by a man of his own blood, he feels in his own flesh the wound inflicted on the other; he discovers his "neighbor."

In the final analysis, it is this discovery that leads to the exodus. Even God will soon be able to say: "I have seen the miserable state of my people." Moses' astonishing "going out" to his people carries in it the seed of future liberation.

An astonishing going out: "He comes to his own domain." The eternal Son will go forth from the Father and to his brothers and sisters. Amid cries of horror an infant will escape massacre by the mighty. God will not cease to rise up on behalf of the oppressed and to take part in the battle of life. "And his own people did not accept him." "Who appointed you to be prince over us, and judge?" Jesus will be cast out from his own people and locked in the darkness of the tomb, but he will return, and on that day the banquet of life will be celebrated. Moses will return from Midian to his own, and on that day the liberation of the people will begin.

∎

Save us, Lord,
* for so many fears overwhelm us!*
Our detractors are too many,

and too powerful those who enslave us!
Send us our liberator;
   let him take up our defense
   and lead us to the place of peace.

Your beloved Son went forth from you
   and came to his own,
   exiled in a barren land.
Since we are his brothers and sisters,
   allow us, almighty Father,
   to go with him to the land of freedom.

WEDNESDAY OF THE 15TH WEEK

BRANDED WITH FIRE

Exodus 3:1–6, 9–12. One day Moses led his flock to the far side of the wilderness and came to the mountain of God. Here he heard Yahweh summon him to set his brethren free. Thus did the story of the exodus begin.

On this mountain Moses entered the presence of the sacred. He was filled at one and the same time with fascination and with a respectful fear. He became conscious that the ground he was walking on was sacred ground, and so he made a detour in order to get closer and see. Later on, Isaiah in the temple and Peter in his fishing boat will have the same experience, for God always calls in the midst of the everyday. At this moment it is a humble herdsman who is chosen to be the shepherd of his people.

But to experience the sacred is first of all to become conscious of one's own limitations as a creature; it is to recognize that one is sinful before the thrice-holy God. As in the case of the prophets and later the Apostles, the experience leads to a mission which causes the chosen person to face up to his own incapacity for it. "Who am I to go to Pharaoh and bring the sons of Israel out of Egypt?"

Moses still has to learn that the Lord who calls also gives the necessary strength. For the moment, a sign is given to him: Once they are set free, the people will come and worship God on the mountain on which Moses now stands. "To offer worship to God on this mountain" is the ultimate objective of the exodus. The people will be set free not in order to lose their identity in an anarchic exercise of liberty but in order to bear witness to the divine kindness among the nations. The former slaves will then become the people of God.

Psalm 103, which probably originates in devout circles within the temple, is an invitation to praise God.

Matthew 11:25–27. "I bless you, Father, for hiding these things from the learned and the clever and revealing them to mere children." These words of Jesus are usually compared with Daniel 2. Both texts are concerned with a revelation. On the one side, the Chaldean sages who are unable to interpret the dream of Nebuchadnezzar are akin to the learned (i.e., the scribes) who are so preoccupied with analyzing the law that they fail to see the signs of the times; on the other side, the mere children (the disciples) are like Daniel and his companions.

What is it that is hidden from the former and revealed to the latter? The coming of the Kingdom of God (Dan 2:44). Daniel has learned of this coming from the king's dream; the disciples see it in the works of Jesus. For, whereas John the Baptist had spoken of a fearsome judge (cf. Mt 3:12), Jesus has shown himself to be "gentle and humble in heart" (11:29) and a mere child, an authentic disciple of the Father who at the baptism had seen himself reflected in Jesus. The mysteries of the Kingdom have been entrusted to Jesus in order that he may reveal them to those who will be judged worthy. For the knowledge of these mysteries is not the privilege of a sect of initiates but is for the "pure of heart," that is, those whom God makes capable of seeing beyond the words and actions of Christ to the intimate union of Father and Son. The pure of heart are true prophets.

■

"Moses was looking after the flock of Jethro, his father-in-law." After returning to his own people and not being accepted by them, Moses the shepherd saw no prospect but to be a permanent migrant, traveling back and forth with his father-in-law's flocks across wilderness scenes void of any landmarks. Now, suddenly, an event sets the story in motion: "The angel of Yahweh appeared to him." The vision turns all points of reference and all norms upside down. "There

was the bush blazing, but it was not being burnt up." "Take off your shoes, for the place on which you stand is holy ground."

What must God be like that he sees the wretched state of his people and soon leads them to a land of freedom? Moses draws near to the blaze, and his destiny will forever bear the mark of this encounter: "Who am I to go . . . ?" "I send you . . . . I shall be with you."

Brothers and sisters, have you ever gazed at length at a fire, a fire at night? It fascinates, it draws, it is alive, yet we cannot grasp it or touch it. We speak of the "fire of love" because love purifies, transfigures, burns, singes. The fire of God! God is "I am"; his name is ineffable, an unfathomable mystery which he bids us contemplate unwearyingly until we become one with him. God will tell us his name, but we will be branded forever with the red fire and will bear within us the scar of his devouring passion. No one can see God without his eyes being seared in the fire of the Spirit. No one can taste God without his heart experiencing a new hunger. No one can believe without his prayer becoming a cry of immense desire. No one can speak of God without experiencing silence, for there are no words to say the name of God.

"No one knows the Father except the Son and those to whom the Son chooses to reveal him." Who has the ability to put into words the glory of Jesus Christ: a man among men, the icon of God in the form of the humblest of human beings? God does not make noise. He reveals himself in the signs of his presence, through faith: a faith that like love is a fire. "I bless you, Father . . . for hiding these things from the learned and the clever and revealing them to mere children." Only a childlike heart has access to true love and to faith. It is good for us that the fire should keep us from drawing near, for it is not possible to stare at God as one takes stock of an idol. "No one knows the Son except the Father." It is good for us to contemplate Jesus with faces veiled, for we cannot speak about him as we demonstrate a theorem.

Moses covered his face because he was afraid to look at God. In a short time, he will truly know God, for when his people leave the land of slavery he will see the God who saw the wretched state of his people and heard their cries. We truly know the fire only when it has burned us. We truly experience faith only when we experience the burning touch of the Spirit. God reveals his "back," for until the time of eternal communion with him when we see him face to face, we shall lay hold of him only when he has passed by: in a fire that burns but does not consume, in words that do not exhaust the mystery, in a face that has always yet to be seen, in a sign that points to a fiery beyond.

■

A burning bush, a fire that burns without consuming,
God allows himself to be known only by a heart
*   that experiences the sting of the Spirit.*
Let us learn his name
*   in the humble signs he gives us!*
Will we have a childlike heart
*   so as to recognize the voice that rouses faith?*

■

Like a fire that goes and comes in the night,
*   so is your gaze in the emptiness of our silences!*
Like a blaze that makes things bright as day,
*   so is your Spirit in the emptiness of our hope!*
Like a spark that sets the horizon aglow,
*   so is your Breath by which our love is quickened!*
Blessed be you, God of the burning bush!

■

Holy is this ground
*   where your love burns without consuming!*
Holy is this place
*   where you call us by our name!*
Do not allow us, Lord,
*   to say your name*
*   without first listening to your word;*
do not allow us to listen to our brothers
*   without revealing your love to them.*

A NAME THAT CREATES HISTORY

Exodus 3:13–20. In order to understand this passage, we must transport ourselves back to the period of the redaction of the Book of Exodus. The time is the eighth century B.C.; the place is the northern kingdom; the situation, that created by the sedentarization of the tribes and the more or less widespread acceptance of the cult of the baals, who were the Canaanite gods of fertility. It is the period of Elijah and Hosea, who came forward as defenders of the God of the fathers; it is also the period of the Elohist, whose writings have the same purpose as the utterances of the prophets.

The Elohist wishes, therefore, to explain the name of Yahweh to his contemporaries. This intention is all the more justified in that in the fertility cults, magical formulas played an important role and called for an exact pronunciation of the name of the divinity being invoked. What explanation of the divine name does the Elohist propose? With the help of a play on words he connects the name Yahweh with a simple form of the verb "to be" (*hawah*); de Vaux therefore proposes translating "Yahweh" as "I am the Existing One."[9]

In any case we must avoid understanding the explanation in a metaphysical sense, for that would not be in keeping with the Hebrew mind. There are several points to be made in this connection. First of all, in v. 10 God had called Israel "my people," thus asserting the existence of special ties. Furthermore, in v. 12, when giving a sign to Moses, Yahweh had added: "I shall be with you." The God of the fathers had undoubtedly also been with Abraham, Isaac and Jacob, but the reason for his presence had been personal or familial. In the present context, "Yahweh is with Moses to serve his people,"[10] that is, to bring them out of Egypt. It is in the exodus event itself, therefore, that the people will learn that their God is the only Existing One,

> a God who did not have a divine history like that of the gods of mythology, because he was simply, totally and constantly the "Existing One." Yahweh was, however, a God who directed man's history and who manifested himself not in the phenomena of nature taking place in a cycle of seasonal events, like the fertility and

vegetation gods, but in historical events following one another in time and moving toward an end.[11]

Psalm 105. "This is the memorial with which you shall celebrate me": Israel will never forget that Yahweh had led it "from servitude to service." Psalm 105 urges Israel to remember and give thanks.

Matthew 11:28–30. "My yoke is easy and my burden light." This saying of Jesus has undeniable polemical overtones. It is aimed at the scribes who set their hopes on a meticulous observance of the law and had therefore ended by laying an intolerable burden on the shoulders of the ordinary people whom, in addition, they despised. Over against their speculations Jesus sets a law that is simple because it can be summed up in a single commandment, that of love.

This law is, of course, a terribly demanding one, and every human being falls short of its full observance, but it is also the law of a God of love and mercy. We must keep in mind that the Beatitudes speak of a gift of the Kingdom and not of a list of virtues to be acquired. The scribes speak of merits, but Jesus speaks of accepting the reign of God by faith. He can therefore legitimately claim to be "gentle and humble in heart," for he is himself first of all a "mere child" to whom the Father has made everything known. If we want to learn what life truly is, we must attend his school of wisdom.

■

"I have visited you and seen all that the Egyptians are doing to you. And so I have resolved to bring you up out of Egypt where you are oppressed, into the land of the Canaanites . . . a land where milk and honey flow." Here is what God says by way of identifying himself: "I have resolved to be concerned for you!" That is the only claim that allows God to say "I am" and to address man as "thou." "Yahweh, the God of the Hebrews, has come to meet us."

Human beings had tried to appoint their own gods: mythological symbols, sacral images, idols whose favors they then tried to win. But these creations of the human mind had no interest in the world of men and women. These gods were regarded as more divine, the more they dissociated themselves from human affairs and withdrew into a world distinct from ours, an ideal paradise. But the God who summons Moses reveals his name, and it is an astonishing and unexpected name. He calls himself "the God of your fathers," "the God of the Hebrews," and "I am."

We have no other basis for speaking of God except his relation to human history. God has no other identity to communicate to us except this: that he has come to meet human beings and that in a sense their future is his future. God does not define himself as he is in himself; his name is connected rather with the relationship he cultivates with his people in a joint history of covenant. He enters the workshop where our history is being made, and we are bidden to focus our attention on our history with him. His name (and for the Bible a name is more than a simple designation; it reveals and to some extent gives power over the reality of the name-bearer), or what he is, we are to learn by building our lives in union with him. What God is is also what he will be. Human history is from generation to generation the ever moving place to which God "comes," the place where he is born and engenders his own being.

A God who has become a "neighbor," a God involved in the destiny of human beings: there you have the foolishness of faith. God has taken sides with man! "I have resolved to be concerned for you! I Am who I Am!" We are here being advised of a name that is not a name at all. God is nameless because no one can have any ascendancy over him. He expresses his being only in his actions. We shall never see God directly but only be able to recognize him where he has passed by. And this passage is clearly marked: "I have resolved to bring you up out of Egypt where you are oppressed." The act which reveals God's identity is an act of liberation. Our faith is a faith in a God-who-becomes-along-with-us, because he has chosen to make our becoming his own.

■

You are not a stranger to us;
and because you resolved to rise up in our behalf
*   we accept the risk of belonging to you.*
As human beings of flesh and blood,
rebellious human beings,
*   we are only dust*

and aliens in our own home.
But your Breath makes us your people.
May he lead us to the light of freedom;
   created anew by his power,
   we will be your inheritance and your domain.

■

Only God, Yahweh, God of our fathers,
God our Father, God of all men and women,
   you are, you were, you come,
   you are always with us,
   you will always be with the human race!
Your name is incised in our memory,
your name creates our history:
   we address you: My God!
   we address you: Our God!
   every being addresses you: God, Lord!
To no one are you a stranger.
To every being you say:
   "I shall concern myself with you!"
To every people you say:
   "I am your God!"
To the slave you say:
   "Here I am to set you free!"
Only God, Yahweh, God of our fathers,
God our Father, God of all men and women,
   we have no God but you.
As long as our history lasts,
   storm-tossed by so many enslavements,
   your name remains engraved in our memory
   and, with all human beings,
   we address you: "God, our Savior,
   our liberator,
   our only God for all eternity."

EATING THE PASSOVER

Exodus 11:10—12:14. The passage, which gives in detailed form all the rubrics to be observed in celebrating the Passover, comes from the priesthood. Its redaction is therefore later than the events it purports to describe.

The rubrics have nonetheless kept the familial character of the feast. From time immemorial, the nomads of the wilderness used to celebrate the Passover at the spring full moon, at the time of departure for summer pastures, during which in addition the young would be born. To ensure a prosperous journey, the herders used to anoint the tent-pegs with the blood of a lamb or goat that had been sacrificed; this gesture was thought to repel the evil spirits that were personified as the destroyer (*mashit*). The absence of any reference to a sanctuary; the fact that the victim was roasted and eaten with herbs typical of the desert and with the unleavened bread of the bedouin; the costume of the herders; the nocturnal celebration by moonlight: all these details bear witness to the nomadic origin of the festival.

How is it connected with the departure from Egypt? According to de Vaux, "one spring, when the feast ensuring the well-being of the flocks and herds . . . was being celebrated, at a time when a scourge was laying Egypt waste, the Israelites left Egypt, led by Moses in the name of their God, Yahweh."[12] Is there anything that can be said about this scourge or plague? The reference is probably to an epidemic, but it must be noted that while the Book of Exodus establishes a connection between the celebration of the Passover and the tenth plague, account must also be taken of the hypothesis of the two exoduses. Tradition links the tenth plague to the exodus-expulsion. We are thus confronted with a complicated mingling of various traditions. In any case, once the Hebrews had settled in Palestine, they established a definitive connection between the celebration of the Passover and the exodus event; the feast thus became a memorial.

Psalm 116 is a thanksgiving psalm. The verses used here express the psalmist's intention of offering a sacrifice of praise. They thus give voice to the gratitude of the Jews as they recall Yahweh's interventions in their behalf.

Matthew 12:1–8. "My yoke is easy and my burden light." The disagreement between Jesus and his enemies often had to do with the interpretation of the law. Thus the Pharisees had reduced observance of the sabbath to a casuistical matter of the permitted and the prohibited. As a result, they missed the deeper meaning of the sabbath as an irruption of the sacred into time.

What is "the sort of fast that pleases me?" Yahweh had asked the prophet Isaiah. True repentance consists of breaking unjust fetters and undoing yokes. The sacrifice and worship acceptable to the Lord consists in an unwearying attention to the neighbor, especially to the lowly. Rather than crush the poor man under excessively heavy burdens, we must show him kindness and mercy.

But in dealing here with the Pharisees, Jesus argues in the rabbinical manner. He appeals first to the example of David; then he recalls another precedent which the rabbis accepted, namely, that the obligations of sabbath observance yield to necessities connected with worship. Though he looks like anyone else, Jesus here asserts his superiority to David and the temple. The Son of Man is truly master of the sabbath.

■

God has come forward to tell us his name. The hour of liberation has struck, the hour for passing from the land of slavery to the path of the promise, the hour of Passover. At this final meal the Lord writes in gestures that stand forever the meaning of the road he is about to throw open to his people. This is an extraordinary night that is linked to the foundational nights: the night of creation, the night of Isaac's sacrifice and Abraham's obedience, the night of the Messiah's coming. Century after century a child will ask: "Why is this night different from all other nights?" and generation after generation a people will give the answer as they eat the Passover: "God resolved to make us his concern!" It is a meal that celebrates God's intervention in behalf of men and women held in bondage. Because they are sealed with blood shed for the sake of salvation, the mistreated will be spared and the oppressors destroyed. A day will come when the Lamb of God, the Spotless One, will shed his own blood for the salvation of the many. On that day God will bear witness in blood and will give his own Passover to be eaten.

This is an exodus meal: "You shall eat it like this: with a girdle round your waist, sandals on your feet, a staff in your hand." The meal will be a viaticum, bread for the journey. There is a Passover only for those who arise and take the road through the wilderness. There is no passage without sacrifice. One must abandon everything in order to receive everything. The Passover is a summons, a pilgrimage feast. It is a "passage" that must be eaten. We who are alienated from our true condition as free men will discover our alienation and be urged to arise so that we may win and receive our freedom.

This is a covenant meal. "This day is to be a day of remembrance for you." God signs a covenant in blood: "The blood shall serve to mark the houses that you live in." An hour will come when the cup will be passed from hand to hand as a sign of the new covenant. God will write in actions of sacrifice the Love that perseveres to the end; he will change the bread and wine into a sign of his irreversible love. The essential passage is the passage of love.

This is a Passover night. God has reversed the course of history: a people is born, brought into being by the promise. In what way is this night different from the others if not because age after age it leads human beings through the great passage? From a land in which they were strangers they pass to a land in which each is the other's neighbor, and in which God has, in all truth, become God-for-us.

■

A people that arises in the night,
a people that shares in haste a meal for the journey.
This night and this meal
will be for all ages a sign of liberation,
the Passover that saves.

■

At the hour when they sacrificed the lambs for Passover,
your Son gave himself up irretrievably.
  By the body and blood of the Lamb
  have mercy on us!

126

A victim without spot or defect,
he shed his blood for the many.
  By the body and blood of the Lamb,
  have mercy on us!

He who eats that flesh
already has life for his inheritance.
  By the body and blood of the Lamb,
  have mercy on us!

■

We are oppressed and exiled in our own country:
  God, remember your promise!
  By the body and blood of the Lamb,
  save our world today!
Seal us with the love that gave itself to the end,
  the blood shed for the many.
  May the bread we share be a remembrance for us.
We shall arise and go toward the road of freedom,
  in an exodus that leads to rediscovered peace.

SATURDAY OF THE 15TH WEEK

THE NIGHT OF HOPE

Exodus 12:37–42. After they had settled in Canaan, the Jews connected Passover with the departure from Egypt. On that night the Lord had kept watch over his people; it was fitting, therefore, that the people should in turn keep watch in remembrance of the divine intervention. This tradition was at the origin of a famous poem in the Palestinian Targum, the poem of the four nights. This poem highlights the fundamental stages in the growth of the people of God: the night of creation, the night in which Abraham received the promise of a son, the night of the departure from Egypt, and finally the night of the world's completion, a night we now experience in hope. The poem thus gives expression to the prophetic aspect of the Jewish Passover, insofar as that Passover heralds the definitive salvation of

127

the human race. And as a matter of fact, the reason why during their Easter Vigil Christians read the story of the crossing of the sea is that they are conscious of the complete liberation which has been accomplished by the death and resurrection of Christ.

Psalm 136, which is part of the Great Hallel, is a classic psalm of the paschal liturgy.

Matthew 12:14–21. In claiming to be master of the sabbath Jesus is accused of blaspheming. His enemies take counsel together on the means of ridding themselves of him, while he for his part withdraws. He continues to work cures, but orders the beneficiaries of them not to reveal his identity. As far as the disciples are concerned, to whom he has already explained the dangers of the mission, there is here a kind of prediction of the passion, for in his withdrawal Jesus is already the suffering Messiah, the "unobtrusive" servant.

The confrontation has to do with his person. Jesus speaks of himself as the Son of Man, while the crowd asks whether he is not the Son of David. The scribes and Pharisees, however, will soon be claiming that he owes his miracles to Beelzebul, the prince of demons. In the final analysis, the thing that dismays them is the newness of the Kingdom. They trust only in their merits and they exclude sinners from salvation, whereas Jesus presents himself as gentle and humble in heart, and he breathes only goodness and mercy.

■

"The sons of Israel went out . . . ." Over three thousand years after the exodus Jews still repeat each year the actions of their distant Hebrew ancestors: they meet as families and gather around the ancestral table to eat bitter herbs and unleavened bread. They "enact" and experience the exodus. The event seems to have become an institution, the miracle a ceremony. But in reality, history has turned into promise.

The reason is that the night of Passover is at the heart of the survival and hope of Israel. It serves as witness and profession of faith, just as it did long ago in Egypt: God (it asserts) is watching over the human race and intervening in history. Already written down in the book of Passover is the unhappy story of mistreated humanity, but the book also sings, in the almost surrealist language of faith, the certainty of salvation. Passover is a night of promise and of the abolition of every enslavement.

This is the challenge of the night of hope: love cannot do everything, and yet human beings continue to desire that in this dark and inhuman world there should be, and be forever, a place of freedom and communion, of festivity and communication.

"This was a night of watching for the Lord." As the prophet of God tells his people of their origins, he still believes, despite so many adverse experiences, that life is good and deserves a generous welcome. God has made us pass over to the other shore: "All the array of Yahweh left the land of Egypt." We believe that our world is not a closed world, locked in upon itself, a ghetto in which every man becomes a wolf preying on his fellows. We believe that we have passed to the other side, into a universe that opens out upon the virgin expanses of a wilderness in which someone dwells and which is therefore habitable by man.

"This night must be kept as a vigil." The book of Passover is written in the lives of men and women, in the courageous, tenacious, persevering struggle of those who refuse to despair of man. Our belief is that every human being who opts for communion and against evil and suffering is committed to God's cause in this world. The night of Passover, celebrated century after century, is something far different from a pious remembrance tinged with romantic melancholy; it is the insurrection of an entire people whom God has raised up; it is an insurrection of hope, today.

■

God, you have visited us in our night;
  you have watched to rescue us from the darkness
  and from all that fettered us.
You have battered down the walls of our ghettos
  and led us to the land of freedom.
Blessed be you for your Son
  who has sown at the heart of our exodus
  the hope of a new earth.
Keep us erect, that your hope may be fulfilled
  and our prayer may be the sign of our watchfulness.

THE TRUE PASSAGE

Exodus 14:5–18. (This commentary will cover the Old Testament reading for tomorrow as well, i.e., 14:21—15:1.)

The "miracle of the sea" separates the period of Egyptian enslavement from the Hebrews' first days of freedom. This fact explains the place of the story in the Passover ritual, as well as the many traditions centering around it. As an example of such many and varied traditions we may point to a detail like the size of the Egyptian group that pursued the Hebrews: 14:6 (Yahwist tradition) speaks simply of Pharaoh's "troops," while 14:7 (Elohist tradition) mentions "six hundred of the best chariots," and 14:18 (Priestly tradition) adds an entire army.

The biblical story thus makes use of the three usual sources, but we shall limit ourselves here to the Yahwist and Priestly traditions, since the Elohist element is more difficult to isolate. According to the Yahwist source, Yahweh personally intervened to destroy the Egyptian army, and the Hebrews, camped beside the sea, had only to wait. First the fog hid them from the eyes of their pursuers; then a strong wind blew from the east all night long, swept away the waters, and thus caused the destruction of the Egyptians when they and their horses ventured out into the dried up crossing, for in the morning the waters returned and drowned them. This tradition (especially 14:19, 21b, 27), which says nothing about a passage of the Hebrews through the sea, likens the divine intervention to a "holy war" against the enemies of Israel. The fugitives "are shown to be in a desperate situation and their rescue is attributed by them to a powerful and miraculous intervention of their God. This act of salvation strengthens their faith in Yahweh (Ex 14:31). The same 'great act' became a fundamental article of faith for all those who became associated with Yahwism."[13]

According to the Priestly tradition (cf. 14:21ac, 22–23, 26–27a, 28–29), Moses divided the sea in two in order to let his companions pass through dry-shod. This story has felicitously been compared with the story of the crossing of the Jordan, at the other end of the entire exodus narrative (Jos 4:22–23). The later story tells how the waters upstream piled into a single mass, perhaps as the result of a natural landslide, and allowed the conquerors to pass dryshod into the Holy Land opposite Jericho. In the

Priestly tradition, then, the miracle of the sea is described as a victory of Yahweh over the sea and the cosmos, for the action of Moses in striking the waters clearly echoes the separation of the dry land and the waters in the first story of creation.

Canticle of Moses. Cf. commentary on Tuesday of this week.

Matthew 12:38–42. The Pharisees have accused Jesus of working his cures with the help of Beelzebul. This amounts to an accusation of practicing magic. Jesus in turn accuses them of bad faith, for they knew very well that healing can be attributed only to God. In their own way these cures proclaimed the breakthrough of the Kingdom, since they terminated the power of Satan—something the enemies of Jesus were unwilling to acknowledge. As a matter of fact, the real issue here is the full meaning of Jesus' message. After the manner of the suffering servant, Jesus proclaims a period of grace and forgiveness. According to him, the Kingdom is to be received as a gift of God; according to the Pharisees, it must be earned. Jesus presents himself as a "mere child," the "Beloved" of the Father; the Pharisees entrench themselves in their pride, demanding a sign but refusing to make out the sign given to them in the person and ministry of Jesus.

The literary history of the sign of Jonah is a complex one. It is possible that the Church added the sign of the three days and three nights, thus making the stay of Jonah in the whale parallel to that of Jesus in the tomb. However, the point of the narrative is to be seen in the conversion of the people of Nineveh who had humbled themselves on hearing the preaching of Jonah, whereas the enemies of Jesus refuse to listen to him. Because they await a glorious Messiah, they are unwilling to see in the humbling of the Servant an authentic sign of the Kingdom. And yet Jesus is greater than Jonah and Solomon, just as he is greater than the temple.

■

They had set out relying on a hope. The vigil had rekindled their desire for freedom and, strengthened by a promise, they had risen up and gone. Then everything fell apart. Pharaoh retracted his decision and sent his chariots in pursuit of the fugitives. To the fear of an uncertain future was now added a more sober appreciation of reality: it was a mistake to rebel against such a master, and the longing for

singing tomorrows was delusive. Realism won out over the dream: "Better to work for the Egyptians than die in the wilderness!" They thought they could liberate themselves by their own power, but now the harsh reality of their situation confronts them with the key question: "Who will save me?" "You will see what Yahweh will do to save you today."

"Leave us alone. We would rather work for the Egyptians." "You will see what Yahweh will do to save you today." The whole truth of the Bible and the faith is to be seen in the conflict between, on the one hand, the realism of the person who can see only the difficulty of his situation and face up to it courageously, and, on the other, the partisan discourse of revelation: God comes to man's help. The Bible presents not only the "happy version" of events, the one in which God is everywhere present as the author of victories, happy outcomes, and events working together unto good. It also gives the other version of events, the idolatrous, rationalistic and rebellious version of them: "Leave us alone!" And the "happy version" is so strongly asserted and repeated only because the other is always there, always present and continually reborn. The Bible presents this "conflict of interpretations": Does our victory come as the result of our calculations, our efforts, our fears and our hopes? Is it the conquest "of our hands" over the fates that rule our lives, or is it a favor revealed to us, a victory to be received? The true passage of the people takes place only amid this conflict of interpretations, this battle between two realisms: "Leave us alone" and "You will see."

"It is an evil and unfaithful generation that asks for a sign!" The conflict of interpretations continues. Jesus claims to take upon himself the yoke worn by human beings, their illnesses and wretchedness. Is he therefore the promised Servant whom God has chosen in order to help his people? The only sign to be given is precisely this: a man who takes upon himself the harsh reality of the human condition, a man who dies. But this man also cries out: "Father, into your hands I commit my spirit." The true passage or Pass-over will consist in confessing amid the scandal of the cross that the Servant has been glorified.

"Leave us alone"—"You will see": two histories in conflict. There is in me the obstinate determination to say: "It is I who save myself," even though I do not succeed, but there is also the conviction that God is not an indifferent witness of our disappointments but takes our part or, in short, that there is a covenant. Faith is a passage: it wins out over what it is not.

■

On the canticle in Exodus 15

I will sing in behalf of God:
 May his victory be brilliant
 in the eyes of his faithful!

Our enemies
 he leaves far behind us:
 in him is our salvation,
 to him our song of blessing goes up.

This God of our fathers,
 his name is "the Lord."
 His glory shines out in the covenant,
 his valor rouses our hope.

The abysses could not hold the Servant
 or death enslave the Beloved.
 God has brought him to the other shore,
 and our victory is called "Pass-over."

TUESDAY OF THE 16TH WEEK

LIBERATION
Exodus 14:21—15:1. Cf. Monday of this week.

Canticle of Moses (Ex 15). The entire set of stories culminates in a vivid hymn in honor of Yahweh. V. 1 corresponds to v. 21, which is sung by Miriam, and is probably the oldest part that provided the base on which the hymn was developed. It is difficult to determine the date of composition, especially since the end of the poem alludes to the "miracle of the Jordan" which allowed the troops of Joshua to cross the river dry-shod. This paralleling of the two crossings gives a glimpse of the same God at work.

Matthew 12:45–50. Who are my mother and brothers? Who is the true disciple? Who is it that accepts the Kingdom preached by Jesus? Like the Sermon on the Mount, Chapter 12 ends with an emphasis on concrete action. Those who do the Father's will are the true disciples.

■

Quite frankly, the Bible has nothing of the impartial chronicle about it. On the contrary, it embodies a very deliberate decision to promote one interpretation of events; it is partisan discourse that seeks to convince: "That day, Yahweh rescued Israel, and they put their faith in Yahweh."

"That day, Yahweh rescued Israel": the Passover will remain at the heart of Israel's survival and hope. But "that day" does not refer primarily to the hazardous crossing of the Sea of Reeds and the exchange of slavery for autonomy. The true "passage" takes place when the claim that rises naturally from the human heart, "It is the work of my own hands," gives way to thanksgiving and praise. True liberation takes place when the believer confesses his faith and passes to a different vision, a different interpretation.

Century after century, men and women would tell one another the epic of the Red Sea, using the almost surrealist language of faith. They would, however, be singing not an epic but their own certainty of being saved and liberated. At the departure from Egypt, a new hour struck for the human race: the hour of its liberation from wretchedness. If the exodus with its two characteristics, an imperious divine will at work along with responsible participation by human beings, had not occurred, the historical course of the human race would have been radically different; redemption would have played no part, even at its very roots. The Jew says in the night of Passover: "Now if God had not brought out our forefathers from Egypt, then even we, our children, and our children's children might still have been enslaved to Pharaoh in Egypt."[14] Conversely, the door which the exodus opened can never be closed again. We are free with an everlasting freedom; the energy which at that moment poured out on the world like a torrent is inexhaustible and invincible.

"That day, Yahweh rescued Israel." In the debate within which our faith is built up we confess that slavery has been forever overcome. This does not mean, however, that we take timorous refuge in a utopian security. Israel lived its freedom in the dramatic events of its history. In the Bible salvation is always glimpsed through opaque and fleshly things. Liberation is a call, and redemption a passage, a Passover.

"You have passed from death to life," cries Paul. Death has not been left behind us like a bitter memory, and faith will continue to involve a conflict of interpretations. For the Easter faith is marked by a paradox, and the transfiguration won turns into light only at the very moment when the darkness is accepted with its painful challenge. We have been reborn with Christ and have passed with him to the other shore in order to continue our journey as risen men and women and to lead a paschal life. The country that opens up before the people is the land in which they will experience their freedom with its shocks and misfortunes. Freedom needs to be lived as a forever expanding liberation.

■

You go before your people, Lord our God,
and lead them to the other shore,
the land of freedom, the covenanted land,
the land of exodus, the land of birth.

With your Christ, first-born of a new world,
make us pass from death to life.
Free us from all that holds us back,
and enable us to live by the grace
which you offer us in Jesus our Savior.

■

To you, God our Savior and our Father,
to you we give thanks through Jesus Christ!
Through him you bring us forth

from the house of slavery
and into the land of freedom.

Your love for us turned to madness
when your Son experienced in his flesh
    the death of a slave
    that we might live as your children.
Because we believe in this sign of Pass-over,
you have begotten us to the freedom of children,
    that we might offer you, with your Christ,
    the praise of redeemed creation.

Reading and Understanding Matthew

The Parabolic Discourse (Chapter 13)

Chapters 11 and 12 placed the person of Jesus at the center of a debate. Chapter 13 does the same, but this time in the form of a series of parables that have to do essentially with sowing and with the soils—good or bad—in which the seed is put. So it is with the word of God in the hearts of human beings: the word is a priceless treasure, a fine pearl, for which no surrender of other things is too great.

The lesson that emerges from the parabolic discourse is one both of realism and of optimism. Soils do indeed differ as good and mediocre, but we must, like the sower, trust in the power of the word. The world is an enclosed field in which the darnel grows along with the good grain. We must therefore be patient and wait for the harvest, when the separation can be done in the full light of day.

The discourse ends on a stern note. The call of Jesus is to be taken seriously; it is the last that God will address to human beings, and its acceptance is therefore a matter of life and death for them. The thrust of the discourse is eschatological, as is suggested by the number of parables (eight, if we include the parable of the scribe in 13:52). Thus we see one group separating itself from the crowd; this group is the disciples who accept the word, even if for the moment they do so with a heart still weighed down with the filth of sin. In Chapters 14 through 17 we shall see Jesus devoting himself in a special way to their formation.

FROM WEDNESDAY OF THE 16TH WEEK
TO THURSDAY OF THE 17TH WEEK

Covenant

It is not easy to be free human beings. The children of Israel learn this truth on the morrow of the exodus. The lesson is a harsh one: the Chinese lanterns have been extinguished, the festival is over. The enthusiastic accents of the canticle of Moses are succeeded by complaints and murmurings. Israel is no longer sure of anything now that it has rejected the concentration-camp world of Pharaoh. It must discover that its life is to come, step by step, from the grace of God, as a gift received from his hand. It must discover that liberation is not accomplished in a day, but that on the other hand God each day takes care of his own and is Providence and Father to them. It is a difficult road that the children of Israel follow in the wilderness, a road on which they try their hand at being free; it is also a marvelous road on which they discover that God is traveling with them; his tent accompanies the people on their journeyings. God too has his exodus.

God turns these escapees, these nameless Hebrews, these survivors of Egyptian slavery into a liberated people. They become his people and his "inheritance." In order to guide them along the difficult way of inventing their own freedom Yahweh gives them ten words which sum up the rights of the risen human person. The Eternal One establishes a community of blood with those who are becoming "his." He takes up residence within their history and pitches his tent amid the caravan that is moving toward the promised land.

The covenant has a history; it is not an abstract ideology. It is woven of flesh and blood, fidelity and sin, revelation and idolatry; it is the adventure of a people who discover, at the critical points in their wandering through the wilderness, that they are the people God loves, the messianic people

137

who are being sanctified by the exodus God is undertaking with them.

■

Father most holy,
it is good for us to praise you
when you make your people pass
  from the land of slavery to the promised land.

You free us in Jesus, the Son of the covenant.
Through him you show us today
  the Easter road
and through your Spirit you give us
  strength to follow him in the wilderness.
It is there that he brings us
  the word that guides our history
  and the bread that sustains our journey.
Blessed be you, God of our lands of exile,
for in our groping quest
  freedom from our servitudes becomes a reality
and we can even now sing the acclamation
  of a people set free by your grace.

WEDNESDAY OF THE 16TH WEEK

VIATICUM

Exodus 16:1–5, 9–15. Why did God send the manna to the travelers in the desert? Two answers can be seen in the verses which are read in the liturgy. V. 4 sees the gift of the manna as a trial decided upon by Yahweh who wishes to test the obedience of the people. V. 12, on the other hand, speaks of a manifestation of divine providence. The first answer is to be understood in the context of the law; the second is connected with the departure from Egypt. The God who set Israel free is also the God who gave it laws. As a matter of fact, the isolation of the sources is difficult: the story is basically from the Priestly tradition, but it has Yahwist elements inserted into it.

However the Priestly concern hardly makes itself felt in the liturgical pericope. A reference to laws regarding the sabbath can be seen in v. 5 with its mention of the twofold harvest; v. 1 speaks of the "community of the sons of Israel" and alludes to the Priestly calendar, since the Hebrews pitch their camp in the wilderness of Sin on the fifteenth day of the second month, that is, on a Friday, the eve of the sabbath.

Another theme emerges more clearly: the theme of "murmuring" to which reference had already been made in Exodus 14:11–12. (Monday of this 16th Week). The Jews who reproach Moses or even Yahweh himself reject the risks of the exodus and clearly manifest their nostalgia for Egypt. This theme, which will be developed in both Jewish and Christian (cf. Jn 6) literature, probably originated in the condemnation of the division of Palestine into two kingdoms after the reign of Solomon. For circles close to the court of Jerusalem, the need, in that context, was to discomfit the northern provinces, the homeland of the tribes of the house of Joseph that had dared to "murmur" against God in the wilderness, and thus to explain the choice of the Davidic dynasty.

The theme of the manna, which was linked to the theme of murmuring, likewise had an extensive theological future. After being regarded by some as a miraculous nourishment (Wis 16) but scorned by others (Num 11), the manna will be transcended in the New Testament by the gift of the bread of life (Jn 6). This messianic vision was already the vision cherished in Exodus, since after the testing of the wilderness the manna was to be replaced by the produce of the promised land (16:35).

Psalm 78 originates in circles at court and in the Jerusalem temple. It too judges the schism of the northern tribes in the light of the conduct of Ephraim's ancestors in the wilderness. In v. 25 the manna is called "the bread of immortals."

Matthew 13:1–9. The parable of the sower contains the essential teaching of the parabolic discourse. It describes the encounter of seed and soil, that is, of the divine word with the human heart. The preceding chapters have described at length the opposition of Jesus' disparagers, but in so doing they have also shown how the irruption of the word effects a separation among human beings. Those who receive this word as a gracious gift deserve the name of disciple; they are good soil that will bear fruit.

The eschatological orientation of this parable is beyond question. In effect, the contrast between the good soils and the barren soils is an allusion to the vicissitudes met in preaching the Kingdom of God but also to the final success of this preaching. In fact, the parable anticipates the final judgment during which the fishermen will sit on the shore separating the good from the bad (cf. 13:47–50).

■

Jesus went out of the house to the vast crowd. "Imagine a sower going out to sow." The prophet arises. After remaining silent for centuries, the Spirit once again reveals the secrets of God. The crowds are bewildered; the harmless little story turns all images upside down. They thought the Kingdom would burst in like a sunny harvest, yet here four of the six verses of the parable speak of failure! How can we countenance so much lost seed, even though some of the seed will ultimately bear abundant fruit?

The questioning and the surprise are ours as well. The word of God has been at work in the world for centuries; how is it possible that our earth should still experience the selfishness that dries up love or the hatred and pride that stifle justice? Why have we continued to be rocky soil, now that the Gospel has been sown in the hearts of human beings? Has God vainly exhausted himself in the effort to make the new man arise in us? Is not the promised liberation only a decoy if tomorrow we must die in the wilderness? A sower who scatters his seed on the road is violating common sense. God is in need of a recycling.

But God's spirit is the poetic spirit of a gardener. He traverses the earth, casting seed in every direction. Could there possibly be a gesture of greater confidence in life? God entrusts his seed to the earth; the rigors of winters and the rough rains attack in vain, for the seed hidden in the furrow will surely shoot up. And God is already rejoicing at the harvest. If the winter is too harsh and the heart of man too hardened, he will scatter his seed again! The wilderness may indeed be only a place of hunger and thirst, but he will accomplish his work of liberation: "You will have bread in abundance, and you will know that I am your God!" God stubbornly takes care of his own.

God has taken man's side; the Son has come forth from the Father to proclaim the time of renewal. When Christ says: "Unless a wheat grain falls on the ground and dies, it remains only a single grain," he is speaking of himself. The sower has become the seed, and the word of God will be scattered in the furrow of Golgotha. The ground grain will be the bread of life, and the word scattered in every direction will be the viaticum for the journey to the promised land—through the wilderness.

■

From the seed that dies, Lord,
   raise up a hundred new grains!
And let our hearts be caught up
   in the foolish hope of a harvest
   that will ripen in the sun of your love!

■

Father, God of heaven and earth,
   blessed be your name!
Yes, it is truly good to give you thanks
   through Jesus Christ, your beloved Son!

Like the grain of wheat that falls to the ground
   he has brought forth much fruit,
   for you raised him from the tomb
   so that with him we may pass
   from death to life.

Yes, Father, blessed be you!
As the seed is hidden in the furrow
until the next spring,
   our life is hidden in your Christ
   until he comes again!
That is why we can already sing your praises.

■

As it did at the dawn of the first day,
your word, Lord, creates the universe,
   a light that espouses our suffering flesh
   to transfigure it!

As it did in the wilderness days,
your word gives us the bread of new pastures,
  a viaticum that sustains us on our journey
  and leads us to the promised land.

Let it be done to us, Lord, according to your word!
Let the hour of our harvest come
  when our history will give birth to eternity!

GOING UP TO BE TRANSFIGURED

Exodus 19:1–2, 9–11, 16–20b. The space occupied in the Pentateuch by the Sinai tradition is enough to show its importance. It begins in Exodus 19:1 with the arrival of the Hebrews in the wilderness of Sinai and continues down to Numbers 10:28 when they leave the area. Sinai is the goal of the Hebrews as they leave Egypt and enter the wilderness: "Yahweh made Israel his people at Sinai. He concluded a covenant with them. He also gave them their laws."[15]

Mention has already been made of the Yahwist and Elohist traditions from which the narrative is constructed. We will recall that the Elohist describes the theophany as a storm, while the Yahwist treats it as a volcanic eruption, something which would have been rather exotic in the time of Solomon but which Israelites might have experienced during a maritime expedition. Furthermore, the liturgy exercised an important influence both on the redaction of the text as we have it and on the traditions which pre-dated the text. Note the mention of a sacred enclosure in v. 12, the emphasis in vv. 14–15 on the purification of the participants, and the use of liturgical objects such as the horn in vv. 13, 16 and 19. Even the cloud—which according to some suggests an active volcano, according to others lighted torches—calls to mind the clouds of incense which symbolized the hidden presence of God in the temple.

The point of the narrative is that at Sinai Yahweh acquired a people. A group of men and women, after escaping from servitude in Egypt, braved fatigue and a harsh climate, forged bonds of brotherhood among them

142

and, above all, experienced the divine presence in their midst. As a result, they had begun to speak a common language. Is it unwarranted to think that the theophany at Sinai represented for the people as a whole what the manifestation of God in the sacred bush had been for Moses?

Matthew 13:10–17. We must recall the context of the citation from Isaiah (6:9–11) if we are to understand the "why?" of the parables. In the prophet the citation serves as a preface to what is usually called "The Book of Immanuel." In dealing with King Ahaz the prophet has just had experience of how men can harden their hearts to the word of God; his contemporaries heard what he said but they refused to understand it.

Jesus has the same experience. The purpose of everything he says and does is to reveal the mysteries of the Kingdom, but many people close their eyes and ears so as not to see and understand. Therefore Jesus speaks in parables; he says simple things that are accessible to "mere children," but enigmatic to the "learned" and the "clever." His practice serves as the occasion for another beatitude: "Happy are your eyes because they see, your ears because they hear!" Many would like to be in your place!

■

They have crossed the Red Sea. They had not been a people, but now they are gathered under a single leader for a joint undertaking. They engage in bitter accusations: when all was said and done, slavery in Egypt was more satisfying than the uncertainties of the wilderness; forced labor was less demanding than the harsh apprenticeship freedom required. The late evening songs and dances were already far behind them, and the journey was becoming burdensome, even if supported by the bread of the manna. Finally, what was the point of freedom if they were simply going to go around in circles? Why all this effort if nowhere on the horizon could the goal and meaning of the adventure be seen?

Yes, the time has come for the people to learn the meaning of the event in which they are a participant. After killing the Egyptian, Moses had found refuge in the wilderness. The man whom the wilderness then welcomed was not simply an outlaw; he was a man betrayed by Egypt, whose injustice had stirred his conscience, and betrayed by his own people, whose inertia made him despair. In the wilderness Moses was under the control of his calling. At the moment

when the bush took fire, everything was made clear; the wilderness had done its work and transfigured this man who had created a space of emptiness and silence within himself; it had filled him with a spiritual plenitude, with words and with prayer. The wilderness had led Moses to the call, to the face-to-face encounter.

Moses treads this wilderness again after the departure from Egypt, but this time at the head of an impressive throng of human beings. This people that is being painfully born constantly asks itself what its foundations are and what the very principles of its existence. In this wilderness the fugitives from Egypt will encounter the God of Moses. The wilderness thus becomes the paradoxical site of an unparalleled adventure, for in its solitudes the covenant is concluded.

God had said to Moses: "You are to offer worship to God on this mountain." And Moses had repeated this to Pharaoh: "Give us leave to make a three days' journey into the wilderness to offer sacrifice to Yahweh our God." The wilderness was to be simply the setting for a mystical moment, the place of a mystical encounter like that of the burning bush, but on the larger scale necessitated by the great number of participants. The setting is the same, but instead of the bush, the entire mountain is on fire; instead of a single individual, a whole throng hears the voice.

The wilderness is thus both a journey and a mystical experience, these two being inseparable. God is not to be sought apart from the experiences of human beings, nor does his covenant have a history independent of the history of the people. God's parable takes the form of a human story, and revelation that of a transfiguration. The God whose name no one can know will link his word to the life of human beings to such an extent that it will become Jesus, the Word made flesh. The mystical encounter will become the journey leading from Nazareth to Jerusalem, and in the transfigured face of the Beloved men will see the splendor of the thrice holy God. "The mysteries of the Kingdom of heaven are revealed to you; happy are your eyes because they see!"

■

God most holy,
you reveal your name to those you have chosen

to become your sanctified people.
You are the Unknowable One
  and yet we can give you a name;
you are the love that creates our history
  and we share in your covenant.

Grant us to persevere in the wilderness
  that we may enter into your mystery.
Purify us of all that might keep us
  from seeing your face,
and let our eyes be those of children
  who are ecstatic at your beauty.

■

On Psalm 29 (Hymn to the Lord of the storm)

Worship the Lord thrice holy,
acknowledge his glory and power.

He speaks, and the earth thunders at his voice,
he makes his light shine forth,
  and the darkness recoils at its brilliance.
He casts his fire,
  and no one can forget the ardor of the Spirit.

The Lord of lords speaks;
he gathers his people
  and blesses them in peace.

FRIDAY OF THE 16TH WEEK

COVENANT

Exodus 20:1–17. Ten words for a free people! The Ten Commandments have come in for a good deal of criticism, with people saying that they enclose the human person in a stifling suit of armor. But if you look at them objectively, you see that they are preceded by a reminder of the divine goodness: the God who gives this law is the God who liberated Israel from the house of slavery. Moreover, by their very structure the Ten Commandments are an abiding call to creativity, since the negative formulation of the majority of them does not simply set boundaries that are not to be crossed; it also leaves the inventive human mind free to explore all the possibilities of love. We can understand, then, why Israel always looked upon the law as a blessing; this people realized that through the decalogue God had given them the possibility of truly living.

What was the origin of the ten words? It is generally accepted that they already formed a unit before they were inserted after the theophany at Sinai. According to Cazelles, they could come from a cultic list that laid down the conditions for admission to a wilderness sanctuary (cf., e.g., Ps 15):

> No statues regarded as embodying the presence of the divinity. No worship of idols. No false oaths sworn by Yahweh, the God who has revealed himself and in whose name the community has been delivered from Egypt. No sanctuary for a murderer. No access to Yahweh after sexual violence, theft, false accusation, or violent attacks on a neighbor's possessions.[16]

It is also to be noted that the condemnation of images (v. 4) is a result of the preaching of the prophets. Though forbidden in the south from the ninth century on, the making of metal images is thought to have continued in the north until the eighth century. In this prohibition Yahweh revealed himself to be a "jealous" God, that is, a God "who reacts passionately, forcefully and energetically to his people's behavior, the God who will not let himself be imprisoned within an image and who will not tolerate another god beside him."[17] In short, Yahweh is a living being.

Psalm 19 is a profession of faith in the divine law.

Matthew 13:18–23. It is a matter this time of hearing and understanding. Some persons do understand, namely, the disciples, those to whom the mysteries of the Kingdom can be confided. The others—those opposed to the Kingdom—hear, but do not understand.

It is to be noted that in the change from parable to explanation there has been a shift of perspective, a shift that betrays the identification of the hearers initially with the seed, but later (in the explanation) with the soils. Whereas the parable had an eschatological orientation, the explanation for its part presupposes pastoral concerns and lays the emphasis on the various attitudes of those who hear the word. Only good soil is able to bear fruit. It is therefore likely that we have here a rereading by the early communities in light of their concerns.

■

"I am Yahweh your God." The entire secular history of the Israelite people will not be long enough for them to exhaust the radical newness of this confession of faith. He who is sovereign and Lord, power, life and light, the One we call God, suddenly reveals himself to be as it were placed in our hands, involved in our human words, mingled with our fleeting hopes, and entrusted to our thoughts. In short, when God reveals his name, he makes known the fact that he is a partner. His title is "God of the covenant," and, continuing along the same line, Jesus will speak of him as "Our Father."

"I am Yahweh your God." The religion that binds human beings to God will be woven of dependence and obedience: dependence on God the Creator, the Master of the universe, and the Lord of all things; obedience to him who delivered his people in order that he might establish ties of tender love and mercy with them. "I am Yahweh your God": it is only in the light of this description that the law yields its meaning. The demands God makes of Israel do not come first; they are preceded by the proclamation of the good news that the people have been liberated. The observance of the law is not to be as it were the fulfillment of a contract, thereby winning the divine favor; on the contrary, obedience to the Commandments becomes a response of gratitude and love to the God who has taken the initiative. Having been set free by God who has come to meet them, the people must henceforth live as a free people. Ten words— that is how Jews describe the decalogue—to shed light on life! Ten words for the sake of effecting a passage. Ten words for passing from slavery to freedom. "I am Yahweh your God." To accept the covenant is to be emptied of all that hinders us. Love him who loves you; do not forget that the Most Holy loves you, as he loves every human being! Do not forget that he loves you in order that you too may love.

Ten words that state the rights of the liberated human being. This is a covenant that risks all on human fidelity. But, then, what would a freedom be that was not committed? A seed that was not scattered in the furrows? The covenant is subject to all the risks of a word that can be rejected; the very fruitfulness of God's self-revelation is dependent on the inclement weather of the human heart. The seed gives wholly of itself for the sake of the harvest, but what risks it runs of disturbances and failures before the abundant harvest comes! The parable of the sower assures us that the harvest is certain and that the Kingdom indeed comes at the end of history, but it also instructs us in the laws governing failure. The word is intended to be heard, the covenant is intended to elicit a response, and freedom is given to us in order that it may beget freedom.

■

You speak, Lord;
  you call us to live according to your law.
Your word asks a response,
  your name elicits love,
  your covenant calls for fidelity.

Open our hearts.
Let the seed you sow within us
  bear fruit
  today and through eternity.

■

Our heart is so often an unproductive soil;
we forget to do your will.
  Lord, confirm your covenant
  and free us by your word!

We are seduced by what is easy;
we bless the work of our own hands.
  Lord, confirm your covenant
  and free us by your word!

So many cares monopolize our lives;
we let our freedom be abused.
  Lord, confirm your covenant
  and free us by your word!

TIES OF BLOOD

Exodus 24:3–8. Despite additions that point to a later reworking of the text, it is generally accepted that Exodus 24:3–8 depends on the Elohist tradition. A covenant has been concluded through the mediation of Moses and sealed by a blood-rite. This rite is quite archaic, as is the action of the young laymen who sacrifice the victims. The blood is divided into two parts and then sprinkled on both altar and people, signifying that the two partners in the covenant are henceforth as it were members of the same family.

The twelve standing-stones, which presuppose the merging of the tribes into a single people, bear witness to the settlement in Canaan. They serve as a memorial, since they are regarded as having "heard" the commitment of the contracting parties. The communion sacrifice likewise points to a revision of the tradition; it presupposes that the blood shed was that of a sacrificial meal, in which offering and communion went together. Jesus will celebrate his final meal in this spirit; in addition, he will use the words of Moses in order to establish the new vital contract between God and the Israel of the final age.

Psalm 50 is modeled on an indictment. It denounces the breaking of the covenant. Psalms such as this come from the northern kingdom and served as an introduction to ceremonies of covenant renewal. The opening verses locate the action in the context of worship, while suggesting that the establishment of a covenant was part of Yahweh's struggle against chaos at the creation of the world.

Matthew 13:24–30. The parable of the sower announced the ultimate victory of God: a good soil will receive the seed and bear abundant fruit. But in the time of Jesus many people wanted to forestall the moment of harvest—for example, John the Baptist who had pictured the Messiah as a judge. The parable of the darnel is a firm response to all these impatient individuals. Just as Jesus has no qualms about being in the company of sinners, so God tolerates the presence of the unjust among the just. In other words, he refuses to turn his Church into a community of the "perfect." This course would in any case be completely unrealistic, since the world contains good people and bad people. God has confidence in the seed he has sown; he allows the earth to produce its fruit. Judgment must await the ripening of the harvest. The infinite patience of God!

■

A lengthy history has led to the table we set, the history of a love, the history of a covenant. This history, which has unfolded in the night of time, had found its appropriate rhythm during the long journey in the wilderness when Israel had no ally but its God. "We will observe all that Yahweh has decreed; we will obey." This people is now committed to becoming a free partner in the holy covenant. The marriage is one sealed by tender love: God has chosen his people, and Israel has replied: "You are my God." At the foot of the mountain the ancient blood-rite proclaims that henceforth Yahweh and his people are of the same blood, a blood shared as in covenants. The blood of God will flow in the veins of chosen Israel. The covenant is a communion, a community of life, a marriage; God and his people are now one flesh. But when the wilderness days are past, Israel will become fickle and bring shame upon its wedding robes. It will cast aside its covenant and prostitute itself. The priests will keep watch and blood will be shed each day in the temple as expiation, in a ritual of forgiveness; blood will no longer signify the humble brotherhood existing between God and man.

But God is preparing a new covenant in which blood, offered out of love, will be a source of life. "This is the blood of the covenant." God himself will renew the forgotten ties, as he did once before in the wilderness. At the time when the people are sacrificing their Passover lambs, Jesus blesses the cup and with this expressive gesture enacts the meaning of his death, of his life that is surrendered. He takes the cup of thanksgiving and reveals that henceforth it is God who will shed his blood in order that all may live by his life.

The covenant, which in the past had been endlessly renewed by the blood-rite, is henceforth brought to completion, for Jesus has died as he has lived: as servant of the covenant. On this final evening he tells of the gift he is making of himself for the success of the age-old pact. When he says: "This is my blood," he signifies that his life will be given, as life has always been given, in order to create ties of blood between God and human beings. Jesus stakes his life in this game of covenant; he puts his life on the table. The cup stands on our table. The ancient blood-rite is no longer a mere rite, for the blood of the Son flows in our veins. And he asks us: "Can you drink the cup that I am going to drink?" They answered: "We can," and they all did drink of it. Can we drink of it? Can we carry our love to the end and live the life of God? Are we able to let the covenant renew us to the point where we are one with him who loves us? Can we be one with him by communicating in his cup? The cup stands on our table, the real presence of the God who persevered to the end. "This is the blood of the covenant that Yahweh has made with you."

■

God our Father,
  we are of the blood of your Son.
  We live by your Spirit.
Renew your covenant.
  Grant that by sharing the Passover cup
  we may pass with your Servant
  into the Kingdom of love.

How can we make payment to you, Lord,
  for all that you have given to us?
How can we thank you
  that your covenant is for us
  the grace of forgiveness
  and the love that always stands first?
In your presence we would be a silent people
  had not you yourself given us
  our words of praise
  and the strength to obey you.

The blood of sacrifices
  could not save us;
we would weary ourselves in vain
  raising to you an offering
  contradicted by our sins and unbelief.
But through your Son Jesus Christ
  you gave us life from your own blood,
and lo! despite our sins,

we belong to your race and your covenant.

Father, accept our sacrifice of praise;
  accept our gratitude,
  for we have no merits to appeal to.

We want to put your word into practice;
  give us a new heart
  so that your own Spirit
  may be the pledge of our success.
Pour out on us the blood of the new covenant,
  that we may be purified
  in the blood of the Lamb,
  who was given to death for our salvation and life.

How are we to thank you
  if not by presenting to you
  the memorial of the death on the cross
  and the resurrection of your Christ?
For it is in him
  that you make us your people,
  sharers in your blood and race,
O living God,
  O God who forgives and raises up.
In your Son, our Savior,
  we proclaim our faith and our praise.

MONDAY OF THE 17TH WEEK

HERE IS YOUR GOD

Exodus 32:15–24, 30–34. The story of the golden calf still poses difficult problems, and exegetes are not likely to agree soon either on the distribution of the various traditions in the text or on the connection between this incident and the religious schism of the northern provinces. Nonetheless it can certainly be said that in its present form Exodus 32 reveals a profound reflection on the future of the covenant that was repeatedly broken and then re-established. In this context, the theology developed in vv. 30–34 is important. On the one hand, it likens Moses to a prophet, since it shows him in solidarity with his people to the point of asking to die with them (v. 32). On the other hand, it emphasizes personal responsibility (v. 33), thus showing a post-exilic viewpoint. V. 34 makes the point that history continued after the break, and thus it highlights the patience of God. The position of this incident is also typical: it comes between the Elohist version of the conclusion of the covenant (Ex 24) and the Yahwist version of its restoration (Ex 34). The concerns thus manifested show the hand of the Deuteronomistic writer. At the same time, we cannot fail to be struck by the attempt to excuse Aaron, which is characteristic of the Priestly document. The episode of the golden calf is truly co-extensive with Jewish history.

The religious schism into which Jeroboam I led the northern tribes was an important moment in this history (1 Kgs 12). In order to promote the independence of the new state, the schismatic king had reopened the ancient sanctuaries of Dan and Bethel; this drew down upon him the reproaches of prophetic circles, especially later on at the time of the Josian reform which emphasized the unicity of worship. It must be noted, however, that the cult established by Jeroboam was not idolatrous. The golden calf was in fact only a pedestal on which the statue of the god was to rest; in this respect, it did not differ from the seraphim in the Jerusalem temple. It is clear, then, that the condemnation of the old sanctuaries reflects the battle waged by both the prophets and the Elohist against Canaanite cults. In addition, Yahwist circles in Jerusalem did everything they could to heap ridicule on the "calves" of Jeroboam.

But what precisely, then, did the first two Commandments of the Decalogue forbid? The First Commandment forbade the worship of any god besides Yahweh; it did not, therefore, deny the existence of other gods but attempted to establish an exclusive bond between Yahweh and Israel, thus preparing the way for the monotheist dogma to be accepted when the people finally became aware of the impotence of these other gods which were nothings in their eyes. The Second Commandment had to do solely with images of Yahweh. It was aimed concretely at the magical practices fostered by the private possession of cultic statuettes; in fact, however, it was safeguarding the divine transcendence and freedom.

Psalm 106 belongs to the genre of national confession. In its present form it may be post-exilic. It may have been used in ceremonies of covenant renewal, which developed the theme of a people who proved unfaithful despite the many gifts of God.

Matthew 13:31–45. A tiny seed, a bit of yeast: the beginnings of the Kingdom are insignificant. We can sense in the background here the bitterness and even the misgivings of the disciples at the obscure beginnings of Jesus or of the Church. Persecutions on all sides: the day of the Lord, which some of the prophets had announced with trumpet blasts, is certainly far distant.

But what is the tiny seed? What is the yeast that makes the dough rise? Ever since the parable of the sower the reader knows that the reference is to the word of God that has become flesh in Jesus Christ. But Jesus was challenged, and the Church is challenged today; this is part of the vicissitudes of the Kingdom.

Nonetheless the tiny seed and the leaven both contain the hidden promise of exceptional fruitfulness. The tiny seed in particular, which becomes a great plant, recalls the teaching in the allegory of the cedar (Ez 17) or the vision of Nebuchadnezzar (Dan 4), which expressed Israel's hope of a final judgment that would humble the arrogant nations. The beginnings are lowly, but the end will be glorious. Parabolic language has thus a prophetic orientation, as the citation from Psalm 78 in v. 35 reminds us.

■

Every human brotherhood, every friendship, every love begins with a season of exaltation, for it is a time of discovery. Then comes the monotony of everyday life; it is then that the bonds established manifest their solidity and depth.

Moses comes down from the mountain; he smashes the tablets of the law at the foot of Sinai. There was doubtless no other moment when this man was more dramatically made aware of the gap between what the conduct of a people worthy of its calling should have been and the reality, which was sinful infidelity. This is a key moment in biblical history. While coming down from the mountain, Moses already knows that the people are adoring the golden calf; he need not fear being surprised by the reality, since it cannot be worse than what he imagines it to be. The shock is nonetheless so intense, the scandal so great, the reality so infuriating, the calf and the law so mutually exclusive, that Moses cannot help smashing, breaking, destroying. No compromise is possible.

At the insistence of the people, Aaron had told them to bring him their gold rings. He had molded a statue from these and had cried: "Here is your God, Israel, who brought you out of the land of Egypt." The people were weary of Yahweh, tired of this invisible God. Like all peoples, the children of Israel would have preferred a divinity that was within reach and could even be grasped, a God present in a given place so that people could come and find him, pray to him, compel him to grant what they expected of him. A useful, utilizable God. Moses had disappeared up the mountain for forty days; the people had been left alone, in distress in the wilderness. They needed security; they wanted their God to be visible in their midst.

And that is why the law and the calf are irreconcilable. The law summons the people to a journey, a future, a risk; the people are to have no certainty save that of a word that has been given, a divine fidelity that has been pledged. The calf, on the other hand, symbolizes a religion that imprisons and encloses; it stands for prohibitions and taboos that rouse feelings of guilt: you must respect the rules rather than live in active freedom. But no one can appropriate for his own profit a free God, such as the God of the covenant is.

Moses acts as defender of this God. He will also act as defender of his people against God himself. This "bosom friend of God" (cf. Ex 5:22–23) is able, by reason of this intimacy, to come out with some very tart answers: "And yet, if it pleased you to forgive this sin of theirs . . . . But if not, then blot me out from the book that you have written." God lets his anger cool. "Go now, lead the people to the place of which I told you." The covenant is made of patience and of faith in the future. For God is well aware of the delays in the harvest. He has learned to be patient, while discovering new ways by which to bring his faithless people back to him. God takes his time; he has all eternity ahead in which to love. For he will never be satisfied with the groveling of slaves.

■

Your covenant, O Lord, you alone can renew;

our infidelity you alone can forgive.
In your patience bring to fruition in us
the seed you have sown;
then we shall be your harvest for eternity.

■

Father, who make your sun to rise
on the good and the wicked,
blessed be your name.

Your word is not taken back,
and your fidelity renews your covenant;
we too shall bless you through Jesus our Savior.

He is the seed cast on the ground,
brought to life by the Easter sun
as the promised future.

He is the yeast mixed in the dough
and today is already bringing forth your Kingdom.
Because you do not weary of our delays,
we bless you, God of endless patience.

TUESDAY OF THE 17TH WEEK

MEETING

Exodus 33:7–11, 18–23; 34:4b–9, 28. Though made up of disparate pieces, Chapter 33 is unified by the theme of the divine presence. In fact, the people are at a turning point in their history and they must face up to themselves. On the one hand, Moses has received orders to leave Sinai and journey to the land promised to the ancestors; but, like Peter on Tabor later on, he asks whether it would not be better to remain on the mountain of revelation. On the other hand, the people realize that they have sinned seriously and they are no longer sure that God will protect them on the journey. In order to answer these alarming questions, Chapter 33 brings together all that the divine traditions said about the presence of God.

First of all, it reiterates the principle of divine transcendence. Because the people have defiled themselves by sinning, Yahweh will live outside the camp in the tent of meeting. We have here an idea that is older than the Priestly tradition, which always locates the tent within the camp; the tent, in any case, is less a dwelling than a place for consultation. The text then goes on to specify the way in which God will be present to his people. While it is true that creatures cannot see God and continue living, God nonetheless renders his presence sensible through signs inscribed in creation and in history. It is in these that Israel will henceforth see its God, whose presence is symbolized by the cloud that descends upon the tent.

The covenant has been restored. In fact, Exodus 34 gives us the Yahwist version of the Sinai covenant; the "renewal" aspect is only a literary artifice rendered necessary by the introduction of the golden calf episode. The "decalogue" in this version, with two exceptions that remind us of the first two commandments in Exodus 20, is made up from a religious calendar that post-dates the settlement in Canaan. Note the language Yahweh uses in presenting himself. It probably comes from stereotyped liturgical formulas which the faithful repeated during worship; their anthropomorphic character suggests their antiquity, as does the notion of collective responsibility, although even here grace wins out over harshness.

Psalm 103, a hymn, once again affirms the kindness of God.

Matthew 13:36–43. The parable of the darnel exhorted the disciple to acquire the patience needed while waiting for the final judgment. The explanation, on the other hand, is concerned only with the judgment itself. It conveys a message of perseverance and trust to a Church that is being persecuted. Christians must be certain that evil will not triumph.

Is the Kingdom of the Son of Man to be identified with the Church or with the world? Like the parable, the explanation does not come down on either side, since the judgment is directed at both the children of the Kingdom and the followers of the evil one. The field in which the good seed and the darnel are sown is the world, a field wherein light and darkness are opposed. Once again, the reference to Jesus is basic, since the judgment will have him for its focus.

■

The biblical writers have the ability to create marvelously tender scenes. Up to this point, the Exodus stories have been marked by grandeur, power and dignity. But once these initial great stages are past, the text seems to change direction: it shows us a Moses who has become the intimate of God. It describes a stirring relationship: "Yahweh would speak with Moses face to face, as a man speaks with his friend." St. John of the Cross speaks somewhere of the "old friends of God." That is what they become who despite all ups and downs have not ceased to maintain communication with God. A familiarity has grown up between Moses and God, so that the tent has indeed become a "place of meeting." As two lovers have their secret nook, so Moses and God conduct their rendezvous in the tent.

While discussing the affairs of the people with God, Moses ventures to make the plea which haunts every human being who has had, in however lowly a degree, the experience of the living God: "Show me your glory, I beg you." He receives a wonderful answer: "I will put you in a cleft of the rock and shield you with my hand while I pass by." Moses, "the confidant of God," becomes the intimate of God as no one else but Jesus ever will. He will see what can be seen of God: "Then I will take my hand away and you shall see the back of me." No one can see God directly and continue to live. God will always be recognized in his passing. The encounter does not exhaust the mystery but on the contrary points to something beyond, to an "always further." Faith is as it were "magnetized" by the mystery of God; the believer will always be a "pursuer." No one can grasp God; he is always up ahead.

Even before the departure from Egypt, God had announced the "place" where he would reveal himself. "I am who I will be": history is to be the meeting place. Moses will see only the traces of God's passing. Revelation takes form in the economy of salvation; God has no other way of unveiling his face except by passing through the history of human beings at every point from Genesis to Apocalypse. As footprints in the snow indicate a presence and invite discoveries, so the action of God in history leads to the manifestation of his identity: God is known only from the back, and the very tent, the place of meeting, shifts along with the people and in dependence on their movements. The covenant is, for the believer, a following of God, while revelation is for God an exodus. I think here of the reflection, in Pharisaic spirituality, on the *shekinah*. Here the "glory" or "presence" of God is used as a name for God that at the same time leaves his mystery untouched. The word comes from the root *shakan* and thus defines the "dwelling place" of God. But in Pharisaic spirituality the *shekinah* is understood as "God in exile." The tent that is the place of revelation is also the place of "God in exile."

"You shall see the back of me." We have locked God up in formulas; we have reduced revelation to a set of orthodox definitions, as if we were trying to see the face of the Wholly Other. But "you shall see the back of me." There is only one place where we can meet the Ineffable and know the Unknowable: our human history within which the covenant has taken flesh. Revelation can only be in the form of a joint exodus, and the meeting can only be a discovery, not a possessive contemplation. Our desire to ask: "Show me your glory" then turns into a humble appeal, the appeal of Moses at the end of his staggering tête-à-tête: "Let my Lord come with us, I beg."

■

On Psalm 42

As the dry earth calls to the fountain,
so I seek you, Lord, and wait for you.
Let my entire being become a single desire,
and let my prayer become an appeal:
  show me your face
  and I shall be saved!
I come to your dwelling place:
will it be the place of our meeting?
Bathe me in your light,
immerse me in your truth;
  show yourself to me as you pass
  and I shall be saved!

■

Who are you:
  you whom we desire,
  you whose love our hearts sense?

Almighty God, vulnerable God,
  God who call yourself Father,
  God of our history, God of the covenant!

Who are you, that you bind yourself by love,
  a God who can be so deeply wounded,
  a God who pardons and restores to life?
God of tender love
  and God whom no one can see and live,
  God of Jesus and God of infinite heavens:
  it is you whom we sing.

WEDNESDAY OF THE 17TH WEEK

WITH RADIANT FACE

Exodus 34:29–35. This section, which is so different from the remainder of Chapter 34, emphasizes the exceptional character of the intimacy between God and Moses. The latter alone had the privilege of meeting Yahweh, with the result that something of the divine glory radiated from his face.

But what do the sources say about Moses? Two points emerge. On the one hand, while all the traditions put Moses at the center of the events they relate, this is the result of a process of harmonization, for neither the ancient professions of faith nor the hymns assign Moses this unique role. On the other hand, the sources show that the person of Moses never ceased to obsess the consciousness of Israel; the picture given of him takes on ever clearer features as history unfolds. Thus for the Yahwist Moses is only an inspired prophet. His mission is to make known the divine intentions, but it is Yahweh alone who performs the miracles (Ex 3:16–17 and 10:13b, 14b). For the Elohist too Moses is a prophet, but his mission has been noticeably extended. Not only does he make known the divine intentions, but he acts in the name of God, intervening in events and performing miracles (Ex 10:1, 13b, 14b). He is thus superior to all the prophets; in addition, his intercessory function is more marked in the Elohist than in the Yahwist. However, it is in Deuteronomy that the picture given of Moses is most complete. Above all, he has become the prophet

160

par excellence, to the point of being the prototype and measure of any prophet through whose coming Yahweh guarantees his own continuing relationship with his people (Dt 18:18–20). Finally, in the Priestly tradition, of which today's liturgical pericope is a witness, Moses is relieved of all the secondary roles which the older sources assign to him, so that his only task now is to converse with God. The image of Moses entering into the cloud on Sinai and remaining there for a long time in intimate dialogue with Yahweh has thus become characteristic of the Priestly document.

Psalm 99 is one of the enthronement songs in honor of Yahweh. It highlights the role of Moses and Aaron, but gives all the glory to the Lord God.

Matthew 13:44–46. In the allegory of the darnel Matthew called upon the disciples to be watchful. The Kingdom demands men and women who are alert and attentive to events. For this Kingdom is in fact something needing to be discovered, and we must discern its traces in history and in our personal lives.

Consider, for example, a farmer who finds a treasure in his field, or a gem merchant who comes upon a fine pearl. These are unexpected discoveries; life becomes brighter, and the two men go and sell all they possess in order to acquire what is beyond price. Would you do the same for the Kingdom? If yes, then you are a true disciple.

■

A farmer discovers a treasure while tilling his field; an antiquarian comes upon such a stone as he never thought he would find. Then each risks everything in order to acquire the wonderful thing. What follies passion leads us to commit! It is impossible to speak of the Kingdom except as seductive; you cannot be a disciple at bargain rates, for the Kingdom will not tolerate half-measures.

Is our faith a passion? Let us admit that our religion is rather a snug affair, without any high points. We have acquired a shelter for ourselves; our religion is a kind of insurance policy, a contract we have made with God. We calculate the risks and we conclude with prudent reservations. Excess is harmful in everything, it seems; therefore we are prudent and opt for moderation, that is, for half-measures.

Risk everything? Jesus is right: you do not risk your life unless you have found a treasure. People commit follies because of some passionate desire. But does our faith bear any marks of love and foolishness? "Go and sell what you own." Risk your life, because the treasure, properly understood, is salvation, love, God's passionate concern for us. Wager everything on the certainty that you have just discovered the priceless pearl. You have found the treasure that fulfills all desire: God believes in you and dreams of your presence with him! That is where your treasure is, and there too is your heart!

Risk everything? God has done so from the beginning. For his treasure is human beings. He has surrendered his tranquillity, his credit, his peace in order to contemplate the human beings he holds in the palm of his hand: these priceless pearls, radiant with the Spirit who breathed life into the kneaded clay. God has done foolish things because of his passionate love: a story begun over and over again with a stiff-necked people. "Yahweh, a God rich in kindness and faithfulness; for thousands he maintains his kindness": thus did God describe himself but yesterday, when he gave Moses his "visiting card." Risk everything? God has sold all that he had, including his dearest possession, for his Son will accept even the cross.

When confronted with such passion as this, how can we fail to risk ourselves in the venture of faith? How can we fail to be overwhelmed by such light as this? After his interview with God, after the revelation of God's name, after having contemplated the traces left by the passing of Yahweh, Moses comes back down the mountain a transfigured man. "Nothing is more beautiful than a face rendered transparent by a life of combat and struggle."[18] Moses has been captivated, and his face henceforth bears the marks of that encounter. How can we fail to be changed by the revelation of God's passion for us? For where our hearts are, there too will our treasure be. How can we discover the pearl with its marvelous texture unless we first train our eye to spot it and unless we set out to gain possession of it? Unless we have tilled the soil in order to give new vitality to the field and unless we have lovingly prepared the ground, how can we discover the treasure buried there? Let God change you, therefore, and you will bring to light his treasure and his passionate devotion.

■

God our Father,
you have put into our hands
  a pure pearl:
  your covenant and your promised future.
May such a gift turn our lives upside down!
Give us the enthusiasm
  of those who have found the secret of life;
then every human being will share
  in the treasure you allow him to discover.

■

We bless you, Father so tenderly loving,
  through Jesus, the splendor of your glory
  and the face on which your kindness shines.
He is the incomparable joy
  of those who seek him without wearying
  and find him present
  within their deepest selves.
For those who know him
  the world contains no other treasure,
  since he alone can satisfy their hopes.
That is why, with all those transfigured
  by this light,
  we bless you, God our covenant.

THURSDAY OF THE 17TH WEEK

TO THE RHYTHM OF HIS STEPS
Exodus 40:16–21, 34–38. Chapter 40 summarizes the sometimes divergent
Priestly traditions regarding the construction of the sanctuary and the
manner of conceiving the divine presence. The role of Moses, a priestly
role, is heavily emphasized here, as is his submission to the commands of
Yahweh. Thus the erection of the sanctuary is seen not as the result of
human initiative but as the carrying out of divine instructions. The earthly

temple is built according to the model of the heavenly temple.

Dwelling, or tent of meeting? The two concepts reflect different theologies as well as the difference between a tent in the wilderness and the definitive temple. The "glory of God" is connected with the idea of a permanent presence; it calls to mind the temple in Jerusalem and heightens the sacral character of the latter. Moses cannot enter into it. The cloud, on the other hand, is the sign of God's coming, and Moses is able to meet this God in the tent of meeting. V. 35 is therefore a clumsy attempt to harmonize the two conceptions. Thus the mystery of the presence of God, whom human beings cannot approach but whom they can meet in order to receive his word, is expressed in a kind of dialectic of cloud and glory.

Psalm 84 contains both the song of the pilgrim who tells the temple priests how happy he is to be in the holy city and the words of welcome with which the priests respond to him and his traveling companions.

Matthew 13:47–53. The shore and the sea: these are precisely the physical setting for the parabolic discourse as a whole, since in order to address the crowds who had gathered at the lakeside Jesus sat in a boat by the shore. The conclusion of the discourse repeats the lesson that has gradually emerged from the reading of the parables. Jesus has been proclaiming the Kingdom, and each listener is now called upon to take a position in regard to it. Each is urged to "understand," that is, not only to pay attention to the teaching of Jesus but to respond with a profound filial obedience. It is natural that the message of the Kingdom should prove baffling, since it is like a treasure containing things both new and old. In his preaching Jesus does not deny traditional Jewish doctrine, but he does renew it from top to bottom and reveal the newness hidden under the ancient garments. Moreover, in the earthly mission of Jesus, final judgment is being passed: those not with him are against him.

At the same time, however, the parable of the dragnet, like that of the darnel, emphasizes the fact that Jesus does not wish for the moment to purge the group of disciples of its undersirable elements. Such a separation will occur in the last times. The highly allegorizing interpretation given of the parable of the dragnet repeats, in terms borrowed from the explanation of the darnel, the threat against those "that are of no use." The threat urges us to take the teaching of Jesus seriously but also to choose joy rather than sorrow.

Finally, it must be noted that the parabolic discourse definitively turns the disciples into a group distinct from the crowd. In this way their apostolic mission is confirmed. They are the scribes of the Kingdom, the teaching body of the Church.

■

There was a time when men thought of God as dwelling on the mountaintops; later on, they built tents or temples for him. But everyone knew that God's dwelling was in fact in heaven; anything else was but a secondary residence or a temporary stopping place. Nonetheless it took time for people to believe that God refuses to be a prisoner of any place.

In the wilderness, God's dwelling is a nomad's tent; he dwells in the midst of his people and adapts himself to the rhythm of their history. The ark of the covenant is located at the center of the caravan, and God's temple takes the form of a temporary shelter. God does not settle down anywhere; he can be distinguished only by the traces of his passing. He is himself the way that leads from slavery to freedom, from death to life, from darkness to light.

Thus the history of the Israelite people and, later on, the history of Jesus of Nazareth become the place where we can discover the meaning of our own lives. Yes, we too have our exodus experience, and it takes the form of a constantly renewed effort to escape little by little from the grip of the determinisms that hold us in subjection. Our exodus is our passage from death to life, a life that must constantly be won back from the forces that would destroy it.

If we have not experienced within ourselves the shifting back and forth from light to darkness, the painful achievement of unity against the forces of disintegration, the ceaseless turning that love requires lest inertia win the day, how can we receive into our hearts as a promise of victory the life of the Witness of God, the life of this man who proclaims, even more by his actions than by his words, that in him light has won the final victory over darkness, unity over division, freedom over slavery, love over despair or, in short, life over death?

Thus the exodus is not only the place where the meaning of our human adventure is made clear; at the same time it reveals to us that God is not a stranger to that adventure. The tent is indeed at the center of the caravan. From the life of a people and the life of an individual, in both of which we recognize our own story, this good news flashes out: our exodus will reach its goal because we are walking in the steps of God.

■

God our God,
  we desire no other God but you.
Your name, which century after century
  echoes in the memory of believers,
  illumines our history and guides our quest.
Blessed be you in the name of all those witnesses
  who render your word eternally young.

Praise to you, O God of Abraham:
  as it did him,
  your word uproots us
  for new departures.

Blessed be you, O God of Moses:
  like him
  we are called to set our brethren free
  and rescue them from the land of slavery.

Blessed be you, O God of Joshua:
  with him we know we have received
  the land in which your people takes root.

O helping God, God of the eternal covenant,
be you blessed in Jesus, the image of your glory
  and fulfillment of your promise.

We cannot look to other guides;
we know
that your word, the Word of God,
  is a word for our future lives.

We thank you for the passage
  you make possible for us in your Beloved:
we have been baptized in the Spirit
and we have crossed the barriers of death

to reach the land,
the promised land,
your inheritance and our own land.
Enable us to dwell there
and make it a haven for all human beings,
so that together we may become a people
called to praise your name.

We pray for all those who seek
the hidden face of things
and the meaning of their future;

we pray with all those whose history
has engendered ours,
those whose lives enable us to see today
the eternal newness of your covenant
as fulfilled in Jesus our Liberator.

Reading and Understanding Matthew

Birth of a Church (*Chapters 13:54—17*)

While some people welcome the word of God, others neglect or reject it. Jesus has already made this clear in the chapter of parables. There are those inside and those outside or, as we might say, the Church and the world, this last term being understood in the Johannine sense.

Matthew now asks his readers to meditate on the birth of the Church. He describes different approaches that are available to the faith of the believer and, by means of these, shows that the Church can grow only if it deepens its relation to its founder.

The first stage in the birth of the Church (13:54—14:36), which can be summed up in the familiar image of the Church as a ship, is seen in an authentically paschal perspective. The account begins with a description of the lack of faith of Jesus' fellow countrymen and ends with the appearance of Jesus who, like the God of the exodus, calms the storm and reassures the fear-stricken rowers. This appearance is an evident allusion to the risen Christ, as is shown by the disciples' act of adoration. But the risen Christ is also the point of reference for the preceding narratives: the story of the martyrdom of John the Baptist, which is told in language that looks forward to the passion of Jesus, and the story of the multiplication of the loaves, in which the eucharistic bread is shared. This is an approach by way of death and resurrection.

In the second stage (15:1–39) attention turns to the presence of pagans in the Church. Their presence points to a death and resurrection on the part of the disciples who surmount the obstacle created by the traditions regarding unclean foods and open the eucharistic table to all who put their trust in Jesus Christ.

Signs are what the Jews want. Jesus tells this adulterous generation that no sign will be given to it except the sign of Jonah; in addition he reproaches the Jews for their lack of faith. Peter experiences the sign of Jonah in the third stage of the narrative (16:1–28). Here we have the Christian journey par excellence: the attainment of glory through suffering. Caesarea Philippi marks the hour of the Church, but of a Church that stumbles.

As we are told by the voice on Tabor during the fourth stage (17:1–27) we must trust in Christ and follow him on his Passover journey. This is the only way for human beings to pass from fear to the freedom of the children of God. Faith transfigures the human person just as it cures the epileptic boy.

FRIDAY AND SATURDAY OF THE 17TH WEEK

GOD THE PLAYER
"I will live in your midst; I will be your God and you shall be my people. It is I, Yahweh your God" (Lev 26:12–13). Israel experienced the covenant as a reality before expressing it in formulas and theologies. God intervened in our behalf: that is the conviction present at every moment in the historical journey of the chosen people. The covenant is first of all a history, and it is

on the basis of their historical experience that believers will subsequently develop this theme which is basic to the entire biblical outlook. Because the covenant is first of all a living experience it finds expression in festive joy. "You shall sound the trumpet; you are to summon the children of Israel; you will proclaim the liberation of all the inhabitants of the land" (Lev 23:37; 25:9–10).

In the Bible and in Christianity a feast is a celebration of the God of the covenant. It is the "carnal" writing down in action of the word never heard, never heeded before, because God has had but a single human history in which to express the prodigality of his gracious love.

A feast is a proclamation, that is, a commemoration. To remember in worship the God who saves is to summon up a past event in ritual form and restore to it its original power. In addition, it is to introduce the rememberers into the very event which the celebration is commemorating. We may recall what Gamaliel said when explaining the Israelite Passover in the light of Exodus 13:8: "Each individual in every generation must look upon himself as having been *personally* rescued from Egypt. Every Israelite must realize that it is *he* who has been liberated from slavery."[19] A feast thus enables us to participate in the history we are commemorating. The history made present to us in the commemoration is doubtless retold as past, and the past is by definition absent; yet we must also say that theologically this past is not dead. For the believer the whole possibility contained in faith is at stake here: the past must be accepted as possible and as a potential revealer.

In celebrating a feast we accept our past as present—"present" in two senses of the word: rendered actual, and gift of grace. When we "play" or re-present (make present once again) the history of salvation, we are caught in its nets and are ourselves "played" (in the sense in which one can play with another); we also re-present or render present what is happening to us today. In its own proper order and manner a celebration establishes the covenant between God and the human race; that is why it is indispensable to faith. A feast is therefore a "symbol" of faith and it "evangelizes" us; because it strikes root in the symbolic and ritual substance of the person it awakens us to God's plan for us.

In addition to being a proclamation and a commemoration, a feast in the biblical sense of the word is a liberation. It does not withdraw us from our life in the world even when it offers this life in sacrifice. It does not establish a gulf between the sacred and the secular, because it shows that our divine life in common is organized according to the structures proper to the human person and because it bears witness that the divinization of human beings is accomplished in and by the humanization of God.[20] Our feast is a liberation because it integrates the individual and collective histories of believers into a "sacred" history.

We celebrate the God of the covenant in order that our own liberation may become a reality. The purpose and the object of our liturgy are the same. If the covenant between God and the human race has as its goal the unity or "communion" of human beings in God, then our Christian feast is the covenant in action here and now. In the sacred rite "we see what the prayers and Psalms, as well as the sacred actions and forms which the liturgy contains, can achieve in us. They purify us and make us able fittingly to receive and to preserve holiness, and to remain possessed of it."[21] The sole object and purpose of a celebration is to bring us together in a festive assembly in order that we may welcome the Lord who is at work in our lives and may enter together into the communion he offers us.

■

It is our joy, Lord,
God of goodness and tender love,
to give you thanks and cry out to you
     the boundless joy that is ours
     as children set free by your grace.
Praised be you for the history
     which you constantly write along with us,
     and for the covenant you are renewing in this feast.
We welcome your kindness!
Behold how full our joy is
     at a love so close to us
     that it is proof against the endless centuries.

THE FESTIVE HEART

Leviticus 23:1, 4–11, 15–16, 27, 34b–37. The Book of Exodus ends with the building of the tent of meeting; Leviticus sets out to explain the proper use of the tent so that it may indeed be a place of meeting between God and man. The last section of this book (Chapters 17–26), which is known as the "law of holiness," gives detailed instructions on what the holy people must do in order to promote its own communion with the holy God. As a result, it pays careful attention to the faithful observance of feasts and holy years.

The feasts, which received their canonical status after the exile, varied greatly in their origin, but all had a twofold purpose: on the one hand, to keep fresh in the memory of the people the countless blessings Yahweh had heaped upon them; on the other hand, to actualize or render present these blessings. For the commemoration was never a sterile contemplation, but rather an expression of the certainty that Yahweh continued to do in the present what he had done in the past. Thus the commemoration was at bottom a profession of faith in God's fidelity. As a result, Passover, which originated among herders, and the Feast of Unleavened Bread, which was agrarian in origin, were both linked to the departure from Egypt. These feasts were celebrated in the spring, and it was during one special spring that Yahweh had sent Moses to Pharaoh. The feasts thus satisfied the desire of human beings to express their faith in communal rituals and in the language of the body.

Psalm 81. The Psalms served as accompaniments to the prescribed rituals. Psalm 81 is an indictment of those who broke the covenant; it emphasizes the element of binding rule that characterized feasts celebrated in honor of him who had brought his people out of Egypt.

Matthew 13:54–58. The teaching in parables has drawn the dividing line between the disciples and those who refuse to listen to the word. Henceforth anyone who is not for Jesus is against him; henceforth, it may be said, there is the Church on one side and the "world" on the other. Matthew now invites us to attend the birth of this Church as he describes the various itineraries open to the faith of the believer.

First of all, there are those outside, those belonging to the "home town."

This term designates a mentality and not simply a geographical location. It situates those who cling to their ideas and refuse to inquire into the new wisdom that emanates from Jesus. Jesus' rejection by his fellow townsfolk thus becomes the symbol of opposition from his adversaries. In their eyes, the person and teaching of Jesus are a stone upon which they stumble and which will eventually cause their fall.

■

I like this rabbinical saying: "There are depths in the human soul which ritual alone can reach." We have perhaps lost our souls in losing our taste for ritual and our grasp of its meaning. Because we calculate our gestures and indulge in endless chatter, because we are afraid to sing and afraid to see, our inner depths have been numbed. But if our depths are never fed except with short-lived promises and gestures that go nowhere, who can keep from being filled with God knows what? It is not by means of ideas that we descend into these depths, but by means of gestures, the senses, singing, and the silences of the body. Tell me, how could you experience your love without embracing or express your joy without laughing and singing? Who can measure the importance of two hands being joined when suffering leads to silence, or the amused conspiracy of two meeting glances?

"Yahweh spoke to Moses: 'These are Yahweh's solemn festivals, the sacred assemblies to which you are to summon the sons of Israel on the appointed day.' " Faith cannot live without festivity, because love and life are impossible without it. Faith is celebration and gesture, a *chanson de geste*. How wonderful it would be if only we could learn to be playful with God! Everyone takes him so seriously that they end up making him deadly boring! We must play our games in God's presence under penalty of otherwise seeing the vigor depart from our confessions of faith.

"You are to summon the sons of Israel on the appointed day." A feast is a convocation: a people gathers to commemorate the deeds of God. Faith cannot live without feasts, because faith is the heritage of a people and not simply the private affair of individuals; revelation is a covenant entered into between God and children set free from slavery. A feast is a memory preserved; the history of salvation is to be periodically renewed, and a people are to return to their beginnings in order to commit themselves once more to a joint adventure with God.

"There are depths in the human soul which ritual alone can reach." We must learn once again to let our faith break out into song; we must doubtless learn once again to live if we are to enter into the meaning of a feast or festival; we must doubtless recover the soul of a child if we are to play in God's presence and in this play, this liturgy, reinvent the world: a festival creates the future in advance.

■

God of our fathers and God of our history,
you call us together to glorify your name
  and to celebrate our deliverance.
Grant that we may keep on saying "Amen"
  at the festival of your love.
It is there that we shall meet him
  whom we proclaim until he comes,
  Jesus Christ, who is our eternal joy.

SATURDAY OF THE 17TH WEEK

FESTIVAL OF LIBERATION

Leviticus 25:1, 8–17. Everyone is agreed that the law regarding the year of jubilee remained a dead letter, but the failure of the law should not cause us to forget the widespread and profoundly religious ideas that found expression in this institution. It has been said that the law presupposed the transfer of property, the lending of money at interest, and enslavement for debts, and this is indeed the situation that prevailed in the selfish society of the monarchical period. But all this did not prevent something of the wilderness ideal from remaining alive in the depths of consciences. Jews would never be able to forget that they were but "strangers and guests" in the land they occupied, for this land had been given to them by God without any merits on their part, and they were only its tenants for life. Nor could they ever forget that Yahweh had rescued them from Egypt in order that they might serve him. The Israel of the exodus was, then, a free people. On a future day in Nazareth, Jesus Christ will take up the torch of rediscovered freedom.

Psalm 67 is difficult to classify. Vv. 4–6 (summarized in the refrain) convey the basic idea of it: that all the nations are to accept Yahweh as God. Israel thus stands forth as witness to the divine glory.

Matthew 14:1–12. No one is a prophet in his own country. As the oracles of Jeremiah had antagonized the false prophets and the priests, so the preaching of Jesus causes a profound division among his fellow countrymen. As a result he will at last experience the fate of the prophets, many of whom met a violent death.

The fate of Jesus is prefigured by that of John the Baptist. Like John, Jesus will be arrested, put in chains, and slain (observe how in this passage Matthew uses the same verbs as in the passion story). But whereas Jesus will truly rise from the dead, the supposed resurrection of John is only a popular tale.

■

"You shall sound the trumpet throughout the land. You will declare this fiftieth year sacred and proclaim the liberation of all the inhabitants of the land."

How is it possible to claim that religion is an opium for the people? Have we so misunderstood the idea of festival that our feasts have turned into a means of evasion, an escape from too harsh a world, a disincarnated and uninvolved rite? For in fact an authentic festival proclaims liberation and makes it a reality.

A feast is a proclamation. In it our faith breaks out into song, for it is indeed true that "there are depths in the human soul which ritual alone can reach." Faith takes on the hues of the feast, because the liturgy proclaims a history that turned into a covenant. We tell each other "the epic of God"; we "play out" what once happened to us. For the Bible is not content simply to describe the part played by God in human history; it also sets before us this history in which God is still involved and in which he involves us.

174

A feast is an act of faith. It reveals the hidden meaning of the human adventure. The object of our celebrations is the action of the living God as he interacts with men and women on their pilgrimage. The liturgy describes God, but does so by telling stories about him and proclaiming him. It does not define by setting clear conceptual limits. It looks at "what happened" and then turns the eyes of the Church to the God who creates history: the God of the covenant.

Our festivals announce, prepare, prefigure, anticipate. When we play out before God the history of our salvation we are "caught in the net" of the covenant. This story of God-with-us comes to us as a promise. As a result, our festival becomes a liberation; it already inaugurates for us what is still to come. God comes from the future.

No, a feast is neither dream nor illusion; it does not cut us off from the present world in order that we may forget the distress of our times. It leads instead to the liberation which we know by faith to be already present. In the festivals of faith human beings, time and history are already living out what is to come.

■

Lord our God,
we praise you for the newness of your word.
It has been in our midst for centuries,
  and yet it remains eternally young.
  How can we be so old?
We praise you that your covenant is eternal.
For centuries now we have had a common history:
  why then are our memories so short?
We pray you:
let your word not pass away
  but be our festival,
and let your covenant renew our future
  and be our communion.

■

On Psalm 95
Come, let us shout for joy because of the Lord,

let us acclaim the God who saves us.
To him let us sing our songs of joy.
He sets us free; on his account we keep festival.

Yes, our God is a great God:
the earth is his handiwork,
and he guides the course of history.
Acclaim the Most High, the Lord of glory!

Come to the Lord who addresses you,
harden not your hearts.
Come to the Lord who sets you free.
Happy the people whose light is the Lord.

■

God of our history,
God of our memories,
God of the covenant, we implore you:
   may the day come
   for completing what you began;
   may the day come
   when you reveal your victory
   and our liberation.
   Yes, we implore you:
   may the day of endless feasting come!

FROM MONDAY OF THE 18TH WEEK

TO SATURDAY OF THE 19TH WEEK

Remember the Wilderness!

Here we are once again in the wilderness. As we start the Books of Numbers and Deuteronomy we launch out upon the "great crossing." We have left the foreign land and the chains for which we were not made. At

God's summons we have entered the wilderness: a parched land where thirst rages, a land of solitude where true communion becomes a reality, a land without landmarks where a route to the promised land must be carved out. But we have not started on our way without purpose or reason. We could, after all, have stayed in our chains, which would at least have provided a certain security. If we have reached the point of risking everything, it is because faith will always entail risk.

The wilderness is a place of testing. Faith makes its appearance there, but this faith does not bring immediate satisfaction nor certainties easily reached. In the wilderness a man must keep going and allow hunger and thirst to scour his being; only then is faith born. In this exodus there is necessarily a painful interspace between the excitement of departure and the tranquillity of arrival. It is not possible to sustain oneself here on what is yet to come, and so there arises the temptation to turn back. The long journey is monotonous; the epic adventure has degenerated into a sorry set of domestic squabbles. One begins to ask oneself: "Is the Lord truly with us?" It is one thing to set out, quite another to persevere. In the final analysis, was not the old servitude preferable? There is a strong temptation to return to "the onions and fleshpots of Egypt," to crawl back into the maternal womb instead of truly living and experiencing risk. But faith is an ever renewed stubbornness, a laborious journey. An exodus is a time of detachment and trial but also a time of liberation and promise.

We entered the wilderness. Now we must at least remember it, make anamnesis of it, for the wilderness will be a constitutive factor in the lives of all the subsequent generations who are called to faith. Moses constantly tells his people: "Remember your history," and the entire Bible never wearies of repeating this after him. Even the liturgy celebrates that history.

"Remember!" But we are not moved by nostalgia for the past. No one can identify himself with the novel that is his past. If we remember, we do so in order to create our own history while at the same time knowing whence we come. For, despite the multiplicity of experiences and even the necessarily divergent ways of living the covenant with God, at every point it is the same divine summons that is heard and the same divine love that signals to us. Past, present and future are inextricably tied together in the eternity of the God "who is coming." Mindfulness is, therefore, a call and a commitment.

In the wilderness we walk by faith. God had said to Moses: "You shall see the back of me." God shows his face and features only in the everyday history of a people like all other peoples and in the conquest of a land little different from other lands. That is how faith works. Events happen to us and at the moment we do not know what they mean; we see nothing in them, we hesitate and we ask questions: Will this road lead anywhere? Is the promised land anything but a mirage? Only later on do we perceive the hidden face of our own history. In our life at the moment we see only the reverse side of the tapestry; tomorrow we will contemplate with dazed astonishment the hidden side of the tapestry we have been patiently weaving.

■

With the entire Old Testament
  which transmitted its faith as part of life,
  we proclaim:
  "Listen, Israel:
  Yahweh our God is the one Yahweh.
  You shall love Yahweh your God with all your heart
  with all your soul, with all your strength."

With Jesus, the one sent from God,
  who lived his faith as a man gives his life,
  we proclaim:
  "I bless you, Father, Lord of heaven and of earth,
  for revealing your mystery to mere children.
  No one knows the Father except the Son
  and those to whom the Son chooses to reveal him."

With the Church, gathered by the Spirit,
  that received the faith
  in order to witness to it by its life,
  we proclaim:
  "If your lips confess that Jesus is Lord,
  then you will be saved.
  For the Lord is rich in mercy
  to those who call upon him."

What name are we to give you,
  God who are always beyond?
What name would we give you

if you yourself had not risked giving us your name
on the winding roads of our history?

What love would we have for you, the covenanting God,
if Jesus had not opened the passageway of Easter?

Because he traveled our roads,
because he shared the turmoil of our exoduses
and ventured out on the waves of our destinies,
the wilderness wherein we are tested
has become a life-giving land.
Let separation come:
love is stronger than death,
and nothing can break the bonds of tender love!
Let doubt come:
love is stronger than the cross,
and nothing will keep the dawn from breaking;
nothing will prevent the feast of Easter.

Because we still experience
the land of thirst and loneliness,
the wilderness of arduous journeys,
hear our plea.
Our hearts are too slow to believe:
give us your Spirit
and teach us to live by your inspirations.
When fear grips us
and darkness overtakes us,
let your word bring us peace and light.
Guide the ship of our history to a safe harbor;
go before your flock
and lead us to the land of freedom.

Deepen our thirst for the infinite,
strengthen our will to communion,
and be yourself our way.
Sharpen our hunger,
and be yourself the bread, the viaticum, of our journeying.
With the mighty breath of Easter purify your Church's desires.

Let it have the first fruits of the land of freedom
where milk and honey flow,

where all barriers collapse
and all divisions cease.
Let your thankful people
   experience the pledges of the Kingdom,
   of the covenant you have made with us
   through Jesus Christ, your Beloved.

MONDAY OF THE 18TH WEEK

THE TESTING OF FAITH

Numbers 11:4b–15. One section of the Book of Numbers recounts the
lengthy journey of the people of God from Sinai (Chapter 10) to their
arrival at the banks of the Jordan opposite Jericho (Chapter 22). The
account has a religious purpose; this is clear from the simplification of the
geographical framework, which serves here as the basis for a profound
meditation on the wilderness experience. It can be said that the crossing of
the wilderness is seen as a period of adjustment in which the salient events
take the form of often dramatic crises. The Book of Numbers calls
attention to the blessings heaped upon the people, while at the same time
it underscores their sin and the punishment to which this sin led. The forty
years in the wilderness are thus seen as a time of purification that cost the
life of an entire generation, with the result that only a completely purified
people was able to enter the promised land.

But what was the sin of which the story tells us? It is one to which Jewish
and Christian commentators alike have called attention: the people
preferred earthly food to the food God gave them. The entire business of
the wilderness made them fearful, and they would have preferred to return
to the security which Egypt represented. The test imposed by the
wilderness took the form of a struggle between materialism and faith, with
freedom being the stake. Moses' prayer shows him to be torn by an interior
conflict, a man utterly discouraged, yet retaining his trust in God.

Psalm 81 shows that the sojourn in the wilderness was the subject of ever
new reflection in Israel. This Psalm contains a full indictment of those who
broke the covenant of Sinai; it probably mirrors the traditions of the

180

sanctuary at Shechem.

Matthew 14:13–21. Filled with pity for the crowd, Jesus heals the sick but does not teach. From now on he will no longer teach the crowds but will devote himself instead to the formation of his followers. Matthew thus narrows the scope of the Master's activity to the point of restricting it to the community, that is, the Church. The latter is now increasingly at the center of this Gospel, for it embodies the Kingdom that had been proclaimed by the Sermon on the Mount and by the parables.

In this Church the disciples take on important responsibilities. Not only do they share the authority of Jesus over unclean spirits and over sin, but they are also in charge of seeing to it that the Christian people share in the blessings of the Eucharist, as the story of the multiplication of the loaves makes clear. For while the allusions to the exodus, which give the Marcan version its richness, have practically disappeared from Matthew's telling of the story, the eucharistic overtones are more evident here and the role of the disciples is more emphasized. V. 19, for example, repeats almost to the letter the Matthean account of the institution of the Eucharist; it is this last, moreover, that provides an historical basis for the activity of the Apostles. Is it not natural, therefore, that Jesus should expect from these men a faith without reservations?

■

Jesus withdraws by boat to a lonely place. These wilderness sites are places of hunger and thirst but also places where the Lord feeds his people and speaks to their hearts. They are the place of the departure from Egypt, the crossing of the sea, a long journey over arid earth; they are the location for a time of truth, of doubts, and of questioning, or, in short, for a time of testing.

When he learned of John the Baptist's death, Jesus withdrew. The times are difficult: the opposition grows ever stronger, the disputes ever more bitter. The precursor has already succumbed to the attack. Jesus himself will soon experience the lot of the prophets. "When evening came, the disciples went to him and said, 'This is a lonely place, and the time has slipped by.' " This is the hour when the passion begins, the same hour when in the upper room, away from the crowds, Jesus will gather his followers for a last meal on the night he was betrayed. It is in this context of trial and distress, suffering

181

and death, that Jesus distributes the bread. This is also why our Eucharist today is well acquainted with the full weight of human suffering, personal and collective.

"As he stepped ashore he saw a large crowd; and he took pity on them and healed their sick." In the presence of this weary throng, the heart of God is profoundly moved; Jesus will break bread. God had already given his people abundant food in the wilderness long ago. The manna and quail which only had to be gathered each morning had shown his solicitude for them. The memory of such forethought lived on. The wilderness, a place of hunger and thirst, would henceforth summon up memories of banquets and festivity.

The wretched conditions of the world at large were of course not eliminated by this action; Jesus did not rid human beings of cruel worry about their daily bread. But at least on one occasion it came to pass that all ate their full and that everyone experienced an abundance. When Jesus revealed himself, they lacked for nothing; the mercy of God had descended upon them, and the wilderness took on a new meaning. "What makes the desert beautiful," says Saint-Exupery's little prince, "is that somewhere it hides a well."[22]

The wilderness is therefore at once a place of hunger and a place of limitless satisfaction. Just think: a dozen baskets of scraps left over! When people have decided on a departure, there comes a moment when they regret what they are leaving and when they do not as yet enjoy what they will later find. They are living in an interspace that tests their resolution. That is why the wilderness or desert will always be a symbol of the testing of faith: we have left behind the illusory satisfactions found in our dreams and the temporary security of our all too easy self-justifications, but we are not yet in possession of the glory of the saved and we do not yet experience the perfect joy of abiding communion. Yes, our exodus is still going on; but a little bread broken for us awaits us at the evening camp and will enable us to journey onward to the promised land.

■

God our Providence, we praise you:
  you do not abandon
  in the land of thirst and loneliness

those journeying in search of the promised land.
Bread for the wilderness and the journey,
wine from a feast yet to come,
  your Eucharist gives joy to the pilgrim.
Praise to you forever, Father,
  for the table that nourishes our hope.

TUESDAY OF THE 18TH WEEK

IN WIND AND STORM

Numbers 12:1–13. According to many critics, Numbers 12 combines two traditions. The first, which is Yahwist but has left only traces, tells of the criticisms directed at the marriage of Moses (probably his marriage to the Midianite woman), but does not make clear the precise point of the criticism. Miriam is punished with leprosy and owes her cure to the very man she had criticized.

The second source, the Elohist, is especially interesting. For in this tradition, above and beyond the debate about Moses' superior position, there appears the whole conflict between the prophets who receive a special call and the professional prophets. This conflict gripped the northern kingdom in the eighth century.

On the one hand, there are the professional prophets; on the other, the charismatics. To the former Yahweh speaks only in visions or dreams; their methods of interpretation do not differ from those of foreign prophets like Balaam (cf. Num 22—23). To these prophets who know God only by feeling their way toward him (cf. Acts 17:27) the Elohist writer opposes the authority of Moses and, in his person, the authority of the prophets who are specially called and are in direct contact with the mind of Yahweh. This chapter also has a connection with the mission of these prophets, since what is entrusted to them is the whole "house" of the Lord.

Psalm 51 interprets the conflict between Moses and his co-workers; it is a conflict between the people and Yahweh.

Matthew 14:22–36 (Years B and C). Is it in order to cut short the

183

enthusiasm of the disciples that Jesus has them get into the boat? In any case, he himself goes off into solitude to pray. Of whom is he thinking, if not of those threatened by the storm? They are in great danger because the wind has risen and is against them. Arising from his solitude, Jesus reassures them. But who exactly is this Jesus? Using language reminiscent of Old Testament theophanies, the incident brings to mind the crossing of the Red Sea. Behind the "ghost" of Jesus can be seen the God of the exodus who commands the sea and protects his people. As for the men in the ship, do they not represent the Church? The role of Peter is heavily emphasized, but when he cries out "Lord, save me!" the entire community cries with him.

To what promised land is this boat sailing? Peter's doubt, the disciples' profession of faith and their act of adoration all suggest an Easter appearance. It is thus the Lord of the Church that Peter is calling upon, and the storm that shakes the boat brings to mind the dramatic moments in the history of the Church and perhaps even the final tribulation before the return of Christ. Then the faith of a community that is filled with eucharistic gifts and strengthened by the presence of its Lord will be tested.

Matthew 15:1–2, 10–14 (Year A). Jerusalem, the guardian of tradition, exercises control even in Galilee. Scribes and Pharisees come there to pass judgment on the free and easy ways of the disciples who eat with unclean hands. Everyone knows how important Jesus' answer was for the life of the early communities, because above and beyond the matter of unclean hands the real issue was the admission of pagans to the Eucharist of the Jewish Christians (cf. Mk 7). It is a pity, therefore, that the lectionary has omitted the beginning of Jesus' answer, where he provides the basis for his argument. Jesus retorts: "Why do you break away from the commandment of God for the sake of your tradition?" and he reminds his enemies of the obligations of children to their parents. In this context, Mark mentions only Moses, Matthew emphasizes the gap between the word of God and human tradition. By stressing the point that evil is in man and not outside of him, Jesus redefines the notion of authentic "cleanness": a human being is clean not by reason of ritual washings but by reason of his fidelity to the divine law. Jesus does not do away with the law, but he fulfills it, while the scribes, prisoners of their casuistry, act like blind men; they show themselves incapable of effectively guiding the people of God who are thus unable to produce worthwhile fruit. God can only decide to uproot the vine.

■

(Reflection for Years B and C. For Year A cf. p. 385.)

A boat buffeted by the winds. The Church shows itself not lacking a sense of humor when it sees itself as this little drifting nutshell. What are we, after all, but men and women controlled by fear? Yet God exists! Of course, but doubt can make itself felt in the biting questions that arise in our depths. The suffering and injustice that affect so many human beings; the constantly renewed despair of our world; the human beings torn apart by life and mistreated in their entire existence: all these are challenges to God, all are testimonies brought to the prosecutor's bench. Perhaps God is dead?

It is doubtless possible for a boat to escape unharmed from wind and storm. We know too that "the gates of the underworld can never hold out" against the Church. Nonetheless each "crisis" makes us tremble to the point of preventing us from facing the real problems with a clear mind and from providing solutions. We are wounded by history and everyday life; we are prisoners of our fears and victims of our uncertainties. To be a disciple is to be torn between doubt and faith. The disciple of Jesus crosses the wilderness in solidarity with his brothers and sisters, the people who live in a shattered and ravaged world, a world that is disquieting yet also surprising and wonderful. Who are we, then, to get up and bear witness against wind and tide that God will lead history to a safe harbor? By what right does the Church, despite its questions, hesitations and even fears, rise up and tell human beings: "Do not be afraid"?

Yet we can do it, and the Church must do it, because Jesus comes by night; he walks upon the waves and comes to meet us in the storm. Have you noticed how God likes to come by night? There was the night of the exodus when Yahweh delivered his people from Egyptian slavery. There was the night of the birth at Bethlehem and the astonishment of the shepherds. There was the night that descended on Golgotha when the Son entrusted his life into the Father's hands. There is still the night of the tomb, when the seed cast upon the ground strikes root in order to shatter the heavy stone. "It is I!" Jesus gives no sign of recognition, utters no name; he alone can speak in this manner. "It is I!" Jesus comes amid the storm to lead his disciples to the shore and to peace.

The God we seek does not force himself upon us; he does not force our hand with arguments and proofs. The God we seek comes by night, in the storms and upheavals of history. Barely recognized, he slips away again, like the wind that refuses to be captured.

"Courage! It is I!" The Church is therefore able not simply to hold the tiller of the boat as it is storm-tossed; it can also venture out upon the very waves. It is not afraid of getting wet, since it belongs there where human beings face the storm of life. Adventure and risk are the normal environment of faith!

■

Almighty God, grant that your Church
may always seek your face.
May it venture out on the waves
and dare to pronounce the name that bestows peace:
"It is you, the Lord."

God our Father, grant that our world
may hold steady in the storm.
May it accept the risks of creating its future
and not let fatalism overwhelm it.

Father so tender and loving, grant that our assembly
may live the adventure of faith.
May it lose its fear of darkness,
its alarm at doubt, its flight from silence.

WEDNESDAY OF THE 18TH WEEK

CROSSING THE RUBICON

Numbers 13:1–2a, 25—14:1, 26–29, 34–35. The narrative has brought the reader to the frontiers of the promised land; it also shows that the spirit of the people has not changed, even though the discomfort of the wilderness has been replaced by the dangers which the invasion of Palestine entails. An analysis of the report of the scouts on their exploration of the country allows us to distinguish two main sources. According to v. 20 the promised land is a land of plenty; the scouts are therefore in favor of an immediate attack, despite the fear which the inhabitants have inspired in them. This source, which is attributed to the Yahwist, echoes the traditions of the south; it would therefore be connected with the exodus-expulsion.

The other source is much later in origin and depends on the Priestly document. Not only does it give evidence of reflection on the events of the wilderness; it also takes into account the fusion of southern traditions with those of the north. It focuses especially on the scouts who are the first witnesses to the fulfillment of the promises made to the fathers; the subsequent course of the whole venture would depend on their good or bad opinion. The Priestly document thus intensifies the contrast between the enthusiasm of the Caleb group, which is full of trust and hope, and the skepticism of the rest of the people (vv. 31–32) who "wailed all that night" and by so doing drew down divine rejection upon themselves. The punishment was made to fit the crime and it affected the entire community with the exception of Caleb and Joshua: the wilderness generation was not to enter Palestine.

At the historical level, Numbers 13—14 thus makes it possible to connect the exodus-expulsion with the exodus-flight on the basis of a stay of Moses at Kadesh, on which the biblical tradition is quite firm. De Vaux suggests a contact at Kadesh of the southern tribes first with the Calebites and later with the Moses group; these encounters would have made possible a first assimilation of Yahwism. However, even after this meeting with Moses, the southern group would have remained independent and would have continued to nibble away at Palestine from the south until the moment when it would have been stopped by a row of Canaanite fortresses in the neighborhood of Jerusalem.

Psalm 106 is a national confession and develops the theme of the people who are faithless despite the generosity of God. This literary genre, which is proper to the north, is probably derived from the Psalms of supplication and from the liturgies for the renewal of the covenant.

Matthew 15:21–28. While in Matthew as in Mark the story of the Canaanite woman illustrates the theme of the admission of pagans to the Eucharist, the special contribution of Matthew is worth noting. In Mark too, of course, the general context is that of faith in Jesus Christ, but whereas Mark only suggests, Matthew is quite explicit. "Woman, you have great faith. Let your wish be granted." The thing that is to decide the admission of men and women into the community of the Church is not their racial or religious affiliation but their faith in Christ and his mission of salvation.

And yet the initial response of Jesus was reserved. He told the woman: "I was sent only to the lost sheep of the house of Israel," and this statement recalls not only the apostolic discourse (10:6) but also the instruction: "Do not give dogs what is holy" (7:6). What are we to conclude from all this? First, that this instruction, despite its seeming harshness, is filled with great respect for the diverse routes traveled by human beings; second, that the missionary discourse is simply pointing to the obvious when it stresses the priority of Israel. In any case, Jesus is now in the territory of Tyre and Sidon, and the pagan woman demonstrates her religious maturity. Does she not address Jesus with cries that recall the liturgy of the churches? Does she not prostrate herself before him? Does she not acknowledge him as Lord and Son of David? Yes, in her person the pagan community is knocking at the door of the Church.

■

Jesus has just crossed the northwestern border of Israel in the direction of Tyre and Sidon, or present-day Lebanon. He has been compelled to take flight, for he has publicly insulted the scribes and Pharisees. We witnessed the confrontation only yesterday. "Why do your disciples break away from the tradition of the elders? They do not wash their hands when they eat food." But Jesus turns to the people and cries: "Leave them alone. They are blind men leading blind men." That kind of subversion was intolerable; Jesus had now signed his own death warrant. But this was not the time or the place for him to die. Therefore, after the skirmish Jesus withdraws to the land of Tyre.

Jesus, then, has just done a dangerous thing: he has knocked down a barrier which constrained human beings. "It is the person's heart that makes clean or unclean." But now another barrier appears before him, when a "pagan" woman asks him for a healing. Shall he cross this dividing line which the Jews guarded jealously in their contempt for those whom they called "pagan dogs"? In "the serious game which Jesus plays with the Canaanite woman" (as Luther puts it), we

may doubtless be astonished by the clear-sightedness of this woman, her shrewdness, her enormous confidence; but in fact faith is first and foremost an impulse toward Jesus. Yet there is more to be said here:

Jesus will learn a lesson from this woman. He will therefore cross a new boundary and do away with a further exclusive right that kept some human beings from God. The Kingdom is offered to everyone. True enough, the children of Israel are seated at the table of God, and the supreme encounter with God has taken place in the life of this people. But henceforth grace is broadcast everywhere, and even the pagans have a right to the inheritance of God's children.

This is a lesson the Church will never forget. When we are familiar with the conflict that divided the first Christian communities as the pagans sought for admission (this was at the very time the Gospel was being written), we understand better what was at stake in this episode of the Gospel. After the example of its Lord, the Church will dismantle boundaries; henceforth, as St. Paul says, "there are no more distinctions between Jew and Greek." A woman's maternal love led to the crossing, somewhat hesitantly perhaps, of an age-old barrier, and with the woman the Church of every age entered the breach.

But—you will object—among Christians as among others there do exist barriers of color, race, language and tradition. Yes, that is true. But after meditating on this passage we can make this promise both to the Church and to the world: nothing counts but human beings themselves, for they are called to enter the Kingdom. We make this promise as men and women who are called to scout the promised land, and we say: "This land does indeed flow with milk and honey; this is its produce." We already yearn for peace, despite our differences and even oppositions; we already profess our faith in the universal Church, despite our sectarianism and disunion. And we hold these signs as treasures in our hands, for they are the tangible proof that we have not been dreaming. They counterbalance the factual admission we are obliged to make: that the promised land is still being eaten up by hostility and divisions; that fortified walls still form barriers which seem impassable.

Jesus crosses the northwestern frontier; he asserts that the inheritance of Israel is henceforth offered to all human beings. He cannot now turn back; he has "crossed the Rubicon." Tomorrow he will have to pull down another frontier-barrier and pass through death in order that life may flow out through the mouth of an open tomb. The Church constantly has the Canaanite woman before it, for the Church is called to universality by way of an ever renewed conversion.

■

God, Father of all human beings,
we believe that you hear our prayers,
   though we do not see clearly
   your answer to our pleas.
We are sure only
   that your paths are leading us
   from the impasses of death.

Blessed be you for the peace you grant us
and the table of brotherhood
   to which your gracious love invites us.
These are the first fruits of the new earth
where all will be brothers and sisters,
   the children of an unmatched love.

God, you batter down the barriers of death
   and bring us, day after day,
   to the land of the living.
May your name be sung
by high and low,
poor and rich,
those who know that they are close to you
and those who think they are far off.
Yes, may your praises be sung
   by all who have access to your supreme dwelling
   through Jesus,
   the gate that leads to the Kingdom.
In him we bless and praise you.

HIS NAME

Numbers 20:1–13. In the main, the account in Numbers 20 belongs to the Priestly document. According to v. 1, the challenge which led to the deaths of Moses and Aaron took place at Kadesh, but this pinpointing of a location is secondary, since the reproaches of the people are out of place in the luxuriance of an oasis. Miriam the prophetess probably died there, and the mention of her death, along with the account of Aaron's death, gives the whole passage a sinister character. Not only will the wilderness generation not enter the promised land; neither will its leaders.

The nature of Moses' sin is not clear. According to the doublet of this story in Exodus 17 it was not Moses who sinned; rather, the people challenged God. The Priestly rereading of the story thus seems to have shifted the sin to Moses, and not without some basis, since Numbers 20 may have preserved the memory of what some clans might have regarded as an error in strategy. Cazelles believes that Moses' sin was to have refused to follow the Caleb group when it went north toward Hebron. In any case, the story in Numbers 20 takes the form of a suit involving Moses and the community of the children of Israel. Vv. 8 and 10–11 are an attempt to show what Moses' sin was: in v. 8 Moses receives an order to speak to the rock, while in v. 10 he chooses to speak to the people rather than to the rock, and in v. 11 he strikes the rock twice. It is possible that the Priestly tradition was blaming Moses for retaining a remnant of the magical tradition: he struck the rock with his staff instead of turning to God in prayer.

V. 13 assigns the name Meribah to the place of challenge; this must be regarded as an effort to explain a place-name. According to de Vaux, the name Meribah had in fact been given to a spring near which lawsuits between individuals were settled, while the spring itself doubtless already had a sacred character. But in Hebrew Kadesh means "sacred," and in Genesis 14:7 it is called Ain-mishpat, "Spring of Judgment." The identification of the two locales is thus understandable, especially if the memory of a dispute between Moses and Caleb was associated with Kadesh.

Psalm 95 combines the opening verses of a pilgrimage psalm with part of an attack on violations of the covenant. It may have been sung in procession to the place where Yahweh pronounced this indictment.

Matthew 16:13–23. Jesus has now devoted himself to his disciples. This is an important work, since he must make clear to them the precise nature of his mission. The first question Jesus asks of them sets the tone, for it is concerned with the "Son of Man," a title generally taken as referring to a glorious being. But perhaps it is brought in here simply to spur the disciples, who must choose between a glorious Messiah and the suffering servant. As a matter of fact, people in general did not have such high expectations: some thought Jesus might be John the Baptist or Elijah; others thought of Jeremiah or one of the prophets. The crowds were looking to the past, and no one imagined that Jesus might be the one meant in the divine promises.

At Caesarea Philippi it is Peter's turn to confess his faith. "You are the Christ, the Son of (*the*) God, *the* living One" (literal translation). Peter had already said the same after his walk on the water, but here the statement is not only more solemn but goes deeper, as the repetition of the article indicates. What Peter is in effect proclaiming is the faith of the Church in the *divinity* of Jesus of Nazareth. Jesus then emphasizes the happy state of his disciple: what Peter has just said expresses his faith or rather the faith which the Father has given to him and which he has accepted, for everything is grace. Peter is perhaps a man of little faith (*oligopistos*), yet Jesus makes of him a rock on which his Church can be solidly built. Just as rain, flood or gales cannot knock down a solidly built house (7:24–25), so the power of death cannot overthrow the Church (it was at Caesarea, near the springs of the Jordan, that the Jews located the entrance to the world of the dead). Nonetheless, though Peter is a rock, he is also a stone of stumbling. But who is it that will stumble? Jesus, whom nothing can turn aside from his destiny, or Peter, who now opposes his master? Caesarea Philippi marks the hour when faith is tested.

■

"Who are you?" In the wilderness where he met God, Moses had asked: "If they ask me what your name is, what am I to tell them?" And God had answered by recalling the history of his love: "I am the God of your fathers, the God of Abraham, the God of Isaac, and the God of Jacob." Only a love that embraced an entire people could be renewed age after age despite the ups and downs of that people's

history: "You are our God who brought us out of Egypt." Who are you? The children of Israel would have to live the covenant for a long time in order truly to learn the name of their God; they would have to experience a lengthy history of misalliances and renewals, deceptions and pardons, repeated exiles and exoduses.

"Who are you?" "Some say you are John the Baptist, some Elijah, and others Jeremiah or one of the prophets." In short, you are the one who proclaims the hour of God, the coming of his day. "But you— who do you say I am?" The response does not come from a worldly book of questions and answers, but from the ardent gaze of human beings who have recognized one another: "You are the Christ, the Son of the living God . . . .You are Peter." "Who are you?" The question is answered by changing a name, for the question itself leads to a true face to face encounter; it forces the parties to say "I" and "Thou" and to exist the one through the other, the one for the other. The question no longer asks for information but involves two lives.

"Who are you?" At Caesarea Philippi, near the springs of the Jordan, that river of covenant and entrance into the promised land, near the place where Jewish tradition located the entryway into the world beyond, the Church of all times bears witness that God answers this question by taking a man's name: he will be God, the Father of Jesus, as we might say "Andrew, the father of Albert." By his confession of faith Peter enables the Church to enter into the new covenant. At Meribah in the wilderness the people had rebelled and Moses had doubted. The waters there were given a name connected with judgment: "Contention." At Caesarea, Peter, a new Moses, leads the people of God to the land of salvation; in the former sinner's confession of faith the echo can already be heard of the stammering voices of men and women who build their lives on God's promise of grace.

"Who are you?" The answer is given in an exchange of glances, but who has the power to capture a glance or reduce to words the mystery in a face? The same question will therefore be asked over and over again, and the answer will always be a renewed relationship, a mystery reborn.

"Who are you?" We too must "confess," and that is something

different from seeing or repeating or knowing. We must perceive intuitively and let ourselves be led and molded by a mysterious gaze; we must risk taking a road on which we will gradually discover a face that will reveal itself fully only in eternity.

■

You are the way,
  and no one goes to the Father
  unless he believes in you.
  Lord, have mercy.

You are the truth,
  and no one knows the Father
  unless he walks with you.
  Christ, have mercy.

You are the life,
  and no one can be reborn
  unless he is immersed in you.
  Lord, have mercy.

Deuteronomy

A Much Misunderstood Book

The Book of Deuteronomy, at least in its first thirty chapters, is presented as the spiritual testament of Moses to his people at the gates of the promised land. As a matter of fact, the history of the book is longer and more complicated than its format suggests. Deuteronomy has one rather odd trait: the alternation within the same discourse and at times even within the same sentence of words addressed to "you" in the singular and words addressed to "you" in the plural (e.g., 6:1–2: "These then are the commandments . . . which Yahweh your [plural] God has instructed me to teach you [plural] . . . . Thus if you [singular] fear the Lord your God . . . "). It is accepted that this alternation reflects successive stages in the formation of the book, with the first redaction not being earlier than the seventh century B.C. The origins of Deuteronomy are to be looked for in the periodical celebrations of covenant renewal as practiced in the north at Shechem (cf. Jos 24). During these celebrations the law was read to Israel as though the people were a single person (origin of the you-singular sections).

As everyone knows, by reason of their exhortations to conversion the prophets played a predominant role in the assimilation of the law by the general population, but we must also take into account the work done by the priests whose function it was to interpret and apply the law. The priests carried on the work of Moses but in the new context of the difficult problems caused by the Israelites' adoption of a settled life; there were religious problems arising from the dangerous presence of the Canaanite gods, and social problems connected with the transition from a nomadic life to an urban civilization.

The Book of Deuteronomy, which was composed under the reign of the wicked King Manasseh by Levites who had fled the north during the threat of Assyrian invasion, exemplifies in written form the ongoing concern to make the law relevant to new circumstances. The book was discovered in the temple in the reign of Josiah and seems to have set in motion the religious reform undertaken by this king. In urging the centralization of worship, the book established continuity with the celebrations at Shechem; it was then enriched with the you-plural sections, which were addressed to responsible individuals. Finally, the traditions about the death of Moses (Chapters 31—34) were added to the book, as was the preface (Chapters 1—3), which is attributed to the redactor of the Books of Samuel and Kings.

FRIDAY OF THE 18TH WEEK

MEMORY
Deuteronomy 4:32–40. This passage is enough by itself to exhibit the theology of Deuteronomy, based as it is on two major themes that are deeply rooted in the people's consciousness of their uniqueness among the

nations. Israel knows that it is God's chosen people and that it can therefore call Yahweh "our God." This deep-rooted conviction is based on experience, for God has revealed himself in the concrete history of Israel, which Deuteronomy continually sets before the people for their meditation. The revelatory events of that history are as it were signs of God's fidelity; the events mentioned in this passage are the departure from Egypt, the theophany at Sinai and the gift of the land to the ancestors. Even the ability to discern God's action in the events of history is regarded as a divine gift (v. 35).

Israel can therefore look upon itself as the Lord's personal possession. At the same time, however, election by God carries with it very serious responsibilities. The fact that God reveals himself to Israel in such a concrete way requires on Israel's part an active response to the divine initiatives. Obedience to the law therefore represents neither moralism nor an ethic of merits, but becomes a response of love.

Psalm 77 is a composite Psalm, but the verses used here belong for the most part to an individual hymn. It invites us to meditate on the blessings God has given.

Matthew 16:24–28. Matthew's Church is a Church that is experiencing persecution. The evangelist therefore endeavors, in the light of events in the life of Jesus, to explain to his fellow Christians the meaning of the difficult times through which they are passing. Can their lot differ from that of the Lord in whom they have put their trust? If they are really living in accordance with the spirit of the Lord, they will inevitably attract the hatred of the world. Like other human beings, Christians want to "save their life"; they must learn, however, to receive it from another. The life of the baptized is a "passover"; like Peter, they must "pass" from purely human reasoning to the divine way of thinking.

■

"Put this question, then, to the ages that are past, that went before you, from the time God created man on earth: Was there ever a word so majestic, from one end of heaven to the other?" When the people ask questions inspired by doubts about the future, or when the children of Israel despair at finding themselves battered by the vicissitudes of history, here is what the age-old faith of the Bible tells them: Look at your past and see God's fidelity at work in the covenant

which he struck with your fathers! Learn today what your Lord and the Master of human history is really like!

"Put this question, then, to the ages that are past." Remembering is something much more than the cold recalling of a dead event; it is proof that everything that ever happened to you lives on. "Put this question, then, to the ages that are past": faith is first of all a message which we hear and to which we respond; it is a gift which we receive. For our memory is not only personal but collective. It is the Church that remembers fully, the Church that celebrates the encounter of God and the human race. In fact, the Church is nothing else but the comprehensive memory of the human race in its joint history with God.

Our common ecclesial memory thus becomes the place of revelation. "Put this question, then, to the ages that are past" is not a commandment from a nostalgic wise man. Rather it indicates the soil which makes possible our faith itself, both communal and personal. We must come to know what we are, beginning with the initial event that shaped our being and continues to do so. If we look at "what has happened to us," we do so in order to be reborn into the faith today. If we summon up our past and celebrate it, we do so in order that what was made known then may come to pass today. If we turn back to the historical actions that constitute the history of the covenant, we do so in order that the power of the events we celebrate may produce its effects today. When we tell one another about the first days in the love relationship between God and the human race, we do so in order to discover, with a sense of wonder, the power they had over the future. Day by day, century by century, the veil is thus lifted from the joint adventure in which God and his people are engaged; the memory of the entire Church is the place where the progressive discovery of God's revelation is carried on in a never-ending process.

■

God our Father,
your name has become part of our history.
We can know who you are
    and accept Jesus whom you have sent.

We ask you:
  let that name be part of our memory
  and let its power illumine our lives!

SATURDAY OF THE 18TH WEEK

LISTEN, ISRAEL

Deuteronomy 6:4–13. "You shall have no gods except me" (5:7). After repeating the Ten Commandments, Deuteronomy applies itself to commenting on the First Commandment with the help of a catechesis which even today still inspires the liturgical prayer of the Jews. For Deuteronomy 6:4–9, together with 11:13–21 and Numbers 15:37–41, constitutes the *Shema Israel*. Deuteronomy exhorts its readers first to love God (vv. 4–9), then not to forget the circumstances that ensure prosperity (vv. 10–25), and, finally, to avoid all contact with pagans.

At the heart of the exhortation there is a principle: God is the one and only God. It is possible that there is reflected here the struggle of Deuteronomy to secure the centralization of public worship in Jerusalem. The meaning of the formula "Yahweh is the one Yahweh" would then be that the God of Israel cannot be divided, as the existence of numerous images and sanctuaries might lead people to think. In any case, commentators are unanimous in pointing out the difference of climate. God is no longer simply one who is to be feared; he is also the God who is worthy of love, "something no one had ever dared to say prior to Deuteronomy. Moreover, there is nothing platonic about this love; on the contrary, it lays claim to the entire person and is synonymous with fidelity in every aspect of life, as can be seen from the pairs of contraries which are such a characteristically Semitic way of expressing a totality.

But behind this exhortation there is also an experience—the experience of becoming a sedentary instead of a nomadic people, as the tribes did once they settled in Canaan. The experience was an ambivalent one, because in both the northern and the southern kingdoms it was accompanied by social injustices and repeated desertions of Yahweh, as the people and their leaders quickly came to prefer the fertility gods of Canaan. As Hosea points out in his prophetic denunciations, the people not only became greedy for material things, but they even forgot that Yahweh was the author of these gifts. We may add here that later on Jesus would denounce the wearers of phylacteries, who had forgotten that a material fidelity not inspired by love is meaningless.

Psalm 18 is a rather complex entity. It is possible to distinguish in it an individual thanksgiving (vv. 3–7, 17–20) and a poem of thanksgiving spoken by the sovereign after a victory over an enemy (vv. 32–51). The other verses are a poem on a theophany (vv. 8–16). The liturgy calls attention to the fidelity of Yahweh, who is compared to a rock, the symbol of stability.

Matthew 17:14–20. The fact that the lectionary has not included the story of the transfiguration should not prevent us from adverting to its importance in the Matthean plan. After the events in Caesarea which are in effect an urgent call to the disciples to accept the messianic figure of the suffering servant, the transfiguration inseparably links the theme of glory with that of suffering. In addition, when the disciples recognize the witness value of John the Baptist's death, they show in effect that they are beginning to understand somewhat the mysteries of the Kingdom (17:1–13).

The time has now come for Jesus to return to the crowds. A man comes to him whose son suffers from epilepsy and whom the disciples have been unable to cure. Whereas Mark attributes this inability to a lack of preparation on the part of the disciples (this kind of demon yields only to prayer and fasting), Matthew has Jesus say that the reason is "because you [the disciples] have little faith." Jesus also criticizes the lack of trust he finds around him: the crowd is as unbelieving as the wilderness generation had been, and even the disciples hesitate to commit themselves more fully. And yet even a little faith would be enough to effect a radical change—even a faith no bigger than a mustard seed, for this yields a plant which grows to an impressive size.

■

Moses is on Mount Nebo. Behind him are long, very long years of authority, struggles and hopes. Now, after so many and such circuitous journeyings the goal is in sight: from here on the mountain top he can see the plain of the Jordan and the sparkling surface of the

Dead Sea. Here at last is "the land which the Lord swore to our fathers that he would give us." Moses is filled with an immense joy, a joy so intense he could die of it. And Moses knows that in fact he is about to die. But first he must speak to the people around him, the people whom so often he has "carried by himself." He must speak and review the past: the struggles and the sins of the children of Israel. Above all, he must remind them of God's gift, his inexplicable choice of this people, his patience as their teacher, his constantly renewed forgiveness, in short, his incomprehensible and unparalleled love. In response, the people must commit themselves: "Yahweh our God is the one Yahweh. You shall love Yahweh your God with all your heart, with all your soul, with all your strength."

"You shall love Yahweh your God." Is it possible that God is really someone we can love? To the religious person, God is beyond a doubt someone whom we respect, fear, and admire and in whose presence we feel our weakness. But can we be required to love this "almighty one," this "one" God? No—unless we recall the likewise unique experience of the covenant. A people that only yesterday were crushed and lacked freedom and a land of their own went into the wilderness and there tasted the divine promises; they learned freedom and benefited from the zealous care of their God. When the eyes of faith read all this, there can be but one judgment: "God loves us." "If Yahweh set his heart on you and chose you, it was not because you outnumbered other peoples: you were the least of all peoples. It was for love of you and to keep the oath he swore to your fathers that Yahweh brought you out with his mighty hand and redeemed you from the house of slavery, from the power of Pharaoh king of Egypt. Know then that Yahweh your God is God indeed, the faithful God" (Dt 7:7–9). God's love for Israel is something quite different than the universal benevolence of the Creator toward all his creatures; it is a matter of a choice and a somewhat mad and unparalleled attachment to them.

Surely, then, it is not surprising that this kind of choice and passionate love should call for a like attachment in return, for a response that matches the love poured out on us: "You shall love Yahweh your God with all your heart, with all your soul, with all your strength." The *Shema Israel*, which every devout Jew recites morning and evening, does not mean simply "Listen, Israel!" It also means

"Be on guard, Israel!" Be on guard because idolatry comes naturally to the human heart; faith on the other hand is of the order of passionate love and commitment. "You shall love Yahweh your God; he is the one Yahweh."

"Let these words I urge on you today be written on your heart. You shall repeat them to your children . . . you shall fasten them on your hand as a sign and on your forehead as a circlet; you shall write them on the doorposts of your house and on your gates." The lover everywhere repeats the beloved's name; everywhere he writes down the name that turns his life into a song. Listen, Israel: your existence is henceforth to be under the sign of love and passionate commitment. Recall and observe: these two words sum up the entire history of your salvation and of the covenant.

■

God of the eternal covenant,
  we remember the mighty deeds
  linked to your promise
  and we recall the blessings
  bestowed upon our fathers.
Blessed be your most holy name;
  blessed be you, the only God,
  the eternal God who has loved us.
We ask you:
  incise your commandments on our hearts
  and write your suffering in the works of our hands,
  so that we may observe what you ask
  and be blessed throughout eternity.

MONDAY OF THE 19TH WEEK

CLINGING
Deuteronomy 10:12–22. This section is the conclusion of the first part of

the book. In the form of an exhortation, it sums up the main demands made by Deuteronomy but adds motivation. Thus, for example, vv. 12–14 list fear, love and service of the Lord, along with fidelity to the precepts of the law, as requirements that are simply a response of the people to God's gratuitous choice of them. This gratuitousness is further emphasized in vv. 14–15, which tell us that the Lord whom no created thing can constrain set his heart on the ancestors out of love for them and chose their descendants as well.

Israel has therefore an obligation to live to the full its vocation as the chosen people; it must cease to be a "stiff-necked people" and instead, to use a favorite phrase of Jeremiah, practice conversion of heart. The past is once again invoked: Israel must never forget that it was a stranger in the land of Egypt. Another motive is also presented: imitation of Yahweh himself who, though so great and powerful and formidable, is no respecter of persons.

Psalm 147 urges the people to glorify God who has endeared himself to Israel by his repeated blessings.

Matthew 17:22–27. Some tax collectors ask Peter whether Jesus pays the tax in support of the temple. Jesus takes advantage of this little incident to show that those who believe in him are free with regard to Jewish institutions. He bases his argument on the fact that in antiquity taxes were levied on subject peoples rather than on citizens ("the sons"). This brings up the question: Who are the true sons of the Kingdom? The answer: those who, like the disciples, place their trust in Jesus; such may consider themselves exempt from the temple tax. Nonetheless, in order not to give scandal to anyone, Jesus will pay the tax.

■

"What does being the 'chosen people' mean, according to Deuteronomy, but the unprecedented, senseless, extravagant choice of abstract obedience preceding any particular attribution? 'Chosen' means postulating a Value which gives value to all values but receives none from them; and this is why it is said that Israel, alone among the nations, decided to 'do' and then to 'listen'; to do, consequently, before knowing what had to be done; to act absolutely before hearing relatively. 'Chosen' also means wagering on an authority which is so high, so removed from the course of history, that it summons me as much as I bow to it."[23]

Moses has urged the children of Israel to review with him the long history of the journey in the wilderness. This history in its entirety must be vividly present in the mind of each individual, so that each may be clearly aware that he who bestows the law is a God of mercy. For the law is indeed not the arbitrary enactment of a god who is an absolute monarch, but the merciful gift of a gracious God. Observance of the Commandments will simply be the visible sign of a choice dictated by love. This is why the recall of the law is preceded by a lengthy act of remembrance and anamnesis.

The law has no meaning in itself; it acquires its validity only within remembrance of the deliverance from Egypt. It binds only within the confession of faith that God has liberated us from the house of slavery. It continues to bind only in order to announce the further deliverances that the future will bring. The law has been given for the sake of the children begotten by God's passionate love for his own. We are far removed here from a code that enslaves human beings and imprisons them in their guilt so as to turn them into potential criminals before the bar. The children of Israel will not have to live in fear and scrupulosity; their obedience will be an occasion for remembering the covenant of grace. The law is indeed at the center of the revelation in the wilderness. Ever since the exodus God has spoken to human beings in terms of perfect equality, and says to each of them *Thou shalt*. The imperative arises from history and the covenant; it is the other side of the covenant, the side of response and human freedom. In the final analysis, the law is not a set of imperatives nor reducible to a series of commandments; its purpose is to make a people participants in the covenant offered to them. The very word "law" is inadequate for conveying the full meaning of the Hebrew word *torah*. In Hebrew, *torah* is not an order but an orientation; it is not "law" but "way," the route by which a common journey is possible.

"And now, Israel, what does Yahweh your God ask of you?" Here are the people who have been invited to journey toward the land of freedom. "What does Yahweh your God ask of you?" The tone is one of petition rather than obedience. What a turnabout in the religious history of the human race: God asking human beings to set out on the way of his covenant! The spiritual men of the ancient world had sensed, if not clearly expressed, that God loves his creatures and is their father, protector and patron. But no one save the God of the Bible could actually invite human beings to love him. It is as though in the torah God were revealing the requirement of love because he felt a need of being loved!

One word sums it all up and is as it were a digest of the covenant: the law is not a set of precepts, duties or regulations; it is a "clinging."

■

God our Father,
we are your handiwork,
  the people you set free to serve you.
Because you have linked your name to our history,
  grant us enough love
  to cling to what you ask for us.

■

On Psalm 19

God of our fathers, your law is the source of life,
your precepts give joy to our hearts.
What happiness to experience the way of the upright,
what joy to observe your Commandments:
they are the light that illumines our future,
the column of fire that guides our journey.

We your servants desire therefore to keep them,
we desire to be guided by their light:
may they be the rock on which we rest,
the guarantee of your fidelity,
and the promise of our freedom.

There is no question now of anything but the Church, a Church already persecuted as its founder had been. Just as the message of Jesus elicits opposition, so the good news which the Church echoes is challenged and put in doubt by men. But this is only the external side of the story, for this man whom they criticize and have already condemned is the one who will pass judgment on those who contradict him. In like fashion, in order to encourage his Christian community and to strengthen their faith amid adversity, Matthew shows them how the judgment passed by the risen Christ continues to be exercised in history through the witness given by the community as such, to the extent that it is faithful to the Spirit."

This sequence continues down to the end of Chapter 23. Chapter 18, which is called "the discourse on the Church" or "on the community," tackles two problems: first, the problem of "the greatest in the Kingdom of heaven," a question raised by the predominant place Peter has had in the preceding section of the Gospel; second, the problem of the presence of sinners in the community.

TUESDAY OF THE 19TH WEEK

PASSAGE OF A PEOPLE
Deuteronomy 31:1–8. The traditions about the death of Moses, which date from the sixth/fifth century, serve as a general conclusion not only to Deuteronomy but to the Pentateuch as a whole. Formed from a variety of traditions, they take the form of a testament in which Moses tells the people of the steps he has taken, in agreement with Yahweh, to assure the succession. The transmission of authority is done in forms which are to be found elsewhere in the Bible and which include successively an offer to step down, a recall (here limited to a few allusions) of the history of the people and its leader, and an appointment of a successor, which is confirmed by

Yahweh. The appointment of Joshua looks forward at once to the conquest and to the division of Palestine, or the plan of the Book of Joshua. To be noted above all is the importance Deuteronomy attaches to the spirit in which these future missions will be undertaken: vv. 6–8, which are addressed alternately to the people and to Joshua, emphasize the need of a complete faith in God.

Vv. 9–13 take up the problem of the transmission of the law, which is ensured by the Levites and elders. The former carried out their function on the occasion of consultations about points of law. For when an individual was unsure of the way in which he should behave in the moral, cultic or juridical sphere, he would consult a priest who then rendered a decision in the form of an oracle. The most important responses were at a very early stage put together to form a series of precepts (the *torot*, from which the name torah is derived), which were intended for the use of the priests first, then of judges, and finally of the people. The collection constituted the apodictic torah (torah in the form "thou shalt" or "thou shalt not"). The second group of transmitters of the law were the elders, the group that supplied the judges whose jurisprudence was the origin of the casuistic law which determined procedure to be followed in a particular case ("If a man strikes another and causes his death, he himself shall be put to death"). Finally, Deuteronomy speaks of a celebration of covenant renewal that was to take place every sabbatical year. Scholars are far from agreement on whether such a festival actually existed, but many of the Psalms that originated in the north are written in the form of an indictment by Yahweh of the failings of the people, and they may have been read at such a celebration.

Deuteronomy 32 takes the form precisely of such an indictment by Yahweh.

Matthew 18:1–5, 10, 12–14. The preceding chapters have described the birth of a faith community to which Jesus has gradually limited his teaching activity. The "discourse on the Church" in Chapter 18 is devoted to a discussion of the nature of relationships within the community. The question asked by the disciples makes this quite clear: "Who is the greatest in the Kingdom of heaven?"—that is, "in the community," since the Kingdom of heaven is not simply a future reality but also takes form during the time of the Church's existence here.

By way of an answer Jesus places a child at the center of the group and urges his disciples to become like little children. V. 5 is enough to show that Jesus is not exalting the state of childhood; what the child symbolizes is Jesus himself. The real point is the "new birth" of which John 3 speaks. Men and women must burn their bridges to the past and thus to sin; they must become the "poor" of the Beatitudes.

It is in this context that Matthew puts the parable of the lost sheep, which evidently has an ecclesial meaning. If each Christian is unique in God's sight (this uniqueness explains the zeal of the shepherd), then he has a right to the solicitude of all the members of the Church; the latter must do everything they can to bring back their straying brother or sister. The Church is a community and not a collectivity.

■

"Be strong, stand firm . . . for Yahweh your God is going with you; he will not fail you or desert you." At the threshold of the promised land, this is the testament of Moses: the people "who were not a people" will enter the promised land, convinced only that God himself will be going with them. And it is for this reason that they must enter together; it is a people as such that will soon be crossing the Jordan.

"You shall not cross this Jordan." Everything seems to militate against the fulfillment of the promise: the walls of the fortified towns, which had astonished the first scouts, and the power of the kingdoms located on the frontiers of Canaan. And to all these ill omens there was now added the news that Moses, the leader and father of the people, was about to die. The people were tempted to remain on this side of the Jordan. "Be strong, stand firm . . . for Yahweh your God is going with you." Come, tie your shoes around your necks and venture to cross the ford which separates you from the farther bank. Let us hold each other's hand, for then our steps and our courage will be more resolute, and let us sing to dispel our fears! The only remedy is to hang on to one another, enter the water together, and cross to the other bank.

Many are uncertain of the place, the day and the hour. They argue about what they should take with them. Does anyone know what they will have most need of? A decision is urgent. What are we to take along that is truly part of us and will provide strength and ardor on the other bank? The people are in doubt, and Moses once again acts as shepherd of the frightened flock: "Be strong, for Yahweh your God is going with you." That is the promise God has kept thus far. And in order that this promise may become a pledge of hope, the old dying prophet gives the people a new chief who will lead them beyond the Jordan.

It is a people that will make the crossing. If we regard ourselves as belonging to the avant-garde, let us not forget those we have left in the rear. It would perhaps be good from time to time to go back to them and tell them that the ground ahead is solid. Let no one be so foolish as to advance alone or think he has no need of all the others. Let each one avoid being contemptuous of the weaker or the littler, those who have trouble advancing or who fall. Courage, brothers and sisters—the promised land is there before us on the other bank. Take one another's hand, listen to the voices of your fathers in the faith, and venture to cross the ford.[24]

■

Your covenant, Lord,
   is the rock on which our hope is based.
When we hesitate,
   raise up guides to lead us;
when fear or discouragement fills us,
   repeat your promise to us:
   "I will be with you until the end of time."

WEDNESDAY OF THE 19TH WEEK

BOUND

Deuteronomy 34:1–12. This account of Moses' death, which is made up out of various traditions, is striking for its brevity. Moses will not cross the Jordan but he is invited to take symbolic possession, before he dies, of the land God had promised to the ancestors.

The text is reserved to the point of being completely non-committal with regard to the place of Moses' tomb. Was there a fear that popular fervor might take possession of the figure of Moses? The final verses eulogize the dead leader, but the eulogy is restrained and emphasizes above all the singular nature of the relation that bound Moses to God. In fact, these verses prepare the way for the remainder of the Deuteronomist's work and in particular for what are called "the former prophets," that is, the books from Joshua to 2 Kings; thus the death of Moses did not prevent the story from continuing. Legend, however, did not remain silent about Moses' tomb; there is one tradition that God himself or his angels provided for Moses' burial, while a Jewish apocryphal book, *The Assumption of Moses*, suggests that the whole world served as his coffin.

Psalm 66 comprises a hymn (vv.1–12) and a Psalm of thanksgiving (vv. 13–20). The psalmist urges Israel to sing out its gratitude: What has Yahweh not done for his people? Some verses suggest the idea of a liturgy that celebrates God's victory over a traditional enemy.

Matthew 18:15–20. If a sheep strays, the community must take charge of the sinner and do everything it can to rescue him from his sin. But if the brother stubbornly persists in his evil way, he puts himself outside the holy Church, which cannot tolerate confusion in its midst. This restriction does not mean that the obstinate sinner ceases to be the object of the community's concern; on the contrary, the fact that he becomes like a tax collector in the community's eyes can only remind his fellow Christians of Jesus' concern for sinners.

In this context, which is different from that at Caesarea Philippi, Matthew has inserted the verse about the power of the keys. He thus gives expression to the Church's consciousness of being a community of salvation and reconciliation. The zeal of the community for the sinner bears witness to God's tender love for that person. The community is thus the place where divine forgiveness is experienced, the first decisive step in the sacramentality of penance.

■

The Church is not a crowd of juxtaposed believers; it is a body, a people. It is a people that experiences liberation, a people that will cross to the other bank of the Jordan into the promised land. "If your

brother does something wrong, go and have it out with him alone." In the time of Genesis, Cain had gotten his back up: "Am I my brother's guardian?" Today's Gospel asks: "What have you done to your brother?"

Is this passage of the Gospel showing us the beginning of a procedure, an embryonic canon law that prescribes steps and sanctions, including even exclusion from the community? In fact, the climate here is utterly different; the last verses in this passage leave no doubt, for all the advice is given within the framework of communal prayer in the presence of Christ. Fraternal admonition, recourse to witnesses, and sentence passed by the Church are simply applications of the patient mercy of God. We are a "community people" and are not bound among ourselves by any law or any necessity imposed by self-interest; we live together because together we experience the same tender love and the same forgiveness. The Church is a holy community because it is sanctified by words of gracious pardon.

"If your brother does something wrong, go and have it out with him alone." Trust and forgiveness are exchanged, grace is shared. In the days of the tower of Babel, human beings had stolen language for themselves; they had preempted it for their own profit and had distorted it by trying to possess it. They no longer understood one another and were scattered in mutual enmity. On Pentecost human beings will receive the Spirit, and a common tongue will rest on each. It is through sharing and brotherhood that the words of gracious forgiveness are exchanged. The obedience of faith creates communication, which is the Church. The covenant is always given to a people in order that they may become a holy assembly.

■

God our Father,
your Son assured us:
  "If two of you on earth agree
  to ask anything at all,
  it will be granted to you by my Father in heaven."

Do not pay heed to our divisions,
but consider rather the confidence of your Church

210

as it unites in asking peace and unity.
Grant it this peace
  that it may live today and forever.

Joshua and Judges

Two Contradictory Books?

The Book of Joshua has all the characteristic traits of an epic. It tells the story of the conquest of the promised land by the people under the leadership of Moses' successor. The invasion of the promised land is presented as a holy war with God as the commander. The version in the Book of Judges, on the other hand, is a much more peaceful affair: Joshua plays no role in it; the tribes do their fighting separately; there are no massacres of whole populations. But if Judges 1 is undoubtedly more objective than Joshua, are we therefore to deny all historical value to the latter book?

In broad terms, the Book of Joshua contains two accounts. The first (Chapters 2—11), which is from the end of the tenth century, brings together and connects with Joshua the Ephraimite traditions proper to the tribes of Benjamin and Ephraim, along with war stories of local interest. The story of the conquest becomes here the story of the occupation of central Palestine by the tribes of the exodus-flight; it has a somewhat extensive liturgical coloring (cf. the crossing of the Jordan or the conquest of Jericho), which was doubtless introduced under the influence of the sanctuary at Gilgal.

In dealing with the second story, we must take into account the reading of traditions by the Deuteronomistic school. In its reaction against the division of David's kingdom, this school presents the conquest as the work of all Israel, and it underscores the need of religious unity by insisting on the extermination of the small conquered groups. The description of Palestine in this story is probably from a document prior to the formation of the Kingdom, in which the ideal borders of each tribe are set down, and from a list of towns and villages in Judah that was drawn up under King

Josiah.

The Book of Judges, for its part, undertakes a consideration of the conquest in the light of faith. It seeks to explain the failures suffered, which are attributed to the infidelity of the people. Judges gives us, therefore, a theological reflection on a very obscure period of Israelite history. The book follows a strict plan: the author states, to begin with, that "the Israelites did what displeases Yahweh"; sin leads to punishment but also to the people's supplications, which win them saviors who are called "judges." The course of history is thus made to display the weakness of the people and the patience of God.

THURSDAY OF THE 19TH WEEK

THE COVENANT OF PITY

Joshua 3:7–10a, 11, 13–17. The story of the crossing of the Jordan is connected with the sanctuary at Gilgal. It reports an historical event, for in fact the tribes of Ephraim and Benjamin did cross the Jordan in the neighborhood of Jericho. The passage required no miracle, since the Jordan was fordable here (cf. Joshua 2, where spies make the crossing twice). The story nonetheless describes an event which was regarded as miraculous, for it emphasizes the point that the Israelites crossed dry-shod at a time when the river was in spate due to the spring runoff of snow. Now various chronicles have reported comparable occurrences. We may therefore suppose, with de Vaux, either that the Israelites at some point in their history witnessed such an event which then served them as a background in describing the crossing of their ancestors, or else that the ancestors themselves benefited by such an event. The story of the crossing of the Jordan would thus be the result of a reinterpretation of a natural event that was regarded as an action of the "living God." Moreover, this story would in turn have influenced the Priestly redaction of the miracle of the sea (Ex 14).

In any event, the narrative certainly has a cultic character. Does it come from a liturgy celebrated at the sanctuary of Gilgal in commemoration of the event? Such a claim has been made. According to this view, the procession started from Gilgal; the priests carrying the ark touched the water with their feet, and the people, who until then had been following at a respectful distance, were invited to pass in line before the ark. But there are strong objections to this hypothesis. For example, Joshua 3—4 supposes that Gilgal became a sanctuary common to all the tribes, and this, in any accounting, puts us in the period of Samuel and Saul or even of David, at a time when the ark of the covenant, which according to the hypothesis played an important role in the liturgy, could not have been at Gilgal. Behind the hypothesis described there lurks the broader question of whether cult creates tradition. De Vaux has maintained the opposite viewpoint; he regards Joshua 3—4 as a "sacred discourse" which was recited at Gilgal "where the twelve stones were displayed, set up as a memorial."[25] But it is also true that the story represents more than a simple recollection, for the crossing of the Jordan was the crossing of a boundary between the wilderness and the land promised by God; the crossing marks the beginning of a new era.

Psalm 114 is a typical poem about a theophany, describing the upheaval in nature that results from the approach of Yahweh. But the poem has been altered to adapt it to the traditions regarding the history of salvation, as can be seen in v. 1 where "When Yahweh came" has been replaced by "When Israel came out of Egypt."

Matthew 18:21—19:1. "If you do not forgive your fellow human beings, your Father will not forgive you your sins." The community is the place where its members experience the forgiveness of God. The preceding verses had brought home this point by emphasizing the need of fraternal correction; the parable of the unforgiving debtor now reveals that God's forgiveness is reflected in the limitless forgiveness which brothers and sisters grant to each other. Peter had asked if he must pardon as often as seven times, seven being the number of completeness; Jesus emphasizes the extent and depth of the required forgiveness by speaking of seventy times seven times, thus stating an exact counterpart to the vengeance sought by Lamech in Genesis 4:24.

The parable shows that God's thoughts are not the thoughts of men. Human relations are ruled by intolerance, spite and meanness. The creditor refuses to cancel a ridiculously small debt, yet believes that he can count on God's mercy for himself. God is doubtless ready to cancel the creditor's own debt, and he actually does so, but the creditor does not see that his own attitude to others is the main obstacle (the "scandal" or stumbling stone) to the exercise of divine mercy. Nonetheless Jesus sets out for Jerusalem; it is there that he will shed his blood for the sins of the many.

■

The wandering people are about to settle in Canaan. The Book of Joshua shows us a people weary of its journeyings in the wilderness, irritated by the discomforts of a nomadic life, disgusted with the insipid manna and aching all over from damp nights in tents. Oh for a land to live in, growing things, durable houses, a town, a little rest! Until now, God's promises had been objects of hope; now, with the taking of Jericho, they are becoming a reality.

The people are about to settle down, and even if the settlement of the Israelite tribes proved as unstable and questionable as all the other conquests of history, it was nonetheless a kind of parable. Entrance into a country is a political act but it is also a symbolic act. The land of Canaan becomes an image of the Kingdom that is offered and given as an inheritance. The Gospel makes a frontier accessible and calls for the abandonment of a country: with Jesus we pass over into a "new land." And this land, which is the land of promise and covenant, is also the land of pity.

Pity: it is fashionable today to reject this as condescending and paternalistic and as inevitably containing a measure of contempt. In fact, pity is the name given to love when the other is in difficulty; it adds to mere sympathy the active impulse to bring help. The land graciously offered to us is a land wherein we live according to the rhythm of God: "Were you not bound, then, to have pity on your fellow servant *just as* I had pity on you?" This great king who wants to settle his accounts shows what God would be like if he were "just" in the current, juridical sense of the word. Happily for us, he is not like that. The good news of the Gospel makes it fully clear that our present state owes nothing to a "justice" of this kind. All of us are men and women who have been forgiven: God has forgiven us a debt of "ten thousand talents." He has simply loved us as we are: shabby, calculating, cheating or ridiculously tiresome. God has forgiven us everything, and this forgiveness is the basis of his covenant with us. We enter a land of new ways that are the reverse of our laws of the

214

jungle: our laws of excessive profit, obstinate vengefulness, violence and coercion of every kind. It is then that we dare to say: "Forgive us our debts, *as* we have forgiven those who are in debt to us." But the land beyond the Jordan is also the land of the cross and of the call to love as God loves: "Love one another *as* I have loved you." This is the land of new beginnings, of a new genesis; as they did in paradise, man and God will live in communion. It is the land of a new creation, since forgiveness grants the other a new opportunity to live.

■

Lord, God our Father,
by giving us your Son
  you show us your pity and mercy;
by raising him from the dead
  you bring us into the land of freedom,
  the land of peace and tender love.

Teach us to live by your Spirit:
  let our mutual forgiveness be the sign of your reign,
  and our fraternal love be already
  the beginning of everlasting joy.

■

Father, whose love for human beings is unfailing,
  and whose forgiveness is never withdrawn,
by sharing with us the bread of your mercy
  you allow us already to have part
  in the life of the Kingdom.
Let your goodness be the source and model
  of our pity for our brethren.

Having reached this point in the Gospel of Matthew the reader is called upon to make a critical choice. He has a better knowledge now of the person and teaching of Jesus; he has watched a community of disciples being formed who wish to live according to the instruction of the Master. Now the reader is invited to join this community, but is he willing to do so? As he has followed the story, he has also become familiar with the enemies of Jesus. Now that Jesus has left Galilee to return to Judea, will the reader have the courage to follow him to the end, knowing that Jerusalem waits at the end of the journey?

In Chapters 19 through 23 Matthew uses a device often found in the prophets. It is the device of a trial, a judicial disputation, to which Yahweh invites his faithless people. In the Gospel there is even a double trial, since we see the accused turn into an accuser. The accused is in effect the Kingdom proclaimed by Jesus and rejected by his enemies. But when Jesus enters Jerusalem and expels the sellers from the temple, he reverses roles: it is now he who summons the scribes and Pharisees before the tribunal of God.

The section is divided into three parts. The first, which covers Chapters 19 and 20, has for its setting the journey to Jerusalem. It is summarized in the compliment addressed by Jesus to the children whom the disciples have scolded: "It is to such as these that the Kingdom of heaven belongs" (19:14). These are prophetic words for those who are learning to follow him and who must first come to understand that the economy of the Kingdom is not one of merits, since merits will always be inadequate.

The second part, which begins with the messianic entrance into Jerusalem, includes Chapters 21 and 22 and focuses on the welcome which the city gives to the Son of David, this disturbing Messiah who curses the barren fig tree, a symbol of rebellious Israel, and expels the sellers from the temple. A series of disputes and parables brings out the increasing tension between the main figures in the drama.

Finally, in Chapter 23, this mounting tension breaks out in reproaches.

However, the indictment of Jesus yields its ultimate meaning only in the call to conversion which he urgently addresses to all who have until now refused to accept his message (vv. 37–38).

RELEARNING GOD

Joshua 24:1–13. (This commentary also covers Joshua 24:14–29.) The twelve tribes, the amphictyonic league, the covenant of Shechem—Joshua 24 has been the subject of many books and articles, especially since the thesis of Noth, who saw in this story the charter of an association of the twelve tribes. On another front, von Rad linked Joshua 24 with other passages in order to attempt a reconstruction of a ceremony of covenant renewal which, according to him, took place during the celebration of the Feast of Booths. These two hypotheses have drawn a great deal of criticism, the first on the grounds that it is not possible to speak of a union of the tribes before Saul, the second on the grounds that neither the historical reports nor the religious calendars attest to such a ceremony— but is this reason enough to reject the hypothesis?

What, then, is the story which Joshua 24 tells? Despite its relatively recent redaction, the story contains ancient elements: the choice between the God of the conquest and the local or Mesopotamian (vv. 14–15) divinities; the response of those present; the concluding of a covenant, followed by the erection of a witness stone. The key issue is what exactly is meant by the "tribes" gathered at Shechem. Since there is no question as yet of "all Israel," the best solution is to think of an association between the Ephraim group and those tribes that had not gone down into Egypt. Thus the Sinai covenant would be progressively extended, first to the southern tribes at Kadesh, then to the northern tribes at Shechem.

An attempt has been made to find in the Shechem covenant the outline of a Hittite vassal treaty. The most that can be said is that certain elements of such a treaty are present, for example, the historical retrospect and the witness stone. The historical prologue takes the form of a confession of faith that recalls the age of the patriarchs, the exodus, the sojourn in the

217

wilderness, the occupation of Canaan, and the people who derive their sustenance from the land given them by Yahweh. As for the stone, it recalls the stones on which treaties were written; its function was to prolong the memory of the covenant made, even if only in the form of a reproach to a later time.

Psalm 136, like the witness stone, recalls the history of Yahweh and his people.

Matthew 19:3–12. "Become like little children." Do not the incidents that mark the journey of Jesus to Jerusalem bear witness that it is impossible to live the Gospel? Is it possible to forgive even seventy times seven times when love so often fails even in the basic community of the human couple? Jesus answers the Pharisees' question by asserting that in the divine plan marriage is indissoluble. If Moses was induced to grant divorce, he did so because "you were so unteachable"; in any case, remarriage is not permitted, for the obligation of fidelity to the repudiated partner remains.

But is it possible to live according to the law of the Kingdom? The reaction of the disciples underscores the difficulties caused by the law of indissolubility. In his answer, Jesus does not deny these difficulties, but he adds to the categories of eunuch by birth and eunuch through mutilation that of eunuch "for the sake of the Kingdom of heaven," that is, in the context of Matthew, those who after separating from their wives remain continent. In modern terms we would say that while bodily separation is legitimate, divorce is not. The Mosaic law is thus radicalized. By insisting on the irrevocability of a repudiation Deuteronomy 24 highlights the importance of the decision that has been made. Jesus now adds that no new marriage is possible. But are the demands of the Kingdom viable apart from him who establishes them? Must not the Kingdom be received as a gift?

■

"Mama, tell me a story!" Children need to dream, to live in the company of their heroes. Stories are a necessity in teaching them what life is about.

At the threshold of their new existence the children of Israel likewise need stories and heroes. Out of a scattering of clans a federation of tribes must be formed that are bound together by a common faith.

Joshua lays the foundations of this federation at Shechem, and he tells the story of the covenant. In this way a unifying creed comes into existence.

God teaches about himself by telling stories about himself; he comes alive only through the story told by believers. And here precisely is the scandal of our faith: that God is God-with-us only when the believers discover him to be such. History is a covenant only because believers commit themselves to such a covenant. God is the God-of-believers, for in the final analysis God has never shown us any other face but the face of men and women who believe in him. Even the disciples of Jesus saw only a man who believed in God, a Son who believed in the Father.

God teaches about himself by telling stories about himself. This is our basic reason for interest in the biblical stories that come from another age. The Bible "tells us stories about God." The events in the wilderness and of the entrance into Canaan are not simply a stirring memory; they are serious, decisive and prophetic, because the promised land is the objective of all the wildernesses in which human beings journey. History as narrated and interpreted by human beings of another age remains the place where our faith is engendered, and all we pray for is: "Tell me a story!"

■

You are the Lord, the God of our fathers;
through their faith you bring us to knowledge of you,
through their hope you enable us
   to be open to your promise.
Praise be yours for those men and women
who have shown us your face down the ages.

May your Spirit give us access to your revelation,
   an icon with a thousand faces
   unveiled century after century.

■

God, Lord of our history,
it is human words

that transmit the message of your fidelity and love;
it is human gestures
  that manifest your covenant.
We pray you that
having been apprehended by your word
  we may put our trust in you,
and having shared your bread
  we may be one heart and soul with you.

SATURDAY OF THE 19TH WEEK

PRESENT

Joshua 24:14–29. Cf. the commentary for Friday of this week.

Psalm 16 recalls Israel's choice. Yahweh is Israel's "heritage and cup." The final verse shows that the choice is a matter of life and death.

Matthew 19:13–15. The incidents accompanying the journey of Jesus to Jerusalem bring out the radical character of the Gospel message, but at the same time they emphasize the point that the Kingdom is for children and for those who are like children. It would be wonderful if neither scandals nor divorces occurred, but in fact they are inevitable (18:7). The Kingdom is not at man's disposal but is given gratuitously by God; it must therefore be accepted as a grace and in the spirit of children. Is it because they do not grasp this that the disciples scold the children?

■

Perhaps we ought to learn anew from the Book of Joshua what is meant by a decision of faith? "Do you decide for or against Yahweh?" The believer is not asked to choose between good and evil; he is confronted not with a moral law but with a person and a history that is already underway.

Joshua demands a decision of faith from his people only after he has recalled the deeds of God on behalf of the children of Israel: God "teaches about himself" and he does so by telling his history; his

covenant is a mighty deed to sing songs about. It is because God chose Abraham, gave him Isaac, sent Moses, brought his people out of Egypt and into the promised land—it is because God did all this for the chosen people that the believer of today is confronted with a decision of faith. The choice he must make requires a decision whether or not to share in this history of salvation.

Joshua receives a land which is a gift from God who fulfills his promise, rather than simply a fruit of conquest. This land "was not the work of your sword or your bow"; it is a pledge that God keeps his word. The believer is made part of a history which God has already begun in common with him. The "present" of faith in which he finds himself comes at the end of a covenant throughout which God has taken the initiative. The believer is a human being who finds himself in a situation of grace even before he makes any decision at all. Given "what happens to him" he is compelled to choose between fidelity and infidelity. The meaning of his life is offered to him as a gift; he does not himself create either the value of his own existence or the values by which he directs his action. The commitment of faith will continue to be a "present," a gift, a today of grace. If Abraham is a model for believers because he obeys the message that compels him to cut his roots, Joshua is likewise a model because he acknowledges that he receives as a gift the land in which his people will strike root.

Joshua receives this land not only as a gift but as a country to be built, a people to be united, a soil to be cultivated, a society to be organized. This land is thus also the fruit of a conquest, a land soaked in blood and sweat, in battles and toil. The land offered him is a land of freedom. God does not smother us with his love; the gifts of God elude us if they do not become a source of life; the covenant becomes a law that creates subjects, unless it leads to mutual love. "Decide for or against Yahweh": the present of the believer is a true present only if it leads into a future of commitment. For it is a person that the believer chooses to serve, and not a code or an idol.

"Decide for or against Yahweh!" Joshua commemorated that day with a stone; in the present of faith, that day brought together the memory of the past and the hope of a creative fidelity.

■

Your name, God our Father,
  has become part of our history;
your covenant has become our inheritance.
Be you praised as we remember your blessings.

We pray you
that today again
  we will choose you as our partner
  and as the meaning and joy of our life.

FROM MONDAY OF THE 20TH WEEK

TO SATURDAY OF THE 21ST WEEK

Nevertheless . . .

Let us be glad and joyful
and give praise to God,
because this is the time for the marriage of the Lamb.
His bride is ready,
and she has been able to dress herself
in dazzling white linen.

(Rev 19:7–8)

The simple fact of being a Christian is once again being felt as something extraordinary. To be touched by God's self-revelation, to believe in his reign, and to carry a concern for this reign in one's heart: all this is once again regarded as something extraordinary—as grace, happiness, responsibility, greatness and danger. With Jesus we "change regimes"; his presence and his word divide history in two. Human existence and human history are not what they used to be. The Kingdom is like . . . . Jesus acts as herald of the reign of God, as spokesman of a new discourse about God. He makes known a new and different image of God: not a new theology but a new history, a new covenant. The Kingdom is like what happens in a story about a king or a landowner . . . . It is not possible to speak of the Kingdom except in parables. In other words, we can speak of the Kingdom only if we allow to penetrate into us what the words and images are conveying: a new relationship. For a symbol is not a comparison; it creates an encounter, establishes a new order of things, confirms a revelation, brings to light what I am and what the other is. The Kingdom cannot be treated as a factual situation or a hard-and-fast reality, but only as a "drama" in the proper sense of this word, that is, as something that happens.

Something that happens and divides history in two, yet something very fragile! What Jesus left behind amounted to disconcertingly little: a few Israelites, just a handful, had faith in this man Jesus; they believed. That was all! And what a fragile thing our confession of faith is! The action of the Spirit, when looked at from outside, shows hardly any visible results. The Church is subject to the human condition and its limitations. We cannot escape the laws of our human reality with all its weaknesses and its potentialities for error and sin. When we speak of the Christian life and of the transformation it should bring about in us, we have plenty of reason to be realistic, and this realism may cause us to doubt the efficacious power of God's Spirit. All this is true. Nevertheless, the fact is that we have indeed "changed regimes." It is our human nature with all that historically weighs it down, and our personal existence with its burdensome stages that God invites to the marriage table. His salvation is utterly real, but it is not the outcome of our efforts and calculations: the covenant is a grace. All the defects that weigh upon the Kingdom are real enough, and we know how serious they are; nevertheless, we ourselves are the living proof that the Kingdom has really come, for we dare to hope and, after a fashion, we make our talents bear fruit. The word of God, when received with joyous faith, accomplishes what it says; it slowly transforms us because it is divine and because we put it into practice. As we wait for eternity and the community of saints, we cause this word to be alive by carrying it out and observing it. The "change of regime" has made us stewards of the Kingdom.

■

Lord our God, it is good
to give you thanks
  and to let your love sing in our hearts
  through Jesus the Christ, our Lord.
It is in him, the eternal Son of your tender love,

that you concluded with the human race
the covenant of your first love.
It is through him, your word of consolation,
that you show forth the power of life.
It is he, the faithful Spouse of your Church,
who enables us to love as you love.
By the power of his word
and the might of his Spirit,
he himself has made fruitful his gifts to us
and strengthens us to watch until he returns.
With those invited to his glorious wedding feast
we can even now
sing your praises and bless you.

MONDAY OF THE 20TH WEEK

WITHOUT BAGGAGE!

Judges 2:11–19. The period of the judges, which lasts for a little less than
two centuries, runs from the conquest of Canaan to the establishment of
the monarchy. From this period the biblical writer has recorded only a
series of infidelities which he contrasts with the serene fervor of the time of
Joshua (cf. Jgs 2:6–10). It is true that the tribes quickly adopted the local
divinities, the Baals and the Astartes, thus betraying the Sinai covenant.
The book describes the events of the conquest, with its raids and its
successes and reverses. But the defeats were felt to be so many divine
judgments; the people saw in them a just punishment for their own
infidelities. The author of the Book of Judges has therefore only given
expression to the way Israel looked upon this period; he has done so in the
form of a very typical four-stage scheme that is well illustrated by today's
reading. Mentioned successively are sin (vv. 11–13) and a punishment (vv.
14–15a) which puts the people in a desperate situation and leads to their
repentance (v. 15b); finally, salvation comes in the person of a "judge."
The latter is essentially a liberator who at a given moment rescues one or
other of the tribes from its hopeless situation. For during the period of the
Judges the tribes were still independent of one another; "every man did as

224

he pleased" (17:6). In this way Israel experienced the patience of God.

Psalm 106 is a national confession which develops the theme of the sinful people. It emphasizes their idolatry but also the fact that the conquest did not wipe out the local population, with which Israel gradually intermingled.

Matthew 19:16–22. "If you wish to be perfect." In the Sermon on the Mount Jesus had already urged his disciples to be perfect as their heavenly Father is perfect. To this man who is a past master at observing the commandments Jesus therefore issues an invitation to transcend himself. "If you wish": the invitation, though urgent, shows a profound respect for the man's freedom.

"The young man went away sad." Did he realize in his heart the difficulties of such a self-transcendence? Was his sadness caused by a realization of the abyss separating the demands of the law from the radicalism of the Gospel? "Who can be saved, then?" the disciples ask. They still need to learn that the Kingdom is pure grace. But we too need to learn that the "counsels" of Jesus are not addressed to a religious elite but are meant for every human being of good will who agrees to open his or her heart to the working of the Spirit.

■

A man rushes up to Jesus, his fervor visible on his face. He wants to be good, to be perfect: "Master, what good deed must I do to possess eternal life?" We know the rest: Jesus asks too much, and the man has too many possessions. "Go and sell what you own and give the money to the poor; then come, follow me." But at these words the young man goes away, for he is very rich. The Kingdom is accessible only to those who set out lightheartedly and without baggage; all the merits, all the knowledge, all the piety in the world cannot open the gates of the Kingdom. Only they will enter who present themselves with empty hands. As St. John of the Cross will comment later on, "What difference does it make whether it is a strong rope or a thread that binds you, if it keeps you a prisoner and prevents your advancing?"

Happy the poor! Only those who set out to follow the Jesus who stripped himself to the point of stretching out naked on a cross will possess the Kingdom. "He went away sad, for he was a man of great

225

wealth." Our joy is to spend our days hollowing out the place in our hands and hearts that can hold the Kingdom of heaven as it passes by.

"Sell what you own!" Set out for God without plans, without memories, without a library. Set out without a road map for discovering him, knowing that he is on the road with you and not only at the goal. Do not try to find him by original methods, but let him find you in the poverty of an everyday life. Abandon your great wealth and rejoice even that your mind is at a loss when it comes to the things of God. And if your prayer lacks fine feelings, keep in mind that God is not reached through the emotions. If you are without courage, then rejoice that you are good candidates for hope. And if you think your lives are too wretched for you to be called to enter the Kingdom, you are close to discovering mercy and living in charity.

"Master, what good deed must I do to possess eternal life?" "Open your hands and become rich in God! Come, follow me; the road which leads to the cross will be your path to life!"[26]

■

You challenged the power of the rich
and you proclaimed blessed the poor who follow you.
Lord, our God,
let your gaze still rest on us,
  for excessive wealth keeps us from advancing.
In your love impoverish us
so that we may walk with no future save yours.

TUESDAY OF THE 20TH WEEK

EVERYTHING IS POSSIBLE!
Judges 6:11–24a. "The Israelites did what displeased Yahweh; Yahweh gave them over for seven years into the hands of Midian" (6:1). Depending on the period in question, the Midianites were the friends (cf. Moses) or the

enemies of Israel. They had remained nomads and used to make seasonal or unexpected raids on the territory of the Israelite tribes and create devastation in their path. Forced to thresh his wheat in a place hidden from Midianite eyes, Gideon, son of Manasseh, decided to counterattack, and he pursued the invaders across the Jordan.

The story told in the liturgical pericope is an etiological legend meant to explain the establishment of the sanctuary at Ophrah, where there was a sacred tree (v. 24: "Gideon built an altar there to Yahweh and called it Yahweh-Peace"). It is within the framework of this legend that the biblical writer has chosen to tell the story of Gideon's call; this call-story is so typical that it is often cited as an example. In it we find the various elements required: mention of a meeting with God (v. 12a); an introductory formula describing the wretched situation of the people (vv. 12a–13); the sending on a mission (v. 14); the objection raised by Gideon who, like Moses, claims to be too young and too weak for such an undertaking (v. 15). The objection enables the writer to emphasize the divine initiative in the form of a word of encouragement: "I will be with you and you shall crush Midian as though it were a single man" (v. 16). Finally comes the request for a sign (vv. 17–19). Such stories occur frequently both in the Old Testament (the call of Jeremiah) and in the New (the annunciation).

Psalm 85 is a Psalm of petition. The responsory verse has been chosen in function of the name given to Gideon's altar.

Matthew 19:23–30. "It is easier for a camel to pass through the eye of a needle than for a rich man to enter the Kingdom of heaven." The statement could not be clearer. We must doubtless add that Jesus loved and called rich men, who had a high social standing, without requiring that they abandon their position. It remains true, however, that he also appreciated the obstacle which riches represent for anyone desirous of entering into life.

The disciples cannot believe their ears. The Master's demands in regard to conjugal fidelity had already seemed to them impossible to meet. Now the detachment he calls for seems equally impossible. If entrance into the Kingdom of heaven requires such sacrifices as these, who can be saved?

But who says anything about sacrifices? The rich man came to ask what he must *do* in order to win eternal life; Jesus speaks to him of *leaving* everything in order to *receive* everything. Here is the dazzling truth: the Kingdom of heaven is not earned but received. Happy therefore those who

227

do not go away sad after realizing their incapacity! If they do not turn away, they are ready to be filled a hundredfold by the Spirit of God, and their hearts, like the world itself, will be made wholly new.

■

"It is easier for a camel to pass through the eye of a needle than for a rich man to enter the Kingdom of heaven." The disciples cannot believe their ears. The conditions for entering the Kingdom of God are such that the anxious question arises: Who then can win through? We need only lend an ear to the groans, snarls and confused murmurs arising from all those around us and we will hear like an echo: "Who can be saved, then?"

Jesus answers firmly, as one who knows what he is preaching and what he is bringing to human beings: "For men this is impossible; for God everything is possible." In the face of the human race's vast and tragic question, God's answer is disconcerting in its simplicity: he sends his Son, alone and disarmed. Those who follow Jesus on the narrow road that leads to Calvary will experience Easter morning and the joy of the Kingdom.

In all truth, there would be reason for despair only if the living word of God were to die out and if the Spirit of Christ were no longer to raise up witnesses of any kind. "We have left everything and followed you." We have begun to cast off our shackles and the riches that kept us prisoners of ourselves; we want to be of service so that the hope of salvation may not be extinguished among human beings. Because our own hearts were converted by the all-powerful word, even though we were no better than anyone else, and because our lives were turned around by a glance from God, we trust in the Lord's word. The most tangible proof that everything is possible in our world and in human history is what has happened to us ourselves.

■

God our Providence,
those who trust in you
*   will never be confounded!*
Be mindful of your eternal covenant

and by your power accomplish
what is impossible by human standards;
let our hope be possible today.

■

If ever God were to abandon us,
if ever the Eternal
    were to hold our sins against us,
who then could stand before God?
Who then could be saved?

But with the Lord there is only grace;
with the Almighty
    there is only a future always offered.
It is he who gives life to his people.
He is the God who loves and forgives.

WEDNESDAY OF THE 20TH WEEK

THE WAGES OF THE HEART

Judges 9:6–15. Abimelech was the son of Jerubaal, but were Jerubaal and Gideon one and the same person? The answer is not that certain, and de Vaux is of the opinion that we must distinguish two personages whom tradition has identified because both came from Ophrah and because Gideon refused to be king while the son of Jerubaal offered himself for the position. In fact the story seems to be explaining an attempt at government that ended in a failure.

The pericope is in the form of an allegory and probably reflects the influence of prophetic circles hostile to the monarchy (cf. 1 Sam 8:11–18). "While the rest of the 'trees' fulfill their role for the good and weal of others, the thorn-bush is the only anti-social good-for-nothing: its 'reigning over the trees,' its call to them to take refuge under its shade, is a piece of ludicrous arrogance."[27]

Psalm 21 is a Psalm for use in royal liturgies. It is thought to have been sung before the start of a procession with the ark and in celebration of a royal victory that is attributed to Yahweh.

Matthew 20:1–16a. "The men who came last have done only one hour, and you have treated them the same as us, though we have done a heavy day's work in all the heat." All the better if we still feel as indignant as the workers did, for then the parable will have accomplished its purpose, which is to challenge the hearer, stir him up, lead him to react to a paradoxical situation.

A man was hiring workers for his vineyard. He agreed to pay one denarius to the workers who came in the first hour; a denarius was at that time the usual wage for a day-laborer. Throughout the day he kept hiring men, but since there were fewer and fewer hours of work done by the latecomers, these workers could expect to receive only some fraction of a denarius. But now the employer gives all of them the same wages. In so doing he shows himself "good," because the wage given is only the minimum needed to sustain life. Conscious as he is of the wretched condition of the workers he has hired, the master is unwilling to deprive the latecomers of what they need in order to live. In the same way, God shows himself generous to the poor.

But the workers hired first have counted on receiving a larger wage and they begin to complain. The complaint would be a legitimate one if the parable were written in a social perspective, but this is not the case, for at issue is the Kingdom (v. 1). Thus when the owner replies to the claims made against him: "I choose to pay the latecomer as much as I pay you," he is expressing the gratuitousness of God's gifts.

Finally, we must not lose sight of the fact that the workers are hired to work in the "vineyard," that is, the Church, the people of God. To work in the vineyard is to collaborate in the building up of the Christian community. The parable thus tries to show that the Church is not the result of human efforts but rather a grace that is to be received.

■

The story is a simple one: the work has to be done, and the owner of the vineyard hires workers as he needs them. Evening comes, the time for paying wages, and the employer gives each worker the same amount. But then he is challenged: Why do those who have worked

for only an hour receive as much as those hired in the early morning? The latter have worked for twelve hours and through the hottest part of the day; their indignation is understandable. Then the owner explains his position: Is he not free to dispose of his money to whomever he wishes?

But why? Is the parable a statement by a landowner: I use my possessions as I see fit? In fact, the problem here is not one of justice or even of morality. It lies elsewhere: "Why be envious because I am generous?" The question is aimed at leading the hearers beyond ordinary "good sense." The parable shocks because it breaks away from reality and reason. It is provocative and challenging. Jesus wants to lead his interlocutors from the realm of reason into the realm of the heart, from the realm of religious faith into the realm of evangelical faith. For at bottom the parables are baffling, challenging, unreasonable. Every parable ends in an improbable, unexpected, outrageous way. The God of Jesus Christ does not act as he should act. God is not a god; he does not behave as a god should behave.

God should stand for righteousness, but here he is, welcoming tax collectors and sinners. He opens his Church to the latecomers, the pagan foreigners, instead of reserving his inheritance for the children of the first covenant. He offers the same grace and shows the same love to belated converts as he does to those who have heroically endeavored throughout a lifetime to carry the burden of existence and make it bear fruit.

God should stand for morality. Where are we if he does not reward the good and the sinful according to their deserts but instead sets about distributing his grace to everyone? We used to have a reasonable religion, but now we are challenged to rejoice in the limitlessness of the Gospel. We are urged to pass from reason to the heart. The Lord's vineyard is not a factory that turns out products; the Church is founded on love. The workers of the eleventh hour did not expect to be even hired; how surprised they were, then, when the employer paid them for a whole day. Astonished human beings: such are the citizens of the Kingdom. The workers hired in the morning would have found it quite natural to receive the salary agreed upon, but those hired in the evening would talk for a long time to come of this incredible vineyard owner who treated them with kingly generosity. And this surprise will accompany them throughout their lives. "Have I no right to do what I like with my grace?" What we hear in this context is not a statement by a capricious landowner but the voice of the heart. Love is a wager laid on the potentialities of the other and not a calculation inspired by justice or a listing of rights and merits.

■

—*You search our hearts:*
the grace you offer us is our blessing.
Blessed be you, Lord, God of tender love!

—*Your word is good news for the poor:*
you give us joy in your life.
Blessed be you, Lord, God of tender love!

—*Your thoughts are beyond our hopes:*
the righteousness you bestow follows no plan.
Blessed be you, Lord, God of tender love!

■

Lord God,
your ways are not our ways.
Our prayer ascends to you:
on the day of your Son's glory
reward us not according to our deserts
but according to your grace.

THURSDAY OF THE 20TH WEEK

INVITATION TO A WEDDING

Judges 11:29–39a. Jephthah was from Gilead, a mountainous region located east of the Jordan and bordering on the territory of the Ammonites. Rejected by his own family, he became leader of a band of outlaws, but was recalled by his fellow citizens when the Ammonites declared war on them.

Jephthah's vow must be regarded an another etiological legend. It is an attempt to explain the origin of a ritual lament unknown elsewhere in the Bible. But the explanation sheds a dismal light on the consequences of idolatry in Israel; idolatry has led the people to adopt Canaanite customs and, in particular, the practice of human sacrifice, although this was forbidden by the prophet Micah:

> Must I give my first-born for what I have done wrong,
> the fruit of my body for my own sin?
> —What is good has been explained to you, man;
> this is what Yahweh asks of you:
> only this, to act justly,
> to love tenderly
> and to walk humbly with your God (6:7–8).

Psalm 51, a Psalm of thanksgiving, sheds light on the efforts of the prophets. Yahweh is not the source of the idea of votive sacrifices; he wishes only that people come to the temple and give thanks. What pleases the Lord is not the multiplication of sacrifices, but the effort to lead an upright life.

Matthew 22:1–14. "The king was furious. He despatched his troops, destroyed those murderers and burnt their town." This verse is probably an allusion to the fall of Jerusalem in 70 A.D. For the parable of the wedding feast, like the preceding parable of the wicked husbandmen, has judgment for its context. Jesus, Son of David, has mounted an ass and entered the city of his distant ancestor for a final confrontation with the leaders of his people.

The parable of the wedding feast has direct parallels with that of the wicked husbandmen. In both cases, the messengers, who recall the prophets of the Old Testament, are harassed and put to death. The anger of the king is quickly felt in both cases. The parable of the wicked husbandmen had announced that the vineyard would be given to other servants. This prediction has already been fulfilled, since the king invites to the feast not a few privileged individuals but all whom his messengers find—out at the crossroads and along the circuitous paths of life. The hall is filled, but those invited are a different breed: no longer Jews, but Christians. The hall in which the wedding feast is celebrated is the Church.

Then a sensation: the master of the house comes to greet his guests, but this visit inspired by courtesy quickly turns into a tour of inspection. The servants had summoned the wicked as well as the good, and here the master finds a guest without a wedding garment. Matthew uses this device to introduce the personal aspect of judgment: the mere fact of being called does not mean that the person is automatically saved. He must also have produced fruit; he must be clothed in the garment prescribed for the wedding feast. And the barren tree will be cut down and thrown into the fire, "where there will be weeping and gnashing of teeth." All are called but few are chosen. All are called, but few allow themselves to be chosen—only a "remnant," Isaiah would have said.

■

Imagine gathering people from the public squares in order to fill the hall at a wedding feast. The parable takes us away from the familiar, from the old-hat; it is a challenge and a stumbling block. The parable speaks of God, and for us God is not an idea or a doctrine. In the eyes of Jesus God "tells stories about himself," and it is these deeds of God that must be proclaimed. Like the troubadours of the Middle Ages who sang the high deeds of knights, Jesus travels the land of Israel to sing of the deeds of God. "The Kingdom of heaven is like what happens in this story I am about to tell you . . . ."

God is like a king who has prepared a wedding feast for his son, amid all the bustle characteristic of such a time of preparation. The king has sent out messengers to say: "Everything is ready for the feast." But though the smell of the cooking is enticing and the table is well laid, though the lamps are lit and the flowers decorate the hall, the essential thing for a feast is lacking: those invited have not come. Imagine the splendid table without any guests. Those who were expected—the old acquaintances, the friends, the relatives—have remained deaf to the invitation. Those regarded as the friends of God—the Pharisees, the high priests—have refused the invitation of Christ. And God is left alone with his banquet. Is he going to put out the lamps? By no means! He sends for the poor, the crippled, the blind and the lame. No one will be excluded from the feast; henceforth the table is set for everyone. The Zacchaeuses will sit at the table, along with the Matthews, the Mary Magdalenes, and people like the blind man at Siloam and the paralytic of Capernaum, the Samaritan who was healed and the adulteress who was forgiven. It is with such people as these that God will celebrate the blood-wedding of his Son with the human race.

Today God still wanders the streets and squares. Is it really true that we are invited to the royal table of God? Invited to the wedding feast of the king's son, to the paschal table? You do not really believe that. Better to find a suitable excuse and not go. Ah, if only human beings realized God's ambitions for them! If while on earth they only took seriously his invitation to them. The feasting would go on forever. But how far off this wedding feast still is! Everything is ready, and nothing is ready, because there must be a response to the invitation. How far has the human race gotten on this wretched, stubborn, painful journey from the initial and always threatening chaos of Genesis to the Jerusalem on high where God will gather all peoples for a delightful banquet? We need only look at the earthly Jerusalem to see that the world is still in chaos and that the city of God, a city of peace and love, is still being rent by the age-old sufferings and resentments of a lame, crippled, blind human race. Yet it is this human race that God invites to the wedding feast, and not a people conjured up in dreams. The joy he offers will not be an artificial exuberance that does not last, like the joy of soulless business dinners. This joy will be the kind that is to be found in the wedding hall, despite handicaps and distress. The conversation will be about the deeds accomplished by the God of tender love. The feast will be a covenant feast at which the surrendered body of the Lord will make clear how unmerited was our call to it.

■

God, whose love is beyond
  any measuring stick of ours,
  blessed be your name.
You open wide the doors of your house,
and we who are poor
  take our places at the feast
  where your Son himself is our food.
Grant that we may sing your kindness
until the day when you clothe us
  in a wedding garment forever.

■

On Psalm 111

With all my heart I shall give thanks to the Lord;
brothers and sisters, join your praise to mine!

Wonderful are his works,
marvelous his deeds:
his mercy is unparalleled,
his tender love and pity unequaled.

The Lord has left a memorial of his wonders;
today he brings deliverance
once again to his people.

He gives nourishment to his faithful
and is mindful of his covenant.

FRIDAY OF THE 20TH WEEK

THE LAW OF LIFE

Ruth 1:3–6, 14b–16, 22. Is this a modern novel set in the time of the judges? As a matter of fact, the language of the Book of Ruth is post-exilic, but the story itself must be older. Like the Septuagint, Christian tradition places this book after the Book of Judges, because the plot is regarded as unfolding at that period. The book thus takes a view opposite to that which emerges from the Book of Judges and is illustrated by the Books of Ezra and Nehemiah. For the danger of idolatry which foreign peoples represented for Israel led to the prohibition of mixed marriages after the exile. And while the Book of Ruth does not oppose the measures taken to safeguard the faith, it nonetheless does represent a reaction against the development of an excessively narrow nationalism.

The story "presents an idyll of simple family devotion and of country life. We see that the virtues of generosity and piety are rewarded and we discern the guiding hand of Providence over all."[28] The personages of the story have symbolic names: Naomi is "My gracious one"; Ruth is "The companion," and Orpah "She who turns her back." The name Bethlehem, which means "house of bread," can also be connected with the action of

236

the Lord in giving bread to his people (v. 6).

Psalm 146. Vv. 5–9 are a Psalm of congratulation addressed to the pilgrims in the temple. The song has the ring of a hymn in honor of the Lord who protects those who are weakest.

Matthew 22:34–40. "The Pharisees got together." The translation at this point misses to some extent what the evangelist has in mind, since the Greek here is an implicit citation of Psalm 2:2 as found in the Greek Bible ("The rulers gathered together against the Lord and his Christ"). The gathering of the Pharisees is thus a conspiratorial gathering; the trial of Jesus is now underway.

The lawyer raises the much discussed question of which is the greatest Commandment. In fact, the real issue is less to establish a hierarchy of some kind than to clarify the foundations of the moral life. Jesus answers by citing the twofold Commandment of love of God and love of neighbor. In both its parts this Commandment is based on the lordship of God, as is clear from the beautiful prayer, the *Shema* (Dt 6:5) from which the First Commandment is taken (cf. Mk 12:29), and from the refrain "I am Yahweh" that goes with the Second Commandment in Leviticus 19:18. The originality of the answer is not to be found in the ideas of love of God and love of neighbor, for these were already familiar to the Old Testament, but in the fact that Jesus brings them together and assigns them equal importance and, above all, in the simplification and concentration of the whole law in these two Commandments. For in fact on these two Commandments depend the whole of the law and the prophets.

■

They still come looking for Jesus; the sects and groups come one after another, all seeking support for their theses or a means of trapping the Son of God. "Master, which is the greatest Commandment of the law?" In the time of Jesus, and during the years when Matthew was composing his Gospel for Christians who had come over from Judaism, the question was an intimidating one. The scribes counted three hundred and sixty-five prohibitions, or as many as the days of the year, and two hundred and forty-eight commandments, or as many as the components of the body. Such was the list that was supposed to guide the life of the devout Jew, and

237

the rabbis made every effort to prove the importance of each commandment and each prohibition. The question was therefore a dangerous one, and the purpose of putting it to Jesus was "to disconcert him."

Christ's answer is simple and utterly traditional; he is content to give in reply the splendid text which every devout and sincere Jew knows by heart: "You must love the Lord your God with all your heart, with all your soul, and with all your mind." There is nothing new here, and yet Jesus avoids the trap by radically altering the terms of the question.

In the eyes of Jesus, a set of rules is not enough, even one so luminously simplified that it might be observed as a code of laws. The real need is to get back to the essential thing, which belongs to the order not of law but of the heart. "It is your heart I want, and not sacrifices," God had already said in the Old Testament. The program proper to the new life is not reducible to musts or oughts; the new life is the challenge issuing from a face: the face of God and the faces of human beings. Jesus rescues the human race from its obsession with taboos and observances, from the fetters of inferior fears and social rigidities. The living sap that flows through any valid morality is not conformity to norms but the love that reaches out to other living beings. Jesus sets himself against anything that can turn the gaze away from what is essential, whereas the rabbis had set protective barriers between the human person and the demands of God. Henceforth the person must keep his eyes on God and his fellows; the important thing is not to be in "good order" but to love.

Love God with your whole being, remembering that love is a passion, not a duty. Love as men love life itself—like one who is intoxicated or infatuated, like one who cannot give reasons for loving. Love God without limit.

Then love your neighbor as yourself. The call is not to construct an argument and then "tolerate" others; it is to go out with an unlimited tender love to those whom God looks upon as he does me, with a passionate love that is willing even to die for love.

Is all this just nice words? Perhaps. But if they were to turn into reality, what a revolution they would cause! Jesus simplified the law. Perhaps it would have been better for us to go on observing the two hundred and forty-eight commandments and the three hundred and sixty-five prohibitions. Then we would at least have realized where our response to the Gospel was taking us. Love is a dangerous thing; it can lead only to the cross. But it can also lead to Easter morning.

■

God our Father, we shall never finish
  praising the immensity of your love.
May this praise lead us
  into a new life bestowed by your Spirit
  and devoted to the service of the brethren.

■

Our joy is to bless you, Father of infinite love.
  Astonished, we find in your creation
  the tender love you exercise in all things.
We praise you for such great love.

Blessed be you too
  for giving us to one another
  as a multitude of brothers and sisters
  called to live by your gracious law.

As we follow the path of this difficult love
  you breathe your Spirit into us
  so that our lives may truly embody
  the words of praise that we utter.

In that praise we join our voices
  to all in this world
  who daily discover
  the many faces of your all-embracing love.

SHOULDER MY YOKE

Ruth 2:1–3, 8–11; 4:13–17. After the death of her husband and two sons, Naomi returned to her native country with Ruth. Here she made shrewd use of the law concerning the redemption of land. This law had for its purpose to prevent the alienation of a patrimony; to this end it provided that a member of the family or clan could exercise his right to buy back land put up for sale because of financial or other difficulties. This "defender" could also ransom or redeem a member of the group who had been reduced to slavery; this was the right Yahweh had exercised in order to "claim" his people who were enslaved in Egypt (Ex 6:6). In the present passage, the law concerning redemption is combined with the law of the levirate, which allowed a man to marry his brother's widow in order to give the dead man a posterity.

The divine favor evidently rests on Ruth the Moabitess who is so zealous in embracing the Jewish way of life. Tradition also emphasized the providential character of the child Ruth conceived by Boaz; it even said that Yahweh had specially intervened so that she might in the distant future give birth to the Messiah. We will recall, too, that Matthew introduces Ruth's name into his genealogy of Jesus (Mt 1:5).

Psalm 128, another song of praise and felicitation, celebrates the joys of the home.

Matthew 23:1–12. "They say, but do not do." They talk, but they produce no fruit. This is an attitude contrary to what the Kingdom requires. Nonetheless Jesus begins by acknowledging what is legitimate about the Pharisees: the scribes sit on the chair of Moses, and every Israelite who is consistent with his beliefs is bound to follow their teaching. But the Pharisees too readily took advantage of their position to place intolerable burdens on the lowly. They were shepherds who did harm, for instead of setting free those for whom they were responsible before God, they kept them from truly living.

A word to the wise is sufficient. Matthew's remarks are valid for Christian leaders too. Vv. 8–12 suppose that some of these leaders were not above striving for honors; it was therefore necessary to remind them of the constant teaching of Jesus on this point. In the Church, the greatest member is the one who serves. The titles "master," "father" and "teacher" can easily inspire a spirit of domination in those on whom they are bestowed; they are all the more to be avoided in the Church since Christians have but one master and teacher, namely, Christ, and one Father, who is God. The community may have need of organization, and some kind of "order" is a necessity, but the organization and the order are for the sake of service, that is, for building up the communion of the body of Christ.

■

This time Jesus attacks openly. He openly accuses the murderous vineyard workers of the parable, the would-be sons. He denounces them before all the people: "You whited sepulchres! You blind guides! You say but you do not do!" There is now open war between this man who is God's face to us and the Pharisees and scribes who arrogate to themselves the right to speak in the name of God: "You say, but you do not do."

These men imagined they could build their own salvation by sheer hard work, to the point where they could soon do without God himself. They had forgotten that God alone justifies human beings, and this as a pure favor. Human beings owe their salvation solely to the fidelity of God, for God never forgets his covenant. Can anyone turn God into a bookkeeper who weighs the merits of human beings? No, God is not like that. The Pharisees utterly failed to grasp the real situation when they excluded the weak, the maimed, the blind, the sinful, in the name of a mass of intolerable prescriptions. The Pharisees ended up excluding God himself so that they might imprison human beings within their system and subject them to their service.

Jesus protests with scathing contempt. He will never allow men to make use of God as a tool of their politics or a screen for their plots. He had overturned the tables of the money-changers in the temple; all the more forcibly does he reject the authoritarianism of those who traffic in God: "You must call no one on earth your father, since you have only one Father, and he is in heaven." Jesus also protests that there must be respect for human beings; he rejects the burdens which weigh upon the weak: "You must not allow yourselves to be called rabbi, since you have only one Master, and you are all brothers." "You have only one Teacher, the Christ. The greatest among you must be your servant. Anyone who exalts himself will be humbled."

But isn't that a utopian dream? Society is ruled by the law of the jungle, the law of the driving piston, the law of the thrusting elbow. To win election, politicians claim to be better than others. How could they get elected without such claims? When all is said and done, the crowd needs masters who can dominate it. So, do not the words of Jesus sound like a pious dream?

Yes, we have to keep looking at Jesus for a long time if we are to learn the truth of his words. "You have only one Teacher." He is a teacher, a master, unlike any other, for he prefers the weak and weakness to the powerful and power. We will have to allow the Spirit to do his work for a long time yet if our hearts are to become like the heart of the Lord, who alone teaches us authentic humility. For only God is truly humble; the Creator of all things does not put out the wick that still smolders or snap off the reed that bends under its burden.

For goodness' sake, brothers and sisters, stop displaying your decorations, don't lengthen the fringes on your cloaks, don't make a list (however long) of your merits (however real). Put yourself to school under Jesus and learn from him humility and truthfulness, along with a good measure of humor, because even when you have done the impossible for God you will still be unprofitable servants. Don't take yourselves seriously. For it is by love that you will be judged: love freely given in the humble service of your fellows.

John the Apostle in his old age realized this full well. He had observed the life of the churches from the beginning, and when he composed his Gospel he told of the washing of the feet, and he did so at the very point at which the other evangelists had told of the institution of the Eucharist!

"I, the Lord and Master, have given you an example!"

■

—*One God and Father!*

242

We are all born of a unique love,
and yet look at all the disputes among us.
  Lord, have mercy on us!

—One Master and Lord!
We experience only the freedom of love,
and yet look at all our pride and vanity.
  Christ, have mercy on us!

—One faith and one hope!
We all live by the one Gospel,
and yet how many empty words are spoken among us.
  Lord, have mercy on us!

You alone deserve the name of Father:
blessed be you, God of the universe!
You give us Jesus as teacher of life:
  may his obedience be a model for us,
  and his mercy the power that makes us act.
He served you to the end;
  because we share his life
  may humility be our source of joy,
  as it will be our source of greatness for eternity.

MONDAY OF THE 21ST WEEK

WORD OF LIFE

1 Thessalonians 1:1–5, 8b–10. 1 Thessalonians is an interesting letter for more than one reason. It is the oldest New Testament document, dating from 51, or only about twenty years after the death of Jesus. The community of Thessalonica, to which the letter is addressed, was the first Church founded by Paul on the European continent. This new community was, however, sabotaged by the local Jewish community. Paul is therefore writing to a community hardly formed as yet, but he has received excellent reports about it.

The first three chapters are a long thanksgiving for the way the

Thessalonians have received the Gospel and for the action of God as manifested in the preacher. For in Paul's view the proclamation of the Gospel is a word of God whose power is at work in him. Did it not convert the hearts of the Thessalonians, who turned away from their idols and "became servants of the real, living God"? Paul is convinced that this power which is at work in his preaching is the same power that raised Jesus from the dead.

Psalm 149 summons the chosen people to praise God.

Matthew 23:13–22. Seven curses against the scribes and Pharisees? This seems unlikely to anyone familiar with the existential weight of a curse as understood by the Bible. As a matter of fact, people are too quick to describe as "curses" what seem to be simple observations of fact. Jesus is here taking note of the hypocrisy of his enemies and saying to them: "Alas!" Admittedly, the context of judgment is always present; in the manner of the Old Testament prophets, and in the form of a lamentation, Jesus is criticizing the leaders of the people.

By comparison with the corresponding passage in Luke, the Matthean text is less homogeneous, since the lamentations are formed into a group with the help of key words. What reproaches does Jesus bring against the scribes and Pharisees? They have "shut up the Kingdom of heaven," that is, they have created obstacles to God's action in history by refusing to acknowledge Jesus as the key to this history. They gain proselytes and then make them "twice as fit for hell as you are," which means that they have converted the proselytes to their own views rather than to God. They have been "blind guides," because they have replaced the simplicity of the law with casuistry, especially in the matter of oaths. In short, they have distorted the law of God; they have been harmful shepherds.

■

Do you realize that words and languages die? Not only those that are now in the past, but those that stick in our mouths or that are trying to well up from our hearts. This death is as old as the human race, but today in our world of verbal waste the word is still in agony. The syllables pour out day and night: radios turned on with no one listening to them, music as "background" in our large stores, hollow words that no longer expect any answer. The syllables pour out, but they crumble and break up; no one attends to them any longer. They

244

are bought and sold: the cleverly calculated phrases of our deceptive ads; the strangely non-committal addresses of our partisan politicians. Our words die; there is no heart to pump out the blood that will bring them back to life.

Words cannot live apart from human beings. True speech is a living grown-up daughter! "When we brought the good news to you, it came to you not only as words but as power and as the Holy Spirit." Paul himself was astonished at what happened: "Your faith is active, your love faces up to difficulties, your hope holds firm." His preaching in Thessalonica has not failed to produce results: the word proclaimed has become the word Christians live by, the Gospel has yielded an evangelical life. For the the word is spoken only in order to elicit a response. Otherwise it remains an empty sound, just talk and syllables mouthed. The word is communication and relation or it does not exist. The word of God is an open book: open to life and to the word we give in response.

Need we despair? Our faith is so uninvolved, our prayer so "wordy," our listening so inattentive. Yes, we would have to despair if the word of God were like our human words: repeated, unfaithful, soulless and fleshless. But God does not utter words into empty air; his words are creative, for what he says, he does. "He spoke, and it was done." His word is generative and creative. He speaks, and his word becomes an event: it lives and exists among us, it enters into history. "The Word was made flesh; he lived among us." The word of God will not let go of us until it has become our life. For God has never spoken his final word. All that we have to do is allow this word to enter into us and resonate there, echoing endlessly. We need only "haggle" with the Spirit; we need only "bring the birds back to life."

■

God our Father, your Word became flesh;
through Jesus, your eternal Word,
you keep your word
and renew the face of the earth.

Since we have accepted your promise,
display the power of the Gospel in us
until the day when it becomes
your final word on our lives.

SERVING THE WORD

1 Thessalonians 2:1–8. In a fuller discussion of the themes broached in the first chapter, the Apostle submits his apostolate to the judgment of the Thessalonians. The aspect of it that should convince them is the note of authenticity that has always characterized his activity: he has never preached to win the favor of men. Seek as they will, they will find neither trickery nor interested motives nor doctrinal errors; even his status as Apostle has never been used in order to gain any advantage. In short, Paul has nothing in common with the itinerant philosophers to whom the Thessalonians were accustomed. His preaching has been carried on under the sign of the purest love; even today he is ready to give his life for those who trust in him.

Psalm 139. If any further proof were needed of Paul's sincerity, God himself would provide it. Psalm 139 is a lament, but the liturgy makes use of the verses which praise the divine omniscience.

Matthew 23:23–26. The Pharisees pay the tax on mint and dill and cummin, but they neglect justice, mercy and good faith. They clean the outside of the cup and the dish, but they overlook the baseness of their own hearts. They are blind guides, for they observe precepts that are quite secondary, but forget the essential and end by being mistaken about themselves. They are true unfortunates.

■

"In entrusting the Gospel to us, God has put us to the test."

Elsewhere Paul will describe all that he endured in the service of the Gospel. The disciple is not greater than his master, and the life of a missionary, too, is a way of the cross. Why then should we be surprised at the seeming contradictions which the service of the word gives rise to in us?

We are not truly "masters" of what we must pass on to others, and yet speak we must. This word is never at our beck and call, and its superabundance always lifts it above us and overwhelms us; but we also know that this word comes to birth only when it rises from our deepest selves and when the words spoken in the past by other believers come to life in us. We have had the experience of a word that is valid for all times but that comes to us in words spoken at other periods of history, and we ask ourselves: How are we to put this word into today's words while still allowing it to be its true self?

The test imposed by service of the word is to be seen first of all in these seeming contradictions which have their origin in the mystery of a word that puts itself on our lips and slips into our ordinary words: it is ours without originating in us. It also comes to birth as the result of a painful necessity: How are we to communicate what we have received? The word summons us from within us: Speak what you have heard and experienced! But it can rise up within the other only if his heart freely accepts it. My words, born of a felt necessity, must die in order that the word of the Other may be born. Fear and trembling lay hold of us in the face of this responsibility, yet we cannot any longer silence the voice that torments us.

To serve the word is perhaps simply to allow the word to enter into our lives and then overflow. For it is to our weak selves that Jesus continues to entrust a Gospel meant for the entire world.

■

God of the word and the prophets,
*   we bless you:*
you entrust your word to us,
removing the veil from the hidden mystery.

Be mindful of us
*   who must face*
*   the contradictions of your Kingdom.*
Let your Spirit be our strength in trial,
your fidelity our source of confidence in doubt,
your patience our pledge of mercy when we sin.

247

THE CHILD, TOO, SHALL SPEAK

1 Thessalonians 2:9–13. Paul continues his defense by emphasizing the disinterested way in which he has carried out his apostolic mission. He was unwilling to be a burden to the Thessalonians during the time when he was proclaiming God's word to them. This is a point he likes to make repeatedly; sometimes he even reminds his readers that he preferred to earn his living with his hands (cf. Acts 18:3). On the other hand, he never made this practice of his own a rule of life for others, and while he was in Thessalonica he even accepted material help from the Philippians for himself.

But the thing that brings joy to Paul's heart and is the focus of his thanksgiving is the way in which the Thessalonians received his preaching. They received it for what it really was: a message from God. They recognized in Paul an authentic man of God. Was he not ready to give his life for them? Was he not both an attentive father and a gentle mother to them?

Psalm 139 is used again (cf. Tuesday). In these further verses Paul's apostolate is submitted to the judgment of him who can probe the heart and the soul.

Matthew 23:27–32. The Pharisees delude themselves and, what is worse, the picture they present of themselves deceives others. One example among others: like Pontius Pilate, they wash their hands of the blood of the prophets slain by their ancestors, even while they prepare to do everything they can to get rid of Jesus.

But the cause is not lost. In the manner of the prophets Jesus gives a glimpse of hope. At the end of his discourse he predicts to the scribes and Pharisees the downfall of the Jewish religion ("Your house will be left to you desolate"), but then he immediately adds: " . . . until you say: 'Blessings on him who comes in the name of the Lord' " (vv. 38–39).

■

After emerging from the womb the child very quickly seeks to go out of itself and establish relations with those around it. It attempts this

248

through very touching gestures: its first cry, its first smile, and then, one day, its first words. But this speaking which introduces it to a properly human level of life would be impossible if its attempt had not been preceded by other words which engender this new level of life. Contrary to appearances, the child's first word is not a call to others; its first "dada" or "mama" is a response. For months now the child's parents have been speaking to it, but the words have seemingly been vanishing into a void. Were they useless words? Not at all: they were words which call, rouse, enable the child truly to exist. Loved before it is capable of loving in return, rendered fruitful by tender words spoken to it before it is capable of speaking in return, the child will soon begin to speak to those who loved it first.

"You can remember how we treated every one of you as a father treats his children, appealing to you to live a life worthy of God." The Apostle has preached the word of God in season and out of season. Now the word that was spoken repeatedly amid suffering and trial has borne fruit: the Church has been born in Thessalonica, and Christians are now speaking in their turn. They are responding to the initiative of God who spoke first. To accept the word will always be a response to a prevenient concern; it will be an act of obedience to a call. Like the child, the world needs to have a word spoken to it if it is to live. And what it needs is not a doctrine from on high, but a word arising out of its own history. The ancients showed themselves well aware of this, for when they spoke of "word" they were thinking less of spoken sounds than of those events in life which are a source of instruction for those able to decipher them. The child can repeat back only what has touched its heart. The believer can say back the word which God gives him, because he has been "apprehended" by the suffering of his Lord.

The word exists only in exchange and communion. The same word in Hebrew means both "obey" and "hear"; in Greek the word for "to obey" means literally "to subject oneself to the word." When another addresses me, he causes me to exist. The child cries "Mama!" and the woman who hears it is summoned to be a mother; a man speaks this woman's first name, and she knows she is being called to be a wife.

"You accepted our message for what it really is, God's message and not some human thinking." Parents find joy in hearing their child finally stammer the words they taught it. God experiences the same joy.

■

God our Father,
we have received your word
  for what it is:
  a covenant that elicits faith,
  a promise that begets hope,
  a mercy that nourishes love.
Let your word be active in us believers
  today and in every tomorrow,
and let it bear a fruit that lasts forever.

Reading and Understanding Matthew

The Eschatological Discourse
(Chapters 24 — 2 5)

The Kingdom has come close to us in the person of Jesus; believers have assembled around the Messiah to form the Church in a first hesitant way. The word, introduced by the Beatitudes, has produced its fruit and can now return to God. A word, a people . . . Before we go any further, we must emphasize how faithful Matthew's Gospel is to biblical thinking. For the Jewish people have always thought of themselves as having been brought into existence by the divine blessing that was bestowed on Abraham; they experienced the day of Sinai when in the midst of a storm a word from God summoned them to a covenant. In like manner the Church, the new Israel, is conscious of having been called by a word from Jesus.

But Jesus has come to the end of his mission. Now is the time for drawing up balance sheets and for questions. As far as the Church is concerned, it is also the time for asking itself about the witness for the sake of which it has been founded. The eschatological discourse does not deal only with the meaning of the passion of Jesus; it also reveals the meaning of the Church's existence. Occupying Chapters 24 and 25, this discourse speaks of the end of time and the definitive coming of the reign of God, in the light of which the choices human beings have made will be judged. From this discourse the lectionary uses only two parables: that of the wise and foolish bridesmaids and that of the talents. The same theme is developed in both: the theme of vigilance, which is the same as saying: the theme of the present reality of the Kingdom.

THURSDAY OF THE 21ST WEEK

STEWARDSHIP

1 Thessalonians 3:7–13. Paul had been very anxious to revisit the community at Thessalonica, which he had had to leave suddenly, but circumstances had prevented him. Happily, however, Timothy, who had been sent on a mission, had reported only good things about the community, and the Apostle, whose feelings toward it run deep, feels revived by the news. Despite the obstacles they have encountered, his Christians in Europe have been steadfast.

His prayer now encompasses three desires: he would like to return to Thessalonica; he wants to find the brethren there firmly established in love and holiness; he hopes that the spark of faith has developed into a mighty flame of joy and welcoming love. The Christians of Thessalonica will then be ready to meet their Lord.

Psalm 90 is a national lament, but its reproaches are not concerned with a disaster caused by war or famine. What the psalmist bemoans is human frailty. Therefore the appeal to Yahweh: let his glory be reflected in those who love him.

Matthew 24:42–51. The eschatological discourse, which ends with a solemn exhortation to a watchfulness that is illustrated by several parables, highlights two events: on the one hand, the destruction of the temple, that is, the rejection of Jewish institutions; on the other, the return of the Lord at the end of time. The parable of the burglar must be read on two levels: first, the level of the Jesus of history, who is convinced that his death will be the signal for the final catastrophe in which his disciples are in danger of being swept away; then, the level of the Church, which is preoccupied by the delay of the parousia and the resultant danger of unresponsiveness on the part of its leaders.

The parable of the steward is likewise addressed to the leaders of the Church. Had the Matthean community had experience of negligent or unfaithful leaders? In any case, the parable strongly emphasizes the obligations of those to whom the protection of the "house" has been entrusted. The Lord will come without warning; the leaders of Israel too had not expected that on Easter morning Jesus would break through the wall of his tomb.

■

"The Son of Man is coming at an hour you do not expect." Is Jesus, then, a sadistic master who waits behind the door to catch out any servant abusing his stewardship? Does he absent himself on purpose in order to return unexpectedly and find his steward lazing about? Will he come at an arbitrary moment to judge and punish?

Jesus puts a strong emphasis on two words: "Stay awake!"

"Stay awake!" Do not let yourselves be invaded by the creeping numbness that paralyzes the powers of attention, lessens the force of the reasons for living, and glosses over the seriousness of human life. Stay awake! Work, no matter what, for it is when the night lasts without advancing that we must instigate the coming of day. Dress as servants, make your treasure bear fruit and pay close attention to the least signs of hope.

"Stay awake!" This means: denounce the sellers of illusions, all those who lull you to sleep and cast spells on you. Be servants who keep watch for their master's return. Let him find you wakeful and at work as men and women enthusiastic for his word.

"Stay awake!" Yet do not let fear get control of you!

How often watchfulness has become a defense mechanism! There is no room for the unexpected; the day one is to receive a visit, one forgets about the friend who is coming and thinks only of all that must be done in preparation. No one can approach our walls that are only too well guarded; we no longer experience the joy of surprise and unexpected good news, because no message is allowed to come to us unless it has been identified in advance. Forget about the passwords that keep you secure; glance outside from time to time and see the first gleam of dawn on the horizon.

The Master of the house has gone off. Stay awake; do not let the darkness and the need of waiting eat away at your hope. He who is coming will surprise you in the midst of your work. He will come at a moment when so much is yet to be done, but happy will you be because you will be able to discern in the dawning day something of what you yourselves have patiently built. Do not fear the Master's return, because his Spirit is keeping you watchful: he is the steward who even now is managing your life.

■

Happy will we be if you find us watching!
Lord, revive our faith
    against the day of your coming.
What will become of us
    if sleep overcomes us?
Enable us to be faithful in your service
    for the salvation of our brothers and sisters
    and for your joy through the endless ages.

FRIDAY OF THE 21ST WEEK

KEEP IT BURNING

1 Thessalonians 4:1–8. After a thanksgiving comes an exhortation, as in other Pauline letters. Paul here begins a new section, reflecting the fact that the Lord's call led to a break in the lives of the Thessalonians. With the Lord's help they must make constant progress.

Paul turns here to face up to some facts peculiar to communities made up of former pagans. Everyone knows about the habitual license that marked pagan cities; the Apostle therefore intends to be realistic. His Thessalonians, good people though they are, are recent converts and will be tempted to fall back into their old habits. Scholars still argue, however, about whether Paul is urging control of their bodily appetites or calling their attention as Christians to the importance of a right choice of husband or wife. The solution of this dispute is not too important, since the thing that really matters is to do everything "in a way that is holy and honorable." That is what the Lord wants.

Psalm 97 is primarily a poem about a theophany, describing the majesty and greatness of Yahweh. It is used here because of its call to holiness.

Matthew 25:1–13. The Kingdom of heaven is like a wedding feast. The comparison with a wedding feast occurs frequently in the Bible as a way of expressing the meaning of God's covenant with his people. Here in Matthew, however, the bridegroom is the beloved Son, and the bride is the Church. The young women symbolize the waiting Christian community.

The young women are ten in number and they carry lamps (probably torches soaked in oil) so that they may dance at the wedding feast of the bridegroom. Oil is an especially evocative sign. For in Judaism it signified both good works and a joyous welcome; in the parable it expresses the measure of the love of those who keep watch. For when the bridegroom finds the young women unprepared, this is less because he has delayed in coming than because they have had to go out to the oil-sellers to replenish their supply. It is a shabby sort of love that is discovered rooting around in a shop.

Love demands daily watchfulness. The number ten brings this out, because it symbolizes human activity (the ten fingers of the hand). It is precisely into the midst of the everyday that the bridegroom comes, to the men working in the fields (24:40) and the women grinding at the millstone (v. 40). But he also comes in the middle of the night: the night of the eschatological time, the night of Easter which saw the First-born raised to life.

Wise or foolish: this is a constantly recurring theme in the Bible. At the end of the Sermon on the Mount Matthew had given an example of this in the men who built, one on rock, the other on sand.

■

How is it possible to offer the "wise" bridesmaids as a model? After all, these young ladies do not manifest a very "evangelical" attitude, since they refuse to share their oil. Then, too, the bridegroom comes very late in the night, without any warning, without having set a time for his arrival. It's easy to understand the young women falling asleep.

"The Kingdom of heaven is like . . . ." A parable always disconcerts in order to awaken the mind to a meaning, to provoke a listening attitude, to prepare the way for a "revelation." We are dealing with God, and God wants to reveal his face to us. A bridegroom, a wedding feast; yes, it is love the parable is about. Who are the provident ladies if not Christians when they set about truly loving? The flame of their lamps is delicate and fragile, like tenderness itself; only love can make it leap up, and it takes a lot of care to keep it burning. The difficulty of the careless young women is that they do not realize the kind of constant vigilance required by love. They allow the flame to die out, and they rush out to the shops to buy oil. As if love could be bought! It is in the heart that love lives, not in trade. Poor careless girls, you have only a notion of love.

"Stay awake . . . ." Wakefulness is a term heavy with tender love and the commitment of the entire person; it is another word for love. A mother stays awake with her child, ready at every moment to alleviate its suffering, ready for anything that may happen. A lighted lamp seen through a window: someone is staying awake, waiting for a late return. When events are in the offing, people gather to form a watch committee and to act at the right moment.

"Stay awake, and keep your lamps lit." Keep your faith alert by constantly relighting your lamp; let the night know clearly that it will not win the victory by its illusions of death; your watchful love will not be caught napping. By carrying a lighted lamp in your hand, you will open yourself to a shared intimacy with God. To stay awake does not mean simply not to fall asleep; it means rather to foresee, to be attentive to the least sign of an arrival, to keep hope alive.

God will never grow weary of awakening his Church. He maintains the Church in this world that it may be a sign, a sign that supports hope, and that means: The night is not endless; do not let the time slip away or get wound up in itself. History is leading to a completion. The Church's vocation is to keep lit the lamp that is set on a stand to

light the human house with its rays.

■

Our impatient God,
it is good to sing your praises through the night,
it is good to sing of your love in the morning.

Awaken our hearts in the fire of your Spirit;
keep us watchful
   when the Spirit comes to meet us
   and the day of the covenant feast arrives.
Let the night not gain the upper hand
   over those you created
   for that morning when life is reborn
   after the darkness of the grave.

■

A little piece of bread on our table
   already speaks to us of the joy of his return:
"The bridegroom is here."
He whom our heart sought is with us;
he opens the hall of the banquet and the great passage.

A cry has echoed in the night:
"Go out and meet him."
It is the song of an endless dawn,
   a hymn of that morning
   when the new wine overflows
   in the goblets of the feast.

God, Father of the human race,
   fill us with your Spirit;
   keep our lamps
   of joy and hope burning.
Let your Church never stop seeking
   him whom its heart loves.
Keep watch yourself over those in charge
   of keeping the Church awake.

Blessed be you,
God of the first evenings and the first mornings,
until the day when we shall bless you endlessly
  in Jesus, your light and our hope.

SATURDAY OF THE 21ST WEEK

RISK

1 Thessalonians 4:9–11. Fraternal love is the second problem to which Paul wishes to draw attention. He gives two instructions. The first is that they should work with their hands; this is something that would be repugnant to former pagans, accustomed as they were to leave manual work to slaves. The second is that they must live quietly; this is probably an allusion to the feverish expectation of the parousia that was so intense in Thessalonica.

Psalm 98 bids us offer praise. The final two verses, however, contain theophanic elements and thus reflect honor on the expectation of the Thessalonians.

Matthew 25:14–30. The master will be away for a long time. The length of his journey thus militates against a belief in an imminent return of the Lord. But what, in fact, is the significance of the length of the master's absence? What is the meaning of the time of the Church, which runs from the first coming of Christ to his return in glory?

The rendering of accounts is the real point of the parable. The first two servants have shown a creative fidelity; they have profited by the master's absence to produce abundant fruit; they have accepted their responsibilities and are now given new ones.

The third servant, however, has chosen to bury his talent; in the eyes of the law this action relieves him of all responsibility. And yet the master's anger does not spare him. Is God being unjust, demanding more than he gives? Or is it not rather the stupidity of the servant that is brought out—this man who has forgotten that love always tends toward infinity? He has not risked the goods entrusted to him; in other words, he has never gotten used to the

257

foolishness of God. The Kingdom is taken from him and given to others.

The parable bids each individual learn the truth about himself. The time of the Church, the time of watchfulness, is the space of freedom that is given to each individual for assuming his responsibilities.

■

He buried his talent; he was protecting himself against the future and taking no risks. The money did not belong to him; better, therefore, to be on guard and prudent. If he should lose it by risking it, how could he pay it back?

Is the parable therefore a short course in economics for a time of inflation and crisis? Do not think of it as calling our attention to our natural talents—intelligence, strength, courage, spirit of enterprise. The parable, like all the others, is about the Kingdom and God; it raises the veil from our relation to God in the medium of our human history.

The Master has gone off on a journey, and the first Christian community finds itself orphaned. Christ has departed and has left the fate of the Kingdom to his disciples. Now we are responsible. What have we done with the message?

The scribes and the teachers of the law were well aware that a precious deposit had been entrusted to them. Jesus blames them for having buried the word that should have borne fruit in the lives of human beings. "What have you done with the word?" This question addressed to the scribes is echoed in the Gospel with reference to us: "And you, what have you done with it?" For there are countless ways of killing and burying the word. Unproductive money quickly loses its value. If you bury love and grace, what will become of them? They are intended to be exchanged. If you bury Jesus, how will he become the living Christ?

We must indeed give the word back and render an account of it. But that is something far different from burying it. Our fidelity has nothing in common with the careful preservation of a patrimony. A Church that does not dare risk its inheritance in the human city has already lost everything. Our fidelity is not reducible to a matter of holding a wake for the dead and cultivating memories. It is something far different from a well-oiled memory machine. It is an attachment to a living word; it involves risk. You can be faithful only if you are up on your feet.

What are you doing with the word? The Church is unfaithful when it hides the word under the weight of customs and habits, under excessive attention to detail or a withering control of any and every point. The word truly exists only when uttered as ever new.

The Church is unfaithful when the word is no longer a cry, a desire that gives rise to life; when questions are smothered on the pretext that they are unfitting; when research is hindered because it is risky; when fear stops us from looking for the new laws of the Gospel; when justice and love, truth, reconciliation and peace remain dead words.

It is necessary to take risks, because the Kingdom is wholly in the form of seeds, and seeds always have a taste for risk and adventure, for the smell of life. The Church has received only one talent, and the name of its inheritance is "Jesus," the living Jesus. Have you noticed that "living" is a present participle? "Believe" is always conjugated as an active verb.

■

You trust us, Lord,
  with the body and blood of your Son.
Grant us to know the happiness
  of working in his name
  throughout our days,
until the Day when you will say to us:
  "Come and join in your master's happiness"
  for ages without end.

■

Let us pray, with hands already extended
  to do what the Lord asks of us:

—That the Church of Christ may never slumber
in a fidelity without soul or breath of life;
that if may be the sign of the God

who constantly invents life anew:
for this let us pray.

—We remember with gratitude all those
who created our past
   by taking the risks of the morrow.
May their boldness inspire us.

—That the mediocrity of some
may not discourage the good will of others:
for this let us pray.

Since you, Lord, have made us
   children of the light,
constantly stir up our boldness.
May your Day come
   through the work of our hands,
   for you are our future.

EVEN YEARS

ORDINARY TIME
WEEKS 10–21

Gospel According to St. Matthew
The chronology of the kings
The prophets:
Amos, Hosea, Isaiah, Micah, Jeremiah, Nahum, Ezekiel
Second Letter to the Thessalonians
First Letter to the Corinthians (beginning)

In even years, the lectionary offers us, along with the Gospel of Matthew, a broad panorama of Israelite history, from the prophet Elijah (on the morrow of the schism between north and south) to the Babylonian exile.

The prophets, from whom many passages are read, were all of them contemporaries of one or other stage of these events: they commented on them, they experienced them, they were often the first victims of them.

What is the connection between the Gospel and this often prosaic history? Does the connection perhaps depend directly on the idea of "reign" which plays such an important part in the message of Jesus? For in him "the reign of God is at hand." And who if not the kings were primarily in charge of this divine reign? The royal commission of concern for the poor and maintenance of religious unity in the nation was in fact flouted by the kings. Only a few of them found favor in the eyes of the biblical writers and the prophets. The reading of history which the Bible sets before us is not a chronicle of events, still less a defense of power; on the contrary, both in the narrative itself and in the prophetic reaction to the events, this history is a criticism of reality in the light of Israel's ideal. It is an ideal which Jesus will take over, but which he will also set on a new foundation.

This is why, without distorting the texts, we might entitle this whole series of liturgical weeks "From one kingdom to another" or, less reservedly, "From corrupt kingdom to Kingdom of God."

FROM MONDAY OF THE 10TH WEEK
TO SATURDAY OF THE 12TH WEEK

The Two Kingdoms

Was not Mount Zion, with its lofty and beautiful citadel (Ps 48), the navel of the world, and was not the house of David established on rock? Had not the Lord chosen Zion (Ps 132) and promised David an everlasting covenant (Ps 89)? Why, then, did the story of the Davidic monarchy end wretchedly beside the rivers of Babylon, where "we sat and wept at the memory of Zion" (Ps 137)? Only a heap of ruins was left of the holy city; the successor of the great king was exiled, blinded and in chains, like the lowest slave and Zedekiah was a puppet on a throne.

Solomon, the son of David, was hardly dead when the kingdom was rent in two; north and south stood opposed, Samaria and Jerusalem, Israel and

Judah. But on both sides of the frontier wickedness reigned, and the covenant was scorned. In vain did Elijah's jealous enthusiasm for Yahweh pursue Ahab; in vain did the wicked King Joash have the prophet Zechariah stoned, an innocent victim, between the sanctuary and the altar; in vain, even, did Israel return to obedience when the law of the covenant was rediscovered under Josiah; in vain all these things. Under the blows of Assyria in the north and of Nebuchadnezzar in Judah nothing was left of the Davidic heritage. There were only lamentations: "Mutely they sit on the ground, the elders of the daughter of Zion." There is no longer any Kingdom of God—except for a little "remnant," a seed, a hope which is promised by Isaiah and, with him, the prophets who experienced the exile as a time of new conversion for the chosen people.

A little remnant, a people of beggars, a kingdom without a crown! In the person of Jesus the Kingdom has drawn near, but its coming was already represented by the poor of the old covenant, so constantly mistreated by the kings: Naboth, the widow of Zarephath and others. "How happy are you who are poor!" will be the message of the new king who is simply a servant and takes upon himself the suffering of his fellows. The constitution he promulgates on the mountain is a covenant with the human heart; it promotes humility and sincerity. "Those who do my Father's will are the children of the Kingdom!"

A new Elijah? So some thought. A new Moses? With the coming of Jesus Israel is indeed reborn, but as a people possessing no citadel save its faith, no buckler save God alone. As a new David, he orders us to build his house upon rock and to offer God the worship of the heart. "Go and be reconciled with your brother first." He locates his treasures directly in heaven so that we may have nothing to fear from thieves and armed foes. Christ the King fulfills the law, but it is an interior law in which love has both the first and the last word. He seeks not his own reign but that of the Father, and of the Father alone.

THE COURSE OF BIBLICAL HISTORY

The story of the activity of the prophets begins with 1 Kings 17 and Elijah. Here are some chronological and historical points of reference that will help in understanding this history.

—David reigned from about 1010 to 970, with the capture of Jerusalem coming about 1000. Solomon was king of Judah and Israel from about 972 to 933. The temple was built in the fourth year of his reign.

—After the death of Solomon the inheritance was divided as a result of the political blunders of Rehoboam. North and south would henceforth have separate histories.

NORTH (ISRAEL, EPHRAIM)

—Jeroboam I establishes the northern kingdom and is enthroned at Tirzah
—Omri (886–75) locates the capital at Samaria
—His successor, Ahab (875–53), marries Jezebel of Tyre
The prophet Elijah
The prophet Elisha (until ca. 800)
—Jeroboam II (787–47)
The prophet Amos (ca. 750)
The prophet Hosea
—In 737 Menahem pays tribute to Assyria under Tiglath-Pileser III
—Pekah enters into a covenant with Damascus against the southern kingdom (the Syro-Ephraimite war); a part of the kingdom is annexed by Assyria
—722–21: Capture of Samaria and deportation; end of the northern kingdom

SOUTH (JUDAH) (Capital: Jerusalem)

—740: Call of the prophet Isaiah
—Ahaz calls on Assyria for help and pays tribute; Isaiah proclaims the threat of enslavement (the Immanuel oracle)
The prophet Micah
—Hezekiah fortifies Jerusalem, but Sennacherib the Assyrian conducts a campaign against Judah, and Hezekiah is forced to pay tribute; Isaiah continues his ministry
—Josiah: Rejection of Assyria, religious reform (Deuteronomy); Josiah dies in 609 in a battle with Pharaoh Neco
The prophet Jeremiah
—Josiah is replaced by his son Jehoahaz, who is himself deposed by the Pharaoh after only three months
—His brother Jehoiakim succeeds him (609–598), and then his nephew

Jehoiachin (Jechoniah) (598–97)
—At this time the Near East is controlled by Nebuchadnezzar the
Babylonian who has won the battle of Carchemish in 606 against an
Egyptian-Assyrian coalition
—Nebuchadnezzar sets siege to Jerusalem; first deportation of the
populace, Ezekiel and King Jehoiachin among them
Reign of Zedekiah, son of Josiah and uncle of Jehoiachin (597–87)
Jeremiah carries on his ministry under these kings
Ezekiel begins his ministry ca. 593
—588: Siege of Jerusalem, which is captured in July-August, 587;
destruction of the temple and second deportation of the populace

The Beatitudes: A Royal Proclamation

"Repent, for the Kingdom of heaven is close at hand" (Mt 4:17). The
Sermon on the Mount sounds like a governmental communiqué in a time
of crisis. A new conversion is urged, a renewal of the basic charter of the
Kingdom. But who are the chosen ones from among the people? In the
eyes of Jesus they are men and women of any and every kind, those whom
nothing suggests that they will some day sit on the benches of the king's
court; honest folk whom no one would expect to undertake an economic or
political turnabout. No one but Jesus Christ could inaugurate his reign by
turning to such people as these.

Among them there are those who weep: trouble has come upon them.
Some are the kind whom others, somewhat pityingly, call "gentle" and
"merciful." Others seem more interested in the renewal of society: they are
hungry and thirsty for what is right, but they have opted for peaceful
solutions; they want peace and not conflict. One thing is sure: all are what
Jesus calls "poor in spirit"; that is, they are completely available and have
an almost excessively naive confidence in the future, along with the kind of
faith that does not calculate costs.

Jesus looks at them; he already knows that they will be insulted for his
sake, that all sorts of evil will be spoken against them, that they will be
persecuted as the prophets were persecuted, once they stop repeating the
official line. Yet the address from the throne takes the form of
congratulations, beatitudes, and encouragements. This king is worlds

removed from those politicians who are constantly pessimistic or inconsistent in their views. He takes charge of these poor folk who are with him, and sets them on their feet so that they may tackle their work. Even before they have accomplished anything at all, he proclaims them happy.

True enough, the moment will come when their work will have to be defined, and the Sermon on the Mount will clearly lay out its radical demands, but for the moment joy fills the king's words to his hearers. The Kingdom belongs to them. The Kingdom is given as a free gift, and it is through fidelity to this free gift, and not by their own native strength, that the poor will observe the new law.

Evangelical repentance and conversion are wholly a matter of this poverty and this joy. In the measure of their desire the poor will receive the promised land and its peace; nothing will be able to take this from them if they remain faithful to their poverty. The Kingdom exists in the human heart, and the joy that the poor have is the joy of a limpid heart that already sees God.

On the mountain this day, human beings have seen God. They have seen a man who told them: "Happy are you!" And because they realized that this man was speaking to their hearts, they immediately saw that he was speaking in the name of God.

■

We thank you,
  God our Father,
  Lord of heaven and earth.
In your goodness
  you revealed your mystery
  to children and the poor.
It is not to the powerful, so full of themselves,
  that you promise the earth as an inheritance,
  but to those who are gentle and kind to their brethren.

In your eyes
  poverty becomes wealth,
  and those who give all
  receive a hundredfold of the Kingdom.

Tears give way to happiness,

and merciful hearts are transfigured
because they receive peace as their inheritance.

Blessed be you, Father,
  for your Kingdom, the new earth,
and for Jesus Christ, your Son,
  who came to seek and save the lost.
He called to his following
  those who grieved under their burdens;
he took their cross on his own shoulders
  and led them to repose.
But before knowing this repose and this peace himself,
he became poor, stripping himself of everything,
  and he pushed mercy to the point of pardoning
  and giving his life for those who handed him over.

Hear our prayer:
  in the school of Christ
  may we, too, become
  simple and peaceful.
Preserve your Church in the happiness
  of the gift you have given it;
  may it give its riches with a generous hand
  to those who hunger and thirst for you.
May your people daily experience
  perfect joy,
  as they sing the praises of you, our Father,
  whom Jesus has revealed,
  and as they bless your Son,
  whom your love has given to us.

MONDAY OF THE 10TH WEEK

THE SUFFERING OF THE POOR MAN

1 Kings 17:1–6. The Elijah cycle. "As Yahweh lives, the God of Israel whom I serve . . . ." The redactor of 1 Kings immediately lets us know that he is not going to provide a detailed biography of the prophet. He is interested in the man of God and his almost superhuman stature. He intends to show us, in the person of Elijah, the irruption of prophecy into Israel. Since the time of David, the territory occupied by the Jews had kept on expanding; this had led to the commingling of the Jewish population with groups of indigenous Canaanites and to the appearance among Jews of alien cults, in particular the cult of Baal, the rain-god. Yahwism was threatened, and to ward off the danger there was need of a voice raised to say who should be God in Israel. The story in 1 Kings 18 shows Elijah stepping forth as champion of the Yahwist cause, while 1 Kings 17 sketches a portrait of the prophet in broad strokes. The man's very name states a whole program, since "Eliyyahu" means "My God is Yah." Elijah was a native of Tishbe in Gilead, an Israelite city across the Jordan, in which Yahwism had been preserved in its original purity.

Psalm 121, which is classified among the songs of ascents, occupies a quite special place. Vv. 5–8 are the two strophes of an oracle assuring the believer of God's protection. It was recited by the priest after the person praying had recited the earlier strophes of the psalm. To be noted is the crescendo that is typical of ancient Jewish blessings.

Matthew 5:1–12. Cf. p. 7.

■

Elijah the prophet is a man of God and almost a man-God. Isn't his name "My God is Yahweh"? Elijah! In the time of Jesus they will still be awaiting his return, which is to occur a little before the coming of God. He was a passionate man who thought the cause of Yahweh worth the dedication of his entire life and all his energies. The history of God's dealings with humankind is filled with men of ardent spirit, with prophets ready for every adventure for the sake of God's name. But soon, as we shall see, Elijah is compelled to learn that all strength is a grace and that a man of God must receive everything from his God. You do not fight for Yahweh as you set out on a crusade or a conquest.

On the mountain Jesus, recalling Moses, another passionate man of God, has gathered a people made up of the poor, the lowly, the humble. Yet does not a mountain suggest the lightning and thunder of Sinai and God revealing himself in the majesty of a terrain torn by supernal forces? But just as Elijah will soon learn that Yahweh reveals himself in the soft breeze of morning rather than in the flashing of the storm, in like manner Jesus will, from the very beginning of his ministry, make his appeal solely to the human heart. Here on the mountain he will speak only about simplicity and poverty, after the manner of one promulgating a new law: the law of the grain of wheat cast on the ground and producing results in patience.

The Beatitudes. They do not offer a cheap happiness or a joy easy of attainment. They express rather the blessing of God on the outcast, on those whose hearts are poor enough to accept the grace and superabundant gift of God. The Beatitudes are not a statement of facts but a revelation. Look, says Jesus, the poor are loved by God; peacemakers are called the children of God, and those whose hearts are pure see God beyond the phenomena of a harsh and intractable world. Even persecution is a blessing, provided it puts its seal on the witness of faith.

Elijah will be persecuted; he will come to know what it costs to be a passionate fighter for God. Jesus will be persecuted and hung on the gibbet of the cross, for the sake of God, for the Father's name. And the Church in its turn will experience the harshness of poverty, the seeming desolation of those who are hungry and thirsty for justice. Christians of all times and all latitudes will learn what lengthy patience is required if the grain is to germinate and the spring yield living water.

But for the moment let us stay with Elijah by the brook Cherith. Let us stay recollectedly near Jesus and allow ourselves to be penetrated by these words from another world: "How happy are the poor in spirit." Someday we will need this nourishment if we are to go further on—with Christ, with Elijah, with Moses. We shall reach the promised land and Mount Horeb, but to do so we must advance by way of another hill named Golgotha, the hill of the Poor Man on the cross.

■

To you we lift our eyes,
to you, our help and our protector.

You are the staff of our journey
  and the blessedness of all the oppressed.
Father, keep us from all evil
  in the name of Jesus your Son,
  who was poor and constantly persecuted
  on the way to the hill and to Easter.

TUESDAY OF THE 10TH WEEK

FORWARD WITHOUT FEAR

1 Kings 17:7–16. By way of an introduction to the story of Carmel the author narrates two miracles worked by the prophet Elijah. The element of the miraculous seems incongruous in the majestic fresco devoted to the prophet's activity, but it serves to locate Elijah in the prophetic movement by showing that this seer has retained something of the spontaneity and imagination characteristic of the "men of the Spirit" who had preceded him. It is probable, moreover, that the doings of Elisha, Elijah's disciple, retroactively influenced the biography of the master—unless, of course, the contrary process was at work: by attributing the actions of Elijah to Elisha, the author would intend to have the glory of the master spread over to the disciple. Let us note above all the promise of salvation that is contained in the prophet's words as he says to the starving widow: "Do not be afraid." Are these not words of consolation for all adorers of the true God?

Psalm 4, which is a lament, voices the distress of the widow prior to the prophet's intervention. V. 3 attacks the enemy, while v. 4 expresses confidence.

Matthew 5:13–16. Cf. p. 10.

■

On Psalm 4

The taste of nothingness invades the world
and each day the land becomes more savorless.

269

Recourse to lies works its destruction
and the light is extinguished on our paths.
Who will enable us to find happiness?
To us, Lord,
your truth and your love
are tastier than the new wine
on days when the joy of harvest overflows.

■

The brook Cherith is dry, and drought is turning the land into a desolation. We must therefore not think of the evangelical Beatitudes as a joyful wandering spring, into which one only need dip one's hands to draw mouthfuls of living water, effortlessly and without having to wait. Let us rather heed the warning of Jesus: we shall be enlightened by him and become a light for the world, *provided* that we follow him on the hard road of this arid and savorless world.

Just look at the poor widow of Zarephath. Is she not a fine model of evangelical generosity? It takes but a word to reassure her in the great distress in which she finds herself. Just a word from a prophet: "Do not be afraid." She humbly does what the prophet asks, and behold, the bread and oil multiply in her hands, without measure or, rather, according to the measure of God.

"How happy are the poor!" But the poor first experience drought. For them the spring has dried up and they have no bread. The poor starve to death. The gentle suffer violence and the peaceful are deceived. Where is happiness? Then fear comes upon them, and the temptation to keep everything for themselves and to lock themselves behind the dividing walls of their anxiety. The world of the poor has its shutters closed. But as a result the world grows dull and sinks into a universal sadness, to which today we give the names of crisis and despair. It is always the third world that experiences drought and famine first. But how can the affluent world long be happy when millions of children die without even being able to put a name to "day"?

Elijah tells us, in the name of the living God, "Do not be afraid. Give and share what you have." And Jesus adds: "You are the salt of the earth." Economic programs will always fail throughout the world as long as human beings are afraid and allow fear to dictate the extent of their initiatives. Do not be afraid. Enter the school of the poor, and measure their expectations. Do not remain closed up in the walls of your fortified cities; cast down the walls of fear, and live according to the rhythm which sharing dictates.

Then your light will shine before men, and all will be able to glorify your heavenly Father. He is a God and Father who makes his sun shine on all human beings. Is it his fault if among the poorest the sun scorches the soil and dries up the water springs? God always gives the earth rain and dew, but we are well aware that this Dew bears the name Messiah, Christ and Savior. Today God expects *us* to make the springs produce their living water.

■

With all the poor
*   we cry to you, God, who are our justice:*
*   "Have mercy on us; hear our prayer."*
Keep us from turning to lies;
*   give us a taste for sharing and not for nothingness.*
Let the plight of our brothers and sisters
*   awaken us to the joy of being salt for the earth*
*   and light for the world,*
in the name of your Son, who is light and peace
*   for all the oppressed, your children.*

WEDNESDAY OF THE 10TH WEEK

THE FIRE OF LOVE

1 Kings 18:20–39. After two years of drought Elijah called an assembly for worship on Mount Carmel, where there was a famous sanctuary of Baal, and there he issued an ultimatum to the people: "If Yahweh is God, follow him; if Baal, follow him." The narrator carefully notes the fact that the crowd gave the prophet no answer. This failure to respond should not be interpreted as an embarrassed silence. If the people gave no answer to Elijah's reproaches it was because they did not understand them; they

271

found nothing shocking about the religious pluralism then dominant throughout the land. Yahweh simply cohabited with other gods in the country promised to the ancestors.

The prophet was therefore compelled to let gigantic forces loose in order to force the people to take sides. In a remarkable narrative the chronicler contrasts the confidence of the Yahwist prophet, who is sure of his God, with the intemperate incantations of the worshipers of Baal. He thus calls attention to a profound insight of the Jewish-Christian religion: it is not man who sets out in search of God in order to draw God to him; it is God who seeks out man.

Psalm 16 has a structure that is not easy to determine. It is sometimes classified as a lament, but it also has traits which link it to the Psalms that celebrate Yahweh's protection of his faithful.

Matthew 5:17–19. Cf. p. 13.

■

Alone against four hundred! According to the law of majority rule, Elijah is defeated before he begins. And with him God too is defeated. God is dead. There is nothing to do now but bow down before the power of the gods who wait nearby. Mightier gods, whose power is based on what the world considers important: gods of fear, of money, of pleasure or of selfishness. False gods, perhaps, but if they have the majority of believers on their side, how can we set over against them the God of Jesus Christ and his seeming powerlessness? Meanwhile, the last followers of the true God lament with the psalmist: "Their idols teem, after these they run." Is the solution perhaps to oppose to these gods the letter of the law, its somewhat nervous attention to detail, its integrism that makes no concession to the enemy?

Would Jesus think of such a solution? After all, he does proclaim: "Not one dot, not one little stroke, shall disappear from the law." Is he then the inspiration for all the stubborn fixations upon the letter of the rule? For the lack of openness to the future or to the world? Does he set over against the idols of the country all the countless canons in the code of ecclesiastical law? Some people think so.

They are mistaken. Jesus came to fulfill the law, that is, to give it its full range, density and imperativeness. He does not spend time discussing this or that precept, but goes straight to the heart of the matter and appeals to the free decision of the human person: You must love with all your heart. He calls upon the person at its deepest level to be completely at the disposal of God. But he refuses to let himself get trapped in the quibbles of those who are always niggling over the law, often in order to get around it. To the legislative code he opposes the law of the cross and of life. Who would dare claim that by this standard even the least part of the Commandment is not given an infinite value?

It is because so many disciples lack this ardent love that God seems dead and the idols can exercise their destructive power. But let the great law of the Gospel revive, and you will see the name of God sanctified once more. Is not the love that surrenders everything mightier than the fire that descended from the Lord atop Carmel at the moment of the evening sacrifice?

■

Lord our God, look with love
  upon the sacrifice of your Church.
Let our praise arise to you
  like an evening sacrifice.

For you do not expect us
  to fall prostrate before you in fear;
what you want from us
  is a heart that seeks you
  and recognizes you in the faces of our fellows.
Grant that we may love you above all else
  and love our neighbor
  as you have shown you love us
  in Jesus, your Son and our Savior.

A COVENANT OF LOVE

1 Kings 18:41–46. A clap of thunder, a small cloud heavy with rain. While this story does have an element of the miraculous in it, it is dominated by the person of Elijah himself, "an historical figure of well-nigh superhuman stature."[29] Just reread this sentence, and you will agree: "As Yahweh lives, the God of Israel whom I serve, there shall be neither dew nor rain these years except at my order" (1 Kgs 17:1).

The essential point of this story is that in the eyes of the king and the whole people Yahweh is presented as sole master of creation and therefore as sole source of life. Baal, his challenger, can only run away. Then, driven by the Spirit, Elijah sets out to meet the king; without stopping, he traverses the twenty-seven kilometers that separate him from Israel.

Psalm 65, which takes the form of a narrative, is addressed to Yahweh and recalls his interventions in the history of Israel. There seems to be a harvest in the background here.

Matthew 5:20–26. Cf. p. 15.

■

Justice can be harsh and calculating, and may be forced into this rigid form by the intransigence of human beings. Imagine a couple driven by anger and asking a judge to give them justice. The last penny must be taken into account. Yet not too long before this same couple had been exchanging vows of loving covenant. But what becomes of a covenant when it stops seeking a justice other than that which weighs pros and cons?

Jesus says: "If your virtue goes no deeper than that of the scribes and Pharisees . . . ." The scribes were zealous for God, but love with its excesses and fantasies, its forgivenesses and new beginnings, had become alien to them. They pleaded God's cause in the same way that human beings try to take a balanced view in a human conflict: "At this point any obligation ceases . . . . You may not commit murder, but after that . . . ."

274

But God had made a covenant with his people. A covenant based on an infinite love. A covenant like that of a man enamored of a woman, and even a covenant far deeper than that. God had put his heart into this covenant, and he expected human beings to live in covenant with their brothers and sisters, loving them without measure. Not a covenant such as people make to protect themselves against a common enemy, but a covenant of joy and peace, of poverty and tender love.

Jesus came to fulfill the law. How, then, could he fail to tell men and women that an insult, a slap, or a grudge can jeopardize the covenant as much as murder does? It is possible to kill a person while leaving him still alive. When you love, everything becomes important: words and silences, glances and judgments. To curse your brother is already to enter the state of final corruption and the hell of fire.

Brothers and sisters, when you come to the altar, remember that you come there to celebrate the great covenant of God with humankind. The body of Christ will be given to you as sacrament of an infinite love. How can you fail first to be reconciled with your brother or sister? Do not calculate in terms of human justice, but let love carry you beyond what justice demands. Remember: in strict justice, Jesus did no evil, and yet on the cross he forgave his executioners.

■

As the rain penetrates the soil,
* let your love, Lord, restore life*
* to our drought-stricken world.*
Do not allow the grudges we hold
* to dry up the spring of your goodness,*
but grant us to live with one another
* according to the justice of your covenant,*
* in forgiveness and joy,*
* and in hope*
* that is daily renewed.*

A TENDER BREEZE

1 Kings 19:9a, 11–16. While the prophet Elijah can be said to have resembled a cosmic force, he was also a man with human weaknesses. Because Queen Jezebel hates him and is persecuting him, and because the people are fickle, the prophet sinks into despair; he flees from adversity. Yet contrary to what he thinks, he is not alone. Yahweh is with him, just as he had been with his people in the wilderness. For it is a wilderness that Elijah is now traversing as a man completely stripped of everything and walking in black night.

He is experiencing a kind of exodus in reverse, a pilgrimage that will take him back to Horeb-Sinai, the mountain where it all began. For forty days and forty nights he journeys with a scone and a jar of water as his only food but at the end a new intimacy with God awaits him. Hidden in a cave as Moses had hidden in a cleft of the rock (Ex 33:22), Elijah hears "the sound of a gentle breeze." The polemical tone is evident. On the one hand, the breeze contrasts with more impressive atmospheric phenomena, such as the fire, lightning and thunder that were the attributes of Baal; on the other hand, we must not forget that these same wonders had accompanied the theophany on Sinai. It is probable, moreover, that the presence of these phenomena on Sinai signified that Yahweh was appropriating the attributes of Baal. If so, then the present passage, which is Elohist in inspiration, would point to a radical purification, along prophetic lines, of the idea of God. However impressive creatures may be, we must distinguish them from their Creator.

Psalm 27 is said by the scholars to have two parts: a royal Psalm of confidence (vv. 1–6) and an individual lament, this last being the part used here. V. 8 protests the innocence of the psalmist, but it is at the same time a beautiful invitation to seek God.

Matthew 5:27–32. Cf. p. 19.

■

"Yahweh, I do seek your face!" How beautiful the face of the Lord is! There our eyes, always misted over by the pollutants of the world,

rediscover the light, in a face-to-face encounter with the inaccessible Light. "Every face turned to him grows brighter and is never ashamed" (Ps 34:5). In order to look toward God Elijah covers his face, because no one can see God and remain alive. But must we not die to all that degrades us if we are to be able at last to look upon anything with the eyes of God? When human beings have contemplated the face of God for a long time, they see the world and other persons in the light of their eternal value.

Love, and especially conjugal love, is such a gazing. How is it possible to say "I love you" without having learned this from God? It is a fact, of course, that a great desire drives human beings to love, but until they have learned that this desire itself comes from God, they are incapable of transforming it into love. They desire, but they think they can satisfy the desire by possessing. And soon they dream of possessing the wife of another. What can we say to such people, except to persuade them to look at the object of their desire with the eyes of God? If they cannot do this, it were better for them to tear out their corrupt eye and throw it away.

God reveals himself to Elijah in the sound of a gentle breeze. Every relationship with God is characterized by delicacy, tenderness and silence. Love has nothing to do with the groanings of mighty passions that set the person atremble but cannot resist the pressures of tomorrow. The love of a man and a woman, as Jesus sees it, is like the sound of a gentle breeze; it is made of contemplation and self-giving, long patience and constantly rediscovered joy. That is why this love is divine, and Paul is not mistaken when he sees in it the "sacrament" of Christ and the Church. In the tenderness of love God is revealed to us as a God whose face shines in the faces of those who love one another without crying their love aloud in public places.

■

Blessed be you, God of tenderness,
  whom we seek without wearying
  and who reveal yourself to us
  in the sound of morning reborn.
God of beginnings and God of silence,
  you created man and woman

that their love might be the face
of your hidden presence in the world's heart.
We pray you:
  grant those united in the name of your love
  to seek your face and your light
  in the depths of the desire
  that brings them to one another.
Then they will know you
  and be able to bless you
  in the joy of being for each other
  the sign of the infinite love
  you manifested in Jesus, your Beloved.

SATURDAY OF THE 10TH WEEK

GUILELESSNESS

1 Kings 19:16b, 19–21. The story of the beginning of the ministry of Elisha ("God has helped") resembles the vocation stories told of the writing prophets. Elijah comes upon his future disciple as the latter is working in his father's fields; Elisha is a native of a village called "Meadow of the Dance" (Abel-meholah). The herald of Carmel casts his cloak on Elisha; this is a way of transmitting his own charism. Elisha's reaction reminds us of the classical objections of men chosen by God; the new prophet wants to return first to his home in order to embrace his parents. Jesus too will have to deal with a disciple who asks permission to take leave of his relatives, but he is less accommodating than Elijah and answers that the Kingdom of God will not allow of any delay (cf. Lk 9:61–62).

Psalm 16, which is difficult to classify, overflows with confidence; the final verses suggest that the prayer of the psalmist has been heard.

Matthew 5:33–37. Cf. p. 21.

■

On Psalm 16

Do not say "Yes" and "No" to the Lord,
but tell him simply: "You are my God!"
Acknowledge what you are before him,
and he will be daily at your side.
Confide even your sins to his love,
with simplicity,
and your heart will keep festival.

■

"It's true—I swear it!" Do you mean that, if I did not hear your oath, I would have to doubt your word? What is the point of invoking God as if without this invocation our dialogues would be only tissues of lies? Paradoxically, the multiplication of oaths highlights the hypocrisy of society. According to Jesus, things should be infinitely simpler; to him, "Yes" means "Yes" and "No" means "No." In fact, people were suspicious of this. We have falsified even the meaning of words. Then we think we can bring people back to truthfulness by hanging God over their heads like the blade of a guillotine. But God is not an inquisitor or judicial officer; more simply, and more profoundly, he dwells in the human heart.

Psalm 16 says: "In the night my inmost self instructs me; I keep Yahweh before me always." But how is it possible to live in this constant awareness without also living in guileless sincerity? If I spend my days cheating on the meaning of words, how can I sleep peacefully with God ever before me? Yes, in the light of the Gospel life becomes a unified whole or it is nothing. The just man is not said to be sinless, but this does not prevent his sleeping in the shadow of God, because he experiences the Lord's mercy and forgiveness. The point is that a conscience is at peace when it calls good good and evil evil. That one point is everything. God, meanwhile, is not looking for the first opportunity to trap us; he is satisfied to be with us constantly as a spring that gives us life even in our moments of weakness.

Perhaps Elisha is a model of this necessary guilelessness at the moment when Elijah calls him without prior discussion and without procrastination? The answer of a disciple is not a "Yes, but" or a "Yes, perhaps"; it is Yes or No. Then it is possible to journey with a joyous heart and a festive soul, because henceforth God takes charge of our destiny. Nor is there need of saying in every crisis: "I swear, I have done what I can!" God knows our capacities better than we do, and he constantly grants us in our weakness what we need in order to be witnesses of his presence—a presence which, even in the night, is light and truth.

∎

True God, faithful God,
  in your Son Jesus Christ
  you have spoken to our world
  your "Yes" of fidelity.
What you give us in him
  you never take back.
He is our pledge
  of your light and your forgiveness.
Grant us to live with eyes fixed on him;
  then our actions and our words
  will reflect your brightness,
  as we rejoice to live with our fellows
  in peace and in truth.

MONDAY OF THE 11TH WEEK

OVERCOME EVIL BY GOOD

1 Kings 21:1–16. King Ahab was a very wealthy man. Not only did he have a splendid estate at Jezreel, but he had also inherited the city of Samaria. Yet is it possible for the mighty of this world to be content with what they have? In addition to the social aspect of the story, there is also an anti-monarchical thrust in Elijah's protest; like Samuel before him, the prophet is conscious of the danger represented by royal claims. Moreover, in siding with the poor, Elijah knows that he is also defending the rights of Yahweh.

At first sight, nonetheless, Naboth's refusal is somewhat disconcerting. Does the king not offer him payment in compensation for his land? But the poor man's refusal is due to more than a simple attachment to his native soil; what he is defending is nothing less than his civil status, since his plot of ground, no matter how small, represents the portion of the country that Yahweh had entrusted to his ancestors. To sell it would be to renounce his civil and religious identity, give up his citizenship, and increase his subjection to the king.

Queen Jezebel, who was accustomed to being an absolute sovereign (she was a Syro-Phoenician), could not understand Naboth's refusal and she therefore ordered a parody of a trial. Her subordinates quickly found two individuals who would testify against this small landowner, and he was stoned outside the town. Much later, another innocent man will again be dragged outside the city for having defended the rights of God.

Psalm 5 must be thought of as spoken by Naboth and all the despoiled of the world. In it they protest their innocence and call for Yahweh's help against their tormentors.

Matthew 5:38–42. Cf. p. 23.

■

"Naboth is no longer alive. He is dead." How many times is this same story to be repeated? The powerful rob the poor to satisfy their own interests, and all resistance is broken through bloodshed and torture. Given such things, who would not cry out in the public square: "An eye for an eye, a tooth for a tooth"? Will the day come, Lord, when you will exterminate the wicked? Let them pay the price which strict justice requires for their crimes.

The story of Naboth's vineyard is a sordid one, and we hear it echoed in countless real estate schemings. "Give me your vineyard since it adjoins my house . . . . I will give you its worth in money." Why does Naboth refuse? Simply for the sake of the dignity that is the final possession of the poor; this patch of ground is his, and it is worth far more to him than any compensation from the king. But when power comes to believe that everything is allowed to it and everything is due to it, it has no concern for the dignity of the people; everything is evaluated in terms of profit, unless sheer caprice determines decisions. People are uprooted as if they were just weeds.

Why are we surprised that the resistance and struggles of the poor

281

lead to torture and bloody repression? Unhappy the man who opposes absolute power; any pretext at all will take his life and get rid of him. How many Naboths have disappeared without trace under all the dictatorships! Therefore I ask again: Why not an eye for an eye, a tooth for a tooth? How can the Gospel be so unrealistic? "Offer the wicked man no resistance."

Jesus rejects the law of talion with its seeming equity, because it is incapable of breaking the chain of human violence and wretchedness. Strict justice is only a makeshift that will never renew the face of the earth. An eye for an eye? But by this norm who would survive?

The social program of the Gospel is certainly revolutionary: to overcome evil by good, wickedness by an excess of love. At first sight such a course is useless and insane. The world continues to sink under the weight of injustices. Yet sometimes a gleam of light peers through.

Another world is possible and is already coming. But let us not forget that it originates at the foot of the cross. It really is a different world: a world in which the Ahabs and the Jezebels are overcome by Christ's forgiveness on the cross.

■

You are not a God who loves evil.
Lord, we pray you,
change the hearts of the mighty;
  let them be just to the unfortunate.

The conceited cannot stand your gaze.
Lord, hear the groans of the lowly;
  enable them to stand fast in trial.

You reject the knave and the shedder of blood.
Lord, forgive our world
  the mounting bloodshed and torture;
raise up witnesses to non-violence.

THE REIGN OF LOVE

1 Kings 21:17–29. Naboth has been executed, and Ahab has taken possession of the poor man's property. The prophet intervenes, because he is defender of Yahweh's cause and because ever since the deliverance from Egypt this cause has been identified with the rights of the poor. In language of unusual violence Elijah accuses Ahab of his crime and communicates God's sentence upon it: just as they have destroyed Naboth, the king and his house will be destroyed in turn. But Ahab humbles himself, and the prophet shifts the punishment to the next generation. The story is not unlike that of David and Bathsheba. On that occasion the prophet Nathan had shamed the king by telling him a story of a man whom a rich man robbed of his only sheep; David had recognized his own crime, and the punishment had been visited on the king's posterity (2 Sam 12).

Psalm 51 expresses the sinner's repentance.

Matthew 5:43–48. Cf. p. 26.

■

Ahab's crime was all the more serious because it was the king's mission to "render justice" to the poor, that is, to protect them against the misdeeds of the powerful. By killing Naboth the king ranked himself with the common enemies of God. The punishment must therefore be a terrible one.

And yet God is softened by the king's repentance. Because Ahab says in his heart: "I am well aware of my faults, I have my sin constantly in mind," because he acknowledges that he has sinned against God, the mercy of the heavenly Father descends upon him and enfolds him in new grace.

True enough. But it is also said that the punishment is shifted to the king's posterity; the misfortune will come on them. Is it possible to gauge better than here the distance that has been traveled when Jesus says: "You have learned . . . . But I say this to you"? The heavenly Father is so perfect that he pardons without qualification, and we are urged to love our enemies.

How is this possible? Martin Luther King has written that Jesus does not command us to fall into the arms of our enemies; he commands us to love them. Evil exists and its wounds cannot be healed overnight. Love is the only effective cure. To love, that is, not to keep grudges and not to try to pay the other back for his wickedness. To love the other with the love of the Father who desires the conversion of everyone.

Let us be clear in our own minds. The thing that makes human relations intolerable is our tendency to want the guilty party to be humiliated at any cost. Only then is our self-love satisfied. But there is no longer any place for self-love; there is room only for God. Pray for those who persecute us. God will know how to get them to recognize the wrongs they have done. The manner does not matter to us; we do not enter the picture; God alone does.

One thing alone is asked of us: to put aside grudges and to greet our detractors with as much love as we do our best friends. An impossible program? But nothing is impossible to God, and Jesus' words acquire meaning only in the power of the Spirit. Let us therefore learn to say with a sincere heart: "Father, forgive us our debts as we have forgiven those who are in debt to us." Everything else is up to God who makes his sun to rise on the good and the wicked.

■

God, you make your light to shine on everyone;
   you love those who do good
   and you wish only the conversion of sinners.
Have mercy on us,
   for our hearts are narrow,
   and we do not know how to love our enemies.
Enable us to look upon each of our fellows
   in the light of your mercy;
then the darkness of our night will be overcome,
   and the world will be reborn
   to the bright day of your grace and your love.
God, our heavenly Father,
   teach us to live

as your Son lived among men,
forgiving to the very end.

THE SPIRIT OF UNOBTRUSIVENESS

1 Kings 2:1–14. The master and the disciple are together for the last time, along with the "brotherhood of prophets." Two events that are associated in time call for attention here: the death of Elijah and the succession of Elisha. I deliberately say the "death" of Elijah, because the point the story is making is that it has always been impossible to find the prophet's tomb. This fact was frustrating to popular devotion, and so the prophet's disciples made up for the absence of a tomb by composing the story of the prophet's being taken up into heaven. As for the second event, it consists in the presentation of Elisha to the brotherhood. 1 Kings 19 has already told of Elisha's calling; the present story has to do with his consecration as a disciple. Elisha receives a double share of Elijah's spirit; that is, in juridical terms, he receives the share of the eldest son.

The "brotherhood of prophets" refers to a phenomenon of the age of the two prophets. For at that time prophets used to live in communities, under the authority of a master. Was Elisha such a master? The expression "Chariot of Israel and its chargers," which is applied to Elijah, designates him as protector of the people; it recalls the time "of the holy wars when Israel was confronted with the chariots of the Canaanites, and, herself not possessing these, was thrown back upon Yahweh alone."[30]

Psalm 31, a lament, expresses the confidence of the psalmist.

Matthew 6:1–6, 16–18. Cf. p. 29.

■

Elijah was taken up to heaven, and for a long time the people of the covenant would look for him to return. John the Baptist and Jesus run the risk of being taken for Elijah. The latter will always be the great prophet whose voice carries across the centuries. For the word of God is not given for the sake of a particular period alone; it shapes the world and remains alive in the memory of the Church. When faith seeks to commune with itself, it does not go to a tomb but to the eternal source, the Word that was once made flesh.

The same was true of Moses, Elijah and the prophets. The same is true, and all the more so, of Jesus, who was taken up to heaven before the eyes of his disciples. From Christ the Church too has received a double share of the Spirit. And it is this Spirit who repeats the words of the Gospel to us when we are tempted to look to heaven in search of him who has left us. He has not left us. He is with us daily through his word and his Spirit. Heaven is not somewhere far away; it is at the heart of our faith.

I like this great scene of Elijah's assumption. And yet does not the Gospel of Jesus Christ call us rather to inwardness, to hiddenness? "When you pray, go to your private room." But there is in fact no contradiction here. The majesty of Elijah's ascension can only be a basis for a Church whose life is the Spirit, and this Spirit breathes deep within, requiring human beings to live an interior, humble life. The impetuosity of Elijah must be succeeded by the patience of Jesus, so that the Scriptures—the law and the prophets—may be truly fulfilled.

At the ascension of Christ the angels send the first Apostles out on the road, and first of all to Jerusalem. And they go off, urged by the Spirit and ceasing at last to look for salvation in the clouds. But the Church will experience the temptation to settle down, to cry out its presence as one might proclaim an announcement of victory, and to derive its glory from itself instead of from its Lord. It will establish public almsgiving and see to it that the human race knows about it.

"But when you give alms," says Jesus, "your left hand must not know what your right is doing." Now that Jesus has ascended to the Father, the Church's sole proper place is in the hiddenness of the Father. Only then can it penetrate to the secret of the world and give the world what it needs most: a new hope.

Perhaps the Church does need, after all, to turn its gaze on high more often. Is it not there that our life is hidden with Christ in God? This hiddenness alone can give our good works their power to succeed and bestow life. But this success is in God's eyes, not in the eyes of

human beings!

■

Blessed be you, Father so tender,
* who know the secret places of our life.*
You are our reward,
* and your love fills us to overflowing.*
May our life remain hidden in you
* with Christ, your beloved Son,*
* who lives with you*
* just as he remains daily with us.*

THURSDAY OF THE 11TH WEEK

THE SPIRIT OF CHILDHOOD

Ecclesiasticus 48:1–14. Ben Sira's eulogy of Elijah helps us understand the fascination which this prophet has had for mystics, both Jewish and Christian. The prophet is here described as a man out of the common. Moreover, Ben Sira brings to light the promise of the future that was contained in the prophet's "assumption": he has a future role to play according to "the prophecies of doom."

For it is the messianic dimension of this prophet that Jewish tradition has emphasized. When speaking of the end of time and of the judgment it will bring, Malachi (3:24) had stressed the role of Elijah in the coming of the Kingdom: he will promote the conversion of hearts and will gather together the new people of God. Jesus will testify that this role has now been filled by John the Baptist.

Psalm 97 is an enthronement psalm and announces the coming of the Kingdom, already glimpsed in the assumption of Elijah.

Matthew 6:7–15. Cf. p. 31.

■

The memory of the prophet Elijah, which is everywhere present in the Bible and in Judaism, continues into Christian history, especially in the world that is centered on the Order of Mount Carmel. The Carmelites, calced and discalced, have adopted the religious tradition of Mount Carmel and Elijah, although it is less the prophet fervently engaged in the struggles of his age whom they venerate, than the mysticism of Carmel and Horeb. Their focus is on Elijah as the man who had such a profound experience of God. Ought we not to continue Ben Sira's eulogy of Elijah by remembering, as part of it, the encounter of the prophet with the living God, both in the wilderness and on Horeb?

Prayer and contemplation, silence and recollection are privileged places for gaining knowledge of God, the kind of knowledge in which the entire being of the person is gradually transformed by the Spirit. Today's liturgy bids us say the Our Father in the same Spirit. The Our Father is a prayer of the heart; the words we have repeated countless times become ever more filled by the Spirit of God. The very repetition prevents any wordiness; those who pray it know that they have nothing more to inform God of, and that they must simply let God take hold of them. The words they speak have been given them by the Word made flesh; they are the word which God speaks to God.

The Our Father is a gift the Lord gives to humankind so that even the poorest may contemplate the mystery and know God. As they repeat the words of this prayer they know that God is a Father and that he cares for us each day; they learn to put aside all useless anxiety and to ask for what is essential: May your name be held holy. They allow God to educate them as they ask his forgiveness and promise that they too will forgive. They dare confront the wilderness of faith, because they know that God will deliver them from the evil one.

Yes, we must thank God for the innumerable throng of unknown mystics who are hidden in the still larger throngs of the world and who live in God with the Our Father as their only book. It is of them that Jesus spoke when he blessed the Father who has revealed these things to mere children.

■

The Spirit you put within us, Lord,

is a Spirit not of fear
  but of trust and power.
Moved by him,
we never weary
  of daring to say your name
  and address you as "Our Father."

■

You are our Father and we are your children;
  in fervor and in weariness,
  in light and in sin
  we are your children.
Father, grant us each day
  the bread we need for that day,
  so that in joy as in distress
  we may remain your children.

FRIDAY OF THE 11TH WEEK

THE KING'S TREASURES

2 Kings 11:1–4, 9–18, 20. Though the reader might have expected to be presented with the Elisha cycle, the lectionary in fact turns back to the chronicle of the kings of Israel and Judah. For the moment, it tells of how Queen Athaliah threatened to frustrate the promise of Yahweh regarding the Davidic dynasty. Athaliah, daughter of Ahab, had married the king of Jerusalem. After the death of her husband and of her son, she takes steps to have all the men of royal stock slain and to take the crown of David for herself. But Johoiada the high priest manages to hide Jehoash, one of the dead king's sons. Later on, following a palace revolt, this prince is proclaimed king of Judah. Note the care with which the chronicler records the details of the investiture ceremony: donning of the royal insignia, anointing, acclamation and enthronement.

Psalm 132 speaks of the covenant which God made with the Davidic dynasty. The poem has a complex structure; the verses chosen for the liturgy seem to be fragments of a more extensive composition that was attached to vv. 8–10 (which are almost identical with 2 Chronicles 6:41–42).

Matthew 6:19–23. Cf. p. 34.

■

Palace intrigues, massacres, violent overthrows of regimes: the Old Testament is filled with these. Is *this* to be regarded as "sacred history"? To some extent, it is, because this is a human history in which God involves himself without thereby suppressing human freedom and sinfulness. In the story of Athaliah the Davidic dynasty is at stake, and if the chronicle of the kings emphasizes this, it is in order to highlight the great king who is the carrier of God's promises. Is it not from David that the Messiah is to come?

Jesus rejected the title of Messiah, because it was too much associated with military and political glory. But God did not blush to have his Son born of David's line, although admittedly this line now had little real prestige. Joseph, son of David . . . . "On the Messiah's brow the crown shall gleam," the psalmist had promised for the glorification of David, but the crown was a crown of thorns and the cloak a cloak of contempt. Such is the human history within which God comes to write his own history.

"Do not store up treasures for yourselves on earth," Jesus says after the Psalm, which sings elsewhere: "Do not put your trust in princes." Thieves break through walls and steal, and the sons of kings are stripped of their thrones by conspiracies which themselves have no future. The lights of this world never shine on eternally.

The people of the Davidic dynasty will soon experience humiliation, deportation and exile. But it is there, in a foreign land, where they have neither treasure nor power, that they will learn the true name of God and the face of his Messiah, who is a suffering servant and a friend of the poor.

When Athaliah is slain, the hour is close at hand when the prophets will begin to speak a new and incisive language, the language of a disturbing religion. Amos, Hosea, Isaiah: these men will not be afraid to talk out unambiguously to kings and the powerful; they will be the word of the God who promised the future to David but without telling him of the extent to which the course of history must change in order that the day of the awaited Messiah might come.

■

Turn our hearts away from idols,
*   and do not let us be captured*
*   by the bait of treasures that have no future.*
God, you abide forever;
*   you alone can ensure our future.*
Let our hearts dwell in you,
*   that we may live*
*   without fearing the downfall*
*   in which the glories of this world die.*

■

Grant, Lord,
*   that those whom you have chosen*
to be shepherds and leaders of your people
*   may put their faith in you*
*   and from you derive their strength.*
For no one can bring the world to the light
*   unless you come each day*
*   to purify the dark hearts of men.*

SATURDAY OF THE 11TH WEEK

A TOUCH OF UNCONCERN

2 Chronicles 24:17–25. The author of 2 Kings passes a rather favorable judgment on the reign of Jehoash (or: Joash); he calls attention especially to the repairs which he made in the temple of Jerusalem. 2 Chronicles also emphasizes the extent of his renovation of the sanctuary, but in addition it points out that the king's conduct was above reproach only as long as the high priest Jehoiada was alive. After the latter's death the king and his court turned to idols.

This situation gives the Chronicler an opportunity to claim prophetic inspiration for the priests. He tells of Zechariah son of Jehoiada being invested with the Spirit of God and uttering reproaches to the king. Furthermore, and this to a much greater extent than the author of the Books of Kings, the Chronicler makes the sinful behavior of the king responsible for the punishment that came upon the country. In addition, the murder of Zechariah left a deep mark on the consciousness of Israel and gave rise to many commentaries. Even Jesus recalls this event in his invectives against the scribes and Pharisees.

Psalm 89 is another dynastic poem that recalls the divine promises accompanying the election of the Davidic dynasty. The Psalm is a very complex one and, in addition to the dynastic poem, contains a prayer for the nation and a hymn to God's action in the universe.

Matthew 6:24–34. Cf. p. 37.

■

Why do we worry so much? "Each day has enough trouble of its own." The Gospel condemns neither work nor the application of intelligence. But once worry takes over a person it leads inevitably to unbelief. Those who put their own livelihood above the interests of God always end up denying God. At least, they deny the God of the Gospel who takes care of us, the God who calls himself "Father."

"Set your hearts on his Kingdom first, and all these other things will be given to you as well." Seek first what makes all human beings live in justice and equality, and your life will be lit up by a joy whose existence you never suspected. Seek first to share with others, and the bare necessities of life will have a new savor. You need not think of yourselves as birds, but you can introduce a little song and a little whimsicality into your daily menu; then your needs will be transformed into a desire for pure air and for freedom. Don't plague yourselves about tomorrow and the day after tomorrow, for each day God keeps you in the palm of his hand. Be realistic: look beyond appearances.

Above all, do not let money become your master. See it for what it is and make use of it for the good of all. Do not risk being torn apart after your death by voracious heirs. Leave to them as their only inheritance the joy of blessing your name just as they bless the name of God.

Yes, live like God, for "the Lord Jesus was rich, but he became poor for your sake, to make you rich out of his poverty." Like him, enrich yourselves and enrich the world with that touch of unconcern that even in the midst of distress is the mark and smile of God.

■

For those who must manage money
   and the goods of the world:
   let them be clear-minded enough
   to set their hearts on what does not pass.

For those who lose heart through too much worry:
   let them recover a taste for living
   through contact with the God who so cares for men.

For those afraid of growing old:
   let them learn again to live
   as if each day were the first and the last.

For those faced with the burden
   of governing the world:
   let them seek and find the Kingdom
   where all are one
   in sharing and in peace.

■

God who takes cares of us,
   blessed be you for the flowers of the field
   and the singing of birds.
Teach us, through contemplation of your work,
   to bless you first of all;
then, sustained by your grace,
   we can live each day with trust in your goodness.

THE POOR DO NOT JUDGE

2 Kings 17:5–8, 13–15a, 18. The end of the kingdom of Israel: Shalmaneser V of Assyria takes the capital city and, after the custom of the age, exiles the elite of the Jewish population, which he is careful to scatter throughout his various territories so as to prevent any desire of rebellion.

The Deuteronomistic historian is now in a position to draw conclusions from his history of the monarchy. If we are to understand his project we must recall that this history was written during the exile, at a time when Jews were asking themselves what had led to the various disasters they had experienced. The question was, then, on everyone's lips: Why has Yahweh rejected his people? As far as the Deuteronimist is concerned, only one answer is possible: the people and their kings had broken the Sinai covenant.

Psalm 60 is made up of two public supplications. The one in the lectionary must have been written on the occasion of an earthquake, perhaps the one that occurred during the reign of King Hoshea in 750 B.C. (cf. Am 1:1). But the Assyrian invasion of northern Palestine was another earthquake.

Matthew 7:1–5. Cf. p. 41.

■

On Psalm 60

There is war and the noise of weapons;
a war of tongues, and the weapons of injustice.
The land is shaken, the people are dizzied by it;
nothing left but to strike camp and flee into exile.

Arise, O God!
O God, disarm the wicked tongues.
O God, restore peace and joy to us,
for in you we are all brothers and sisters.

■

294

Does God hold grudges? Will he really judge us according to the standard we follow in our judgments of others? And was the exile of Israel really a punishment for the sins of the people? If God is merciful and finds his pleasure in forgiving, why does he reward the good and punish sinners, as any human judge would do?

Our trouble is that we do not have a proper understanding of mercy. We invoke it in self-defense without thinking of imitating God and becoming merciful ourselves. God does not punish. But Jesus, like the prophets, warns us that a world in which the human heart grows hard quickly dooms itself to destruction. It is not God who leads the people into exile, for how is it possible not to see the exile as inevitable when no one tried to live according to the law of love? And yet it is remarkable how many human beings learned to live as brothers and sisters in the prisoner of war camps.

It is said over and over; and in every circumstance, that God is love. We sing of this love, but we hasten to condemn our brothers and sisters. How can we not see the scandal of this situation? Quite naturally, therefore, the Israelite people in exile were advised that the source of all their ills was their own disobedience to the covenant and to God's Commandment of love.

Must we, then, suffer exile and imprisonment before we realize that the splinter in the eye of our brother or sister does not justify all the judgments we pass? As in the case of Israel, it is abundance that hardens each of us to others. In the wilderness, on the other hand, people were forced back into their own poverty and then suddenly realized that God is a God of tenderness and that the face of their brothers and sisters is a sacrament of him. Amid deprivation a community of brothers and sisters becomes possible; then, instead of brooding over the faults of their fellows, individuals begin to extend a hand to them and to join them in carrying the common burden.

■

We have not obeyed your word;
we have weighed down our brothers and sisters
with the burden of our judgments:
  Lord, do not deal with us according to our sins.

We have scorned your law;
by crushing our brothers and sisters
we have sinned against you:
  Lord, do not judge us according to our offenses.

In our self-sufficiency we have gone astray,
and we have created a world
that is hopeless and joyless:
  Let your mercy descend upon us, Lord.

TUESDAY OF THE 12TH WEEK

A SMALL REMNANT IS ENOUGH

2 Kings 19:9b–11, 14–21, 31–35a, 36. After the kingdom of Israel it is the turn of the kingdom of Judah. This time the chronicler provides many more details. As a matter of fact the southern kingdom had felt itself under threat ever since the first assertions of Assyria's policy of annexation, and the fall of Samaria in 721 had dealt a harsh blow to the morale of the Jerusalem populace. On the other hand, all was not well at Nineveh, the Assyrian capital; disputes about the succession had for a time shaken the stability of the throne, and this caused hope to spring alive both among the exiles and in the vassal territories of Assyria. Hezekiah, king of Jerusalem, therefore attempted—in vain—to rebel against Sennacherib. The latter, who was in a hurry to gain free access to Egypt, sent two ambassadors to Jerusalem in order to threaten the Jewish king and to stir up the populace against him.

The narrative reports the despairing prayer which King Hezekiah addressed to Yahweh before calling Isaiah to his side. The prophet was in a difficult position. On the one hand, he had always attacked royal diplomacy and, in particular, the alliance with Egypt; on the other, he regarded Sennacherib's punitive expedition as the punishment Israel had merited by its sins. He therefore contented himself with repeating to the king what he had already proclaimed: despite the evils of the time God will not abandon his people; there will be a "remnant" left in Jerusalem.

Psalm 48, which is a canticle of Zion, reminds the Israelites, amid the

296

threats weighing on Jerusalem, that Yahweh has always enveloped the holy city with his protection.

Matthew 7:6, 12–14. Cf. p. 44.

■

"A remnant shall go out from Jerusalem." The prophet's oracle is an act of faith in the future, but even though he predicts a resounding defeat for the enemy king in the near future, nothing will prevent the final destruction of Jerusalem. Only a remnant will survive.

The Church is this remnant, today more than ever. The time is past when religion built cities and Christians ruled from their fortified places; we are now a remnant, a small remnant, in the world. Not a "remnant" in the sense of a few survivors who are left after a defeat and are awaiting extinction, but a "remnant" in the biblical sense of a sucker or a seed cast into new earth. We have come to realize as a result of trials that the road to life is narrow and that we must search in order to find it. Jerusalem is no longer the capital where Christians are strong, nor is Rome or any other place. Our holy city is to be found wherever men and women live their faith humbly, as people live a hope.

There was a time when we carried our wealth ostentatiously, as overly rich matrons display their jewels. And without our even adverting to it, we have allowed our treasure to be devalued. Because we have confused fine pearls and shoddy goods, we have allowed the world to trample down our faith along with our outdated ways of acting. And the structure has been shaken. Perhaps it has even collapsed? We are a small remnant, possessing no treasure now but our hope.

But this treasure is enough. The Gospel does not promise us the conquest of the world; it distrusts avenues that are too broad, on which men and women think they can reach salvation without renouncing themselves. The gate into the Kingdom is a narrow gate. When Jesus entered Jerusalem, the crowds pressed around him, thinking that the splendid days of triumph had returned. But our Savior was only passing through the city on the steep way of the cross. Abandoned and left to himself, he passed through the narrow gate of Golgotha, and there, as an abject remnant, he underwent the trial that leads to life.

Can the Church live differently than its master did?

■

Keep us, Lord,
from wasting the treasure you entrusted to us;
remove from us the temptation
to pile up wealth that comes too easily.
Lead us along the way to life;
may our only strength
be our hope in your word,
for you are the God who remains with us
when no treasure is left but you.

WEDNESDAY OF THE 12TH WEEK

THE TREE OF LIFE

2 Kings 22:8, 10–13; 23:1–3. Josiah, a ray of sunlight amid the dynastic shadows! With David and Hezekiah he is the only king to escape severe judgment by the Deuteronomistic chronicler. Like Hezekiah, he undertook a vast religious reform; it was he in particular who suppressed foreign cults and centralized the Israelite religion in Jerusalem.

According to the historical annals he based his vast reform program on a "book of the law" that was discovered in the temple during restoration work there. The book seems to have contained the legislative sections of our present Deuteronomy (Chapters 5—28); it probably originated in the northern kingdom and reached Jerusalem after the fall of Samaria. It is possible that the book had already served in the reform of Hezekiah and had then been lost from sight.

Josiah also took advantage of the weaknesses of his enemies to reassert the independence of his country and to occupy the northern kingdom. The Assyrian star was rapidly waning and would soon dash itself to pieces against the might of Babylon. The Egyptian Pharaoh wanted to cross Palestine in order to come to the aid of Assyria; he was blocked by the army of Josiah at Megiddo. The king of Jerusalem was defeated here and died in battle (509 B.C.).

Psalm 119. No Psalm is better suited than this one for expressing Israel's wonder and gratitude for the law.

Matthew 7:15–20. Cf. p. 48.

■

When King Josiah "read out everything that was said in the book of the covenant, all the people gave their allegiance to the covenant." This marvelous word, "covenant," which suggests military treaties as well as commitments of love, runs throughout the Bible. Every renewal of religious life was a renewal of the covenant, down to the new and everlasting covenant which was sealed with the blood of Jesus and which we celebrate in every Eucharist. God has made a covenant with the human race, and there is nothing better that we can do than to renew our allegiance to it every time that infidelity takes us from it. To renew allegiance to the covenant as we rediscover the demanding but exalting way of love and fidelity. For, in contrast to the military covenants which Israel too readily entered into, even putting its trust in them, the covenant God wants is a covenant of the heart, a covenant of love, a covenant of fidelity to a word that is more reliable than any weapons of war. The religious reform of Josiah bears witness to this.

The words of Jesus on the mountain also propose a covenant; they already anticipate the covenant of the cross and the Spirit. "You must bear fruit," Christ says. It is not enough to take pride in an outward membership in the people of God; a tree can, after all, be dead and no longer bear fruit. And how are we to bear good fruit once again unless God comes and renews our hearts and unless his grace renders our arid earth fruitful again? The sap we need is a gift, a love poured out in the human heart by the Spirit. The difficult sayings of the Lord cannot, therefore, become spirit and life in us unless the Spirit comes and renders our faith fruitful. Obedience to God, too, is a grace; it is up to us to receive it and not put any obstacle in its way.

It is the Lord himself who teaches us the way to life; it is he who guides and enlightens us. Perhaps the enthusiasm of the moment may make us think that we can by our own power commit ourselves to God; if so, it is good that sin should come and teach us our limitations. Only then does obedience turn humble and trusting. We must distrust those false prophets in particular who turn faith into a form of human morality and act as though we could please God without the aid of his grace. Jesus bore fruit on the tree of the cross, not by the strength with which he withstood every trial, but by the faith with which he painfully abandoned himself to God his Father. He bore fruit, and his blood that was shed is for us the sacrament of the new covenant, a covenant based on grace.

■

We thank you for your grace,
  O faithful God
  who ceaselessly renew your covenant with us.
In your Son Jesus
  we acknowledge the prophet you have sent.
His word is spirit and life,
  and those who remain in him
  can bear much fruit.
On the tree of the cross
  he renewed your covenant in his blood;
and in his flesh that was handed over to death
  we have received the source of all grace.
That is why,
  led by the Spirit,
  we bless you with all our brethren
  who put their faith and hope in you.

THURSDAY OF THE 12TH WEEK

SOLID FOUNDATIONS
2 Kings 24:8–17. The history of the two Jewish kingdoms was constantly affected by the rivalry between Egypt and the empires of the

Mesopotamian region. Palestine, unfortunately, was on the route followed by the armies of these two rivals.

A series of events prepared the way for the end of Jerusalem. Egypt was conquered by the troops of Nebuchadnezzar in 605 (cf. Jer 46:2–12), but the Babylonian prince, who became king shortly afterward, himself suffered heavy losses some years later. Josiah's second successor took advantage of the situation and rebelled; this cost him his throne and his life. In order to avoid the complete destruction of the kingdom, Jehoiakim's son, Jechoniah, chose to go into exile with all his house; the prophet Ezekiel was among the deportees. Desirous of maintaining the little kingdom of Judah near the frontier of Egypt, Nebuchadnezzar appointed to the throne of Jerusalem an uncle of Jechoniah, Prince Mattaniah, whose name was changed to Zedekiah (as a sign of his subjection?).

Psalm 79, a national lament, accuses the enemies of Israel and entreats Yahweh to take away the evils they have inflicted.

Matthew 7:21–29. Cf. p. 51.

■

On Psalm 79

Lord, if you hold our past sins against us,
how can your Church remain steadfast
amid the storms of the centuries?
We ourselves can no longer stand by our own power;
if you do not come and take our side,
your inheritance will be destroyed.

■

A man of foresight had built his house on a rock. Was any city more solidly built than Jerusalem? Was any hill more invincible than Mount Zion? But now the storm beat upon the house of David. How could the foundation stone of the temple have proved to be but sand and dust? Who will denounce the improvident and foolish builder? And how is it possible to think that a Nebuchadnezzar should have carried out what the Lord commanded?

Did David's sin effect his posterity? Yet after the great king had fallen on the stone of stumbling, he had through his conversion signed a covenant of forgiveness with God, and his son Solomon had been able to build a solid, proud temple for the Lord. No, as Ezekiel will tell the exiles, God does not visit the sins of the ancestors on the heads of their children. Each person is responsible for himself.

Yes, but we must add that in God's sight we are members of one another and that the foresight of some can clash with the folly of others. Each individual will certainly be required to account for his own conduct, but the life of the Church also supposes that all have faith and that all are faithful. If the foundation of the temple is attacked by the unbelief of the faithful, it will not be able to resist erosion, and the entire edifice will collapse. A Jerusalem without living stones is nothing but a lifeless house and ready for destruction.

Jesus' Sermon on the Mount, which ends in today's liturgy, is not a document detailing an individual morality; it is rather the foundation of the Church and of the new covenant. A covenant in which each individual is integrally linked to his brothers and sisters and in which personal responsibility is the cement that holds the entire building together. Every time the Church is assaulted by Nebuchadnezzar and must experience for a while the sorrows of exile, each of us must ask whether he or she has been a living stone in this Church or, on the contrary, dust that is tossed about by the wind.

■

Lord, you built your Church
   on the rock of your word,
and you have left the power of your resurrection
   as a pledge of the future.
Do not let dispersion
   shake our fidelity,
but make us living stones
   for the building up of your dwelling
in every period of history
   and into eternity.

THE SONG OF HOPE

2 Kings 25:1–12. In 594 Babylon found itself in new difficulties. Relying on the support of Egypt, Zedekiah rebelled against his overlord. This was unlucky for him, because Nebuchadnezzar decided to make an example of him. The Babylonians confined the Jewish troops in their various fortresses and reduced these one by one. In 587 they captured Zedekiah and took him to Nebuchadnezzar's headquarters at Riblah. There the sons of the conquered king were slaughtered before his eyes, and then, so that this terrible picture might be ever before his mind, his eyes were put out and he was taken in chains to Babylon. The remainder of the people accompanied him into exile, and Jerusalem was razed to the ground. But the Second Book of Kings ends on an optimistic note: Nebuchadnezzar's successor pardoned the previously exiled king, Jechoniah, and ordered him to be released.

Psalm 137 cannot be put into a category. It sings of the exiles' longing for their home; Jerusalem remains at the center of their thoughts.

Matthew 8:1–4. Cf. p. 56.

■

On Psalm 137

Exiled to a foreign land,
how shall the leper sing
when all turn their faces from him?
What song, what hope
can restore life to flesh already dead?
Yet it takes but a prayer
for life to be reborn:
a prayer and a cry—
"If you wish, you can save me."
And out of the cry comes a new song.

■

Jesus has proclaimed the charter of the new Kingdom. The poor and

the outcast are the first ones called to it. But here comes a leper, a man sick and condemned, since leprosy was not simply a bodily uncleanness; in the judgment of the ancient law it was also a sign of divine displeasure. No one can approach a leper; above all, no one can touch him. He is an outcast and in permanent exile, cut off from human society.

Jesus has proclaimed the blessedness of those who are persecuted. But what good is a discourse unless it is acted upon? The Kingdom of God is not a project located in the clouds, but an earthly reality. Jesus touches the leper and heals him. The Kingdom is at hand. Nonetheless, this reign of God does not achieve its victory without a struggle, for by touching the leper Jesus has taken the sickness upon himself and must soon be exiled in his turn from the religious community of his fellows. He will be banished and put to death outside the city, where all will look upon him as a leper, "a man to make people screen their faces."

The Kingdom of God can transform our earth only if its apostles are willing to share the exile of this world's outcasts. Evil will often seem to have the upper hand, and we shall weep as exiles in a foreign land. Beside the streams of Babylon . . . .

How splendid it would be if the earth were already changed into a paradise and the leprous were never again made outcasts. Who does not dream of a world without sicknesses and without injustices? Of a new Jerusalem in which there is no weeping and crying, no sorrow and sin? Of a Kingdom of universal peace, of singing to the harp, of chanting a new song to the Lord?

Brothers and sisters, the harshness of life must not discourage us. The word of the Lord retains its authority amid the trials of time, and the risen Jesus does not abandon our world. We cannot forget him, we who remember his death and resurrection in each of our Eucharists. But our nostalgic songs must be transformed into actions, for on our commitment to all lepers, to the point even of sharing their lot, the coming of the Kingdom depends. And this not only in the shelter of our age-old churches but also beside the streams of all the modern Babylons where the human race waits more than ever for us to sing to it the song of hope.

■

Let our voices remain silent, Lord,
   if we can no longer proclaim to our brethren
   the words that lift up and heal.
You have promised peace and happiness to the outcast,
   you have taken on yourself the world's sin.
Change our songs of lamentation
   into songs of hope,
and, above all, turn our lethargy
   into passionate concern for all who suffer.

SATURDAY OF THE 12TH WEEK

THE TABLE IS SPREAD

Lamentations 2:2, 10–14, 18–19. Jerusalem is no more. A light has been extinguished at the crossroads of the civilizations, for, though Israel was but a small people and spoke the same language as its neighbors, it also gave words a new meaning. Its destruction meant the disappearance of a specific idea of the human person; a way that had been opened to the Other was now closed.

Has God become the enemy of his people? Is it he who has swallowed up the pasture lands of Jacob? The policies of the kings have indeed played a part, but when the people dies, is this not a sign that God himself is dead? And what of the prophets who instead of true visions have no longer aught but tinselly delusions to offer? They are rogues who could not bring themselves to denounce the sins of the people, toadies who even now do not disclose the people's perversity. How can Israel come back to God? The eyes of the elderly are wasted by tears, the daughters of Jerusalem are prostrated, and their children cry their hunger on the street corners. Even the walls weep. How could this have happened? How could it have happened?

Psalm 74 is a Psalm of national supplication and continues the questions asked in the Book of Lamentations.

Matthew 8:5–17. Cf. p. 58.

■

On Psalm 74

God never forgets his covenant.
Let a foreigner come, murmuring
"I am not worthy,"
and the doors of the banquet hall open
to welcome and save him.
Forget your privileges,
people who have inherited the promises;
turn to your God and pray:
"Lord, I am not worthy."

■

"He took our sicknesses away and carried our diseases for us." The song could be one of triumph and acclamation, but on a certain Friday in the streets of Jerusalem it will be a song of mourning and condolence. Women standing along the way will veil their faces as before a leper. The Lamb of God will go forth, bowed under the weight of our sins. But to the veiled women the Lord will say, "Daughters of Jerusalem, weep rather for yourselves."

A song of lamentation has risen over Jerusalem, because the city is no more—only ruins and desolation. Because they have put the Innocent One to death, not a stone of their houses will be left standing. He healed the sick, welcomed sinners, and revealed the Kingdom of God, but they preferred their own strength and glory. Exiles, banished, reduced to wretchedness, they will go forth as vagabonds on the ways of the wilderness. "Daughters of Jerusalem, weep rather for yourselves."

Has God forgotten? Is he taking revenge for the evil human beings have done? "Why, God, this vengefulness, this anger of the shepherd against his flock?" They have set fire to your sanctuary.

But God has not forgotten his covenant; his mercy cannot be suppressed. He has not forgotten his Son's prayer and the cry of the innocent. He has raised up his sanctuary in three days. But the temple of God will be found henceforth wherever human beings put their trust in Love made flesh.

A centurion, a pagan, a foreigner is declared blessed with the blessedness which no lamentation can destroy. The blessedness of faith! Whereas a sinful people put its trust in its own strength, a human being gives voice to his own unworthiness. He makes no claims; he makes a request and expresses immense trust: "Just give the word."

"Go back, then." The city of God will never again take the form of a lofty fortified citadel. Henceforth God dwells wherever men and women dwell who are able to say: "I am not worthy to have you under my roof; just say a word . . . ."

■

Lord, for those who put their trust in you
  you change cries of mourning
  into songs of joy and hope.
Look upon us, your servants,
  paralyzed, slaves of our wretched state.
We are not worthy of your blessings,
  yet say but a word
  and we will be able to thank you
with all whom you invite to the feast of the Kingdom,
  where the table is spread
  for the sinners and poor of the world.

FROM MONDAY OF THE 13TH WEEK
TO TUESDAY OF THE 16TH WEEK

Planning a Strategy

"The harvest is rich." This is not the time to be idle. For a people who had gone astray, a degenerate people, God had raised up prophets. For a world that is weary and without a shepherd, Jesus calls the Twelve. The harvest is rich because instead of condemning and annihilating God shows favor. The prophets and the missionaries are to be the harvesters of this favor. They will give freely what they have freely received.

Yet from every side rumors of defeat reach us. Like a licentious wife, Israel has turned back to its old gods; it has sinned with them and borne children in pain, but it has reaped only wind and storm. In the king's domains the upright man is sold for money, and justice is put to death. The scribes of Jesus' day plot his destruction; Capernaum hardens its heart. Sin paralyzes individuals and society. The Apostles will soon meet with persecution for the name of Jesus. Even families will be divided.

How could God fail to bring suit against his people? "Capernaum, you shall be thrown down to hell." But a suit brought by God can only be a suit brought by a lover. The indictment is an impassioned one, but its wording betrays God's heart. "My people, what have I done to you? Do you not remember your youth, your infancy, the wilderness where we were espoused and you took your first steps, when I myself taught you to walk?" God has even gone so far as to teach his spouse the first steps in love, a spouse even then paralyzed. So, if there is a suit brought now, it is brought not for the sake of a divorce but the sake of a new covenant. God likes to show favor.

Look now at Jesus. He raises up the paralytic, calls the tax collector, raises the little girl from the dead, and forgives sins. He does not condemn, he heals. Then he sends the Twelve; to aid them he develops a mission strategy. He puts his yoke on their shoulders so that like him they may be gentle and humble and may be able to bring peace to the hearts of the poor. They must lose everything, give everything, risk everything. Their strategy will be to give men and women a living image of the Master who is first of all a servant.

"The harvest is rich." God, unhappy apart from his adulterous spouse, dreams of bringing her back into the wilderness and re-establishing their love. A new wedding will be celebrated, and the new wine will flow in abundance. The harvest will be magnificent, "seeds of justice and harvest of mercy." And even though the grain cast on the ground seems dead, it will yield much fruit, for God has never been able to bring himself to let love rot away in the earth. How could God forget the grace he gave on the first morning?

Israel and Prophecy

Israel did not have a monopoly on prophecy. Egypt too had its seers, Mesopotamia its *baru*, and Canaan its possessed. The phenomenon of prophecy occurred therefore throughout the entire ancient Near East, and the prophets of the countries who were Israel's neighbors manifested traits that would subsequently be found in their Jewish counterparts. Thus the Mesopotamian *baru* may be described as an official who was connected with a sanctuary and whose role was to give advice on affairs of state. That he did this with the help of divinatory techniques does not alter the fact that his successors in Samaria and Jerusalem would constantly intervene in the political life of their country.

Israel must have come into contact with such prophets from the time they settled in Canaan; in addition, some kings, Ahab for example, introduced foreign prophets. It seems, nonetheless, that there was a world of difference between the great prophets of the Old Testament and their Canaanite predecessors. It was Elijah who finally made it quite clear that things were different in Israel; he lived in community with the brotherhood of prophets, subsisted on alms and gifts, and wore only a sheepskin for a garment, this last soon becoming a sign of protest against the bourgeois ways that had been adopted by a formerly nomadic people.

As a matter of fact, the activity of the prophets may be summed up as one of challenge: challenge to society and its pervasive idolatry. Urban civilization had replaced the wilderness, and with civilization had come the opportunity for private property and a taste for comfort. The solidarity among the tribes that had been so vitally important on the steppe had declined and given way to social rivalry. In the religious sphere, on the other hand, Israel had turned to the Canaanite divinities that were the patrons of agriculture and stock-breeding. Baal began to rival the "God of the fathers," and the covenant was forgotten. It was then that the prophets arose as critics of this destructive development and as defenders of the lowly and champions of Yahweh.

But who were these prophets? They are noticeably reserved with regard to their personal lives, being wholly absorbed in the message they are to communicate from God. Jeremiah is certainly the most explicit about his own interior life. He presents himself as a man of the word. A kind of implacable force has seized hold of him and will not let him go. The prophet has no particular desire to exercise his ministry; on the contrary, he bears witness to a continual interior tension between his personal desires and the word that devours him and isolates him from his contemporaries. But Jeremiah also knows that he will be even more unhappy if he does not speak out.

A prophet is also a seer. He is this first of all by reason of his ability to challenge, since despite his isolation he never takes his eyes from contemporary events. Crises, wars, exile: he shares the good and bad times of his people, but, sustained by the faith that inspires him, he sees these events differently than others do. At the same time, he proclaims that his vision is the work of the Spirit. But the world into which his vision brings the prophet is not an imaginary world. Isaiah's inaugural vision, fantastic though it is, has its roots in human experience; the liturgy is the liturgy of the Jerusalem temple, and the Thrice Holy God has Davidic traits.

It must also be observed that the prophetic movement is correlative to a political situation that was extremely critical for Israel. When Isaiah began to speak, the existence of Judah was threatened, and this fact inevitably raised the question of the permanence of the covenants (in this case, the covenant with the house of David). The political crisis was thus seen as the earthly manifestation of the struggle between Yahweh and the powers of chaos, between good and evil. The prophet therefore tries to convince his countrymen of the need for a conversion which, however, God alone can make possible. Only after such a conversion is a new historical period possible in which the hopes of Israel, based on the Sinai covenant or the Davidic monarchy, will be fulfilled.

But what will happen if the promise is not fulfilled? Despite all the oracles promising salvation, Israel fell into the hands of Nebuchadnezzar. A disciple of Isaiah quickly grasped the problem raised by the unfulfilled promises; he writes in his introduction that "the word of our God remains forever" (40:8). Convinced of the fidelity of their God and at the same time concerned to preserve their political freedom, the Jewish people will safeguard the relevance of the prophetic message by projecting it into the final age. As long as the promise has not been fulfilled, the prophetic word will remain valid, even though events may give it the lie for the time being. Because the future of God remains open, the disciples of a prophet will go on reasserting the ancient prophecies in order to feed the hope of their people in successive new situations.

■

O God, who patiently guide our history,
  we bless you for your apostles and prophets.
They believed in your word
  and they fought the good fight
  until persecution struck them down.
In the midst of everyday life they felt
  their mission as a sword
  that pierced their hearts
  and compelled them to surrender everything for you.
They did give everything:
  their time and their rest,
  their reputation and their future.

They spoke the word that causes consternation,
  they opposed the powerful,
  they raised up the weak who were abused,
  they took the side of justice.
God, we bless you
  because you never abandon your people
  when the punishment of their infidelity weighs them down.

We pray you: in this time of disarray
  be with us despite our sins;
  save us despite our covenants with the world.
In your presence we acknowledge our sin:
  we have brought forth only wind,
  we have lost all in trying to save all.
We have concealed your name
  that we might ally ourselves with those who blaspheme you;
we have denied justice and love
  that we might despoil the unfortunate
  and enrich ourselves with fruitless things.
Now on our shoulders rests
  the yoke of slavery
  that keeps us chained to ourselves.

Lord, do not abandon your Church.
Raise up new workers for your harvest.
Call prophets who will revive our faith.

Accept us too, despite our unwillingness.
Your Kingdom is at hand:
  make us apostles of your reign.
Let us be for our brothers and sisters,
  the sign of your peace and your pardon.

MONDAY OF THE 13TH WEEK

GOD TAKES SIDES

Amos 2:6–10, 13–16. Like the preceding poem, which was directed against the nations, this oracle against Israel accuses the people of contempt for the law. It reminds them that Yahweh will not tolerate any violation either of the rights of peoples or of the rights of individuals. But because this poem is like a musical pause, it also contains some of the most trenchant and circumstantial reproaches. Israel has received greater kindness than any other people; its responsibility is therefore the greater, and the sight it presents is the more desolating. Its judges are corrupt, and the lowly are treated arbitrarily by the rich. Even its public worship has been dishonored, for the robes in which men loll at their sacred banquets, as well as the wine they drink there, have been confiscated from the poor. Creditors have even forgotten their obligation to restore a debtor's cloak before nightfall. In short, the ancient solidarity of the tribes has given place to the sordid exploitation of the weakest among the people.

Israel will be punished; the Assyrians are at the borders, and the people are rushing toward military disaster. On that day—the day of judgment—no one will escape. Neither archer nor foot soldier nor cavalryman will be spared; all shall run away naked on that day.

Psalm 50 is an indictment of Yahweh against his people, whom he accuses of hypocrisy.

Matthew 8:18–22. Cf. p. 62.

■

On Psalm 50

312

God is prosecuting his people,
and the indictment is a severe one;
at the tribunal of faith
who will leave forgiven?
Hear then the Lord's reproach against you,
and allow grace to convert your hearts,
you who constantly talk of the convenant
but live exclusively by pillaging others!

■

Amos is not a mealy-mouthed prophet, and, on hearing him, more than one Israelite must have frowned, thinking that this man should not be mixing religion and politics—all the more since Amos tends to derive his language from the left. But how could a prophet worthy of God keep silence when a poor man's life is worth less than a pair of sandals and when the heads of the poor are crushed in the dust? The God of the covenant is not an easy-going idol, to be lulled with incense. God takes the side of the unfortunate, and so much the worse if the throng of unfortunates are on the left. As a matter of fact, human beings are everywhere trodden underfoot by their fellows, and the poor have nowhere to lay their heads.

God sides with the mistreated poor. Jesus, the Son of Man, will direct his mission solely to those whom everyone abuses. Here is a scribe ready to follow Jesus wherever he goes. What does Christ promise him but an itinerant, uprooted life, with no fixed home and no social standing? The man will not even have time to bury his relatives. God's work is urgent; it means life to those reprieved dead whom no one gives a thought to. "My sentence is irrevocable," says the Lord. "He who is not unhesitatingly with me is against me," and God is with those who hunger for justice. One cannot recite the Beatitudes and at the same time fail to react against the continual violation of human rights.

On the point of embarking, Jesus says: "Follow me." And he leads his disciples to the other shore of the lake. On that other shore are there not people to be found every day who have been rejected by the self-satisfied folk "on this side"?

We want to follow you, Lord,
  to the very heart of the world,
to the very foot of the cross.
Do away with our resistance:
  grant us a hunger and thirst for justice
  and be our support.
Let the cry of the oppressed
  not condemn us,
since you gave your life
  to save the poor
  and open a new future to them
in your Kingdom of peace and hope.

TUESDAY OF THE 13TH WEEK

AGAINST THE STREAM

Amos 3:1–8. "Listen, sons of Israel, to this oracle." Yahweh addresses the children of Israel and reminds them of his choice of them. He has "marked" Israel out from among all the peoples of the earth; now he means to "concern himself" with them. He will demand an accounting from this people that has neglected the obligation imposed on it by the covenant.

The prophet's destiny is a strange one. Amos will defend himself against the charge that he had sought to be a prophet (7:14); no, it is Yahweh who compels him to speak. Is his subject the Assyrian threat? Or the excessively untroubled hope of the people? A day had dawned when Israel's impenitence seemed to him like a challenge that had to be accepted. No one can muzzle the word of God; it forces itself upon a man and bursts forth like the roar of a lion.

We may admire the subtlety with which Amos explains his vocation to his audience. Seven questions precede the key question—seven questions, and only then does he say: "The Lord Yahweh speaks: who can refuse to prophesy?" The Jewish mind proceeds inductively, moving from the known to the unknown. There is no smoke with fire, according to popular wisdom. If a lion emits a satisfied roar, it is because he has caught a prey; if a prophet speaks, it is because Yahweh is compelling him to speak. Yes, but when the lion roars, he stirs fear; when Yahweh speaks, we must heed the prophet.

Psalm 5, an individual lament, is a protestation of innocence: "You have no room for the wicked."

Matthew 8:23–27. Cf. p. 64.

■

On Psalm 5

In the suit brought by God
the prosecutor speaks:
Here are the poor,
victims of the knave and cheat,
those whom the conceited scorn.
Shall God not do justice
to the unfortunate who have no defender?

■

We must set out for the other shore, where human beings are in danger. But how is it possible to reach that strange country without facing up to the countless anxieties of an unfamiliar crossing? The sea is in violent upheaval, the ship is sinking. Yet Jesus sleeps. How often God seems to be asleep when our crossing is marked by storms and contrary winds! We know we must go out to other human beings, but why does God leave us so helpless and alone? Is God dead? We are lost, confronted with a world from which there is no way out. Has Christ truly risen from the tomb?

"Why are you so frightened, you men of little faith?" Fear will always be the last trick of the evil one. On the storm-tossed sea we grow afraid and we abandon the cause. We turn our boats back to harbor and, ashamed, we return home. The evil one has won the day, and the world can go on killing human beings. On the other shore there is only a wilderness.

315

"You men of little faith." To overcome the evil one and change the face of the earth takes a great deal of faith: a faith that matches the gift God has given to us in Jesus Christ risen from the dead. A little bit of faith is not enough, for the least squall exhausts it. It is not enough to say that the Lord will perhaps be with us. We must believe that in every circumstance he is indeed with us, standing up there and commanding the winds of the sea.

How are we to know this when everything seems to argue the contrary? But faith alone can make us know it. Faith has its solidity within itself. When Jesus calmed the storm, he continued the journey with his disciples, and it remained a journey of faith until it was finished. There is only one remedy for the lack of faith: to believe more strongly and, above all, not to be satisfied with half-measures.

■

Father, do not subject us to temptation:
  let trials not overcome our faith,
  for then we would be lost.

Rescue us from the Evil One and from death,
  for we cry to you,
  and our boat is already in danger of sinking.

Arise, O God; awaken, O Christ.
  It will take all the aid you can give us
  for our faith not to founder.

Forgive us for our lack of faith.
  Grant us strength to stand erect,
  for you alone are our source of confidence.

WEDNESDAY OF THE 13TH WEEK

STRUGGLING WITH DEMONS

Amos 5:14–15, 21–24. "I hate and despise . . . I take no pleasure . . . I reject . . . and refuse to look at . . . ." Could there be a stronger indictment than this? Is the cult irrevocably condemned? In fact, what the prophet is emphasizing is the divorce of worship from daily life. The Book of Leviticus makes clear the care which Israel devoted to everything having to do with the liturgy, but of what value is a liturgy that has been reduced to lifeless rubrics? When worship becomes remote from human beings it does not thereby draw closer to God.

Authentic worship is rooted in a demanding daily fidelity to the covenant. It helps us to develop a passionate human commitment to all that concerns God—but what, after all, concerns God if not the human person and his dignity? Let Israel first make justice reign, and let its integrity flow like an unfailing stream. Then Israel has reason to hope that the Lord will have mercy on his people.

Psalm 50 is an indictment of Yahweh against his people, whom he accuses of hypocrisy.

Matthew 8:28–34. Cf. p. 67.

■

Exorcisms can easily occupy a good deal of space in forms of worship. But fear is not always a good counselor; in this case, it drives people to multiply rituals and spells, sacrifices and prayers in order to ward off the evil one or even to do violence to God and thus win his favors.

When God cries out to us today through the mouth of the prophets: "I hate and despise your feasts, I take no pleasure in your solemn festivals, I refuse to look at your sacrifices," we should not too quickly conclude that our God is opposed to public worship and liturgy. What he cannot feel drawn to, however, is a multiplication of prayers and sacrifices, an uproar of singing, and celebrations rendered unauthentic by daily injustices. A liturgy of the lips, when the heart is like stone before the wretchedness of the world.

Yes, when fear lays hold of us because the world is slipping irresistibly into the abyss of hell, it is useless suddenly to multiply sacrifices and exorcisms. What is needed, says God, is first of all to make justice reign and to give integrity its proper place. Then our assemblies will be able to offer God a sincere and upright thanksgiving.

What an odd liturgy Christ performs in the country of the Gadarenes! Everything suggests an exorcism, with a scenario worthy of the most ambiguous kind of religious feeling. The possessed are set free; the demons return to the place par excellence of uncleanness: swine; and the swine are engulfed in the sea where they can return to the wellsprings of death. Is Jesus simply an exorcist?

But did you notice the disturbing fact that the two possessed men, who are pagans, immediately recognize Jesus as the Son of God? What a mysterious connivence between Good in its pure state and the evil one who dwells in human beings! The demons plead not to be expelled "before the time." We know that when that time comes, on the cross, the Son of God will make himself known through the extreme poverty inflicted on him by his own love. On that day he will celebrate the sacrifice that saves human beings once and for all. No exorcism then, but rather the gift of himself to the very end.

Today the inhabitants of the other shore are unable as yet to comprehend. They become more afraid than ever and ask Jesus to return whence he came.

It will always take a good deal of time for human beings to pass from fear to faith, from ritual to justice, from exorcisms to true sacrifice. Let us at least bear in mind that our liturgies have no other purpose than to make that day possible and to hasten its coming—the day when justice and love will reign.

■

God, our God, do not indict us
  for our lifeless sacrifices:
through your Christ, handed over to love on the cross,
  forgive our injustices
  and change our hearts.

BINDING AND LOOSING

Amos 7:10–17. A representative of the official priesthood is here
condemned by Amos. Bethel was an ancient patriarchal sanctuary
connected with Jacob; it had its hour of glory after the separation of the
two kingdoms. Although himself a Judean, Amos spent the major part of
his prophetic career at Bethel, thus bearing witness to the fundamental
unity of the chosen people despite its human vicissitudes. The priest in
charge of the sanctuary accuses the prophet of conspiring against the king;
the accusation was all the more serious since unlike Jerusalem the
northern provinces did not have a hereditary monarchy. The priest then
decides to expel Amos from the temple and send him back to the south, on
the pretext that he works for money.

Amos gives a proud answer. Just as Elijah and Nathan retracted nothing
when confronted with their sovereign, so Amos will not change a word of
his message. First, he makes it clear that he is not a professional prophet;
it is Yahweh who has called him, and it is in Yahweh's name that he
speaks. Then Amos turns to threats: Amaziah will be stricken in his
person, his family and his possessions. When the troops of the enemy pour
out over the country, his wife will be violated in the city and his children
will perish; he himself will be exiled, and his possessions will be
confiscated.

Psalm 19 is a hymn proclaiming that the person praying is faithful to the
word of Yahweh.

Matthew 9:1–8. Cf. p. 70.

■

Jesus is engaged in a ceaseless struggle with the evil one, and the
sole purpose of the authority he has received is to bring him wherever
human beings suffer and await deliverance. Hardly has he returned
home to Capernaum when he is faced with a paralytic.

The scene is an imposing one. Here, face to face, are the Son of Man,
who will come on the clouds to judge the living and the dead, and a
poor fellow who is incapable of standing erect and has been laid low

319

by sin. Here, face to face, are the one whom God has set upon a royal throne so that he may bring justice to the unfortunate, and a man who has only the faith of others to plead his cause. The hour of judgment has struck, and the man's sin will be overcome. "Pick up your bed and go home." Supported by the faith of a group, the man is at last able to take control of his own history and go away a free person. The authority of the Son of Man is that of the free and holy God.

But this power has been shared with human beings, with the faith community of the Church. Is there any nobler and more imposing liturgy than the liturgy of reconciliation—a sacrament celebrated out in the open, face to face with life and the future? Because the Son of Man, now risen, abides at the heart of our earthly dwelling, the ecclesial community has received the power to bind and loose in his name. When the faith of the brethren enables the paralyzed man to draw near to the Savior, the latter gives a share of his authority to believers, and each can truly say to the others: "Arise and walk."

Yes, as on that day at Capernaum, whenever faith lives in the community of believers, a great breath of hope passes across history. And every sinful human being can stand erect and walk freely, liberated now from fear and paralysis. For if God has placed judgment in the hands of the Son of Man, it is in order that the evil one and his somber retinue of fear and anxiety may be conquered once and for all.

■

Almighty and merciful God,
how wonderfully you created man
and still more wonderfully remade him.
You do not abandon the sinner
but seek him out with a father's love.
You sent your Son into the world
to destroy sin and death
by his passion,
and to restore life and joy
by his resurrection.
You sent the Holy Spirit into our hearts
to make us your children
and heirs of your Kingdom.

You constantly renew our spirit
in the sacraments of your redeeming love,
freeing us from slavery to sin
and transforming us ever more closely
into the likeness of your beloved Son.
We thank you for the wonders of your mercy,
and with heart and hand and voice
we join with the whole Church
in a new song of praise:
Glory to you
through Christ
in the Holy Spirit,
now and forever.
Amen.[31]

FRIDAY OF THE 13TH WEEK

PHYSICIAN TO THE WORLD

Amos 8:4–6, 9–12. "See what days are coming—it is the Lord Yahweh who speaks": terrible days, days of punishment. While it is possible that the prophet is here drawing on an ancient tradition—the darkening of the earth during the day is part of all the eschatological scenarios—this does not prevent his being the first to describe the day of Yahweh: a day of repentance, lamentations and obsequies. The mourning on that day will be like the mourning for an only son, when any future seems blocked. Men and women will hunger and thirst for a message they had been unwilling to hear when it was given to them, but now they will not hear it again.

Whom is the prophet addressing? Various greedy individuals to whom God is an embarrassment; some upstarts for whom the sabbath is only a day lost to their enrichment. Society is organized for the profit of a few, who tamper with the scales, arrange prices, and sell into slavery those who cannot pay their debts. But God will never be on the side of exploiters.

Psalm 119 sings of the benefits of the law to those who are hungry and thirsty to hear the word of the Lord.

Matthew 9:9–13. Cf. p. 74.

■

Matthew was a tax collector. After the Gospel's eulogy of that class of men, we're almost tempted to add "humble and poor" to the term "tax collector." But that would be far from the truth. We can apply to tax collectors what the prophet says about the greedy men of his day: "They raise prices, they buy the poor for a little money." Matthew the tax collector was simply a thief whose thievery was ill disguised under the appearances of legality. And the people whom Jesus found at table with him were certainly no better than he. They were the people of whom God says: "I am going to turn your feasts into funerals, all your singing into lamentations." Well, then, does the word of God convey the terror of the dies irae or the tender love of a merciful Father? There is an even more serious question: Is God overly good or (what would really please us more) is he strictly just?

But when we ask the question in this form, are we not putting ourselves on the side of the Pharisees? We want a just God who will punish the wicked, because we rank ourselves among the upright. We, of course, have never tampered with the scales. We have never sold the sweepings of the wheat. We have done nothing, as children who are caught red-handed say. That describes our virtue: we do nothing. We are not sick. We are nothing and have need of no one. And if the sun is to be eclipsed at midday when God comes to render justice, this certainly won't happen in our house, because in our house the sun has not shone at all for a long time now.

At Capernaum on this evening the sun has shone a thousand times brighter. A sun shining for human beings who are weary of being lost in the darkness of their cheating. A table set with bread and wine for sinners who hunger and thirst to hear the words of the Lord. For just as a physician can only heal patients who will cooperate with him, so the table of God can satisfy only those who are conscious of their hunger, and his sun can warm only sinners whose strength has been drained by the night.

If on the day of judgment the sun is to be darkened over the world and if the people of the land are to weep as at the burial of an only son, the reason is that for too long those supposedly righteous have refused to let the sun shine on all human beings. These reputedly upright people have been fettered to the injustices of society and without saying a word in opposition have collaborated in the murder of the only Son—this Son who was nailed to the cross one day for having eaten with tax collectors and sinners. Did not the sun hide itself at the moment of his death? Only a repentant robber saw the light of a new dawn.

God is not overly good. He simply teaches us that true righteousness takes the form of forgiveness and hope for us who are sinners.

■

God, you make your sun to shine
*   on the world of the poor and the scorned:*
Do not condemn us to our night
*   because we have distorted your justice.*
Grant us to acknowledge our sin
*   so that the sun of your mercy*
*   may fill our hearts again*
*   with a taste for the feasting and the peace*
*   of the day of judgment.*

SATURDAY OF THE 13TH WEEK

RIGHTEOUSNESS AND PEACE

Amos 9:11–15. "That day . . . ." The preceding oracle ended with a threat; now Yahweh speaks of re-erecting the hut of David that has been tottering. It is likely that this epilogue to the Book of Amos was composed during the exile. The deported have acquired through experience the conviction that God does not will to wipe out his people completely. In addition, David's people had always taken seriously the commitments of Yahweh to the Davidic dynasty. The destruction of Jerusalem had not destroyed their faith. The royal hut would be re-erected, and the little kingdom of Judah would recover the splendor it had had in the time of David and Solomon; even Edom, its hereditary enemy, would lie at its feet. Those in exile would return to their ancestral land, but a land henceforth so fertile that there would be no interval between toil and harvest, sowing and reaping. Finally, as if desiring to authenticate the whole of this prophetic book, the final redactor adds: "says Yahweh, your God."

Psalm 85 is a national lamentation; its final verses, 8–13, provide a response which enabled the believer to expect an oracle from Yahweh and to presume that this oracle would be a favorable one.

Matthew 9:14–17. Cf. p. 77.

■

On Psalm 85
Hear what the Lord says:
he speaks of peace and righteousness
and announces a harvest of truth
that is filled with the rich juice of love.
He says it, and what he says he does.
Our land will bear its fruit,
righteousness and peace will embrace.

■

A beautiful wedding! A fruitful covenant! Righteousness and peace embrace, and those invited sing for the feast! The bridegroom leads the dance, and the wine flows abundantly. Nature too joins in the celebration: the hills flow with wine, and our land bears fruit a hundredfold. Loyalty springs from the earth, and love unites all human beings in peace. Never again, says God, shall the days of want and lamentation return. For God's covenant with our world is an eternal one. Hear what the Lord says. What he says is peace for his people.

Brothers and sisters, let us not return to our folly. No one puts new wine into old wineskins. Let us stop complaining about what goes wrong. Love and truth, righteousness and peace have been given to us: now is the time, not for fasting, but for restoring life and joy to our world. At the banquet which was the Last Supper Jesus put a new wine into our hands; he offered himself for the sake of righteousness and peace among his fellows. How can we who celebrate his covenant

324

refuse to be the singers of a new world in which righteousness and peace embrace?

Ah, we know only too well that echoes of the world sadden us daily and that the Bridegroom seems once more to have been taken from us. The cross remains standing at the heart of the human wilderness. But we are not the gravediggers of a lost world; on Easter morning God gave us access to the garden once again and a new soil to cultivate. He himself gives the nourishment and sun that are needed if our vine is to bear fruits of happiness. When everything seems to be drying up from drought, he invites us to the wedding feast of the Bridegroom. Will not our real repentance show itself by our persevering in the joy of hope and the truth of righteousness—a repentance which itself has for us the taste and savor of a new wine?

■

God, you make all things new;
  we praise you for the wedding table
  where you give us the new wine
  and the joy of a reborn future.
Through your Spirit and his kindly inspiration
  our earth bears its fruit:
  righteousness and peace embrace
  at the feast of your eternal covenant.
Grant us a fervent love
  and fill our hearts with the joy of praising you.
Let our communion with our brethren
  in truth and righteousness
  be the sign that you are a faithful God,
  the Bridegroom who never fails us.

MONDAY OF THE 14TH WEEK

A GOD WHO SEDUCES

Hosea 2:16–18, 21–22. The Book of Hosea tells two dramatic stories. The prophet has married a woman named Gomer; she however is a cultic prostitute, a fact which links the conjugal drama with the national disaster. For in the time of Hosea, which is slightly later than that of Amos, the promised land gave evidence of Israel's infidelity to Yahweh: alongside their own God the people had adopted the divinities of the country, who were real specialists in country life. The rituals of these nature religions were geared essentially to promoting the fertility of the soil, of animals and of human beings. As a result, prostitutes, both male and female, played a part in the liturgy of cultic marriage. Such was Gomer's "profession."

Yet Gomer continued to be passionately loved by her husband. When his initial anger passes, Hosea wants to take her back. These conjugal difficulties enable the prophet to gain insight into the power of love and thereby to discover God as well. He tells himself that if a human being is capable of so much love, much more so God, who is Love itself. Yes, Yahweh likewise wants to renew his intimacy with his people. In addition, he wants to allure her again, and to this end he wishes to lead her back into the wilderness, as he did at the time of the exodus, the time when Yahweh and Israel were espoused.

Happy the woman who arouses such passion! Happy a people when they experience the love of God!

Psalm 145, which makes use of older forms, belongs to the genre of hymn. It is placed on the lips of a repentant people, where it echoes the words of the Lord.

Matthew 9:18–26. Cf. p. 81.

■

God desires life; he is comfortable only on the side of life. Let them laugh at him; he does not care. A dead young girl is worth making a journey for, and a faithless wife calls into play all the tricks of a seducer. God does not will death, above all not this death that is more tragic than any other and goes by the name of failure, separation, divorce. God will play seducer to the faithless wife, and he does it extremely well. For no life is possible except where seduction is at work—the genuine kind of seduction.

Death, infidelity, the temptation of idolatry, evil in all its forms: these seem inevitable. "That's life," say the disillusioned; they resign themselves to it, but they sink into sadness and despair. There was a

time when love and beauty seduced them, but they had not understood the value of authentic seduction. They preferred the stagnation of fatalism. The happiness of engagement lasts, it seems, but a short time.

But now look at this woman who has been suffering from hemorrhages for twelve years. Life seeks to leave her; life flows out of her to no purpose. She could already be sinking down into death. But nothing can stop her, not even ridicule of her going up and touching the hem of Christ's garment. This woman, at least, has been seduced. She has faith—a rather bizarre faith, but what difference does that make? We've already seen this: when one is seduced, what difference does it make if others mock? Faith reaches beyond the mockery, and life is reborn.

They must have made fun of Hosea when he took his prostitute wife back into his home and showered countless marks of affection on her. He, a prophet, the husband of a professional prostitute in pagan temples! But then, why not make fun of the God who looks back to the exodus like an unfortunate husband who cannot forget the time of his betrothal?

Yes, many make fun of God and Jesus. These people claim to be serious, but their seriousness already has the wrinkled features of death. They claim to be facing up to the meaninglessness of fate, but they can do nothing for the good folk who simply want to live. God for his part wills life, even if this makes him seem ridiculous. For life is the best thing there is, and life will never die out completely as long as there is a man to say to a woman: "Come, I will speak to your heart. Come, the future is before us. Come, rise up, and let us live."

■

When we are tempted to seek elsewhere
  a joy which eludes us,
then, Lord, seduce us
  and speak once more to our hearts.

When death obsesses us
  and everything speaks to us of calamity,
seduce us

and take us by the hand.

When the burden of sin tells us
  not to expect any further tenderness,
seduce us
  and lead us to your hidden wilderness.

THE RIGHT TO SPEAK

Hosea 8:4–7, 11–13. Here is an oracle that paints a very unflattering picture of the internal state of Israel. The first complaint: the anarchic succession of kings. Instead of consulting God's prophet, as was customary in the northern kingdom, the Jews of the southern kingdom allowed violence to carry the day. The result: ten kings in five years. The second reproach: the religious schism. The two golden calves were doubtless not wrong in themselves, since they were simply a pedestal for the divinity, but the apostasy could only scandalize true worshipers of Yahweh. This oracle of Hosea will prove extremely important, since it will be the source of the prohibition of images of God (Dt 5:8; Ex 20:4).

But the worst of Israel's sins was that it scorned the divine law. It was looked upon as the work of a stranger; meanwhile the cultus was turned from its proper purpose. The situation can have only one outcome: since the people refuse to turn back to God, they must return to Egypt.

Psalm 115 does not belong to any well-defined literary genre; it contains an attack on idols as well as an exhortation to fidelity to Yahweh.

Matthew 9:32–38. Cf. p. 83.

∎

On Psalm 115

The money-god has no heart;
the power-god is impotent;
the learned god is struck dumb;

the god of the depths is powerless.

*May those who put their trust in idols
become like them.*

*Our God is our heavenly Father.
We can rely on him:
devaluation will never affect him
nor fever consume him.*

*We, the living,
put our trust in the God of life.*

∎

In the judgment of a Pharisee, if a dumb man begins to speaks, there must be some demonic spell at work. For it is understood, once and for all, that the function of the dumb is to remain silent. The world is what it is, and, in any event, it is for the righteous to speak; they have all the means at their disposal for placing the full burden of their pride on the weary and dejected crowd. In the view of a self-respecting Pharisee the crowd's role is to be silent, since it is utterly ignorant. In addition, those really mute are also deaf; they hear and understand nothing, therefore let them remain silent. If Jesus heals them, he must be in cahoots with the demon, who, as everyone knows, speaks only to whisper evil. A short time hence, and the Pharisees will be duty-bound to impose silence on Christ. After all, you can't let just anybody say just anything. If Jesus has nothing but words of encouragement for sinners, he must be forced into silence.

True enough, there are some odd things said in the community of the disciples. Gather together the Matthews, the healed paralytics and lepers, the young girls raised from the dead, and the Apostles who panicked on the lake: you can hardly avoid getting some very odd conversations. Stories about what lies beyond the sea and beyond the tomb, beyond sin and beyond exile—those are not the sort of things usual among Pharisees, imprisoned as they are in the strict letter of religion.

But what a lesson for all future ages! For the wearied and shepherdless crowds were not fooled; they had never seen anything like this before in Israel. The Church of the pure and the righteous never understood the crowds, but with a single glance the man from Nazareth understood their plight. He told them: "Come," and they discovered a Church in which the poor have the right to speak about their poverty. What a lesson for today's Church that is so often mute, even though the harvest has never been so rich.

One thing is sure: the workers who gather in this harvest will never come from the ranks of the Pharisees. The only workers capable of restoring speech to the dumb are the poor who have discovered a different word.

■

Lord, open our lips
  and our voices shall proclaim your might.
You speak words of encouragement for the future
  to those reduced to silence.
Blessed be you
  who restore to the dumb
  the joy of singing your praise.

WEDNESDAY OF THE 14TH WEEK

TWELVE APPRENTICES

Hosea 10:1–3, 7–8, 12. "Israel was a luxuriant vine." Such were the advantages of the settlement in Canaan. The former nomads were transformed into farmers proud of their land, and the northern kingdom in particular experienced years of enviable prosperity. But the Israelites soon forgot that they owed this new good fortune to Yahweh; they began to court the gods of the land and to set up sacred stones and altars to them. Their ingratitude brought disaster and will cost them dearly now that the Assyrians are at the gates: no more king, no more altars, and soon no more native land—unless they return to God and begin again to practice integrity and mercy. If they do, they may have hope again: Yahweh will continue to give rain to the soil and salvation to the people.

Psalm 105 is a hymn. The few verses cited from it here may seem a

330

surprising choice in the context of Israel's sin. In their own way, however, they reassert the steadfast confidence of the people in Yahweh. In fact, while Israel was aware of its sins, it believed even more in the fidelity of God.

Matthew 10:1–7. Cf. p. 92.

■

There are twelve of them, and they represent the twelve tribes of the chosen people; they are the true Israel and the first-fruits of the future Church. In Christ's name they will go forth carrying the good news, so that the human race may know of the fidelity of God, who never abandons his flock. They will be the shepherds of the lost sheep and will have the Lord's own power to preserve from death those entrusted to them. As a good shepherd should, and as so many kings and leaders of ancient Israel failed to do, they will have to give their lives for their fellow human beings.

These men are also called Apostles (men sent) and witnesses of the resurrection. This title is, however, not reserved to them; others are given it in the New Testament, because every witness to the Lord is an apostle, and Paul, a convert, was doubtless the first to lay such forceful claim to the title. It is true, however, that for us the Twelve are par excellence "the twelve Apostles." The reason is that in their persons the witness to the resurrection has its roots in the human and fleshly lifetime of the Son of God. As disciples of the first hour, they link the Church of Easter to the Church that traveled the roads of Galilee and Judea.

What more can be said of this title of theirs? Nothing, save perhaps to express our surprise that several among them are not better known to us. We know hardly anything of them as companions of Jesus, and even less of them as Apostles and missionaries of the Gospel. What more is to be said of them except that one of them, Judas Iscariot, was "the one who betrayed the Master"? The Church is thus not preserved from the danger of being betrayed by its own. The Lord has not built the new Israel on the rock of guaranteed holiness. Until the final day, the task still remains of transforming an evil world through the Gospel.

Did these men disobey Christ by going out to the pagans or even among the Samaritans? Or are we to see in their action a break with the missionary attitude of the first post-Pentecostal generation? One thing is certain: history cannot stand still, and even though Jesus—perhaps—decided to limit himself to the lost sheep of his own people, we know that it was the Spirit of Jesus himself who made the Church a universal Church. The Gospel is a point of departure; it can never become a rein.

One thing, and one thing alone, matters: that the name of the Lord Jesus be proclaimed. That is the very essence of the apostolate: To tell every human being who is being lost that "the Kingdom is at hand."

■

You founded your Son's Church
  on twelve men, poor in everything,
  who were sent out into the world
  as defenseless shepherds.
Lord our God,
  deign to preserve your Church in this faith:
let your word never be adulterated
  by the power of the world,
for you alone are our strength
  and our surety through the centuries.

THURSDAY OF THE 14TH WEEK

TWELVE POOR MEN ON THE ROAD

Hosea 11:1, 3–4, 8c–9. A father . . . . Yes, we are confronted here with a father who complains of the ingratitude shown him by a child whom he nonetheless still loves tenderly. "When Israel was a child I loved him . . . . I was like someone who lifts an infant tenderly against his cheek; stooping down to him I gave him his food."

But can a father abandon his child? Yahweh is the holy God; his thoughts are not those of men. Where a legitimate grievance might bid him give vent to anger, love orders forgiveness. A day will come when Yahweh again calls his Son up out of Egypt (Mt 2:15); salvation will then be close at hand for the human race.

Psalm 80 is a psalm of national supplication that perhaps originated in the north at the time of the Assyrian invasions. It harmonizes perfectly with the prophet's meditation on God's "repentance"; it thus expresses Israel's confidence in divine mercy.

Matthew 10:7–15. Cf. p. 94.

■

On Psalm 80

The true shepherd gives his life,
the true vinegrower prunes his vine.
That is what our God is like.
In order that we may bear fruit
he cuts off our withered branches;
in order to save his scattered flock
he struggles to the point of dying.

■

"I am God, not man." These infinitely tender words seem to be in Jesus' mind when he sends the Twelve on a mission: "Be like God," he tells them, "and not like men."

"You received without charge; give without charge." Remember that all you have you have received from this God who taught you to walk, like a father supporting his child by the arms. Lead human beings by the guiding strings of human nature; do not put on them a burden too heavy for their shoulders. Be witnesses of peace, not of law; in God's eyes human beings will always be infants.

Be children yourselves. Go forth on the roads unencumbered: no weapons, no money; be content with what they offer you. It is through this kind of exchange that men and women will come to understand the love bestowed on them, for there is as much joy in giving as in receiving. Be content with your daily bread; resist the temptation to look for something better, for nothing is better than to live from day to day while resting in the hands of God.

True enough: if they refuse to welcome you, you must depart and shake the very dust from your feet. True enough: a terrible punishment awaits those who have rejected the good news of peace. But do not on that account let your hearts be hardened: God never gives full vent to his anger. Who knows? Perhaps tomorrow other Apostles will find changed and repentant hearts. As for yourselves, be content to bear humble witness to God, his tender love, his patience. Give freely, and leave to God the task of claiming the price of your weariness that was seemingly suffered in vain.

"Truly," says the Lord, "I am your reward."

■

God our father,
  full of love and tenderness,
we come before you
  like children,
  to thank you.
You have given us all things freely:
  life and faith,
  hope and bread.
Teach us,
  as we teach children,
  to share everything
  joyously and wholeheartedly.
In this world may we be
  your Church that is ever young,
  a Church filled with wonder,
as children are
  who discover each day
  their father's love for them.
You are our God:
  blessed be you.

LIVES OF SACRIFICE

Hosea 14:2–10. "Israel, come back to Yahweh your God." The purpose of the prophetic preaching is to bring a sinful people back to God. Relations between Yahweh and his people are like a lovers' game: when Israel plunges into disobedience, Yahweh draws back, but the urgent calls of the prophet force the people to reflect on their conduct, while the absence of God enkindles their desire for him. When Israel is converted, God returns.

But conversion does not consist in the offering of extra sacrifices; what God requires is circumcision of the heart, that is, the trusting surrender of his people to him. They must abandon their policy of alliances with pagan nations and reject useless idols. Then it will be possible for Yahweh to reappear and, as in the days when Israel was a child, to be prodigal in his attentions to his converted people. Then they will see "fruitful" Ephraim live up to its name. The return of Israel to its God will coincide with the return of the exiles, and the people will be as fragrant as Mount Lebanon, which was famous for its aromatic plants.

Psalm 51, which is an individual lament, must have formed part of a penitential ceremony presided over by the king. It is to be noted that the one praying does not dwell on himself but turns immediately to God, whose love and mercy he praises.

Matthew 10:16–23. Cf. p. 96.

■

"We offer you in sacrifice the words of our mouths." This translation brings out the connection between word and sacrifice, which cannot be separated any more than the cross of Christ and the Gospel message can. The word of God, whether descending to human beings in the good news or returning to him in thanksgiving, is always heavy with the love that brought Jesus to his sacrifice. We must heed him, the Word of God, as he says, with a final sigh on the cross: "Father, I offer you in sacrifice the words of my mouth." There the word is efficacious and saves the world.

The same will be true of the Apostles and messengers of the Gospel until the end of time. To the extent that they speak the word of God while first living it themselves, they will be handed over to tribunals just as Christ was handed over to his judges. "You will be hated by all men on account of my name," the Lord tells them. But what is hateful about the name of Jesus? It is not in and of itself that it arouses the ill-will and malice of others. For as long as "Jesus" remains simply the name of a religion attached to heaven and the virtues, everyone hastens to flatter the Church; as long as sacrifices are celebrated with rituals and canticles, everything is fine. But let the name of Jesus be used in denouncing the injustice by which human beings are sacrificed like cattle in the slaughter-house, and let the Gospel be preached as applicable to this world and in behalf of the condemned of our societies, and let the Apostles proclaim the Beatitudes as valid here and now—then immediately comes persecution from the "right-minded" and from those with secure positions in this world. A brother will hand even his own brother over to death. The authentic word of God and sacrifice are inseparable.

It is through this association with self-giving that the word becomes efficacious. "The Spirit of your Father will be speaking in you," says Jesus, but the Spirit can speak only in those who have entrusted their lives to him without reservation. Every apostolic life is a sacrifice, an entrusting of oneself to God and to human beings; otherwise the word remains an insubstantial breath of air.

This, however, is not a reason for running out and seeking martyrdom. We must first do all we can to change human hearts and to reach that part in them which is as resistant as stone. This is a fine opportunity for us to review our apostolic dexterity. "Be cunning as serpents," Jesus says. And if he adds, "and yet as harmless as doves," it is because he is well aware that the Christian diplomacy will sooner or later lead to persecution. The point is not to rouse persecution beforehand.

■

We return to you, O Lord,
  for you have first come to us.
  Change our hearts, and we shall be saved.

We return to you, blessing your name;

accept the sacrifice of our mouths.
Grant us your Spirit, and we shall be saved.

We return to you amidst our cowardice;
there is still a long way to go.
Teach us to persevere to the end,
and we shall be saved.

SATURDAY OF THE 14TH WEEK

FEARLESS HEARTS

Isaiah 6:1–8. The account of Isaiah's call serves as an introduction to the literary unit that usually goes by the name of "The Book of Immanuel" and is a collection of some of the most important messianic oracles. But in this passage there is much more than the recollection of a call; it also contains the essence of the prophet's preaching: on the one hand, the irruption of the thrice holy God into a human life; on the other, the clear insight of this man as he acknowledges himself to be a sinner. Thus, in the year of King Uzziah's death (probably around 740 B.C.) this man who was soon to show himself a prophet of exceptional temper became aware of the abyss separating God from his creatures. In the depths of his own being he perceived how the human person is divided, dislocated as it were by sin, and this experience matched that of the people to whom Isaiah belonged and with whom he proclaimed himself to be in profound solidarity. However—and this is also an essential element in Israelite religion—this perception never led to an unhealthy sense of guilt, but was accompanied rather by an unreserved faith in Yahweh. For while God will not tolerate evil in any form, he is able to purify the human person of evil. Better still— and the prophet's own call is proof of it—this God wants to be present to the world and to bind himself to human beings by a common history.

Psalm 93 is an enthronement song. It must orignally have been sung in the processions that brought the ark of the covenant back in triumph after a victory over an enemy. The formula "Yahweh is king" was at first an independent one; it was connected with the proclamation of a military victory. After the cult was centralized in Jerusalem, this song became one

337

of the liturgical formularies for the Feast of Booths.

Matthew 10:24–33. Cf. p. 99.

■

God does not call men and women because of their character or human gifts; he makes Apostles of the timid as well as of the impetuous, and to all of them he says: "Do not be afraid!" Yes, whoever we may be, "our help is in the name of the Lord."

Isaiah is conscious of his unworthiness. God is holy, while Isaiah belongs to an unclean people. How can his lips proclaim the word unless God purifies them? But once God has sanctified him, the prophet hesitates no longer. "Here I am; send me." No boasting here but simply a consciousness of the living God. An Apostle never labors for his own interests.

This is why he is able to banish fear. He knows the kind of treatment that awaits him, but he knows even more surely that God cannot abandon him. He knows our value in the Father's sight.

We were unclean, soiled, sinful. But in his resurrection Christ made of us his body. Our words are henceforth his; we bear witness to him and not to ourselves. His holiness constantly purifies our weakness. The only serious sin that could condemn us would be to deny before men him who is our salvation. But if we persevere in faith, nothing will ever be able to keep our uncleanness from being burned up and sanctified in the great fire of love of God. This we can proclaim publicly, without boasting but also without reserve.

■

Holy God, thrice holy God,
  who are we to utter your name?
We have profaned your love;
  we have concealed our faith
  as one might conceal a dangerous child.
But you, who are a forgiving God,
  have made your name holy
  in Jesus, your Word who is never concealed.

338

May he, our Savior, be blessed,
for despite our unworthiness
he has entrusted us
with his name and yours before men.

O God, do not cease to send us,
and everywhere we shall sing to our brethren
the hymn to your mercy
which the angels and seraphim
sing throughout eternity:
"Holy, holy, holy
is Yahweh Sabaoth.
His glory fills the whole earth."

MONDAY OF THE 15TH WEEK

A THIRST-QUENCHING RELIGION

Isaiah 1:11–17. On reading this oracle many will ask whether the prophet is not radically rejecting all cultus. But in fact Isaiah is not attacking liturgy as such; he is rather stating some criteria of discernment. Too many Jews—Jesus would utter the same reproach—believed that the presence of the temple in Jerusalem guaranteed them an automatic salvation. The prophet therefore calls for an authentic worship, that is, one that is nourished by the way life is lived. Far from multiplying hypocritical rites, religious persons must make life itself a liturgy pleasing to God (cf. Rom 12:1), for God cannot find pleasure in both crimes and feasts.

Psalm 50 has the ring of an indictment. Because it attacks violations of the covenant, scholars like to link it with the traditions of the Shechem sanctuary. The verses used in the liturgy make it clear, however, that what is being rejected is not the cultus as such but religious hypocrisy.

Matthew 10:34–11:1. Cf. p. 109.

■

Who is it that falsifies a human being

if not he who scorns his thirst for justice?

But a cup of cold water
given in the name of the Lord
can, by itself, change evil into good.

Let your righteousness therefore leap forth
like a spring of living water
amid the wilderness of falsified human beings.

■

We may end up feeling uneasy on reading Isaiah and the other prophets, especially when we read them in the course of the liturgy. If God really looks with horror on our incense, our assemblies, our solemnities, would it not be better to abandon our churches and struggle for justice in the world? After all, is not the important thing to do justice to the orphan and defend the widow (remembering, of course, that nowadays the orphan and the widow may take the form of those who are hunted down by society or of the handicapped and rejected)? "Bring the oppressor to heel," God says; is not that the true liturgy?

Nor does the Gospel speak a different language. Jesus prides himself on bringing a sword into the world and division into families. Obviously, incense has never started a war. A public worship that is calm and peaceful, as devotional as we like, and remote from the struggles of human beings, suits us better than this general mobilization of the disciples for the elimination of oppressors. But are we wrong here? Should we really feel so guilty for resting a moment in God, in the shadow of his temple? Must we be constantly up and doing battle?

Surprisingly, the Gospel is familiar with a different temple and a different kind of rest, with a liturgy full of peace and self-abandon. "Anyone who welcomes you welcomes me . . . . If anyone gives so much as a cup of cold water to one of these little ones, because he is a disciple, he will most certainly not lose his reward." A cup of water and a warm welcome, an act of faith in the word of an Apostle, and, lo, a simple home is transformed into a church in which God is present. For God needs no other sacrifice than that. The liturgy of the

Gospel consists first and foremost in faith and love.

What both Isaiah and the Gospel condemn is the continual lack of coherence between our prayers and our manner of life. The peace of God is not an evasion, not even a liturgical evasion; the only peace of God is the peace Christ won on the cross. Evidently this peace is a sword in the human heart and cannot make concessions even to family ties. And, we must add, neither can this peace, which is celebrated in every sacrament, make any concessions to liturgies in which there is no real human commitment.

If in church we speak of peace but refuse to change our lives so as to bring justice to the unfortunate, then, yes, God will shrink in horror from our incense. On the other hand, what peace fills even the humblest dwelling in which the word of God is taken seriously and with faith! The peace in that house has in it the savor of a cup of cold water in midsummer.

■

Let your word, Lord,
  be the light of our lives,
and even if its cutting edge
  must cause the loss
  of what enchained us,
be gracious and grant us
  to save our life
  by following you unwaveringly,
for you bring justice to the poor
  and defend the rights of the oppressed.

TUESDAY OF THE 15TH WEEK

EMMANUEL AT CAPERNAUM

Isaiah 7:1–9. "A large army will not keep a king safe . . . it is delusion to rely on the horse for safety" (Ps 33:16–17). The times are difficult ones for the little kingdoms of Palestine. Assyria is a heavy sword held over their heads, and the kings of Syria and Israel are urging their colleague in Jerusalem to join them in a coalition against the enemy. The king of Judah at first refuses, but when he sees the armies of the coalition camped outside the walls of Jerusalem, he panics, all the more so since the internal situation of the country is likewise unfavorable to him and an opposition party led by the son of Tabeel is becoming a threat. The king is now ready to ask for Assyrian help, doubtless to be bought by a heavy payment of tribute.

Isaiah cannot tolerate the idea that national independence may be lost, for this would show contempt for the promises Yahweh had made to the house of David. The prophet seeks out the king as the latter is examining the fortifications, and he urges upon the king confidence in the divine word. Who after all are Razon and Pekah? What do these two amount to as compared with a child? For the divine pledge comes in the form of a child: today the prophet's own son with his name indicating a predestination; tomorrow the Messiah, the sign of God-with-us. While human beings are always tempted to put their trust in force, God puts his in a child, for the child is the human race's future.

Psalm 48 is one of the songs of Zion. The principal subject developed in these in the protection Yahweh gives to his city. Enemies may be leagued against it but it is inviolable. The songs of Zion may have been used for the Feast of Booths, which was connected with the victories Israel had won over its enemies. The ark was conducted in triumph to the sanctuary, while the flight of the hostile armies was represented in a ritual drama (cf. vv. 5–8).

Matthew 11:10–24. Cf. p. 114.

■

Just look at King Ahaz, shaken as forest trees are shaken by the wind, because two enemies, two smoldering stumps of fire-brands, have come up to attack Jerusalem. As if the city of God owed its strength to human victories! And as if it were the power of a king that was to save the world! Take stock, rather, of your own weakness, Ahaz, for salvation will come from a child when everything is brought to completion. A child whose name is "A remnant will return," "Emmanuel."

God is not concerned with the strength of human beings or their reputation or their skill. Capernaum was a rich commercial city, a crossroads near the frontier, a strong city. But when the voice of God within its walls adopted the accents of a child and began to denounce riches and call sinners back, the city shut its ears, and the springtime of the Gospel made way for the hot toil of summer, in preparation for a harvest in which the grain of wheat would be the sacrificed body of the only Son. Capernaum refused to put its faith in a poor God, for what then would be left of its glory? Was it then that people began to speak of "a precious Capernaum" in derision of heaped-up wealth for which there was no future?

God is not concerned with the reputation of human beings, for their past and for all their claims to salvation. If Sodom believes in God, it will be saved despite the sin of the Sodomites, which is less serious than the unbelief of my people, says God. And if it pleases me someday to call a Cyrus, a pagan king, to save my people, then I am free to do it, says God.

Meanwhile, stop trembling, Ahaz; and stop your panicking, all you who see the Church in the snares of its enemies. There is no salvation except in the name of the Lord. Look rather at what God is doing for the human race in his Son who is always present among the poor, and believe in the good news. Believe in the Gospel and be converted, lest on the day of judgment you suffer a fate worse than that of Bethsaida and Chorazin.

■

In you, Lord, is our strength
  and our hope.
When we are harried
  and your Church is taken by assault,
we cry out unceasingly to you:
  You are our salvation
  in your Son Jesus, our Lord.

343

CHILDREN UNDERSTAND

Isaiah 10:5–7, 13–16. This oracle against Assyria anticipates the collection of prophecies against the pagan nations in Chapters 13—23, and amounts to a negative summation of Assyria's conquests. What is the reproach leveled against the conqueror (probably King Sennacherib)? That he had mistaken himself for God when in fact he was only God's instrument; that he took himself for the worker when in fact he was only the "axe" or the "saw." The prophet thus offers a critical interpretation of the political events of his time.

Israel's conduct had earned it punishment, and it was Israel's powerful neighbor who was to administer it. But whereas in the prophet's eyes Sennacherib was only the instrument of God's anger, the king thought of himself as acting on his own initiative. It is with this folly that he is now reproached; he has gone beyond the bounds of the mission Yahweh had entrusted to him. He should have been content with pillaging Israel and forcing it to pay tribute; instead he took advantage of the situation to wipe out neighboring nations. With his conquests and massive deportations he has attacked the cosmic order by eliminating frontiers. He must therefore be punished in turn: Assyria will be destroyed; only a "remnant" will remain (v. 19).

Psalm 94 in its present form joins some verses of a sapiential kind (vv. 7–11) to a individual lament. After having drawn God's attention to the ravages which pagan nations have inflicted on the Jewish people, the Psalm denounces the stupid thinking of those who do not take God seriously.

Matthew 11:25–27. Cf. p. 117.

■

On Psalm 94

All you of upright heart, applaud!
All you who thirst for justice, rise up!
In vain have they slain the Innocent One,
for God has not spoken his final word.

Sooner or later the narrow-minded will understand:
God grant it may not be too late.

■

God does not disdain intellect, but he has no use for those "sharp minds" that claim for themselves a glory that belongs to him.

The Assyrian king represents the martial, military mind and political wisdom. God makes use of this in order to teach his people a lesson. Very good—but what stupidity on the part of this king who believes he has won the victory by his own strength! What a fool! Soon he and all his glory will be reduced to ashes.

The scribes represent the theological and moral mind, the wisdom that comes from books. God has made use of them in order to keep his people on the right path. Very good—but what stupidity on the part of these scribes who claimed for themselves the glory of a morality of which they were only the trustees! What fools! So swollen with pride had their books made them that they did not even listen to the voice of the Son of God.

Mere children did understand; they listened to the word and recognized Jesus as Son of the Father. Their hearts opened wide to the revelation of the mystery hidden in God. They are happy, and Jesus can give glory to God for them.

How wonderful the action of the grace of God's Son! But do we realize to what extent this grace throws down the mighty from their thrones and the learned from their professorial chairs? The reason for this overthrow is that the mighty and the learned are unable to give thanks; their very strength keeps them from it. Only the child, the poor person, who is open to the new and unexpected, can join Jesus in singing the praises of God who has concealed the whole mystery of the world in the secret of his eternal love, where he says to his Son: "All of my love is yours."

■

Father, Lord of heaven and earth,
*   with your Son Jesus*

we proclaim your praises,
for what you hid from the learned and the clever
    you revealed to mere children.
Yes, Father, in your goodness
    you willed it so.
No one knows your Son
    except you, from whom he came to us,
and no one knows you, the eternal God,
    except your Son
    and those to whom he chooses to reveal you.
For this revelation
    made to mere children,
we praise you, Father.

THURSDAY OF THE 15TH WEEK

YOUR YOKE UPON MY SHOULDERS

Isaiah 26:7–9, 12, 16–19. This passage is a prayer or rather a meditation in the manner of Psalm 1. Two ways are open to human beings: the way of uprightness and the way of wickedness. The reading as contained in the lectionary has omitted everything having to do with the second way and preserved only the references to the desires of the just: first, their desire of an interior religion (keeping watch with the Lord day and night) and then their longing for the divine interventions that will be so many occasions for the education of the nations.

But the poem suggests above all the perspective of a national resurrection. It is probable that the people at large did not understand the reason for the sufferings of the time; these sufferings seemed in fact to be entirely useless. The prophet therefore proclaims a message of hope: these sufferings are birthpangs, the prelude to a new world.

Psalm 102 is an individual lament. The verses used in the lectionary list Yahweh's motives for intervening in behalf of his people: first, the favor he has always shown to his capital city; then, echoing the prophet, the reputation he must maintain in the eyes of the pagans.

Matthew 11:28–30. Cf. p. 121.

■

Here is Jesus, far now from Capernaum, traveling the roads with his disciples. He does not tire of calling men and women: "Follow me!" He teaches them; patiently he stakes out the ground for the Church— a Church that has no other foundation but the faith of these little ones.

He speaks to them in a way different from that of the scribes, for his teaching sets them free; they can journey with him without being bowed down under the weight. The law of Christ is simple, and the simple understand it. They can take his yoke upon them, because it is light.

His burden is easy to carry. "Love," says the master, "and go wherever your steps lead you." Not because love takes just any form at all, but because its burden, its demands, are light when everyone helps everyone else to carry them. The Church of Christ draws its vitality from this kind of rivalry.

The scribes for their part lay burdens on shoulders and consciences, but they themselves carry nothing. They leave human beings to their own resources. Jesus is the first to carry the burden of others; he is the first to go wherever his steps lead him. He will go even to the cross, and the Church with him.

But Jesus will never put pressure on the freedom of human beings. His word is gentle and his heart is humble. He proposes and shows the way. In him, men and women can find rest even on the days when love scorches them. For his is the repose of the heart and the soul.

The law of the scribes leaves no repose; it ceaselessly harries, but in the final analysis does not go very far. The person becomes mired in a good conscience or in despair. The Gospel is utterly different; it frees the human heart and brings it true rest—the repose of love.

"Your dew, O Lord," Isaiah said, "is a radiant dew. From daybreak my soul seeks you." Yes, blessed be God!

■

Lord, you are gentle and close to humankind;
  make level the road to which you call us,
  for our souls long constantly for you,
  and we desire to take your yoke upon us.
We have suffered:
  the law and its precepts
  were a burden too heavy to bear,
  and we gave birth only to wind.
Lord, you are righteous,
  and you go before us on the road of love;
lead us to the place of true rest
  where our souls will experience life
  through full abandonment to love.

FRIDAY OF THE 15TH WEEK

THE FREEDOM OF SUNDAY

Isaiah 38:1–8. The Book of Isaiah ends with an appendix of four chapters containing stories about the life of the prophet; they are repeated almost without change from 2 Kings. Chapter 38 reads like a golden legend.

The account here has to do with King Hezekiah who, along with Josiah, is one of the few kings to escape negative criticism in the Books of Kings; he had to endure the campaign undertaken by Assyria in order to ensure its control of the Palestinian corridor leading to the gates of Egypt. The story, which highlights the role and effectiveness of prayer, tells of an illness of the king; because of the illness the prophet advises the monarch to set his affairs in order, but then announces a miraculous healing for him and the deliverance of the country from the Assyrian threat. A sign is given to the king: as the day is miraculously prolonged (the shadow of the sun retreats ten degrees on the sundial or ten steps on the outside staircase leading to the royal chamber), so the life of the king will be prolonged.

Canticle of Hezekiah. It is natural to find some verses used here from the Psalm which the king is supposed to have uttered in the temple after his cure. The canticle takes the form of an individual thanksgiving; the

348

psalmist first describes the distress of the king and then gives thanks for the healing he obtained.

Matthew 12:1–8. Cf. p. 125.

■

Mercy is more important than the temple, and the sabbath may never be turned into an absolute. With a few words Jesus overturns an edifice full of cracks and replaces it with the freedom that love brings. The Son of Man is master of the sabbath, not in order that he may give it added binding power but that he may replace it with a freedom that has its source in God. Can any gesture be freer and more spontaneous than that of nibbling at a few ears of corn while walking amidst God's creation? Even on the sabbath!

This day, the sabbath, was meant to bear witness in Israel to the freedom of God; it was meant to break the alienating rhythm of toil, make human and fraternal contacts possible, and set aside time for praise. At the heart of time, which bears the mark of death, the sabbath was to be the day of life and of the beyond; it was to be a testimony to God as friend of human beings. But what did the Pharisees make of it but a day of universal "low spirits," a kind of premature entrance into death, even though God is life and the unforeseen?

In a sense the Pharisees did not believe in life. Their religion had about it the sadness of shrouds and funeral laments. In vain did they profess some kind of resurrection on the last day, for they did not allow the God of the living to break through now into our present time and to free it even now from the bonds of death. Their sabbaths brought the heavy silence of death upon the world, a silence broken only by laments raised to an impassive God.

Has any more poignant text been written on the drama of death than the extraordinary prayer of Hezekiah? What would death be like if God had not overcome it? Above all, what would it be in the face of a God who could not deliver us from it? "In the noon of my life I have to depart for the gates of Sheol . . . . I shall never look again on any man of those who inhabit the earth. My tent is pulled up . . . . Like a weaver you roll up my life to cut it from the loom." Can God allow

349

this to happen?

The God of the living did not allow it. His Son came forth from the world of the dead and his risen face is our icon of life. We shall no longer die but shall enter into life. That is why our Sundays have nothing in common with the sabbatical rigidity that foreshadowed death without being able to transfigure it; our Sunday is the day of resurrection, and nothing can be dearer to God than to see us free on that day. Yes, on Sunday we love and do what we wish. And during this time of the Church the Pharisees of every persuasion will long continue to lament this freedom.

■

For David, who danced before the ark
  and loved freedom to the point of succumbing to it,
  blessed be you,
  the God who wants mercy and not sacrifices.

For the fields of grain under the sun
  and for the wild freedom of your creation,
  blessed be you,
  the God who gives rest to man so that he may live.

For your Son who rose on Easter morning
  and for his transfigured human face,
  blessed be you,
  the God of our Sundays and our human feasts.

SATURDAY OF THE 15TH WEEK

WITHOUT UPROAR AND WITHOUT INTOLERANCE

Micah 2:1–5. Micah of Moresheth was a contemporary of the prophet Isaiah. The political and social circumstances of his time explain his message. On the international scene Assyria represented a constant threat to the little kingdoms of Palestine. Internally, the rise of the monarchy led to the appearance of a class of parvenus who crushed the poor masses under increasingly heavy taxes. Unlike Isaiah, Micah did not mingle in politics, but strongly denounced social injustices, which he regarded as so many failures to meet the community ideals of the covenant. In his view, punishment would not delay long, for he knew that God does not tolerate injustice. The land would be shared out among the pagans.

Psalm 10 is an alphabetical psalm; it is also an anthology of disparate fragments. The second part, which resembles an individual lament, is directed against the wicked who flout Yahweh and kill the innocent.

Matthew 12:14–21. Cf. p. 128.

■

"The first will be last." The Gospel is not satisfied to draw a moral lesson regarding the emptiness of false greatness; it proposes to us a lifestyle that conforms to God's idea of man: "Anyone who wants to be first among you must be your slave." The social order must be based on a hierarchy of service. Jesus bears witness to this truth by the washing of the feet, which occurs during his farewell meal with the disciples. "I have given you an example so that you may copy what I have done to you."

Almost by compulsion, however, the world develops according to a model in which the powerful oppress and exploit the lowly. At daybreak everyone sets busily about getting all he can from others, even to the point of stripping them, materially or morally, if that is feasible. Worse still, the entire organization of society is against the defenseless, and the poor become daily poorer. The bruised reed is immediately snapped, and the smoldering wick is extinguished. There is no time to be spared for humanitarian hesitations. The spiral of violence and power does not allow it, for he who hesitates to get the better of another knows full well that others are already endeavoring to get the better of him.

Amidst the vast prophetic literature, in which conflict with the injustices of the mighty bulk so large, the mysterious figure of the servant appears. Who is he, this poor man who is loved by God and who without wearying takes the side of the weak to the point of becoming one of them? Who is he? An image of the whole people who are jeered at but then raised up by God? An image of some prophet, for example a Jeremiah who is constantly persecuted? An image of a coming Messiah, of whom one never knows whether he is not already on the scene? Or perhaps all of these simultaneously?

Jesus claimed to be the Servant. He sought no other glorious title but this one. With endless patience he fought for the oppressed and became one of them. He took the last place in order to challenge the mighty and renew the world without owing anything to the tactics of this world. He took the risk of preaching God to humankind and did not withdraw from an infamous death.

This is why, as long as the Gospel is read and lived, as long as the voices of the prophets are heard in the Church, the social model set before Christians will always be utterly opposed to the ways of the world. The risk, of course, is that the power of the Gospel may appear as weak as it must have appeared to the disciples when Jesus washed their feet.

■

Lord, do not forget
  the cries of the unfortunate,
  for the weak rely on you.
Enable your Church
  to be poor and a servant
  for the sake of oppressed mankind.
By sharing their wretchedness
  may we reveal to them
  your presence and your concern for them.

MONDAY OF THE 16TH WEEK

WHAT DOES THE SIGN OF JONAH PROVE?
Micah 6:1–4, 6–8. The prophets often composed their oracles in the style of the courtroom; thus Micah here invites us to an imaginary trial. He calls heaven and earth, which are symbols of stability, to give testimony, and

then he has God and the people speak in succession. Yahweh is the plaintiff; he lists the fatigues he has borne for his people (cf. the "Reproaches" on Good Friday); he brought them out of slavery and gave them leaders.

The people then present their defense, but it is a poor one. The Israelites have reduced the covenant to a set of ritual prescriptions, to the point even of sacrificing infants as the Canaanites did, even though the law actually forbade this infamous practice. All that remains now is to await the verdict. In the name of God the prophet describes what the conduct of the people should be: the cult has meaning only if it is rooted in a life totally consecrated to God.

Psalm 50 is likewise an indictment of the betrayals of which the people have been guilty. Like Micah, the psalmist denounces the stupidity of a cultus that is separated from life.

Matthew 12:38–42. Cf. p. 131.

■

"We should like to see a sign from you." The apparent politeness conceals a sinister demand: the sign or proof will have to be visible, manifest, evident, and must come directly from Jesus so that it will establish his authority. But what sign, what clear proof could Jesus furnish to enemies so set in their pre-determined rejection? No other sign will be given to them except the sign of death and resurrection. But how can such a sign be an evident one? What eyes will be able to see the power of Christ at work in his Easter action? Faith alone can recognize the living Lord, and there is no more faith in the hearts of the Pharisees than there is the kind of good will that can lead them out of their blind alleys.

The Gospel is not proved; it is lived. If Jesus had remained dead and if he had been only a pitiful servant, the Gospel would present its marvelous ideal in vain, for it would not be the word of God. It is Christ's resurrection that bears witness to the perennial power of the Gospel. But this resurrection itself will always depend on our faith: for those who have eyes but do not see, the risen Lord will always be a mirage, and the Gospel a dangerous utopian vision. Thus faith lives in a constant back-and-forth in which the light of Easter illumines the

Gospel message, while at the same time the risen Jesus is able to reveal himself only to those who travel the way of the Gospel with him. A sign is given, but it is a sign that is internal to that which it is to prove. The logic at work here is not like other logics—and with good reason.

The drama of pharisaism is that it reduces religion to a human logic, of a higher kind perhaps but still human. God's work is judged in terms of religious traditions. But Jesus was not a religious man in the traditional mold; he produced an unparalleled revolution in religion, putting mercy and righteousness before sacrifices and the law. He carried to the utmost point the message of the prophets who, like him, were also disturbers of the peace. What proof could he have given except this sign that was located beyond the evidences of religion, namely that death did not overcome him? But this sign does not belong in the realm of logic, even a religious logic. To enter the world of the resurrection one must love. But this was not provided for in the program of the religions, which were much too busy satisfying a God who had nothing to do with such programs. That is why the religions are mortal; one after another they pass away. Only the sign of Jesus remains.

■

Do not go to trial against us, Lord,
  for you alone can come to our aid
  in the unbelief that enslaves us.
Make your risen Son manifest in us,
  for we have no one else
  to plead our cause.
Despite our coarseness
  we love him:
he is our Lord and our Savior.

WITHOUT THE LEAST FAVORITISM

Micah 7:14–15, 18–20. The commentators like to speak of a "liturgy" in connection with these verses. And in fact we do have here four fragments which alternate between an act of faith and a supplication on Israel's part (vv. 7–10 and 14), and a promise of salvation and an announcement of divine marvels on God's part (vv. 11–13 and 15–17), the whole being crowned by a hymn (vv. 18–20). This dialogue between Israel and its God opens up perspectives of hope. The liturgical reading singles out the supplication (Israel wants to regain the rich lands taken by foreigners) and the hymn to the merciful God who now wishes to recall only the promise made on oath to the ancestors.

Psalm 85 is a psalm of national supplication; it mingles professions of trust with reproaches to Yahweh. Will his anger last forever, even though in the past he always gave evidence of his good will to the fathers? The psalm goes on to announce a favorable oracle (vv. 9–14), one that is often repeated during advent.

Matthew 12:46–50. Cf. p. 134.

■

On Psalm 85

A song for the return from exile:

In a distant land,
prisoners behind death's barbed wire,
our companions have already lost
even the meaning of life.

Blessed be God
who has bethought himself of his love:
from the doorless tomb
he has rescued the captives.

They return to the Land
and we sing the hymn of life.

■

To plead our cause shall we invoke some privilege, some ties of blood uniting us to Christ, some membership in the clan of his Church? When a plea thus endeavors to avoid the truth by the subterfuge of favoritism, it can only be condemned without further trial.

I am not saying that the mother and brothers of Jesus tried to take advantage of fleshly ties; besides, what advantage was to be gotten from a relationship with a prophet already rejected by the people higher up? But the Gospel has not been given to us as a pond in which to fish for anecdotes; it is the word of life for us, and it is we who are the real issue.

Is there anyone who has not tried to substitute his or her position for the necessity of doing the Father's will? Has it never happened in the Church that social position was more highly regarded than the duty of charity? Is it fitting, after all, that a prelate should dirty his garments in the blood of the oppressed? Thank God, more than one has done so, for such is the Father's will.

Such, too, is God's family on earth. The disciples, the poor, the peacemakers, those hungry for righteousness are the brothers and sisters of Christ. God has exchanged his own patents of nobility for others derived from the eminent dignity of the poor. At the family table Jesus shares his bread with sinners and outcasts.

But we must add that there is no favoritism shown even to poverty. The poor person who does not do the Father's will is no longer the brother of Christ. But what is the Father's will if not that the poor— and every human being—should trustingly acknowledge their poverty? For those who accept being poor acknowledge at the same time that they look to God for everything. God has no other will than this for us.

It was thus that Mary became fully the mother of God on the day when she said: "I am the handmaid of the Lord"—a handmaid, that is, a poor woman who was henceforth simply one with her Son, a servant and wholly in the hands of the Father. Like every true believer, Mary has no other patent of nobility.

■

356

Father,
  may your will be done
  in us as in your Son Jesus.
May we be his disciples,
  sacrificed to the very end
  for the coming of your Kingdom.
Then our poverty will be transfigured
  into a patent of nobility,
  for we shall be your children
  and heirs of your grace
  that remains forever.

FROM WEDNESDAY OF THE 16TH WEEK
TO SATURDAY OF THE 18TH WEEK

Parables for A New Covenant

Jeremiah: people talk about his "jeremiads," but what would they have done in his place? Most would have gone back and hidden at Anathoth. Besides, Jeremiah did not spend his whole time lamenting. He lived through the dark years that heralded the exile, and he fought against the soothsayers of a false happiness, false prophets who hid the truth lest they have the authorities on their back. His life was like a long parable for a time of crisis.

Jeremiah realized that God could not avoid having to strike a new covenant with his people if he wanted to save his work; he also realized that this new covenant would be a covenant of the heart, a law written into the flesh of human beings, a "new spirit." For the last glorious sparks of the majesty of Sinai were now but ashes; God would have to light a new fire in the hearts of human beings. And Jeremiah said as much, taking the risk of demoralizing the last survivors of the glory now past. The risk could not be avoided.

The Church which Jesus has patiently been gathering since he called the Twelve will not be any different. It will be a Church of the heart and of humility, a Church in which parables take the place of a legal code—in short, a Church in which the most important things find expression in the smallest things: a sower who sows without watching the terrain and risks wasting the seed; a woman who makes the dough rise with a little bit of yeast; a crowd of people drawn by Jesus into the wilderness and five small loaves to feed them; a little dog who gathers up the crumbs; a tiny seed that becomes an immense tree; a bit of faith that is enough to move mountains. Are you familiar with all these? Are you familiar as well with the story of Jeremiah's loincloth, his visit to the potter, his sojourn at the bottom of a well? There are piles of such little stories—stories by which the Church is built. For when the world begins to collapse and exile is near, the Church has no war strategy to propose but rather a renewal of hearts, a new covenant based in new values—and these values will be simply those of everyday life.

It is in this respect that the parables are startling to us: they give expression to the extraordinary by means of the very ordinary. But it is the ordinary seen from its other side, the side that God sees. The right side of the world becomes visible when everything is turned inside out. But few people are able to turn their minds inside out in the same way. This is why the final parable always takes the form of the prophet's death. That too is quite in the ordinary run of things—as ordinary as Jeremiah and Jesus.

■

God, you continue to sow your field;
whether the sun warms our soil
  or night shelters it in its shade,
the seed buried in the cracks of the earth
  is preparing an abundant harvest
  and fruit a hundredfold.
The smallest seed, humble and unobtrusive,
  becomes a majestic tree
  in which men find food and strength to live.

Yes, we believe this:
if the grain of wheat does not die
  it remains alone;
if your Son had not been buried at sowing time,
  the harvest would never have ripened
  that gives us the bread of life.

Christ is the bread we share;
  he is the new wine
  and intoxicating eternal joy.

God, you did not create life
  in order to see it swallowed up by death;
Jesus Christ came to life again on Easter morning,
  and his Spirit renders our vine-shoots fruitful.

Father, we pray:
let your workers sow with generous hand
  the seed of an always unexpected harvest.
Let them work to your patient rhythm
  and not pull up too soon
  the weeds that grow with the grain.
Let them be disinterested and free,
  giving without calculation
  what they received as a free gift from you.
Reward them for their labors:
  may they receive from you
  a wage more abundant
  than the toil they gave so generously.

Through your Spirit heal our hearts of stone,
  that your seed may strike root
  in those who hear your word.
Prune our vines,
  that your fruit may ripen
  for a festive vintage.
And let us be filled with joy
  in Jesus, the first-fruit of a new world.

WEDNESDAY OF THE 16TH WEEK

THE STAMMERER WILL SPEAK

Jeremiah 1:1, 4–10. Jeremiah 36 tells us that in 605 the prophet put together a first edition of his oracles and that this was immediately destroyed by King Jehoiakim. It was probably for this edition that Jeremiah composed the account of his call, in order to give his mission a divine guarantee. In this account the prophet emphasizes the special care with which God set him apart with a view to his future ministry; it was necessary for Jeremiah to enter into a close relationship with him whose messenger to the people he was to be. Moreover, while not hiding his own inexperience, the prophet stresses the support Yahweh gave him. Finally, in a kind of ritual of enthronement, God touches the mouth of Jeremiah, thus entrusting his word to him. The gesture is especially meaningful in the case of this prophet who, more than any other, was a man of the word and devoted his whole life to it.

Psalm 71 is a very beautiful individual lament. It seems to have been written by an old man who, at a time when difficulties assail him, unhesitatingly voices his complete confidence in God. Has not God been his teacher since he was young?

Matthew 13:1–9. Cf. p. 139.

■

On Psalm 71

You see that I cannot speak:
whenever I open my mouth
they persecute and torture me.
Look, Lord, I totter.
A little more, and I would begin to doubt you . . . .
If you were not my rock,
humiliation would long since
have reduced me to nothingness.

■

"I do not know how to speak: I am a child." But it is God's practice to choose what is humanly weak in order to manifest his own power. A prophet too sure of himself would be in danger of regarding as his own a glory that belongs to God. If Jeremiah is not naturally equipped for haranguing crowds, all the more reason for God to choose him and say to him: "I am setting you over nations and over kingdoms." But we still have to try to get inside this prophet's skin and understand what violence God did to him.

A vocation is something quite different from a natural inclination. When taken in its full and undiluted sense, a vocation is a word from God. Those who are to proclaim the word must first hear it as a personal, demanding call. Jeremiah is a man whose consciousness of God is at the very center of his life; he may struggle with this consciousness, but he cannot deny that the hand of the Lord is upon him. A call is a free act of God before being a free human response. Is it a kind of predestination? No, because the human person can refuse, flee, turn his back. But when God asks something, he does not do so on a sudden whim. "Before you came to birth I consecrated you." The prophet can, however, still reject this consecration; in any case, he will understand the hard work it demands.

We have become too accustomed to looking at everything in terms of ourselves, including the things of God. But Scripture shifts our center and surprises us by seeing everything from the vantage point of God. God is at work. His word is being sown far and wide, on all kinds of soil, without regard to expense. Yes, God wastes his energy for the sake of human beings; otherwise he would choose only candidates with natural ability. But his Kingdom is of a different kind, and the workers in the harvest will always have to learn that it is God who has chosen them, and not the other way around. Their incompetence, sustained by the strength of God, is the best test of whether they have learned this lesson.

■

Your eyes are on us, Lord,
and your word anticipates in us
the day of our awakening.
Before we were able to answer you,
you were already calling us
and longing to send us.
Look upon our weakness
and deign to put on our lips
the words that will make clear
how your power shines forth
despite the smallness of our talent.

THERE IS NO WORSE DEAFNESS . . . .

Jeremiah 2:1–3, 7–8, 12–13. These verses contain two oracles, each of which is characteristic of Jeremiah's manner. First, in an oracle of salvation, the prophet recalls the time when Israel cleaved to Yahweh. Like Hosea, and perhaps influenced by him, Jeremiah contrasts the conduct of the people during the exodus with their attitude after the settlement in Canaan. The period in the wilderness now seems like an idyllic time; deliberately forgetting Israel's rebellions back in those days, the prophet remembers only the wonderful things God did.

Second, Jeremiah calls the heavens to bear witness to the present betrayals of his people and especially those of the authorities: the priests whose mission is to interpret the law; the kings; the prophets who dare to speak in the name of alien divinities such as the Baals. The people have forgotten the fountain whence their life comes; they prefer stagnant water and leaky cisterns.

Psalm 36 has been chosen because it too speaks of the "fountain of life." The psalm is a composite one; vv. 6–11, used here, are a hymn to God's fidelity.

Matthew 13:10–17. Cf. p. 143.

■

On Psalm 36

They have forsaken you, Lord,
the fountain of living water,
and dug for themselves cracked cisterns
that hold no water.
But you, the God more precious than love,
are the fountain of all life;
you slake our thirst
in the streams of your paradise.

■

"The mysteries are revealed to you, but they are not revealed to them . . . . They listen without hearing or understanding." Is there a predestination of good and wicked, to the point where "from anyone who has not, even what he has will be taken away"? Is God a sadist, and is it the sole purpose of parabolic language to imprison in their deafness the "poor hearers" of the faith?

All this may surprise us, especially since the parables seem to us to be the simplest and most accessible part of the Gospel. Well, let us begin by becoming conscious of our own deafness. Yes, we too are hard of hearing, and our hearts are coarse. What do we really make of the point, the unexpected sting in each of the parables? How often have we not dulled the striking force of the language of the parables by making it fit in with our sluggish habitual ways?

Recall, for example: "Suppose a man had a hundred sheep . . . ." Is this the normal way for a shepherd to act? Are our hearts spontaneously attuned to such a waste of time and energy for a single lost sheep—one evidently lost by its own fault? Or recall this other one: the darnel and the good grain. Are we spontaneously disposed to let the darnel grow until the harvest? Are we ready to be as patient as God is?

No less than our fathers, we have replaced the fountain of living water with cracked cisterns that do not hold water. We have enclosed the word in lifeless formulas, and God speaks to us in vain. We try to be shrewd, and we have ears only for what suits us. Where has the ardor of the young bride in us disappeared to, our longing to live the Gospel without evasion or accommodation? We look without seeing and we listen without hearing and understanding. "A man had two sons . . . ." We've heard the story a thousand times but never put it into practice. Yet God continues to speak to us in parables. Hear well, and you will be saved.

It is only the children, the humble, the people of no rank who understand. A parable enthuses them and they go away without discussing it. They see and understand. They are happy. Others call them naive. Just like Jesus! Just like two lovers in the wilderness! Just like God who has not forgotten the tenderness of our youth!

Meanwhile the wise, the shrewd, the honorable and the virtuous imprison themselves in total deafness. They lock their treasures in the strongbox of their withered hearts. They tremble with fear of losing everything on the heady paths of the Gospel. But even now they have already lost everything; their hearts are empty and their virtue has faded. They have nothing now. And even that will be taken from them.

■

God of the poor, fountain of living water,
  do not let our stony hearts
  keep your word from gushing up in us.
Open our eyes to your light,
  open our ears to your call,
and restore the ardor of that first springtime.
Let your good news
  be ever fresh in our lives,
  always waiting to be discovered.

FRIDAY OF THE 16TH WEEK

A WORD SOWN ON EVERY SIDE

Jeremiah 3:14–17. Archeological study has shown that the Babylonian invasion brought the complete devastation of the country. In addition, the ark of the covenant had disappeared during the destruction of the temple. All this does not keep Jeremiah from pronouncing an oracle of happiness and picturing a time when there will no longer be any need of the ark, which had been too material a symbol. Henceforth, Yahweh's throne will be the holy city, where the nations will gather. But if this is to come to pass, the people must be converted.

Jeremiah 31. The canticle from this chapter pictures the return from exile, when the people will come as pilgrims to Zion. The pilgrimage seems to be the one for the Feast of Booths, which marked the beginning of the rainy season on which the prosperity of the following year depended.

Matthew 13:18–23. Cf. p. 146.

■

On the Canticle of Jeremiah

To ransom his people
God paid the great price.
To end their mourning
he gave himself even to death.
On the morning of the new day
let dances and processions be held;
let grace be poured out
like light at midday.

■

Our God is not mute; he is not like the idols which have mouths but do not speak. His word has not dried up; our God is not the God of the scribes who imprison the law in their dead books. God still speaks, for he is Word. The Gospel is not a story about yesterday; it is a seed cast daily into the soil, a word meant to bear new fruit until the end of time. The Gospel will never close in on itself, for it is a book that is open to life; it is the word of God for the people of today, a seed cast into any and every soil, a call issued to all hearts. Happy they who hear the word of God and keep it—not in order to preserve it but to multiply it.

Under the old covenant and down until the exile, the ark of the covenant remained in the temple; its sacred presence signified that Israel was before all else the people of the word. But the ark too quickly became a sealed chest; the law degenerated into a set of niggling rules; the living word dashed itself against the stubbornness of its guardians. Then the ark was destroyed with the temple. Henceforth the word of God was in human hands. Jesus Christ, the Word of God, wrote nothing, composed no code.

Brothers and sisters, you are temples of the living God; you are the echo of the word of life. In you the seed has been sown, and the only harvest God will have among men is the fruit you yield. The stony world, which is such an inseparable mixture of good soil and thorns, will be given no word besides your witness. How do you receive the Gospel of Christ? If your soil does not allow the word to take root and bear abundant fruit, then you will be called to account for the world's unbelief. For God now has no other platform from which to be heard.

■

On the path of our lives
  your word, Lord,
  is sown widely, generously.
On the edge of the path,
  at the mercy of our distractions,
  your word has been carried away by the wind:
do not cast us off,
  but lead us further on your way.
On the rocky ground,
  on the stony soil of our carelessness,
  your word has withered for lack of roots:
do not condemn us,
  but lead us further on your way.
Among the thorns,
  strangled by the attraction of riches,
  your word has remained barren:
do not abandon us,
  but lead us further on your way.
Lead us to the land of your grace,
  where our faith, touched at last by your concern,
  will produce for the world
  a superabundant fruit,
  a fruit that remains in eternal life.

SATURDAY OF THE 16TH WEEK

PATIENCE

Jeremiah 7:1–11. The "discourse at the gate of the temple" was uttered in 608, at the beginning of the reign of Jehoiakim. It attacked the illusions which the Jews cultivated because of the presence of Yahweh's temple in their land. The illusions were to be explained by the fact that the political situation was favorable to the little kingdoms of Palestine. On the one hand, the Assyrian threat had ceased; on the other, Babylon, whose star was ascendant, was not yet worrying anyone. As a result, King Josiah, Jehoiakim's predecessor, had pursued a policy of independence; he had increased the nation's territory by recovering the northern provinces and had been actively engaged in centralizing the cult at Jerusalem. Throughout this entire period Jeremiah constantly called attention to the danger from Babylon and therefore to the possibility of an invasion from the north.

The time was not ripe for such preaching, and the prophet was several times accused of defeatism. The confidence of Jewish leaders in their institutions was all the blinder because it was Yahweh himself who had chosen the Davidic dynasty and had settled on Mount Zion as the place of his dwelling among his people. Jeremiah courageously undertook to denounce these false securities. After so many others, he reminded the people that only an interior religion could give meaning to the official cult.

Psalm 84, a composite Psalm, contains a very beautiful pilgrimage song. The psalmist addresses the priests and tells them of his joy at being in the house of the Lord. The song is generally assigned to the final decades of the monarchy; it seems to show that the centralization of the cult had by now been brought to pass.

Matthew 13:24–30. Cf. p. 149.

■

There are many forms of intolerance, but all are based on a good conscience and the rejection of "others." Jeremiah was persecuted because the good conscience of those in authority could not allow him to denounce the injustice of the secure and the thoughtlessness of the politicians. In the parable of the darnel Jesus condemns the excessive self-assurance of those who seek to reject the "wicked" because they themselves are good. There is intolerance on both sides. "Let them both grow till the harvest," Jesus says.

God has never met the intolerance of human beings and believers with an intolerance of his own. The history of the chosen people is a long litany of God's forgivenesses. The story of Jesus is that of a cross

367

on which the Father's Mercy made flesh dies after long patience. But what is this harvest in which the harvester will at last remove the darnel from his field?

The harvest takes place daily during these last times, because the risen Christ has received all power and all authority over the world from the Father. "But," you say, "we find darnel every day; every day the enemy pillages our land." True, but every day God also sends workers into his harvest. It is not, however, a harvest as the world understands harvests.

The darnel is separated from the good grain because God recognizes his own. And this is his work, not ours. It is useless to cry "The sanctuary of Yahweh!" or "The Church and all its privileges!" God recognizes his own; he prunes his vine and purifies his soil. For our part, let us practice righteousness, follow the path of the Gospel, avoid oppressing the immigrant; let us come to the aid of the innocent, and let us pray God to recognize us in accordance with our merits and also in accordance with our poverty. For the darnel is pride, and the good grain is the grain that dies in the earth so as to bring forth fruit—a fruit of humility and grace.

■

When the enemy ravages our work,
  keep us, Lord, from all intolerance,
  for you are patient
  and carry on your work in accordance with your mercy.

When the darnel invades our hearts,
  keep us from all impatience,
  for you know us better than we do,
  and you never close the door of forgiveness.

When nothing is any longer clear to us in this world,
  keep us from all discouragement,
  for you begin over and over again,
  and you bring good out of evil.

LITTLE THINGS ALL

Jeremiah 13:1–11. An allegory or a symbolic action? Opinions differ on the point. Jeremiah buys a loincloth and ties it around his waist, but does not wash it in order that sweat and dirt may finally make it deteriorate. When this has happened, he goes to the Perath (a Hebrew word usually meaning the Euphrates but here perhaps referring simply to the Wadi Fara, an hour's walk from the prophet's native town) and hides the loincloth in a hole in the rock. "Many days afterward" the prophet returns to the Perath and sees that the loincloth has rotted completely.

The loincloth is Judah and Jerusalem. The Lord had attached himself to his people just as one ties a loincloth around one's waist. Yet, despite Yahweh's tender love for it, Judah had separated itself from him and gone off to rot through contact with Babylonian idolatry.

If this was a real action performed by the prophet, we must be sure to grasp its full weight of meaning, for according to the mind of that age such actions were not simply external illustrations but rather affected the future just as the prophetic word did. In fact, such actions derived their effectiveness from the power of the divine word which they suggested.

Deuteronomy 32. This canticle, attributed to Moses, illustrates the meaning of Jeremiah's gesture. Judah has forgotten the Rock of Israel that gave it birth; it has abandoned the Rock for empty idols.

Matthew 13:31–35. Cf. p. 154.

■

"Listen to this further parable! As a man ties a loincloth around his waist, I bound myself to Israel. Holding it to me, I embraced it and guided it. And now? Just as an abandoned loincloth finally rots, so the pride that rejects my tender love is condemned to rot, says the Lord."

God's love for his people is comparable to many things, but they are all small and insignificant, without pride or haughtiness—a mustard seed, a bit of yeast, a loincloth, an unobtrusive pearl, a love that makes no show, an everyday tenderness: little things all, but they suppose affection, patience and faith.

It is true that love of God can seem a little thing to us. We dream of glorious actions; we dream above all of being free, free with an isolated freedom—as if tenderness and the long patience of the grain cast into the soil took freedom away, as if to be free meant to accomplish everything, immediately, all by ourselves. Freedom is in fact the royal gift of God the Creator, the secret hidden from the beginning, the seed buried in the inmost recess of our life. To be free is to live according to the rhythm of God. But pride seeks to ravage everything and corrupt it.

Listen carefully to the parable. Is any bread more tasty than the loaf in which a woman placed a bit of yeast and which with loving eyes she watched rise, because it was to be the daily bread of her family? Is any jewelry more beautiful than the love of God in which we are clad? Is any secret more wonderful than the one hidden from the beginning when God saw man's astonishment at being free and loved?

On the other hand, is there any pride more rotten than that which grows impatient and grumbles: "The seed is sorry stuff, the earth too frozen. God is of no use. I will be my own God"? "Amen, I tell you, such pride as this will rot away and will render unclean everyone who comes in contact with it, and my people, who were willing to listen to me, will perish before spring comes and the new bread is broken."

For the love of the Lord is a bread that rises patiently and fills the house with its odors of spring. The bread of Easter and a leaven for the world: a humble sign hidden from hearts hardened by pride.

■

You are the grain sown in the earth,
  you are the yeast that gives life
  and makes the bread rise on our table;
you, Lord, are this bread broken
  and you are the seed of a new world.
Do not let pride harden us;
  let us rather be like you,
  a leaven and a hope for the world,
  a seed and a future for our earth.

IN THE SUNSHINE OF THE FINAL EVENING

Jeremiah 14:17–22. Chapter 14 tells of a penitential liturgy celebrated on the occasion of a prolonged dry spell. Vv. 2–9 and 19–22 are a good example of a national lamentation, which ordinarily contains a series of reproaches directed against Yahweh, a description of the misfortunes of the nation, and accusations, sometimes quite strong, against the enemy. The verses used in today's liturgy contain, in effect, reproaches that are formulated as questions (v. 19), together with a plea for help that is presented as a bit of blackmail exerted on God: Yahweh must help his people or he will become the laughing-stock of Israel's enemies (cf. v. 20).

Vv. 17–18 belong to a different literary genre; they imitate the Psalms of individual supplication. Presented as oracles of Yahweh, they describe the unhappy situation of the country and may mean that God suffers at seeing his people thus ravaged.

Psalm 79 is a Psalm of collective supplication, with a long prayer of petition and a promise to give thanks when the prayer has been heard.

Matthew 13:36–43. Cf. p. 157.

■

On Psalm 79

Your people are exhausted;
do you not hear the cries of the prisoners?
Must we pay to the bitter end
the price for our past sins?
Must we experience death
in order at last to be able to bless you?
God, do not delay!
God, save us!

■

Each day God recognizes his own and prepares for his harvest, but this harvest will be determined once and for all on the last day when this world ends and all things come to light. On that day, the just will shine like the sun, while those who have spent their time knocking down their brothers and sisters will end in the blazing furnace in which the noxious weeds and the darnel are burned. For evil is not eternal, and God owes it to himself to encourage the upright by a promise that in the end truth will be established. After all, of what use is it to be patient with the darnel if the good grain is never to be separated out and to produce a bread of gladness? God's patience would be meaningless if he were never to acknowledge the good and bring it out fully into the light. God cannot declare justified those who knock others down.

"For your name's sake . . . for the honor of your name . . . remember us!" We are not better than our brothers and sisters, we have profaned your covenant, we are sons and daughters of the evil one, but has not Christ saved us by his cross? How terrible if on the last day the Son of Man must be ashamed of those who have been sealed with his name! For if God judges, he does so unwillingly, and he will do everything he can to win our conversion. Let us begin therefore by imploring this conversion as a grace, an act of divine power. God alone can change our hearts, but he demands that we ask him to do it. However low we have fallen, our prayer will always be the door that opens to the final grace.

"Just God, God just and good, show us your righteousness, and as long as the time for conversion lasts, come and transform us. Let the darkness of our sins be changed into the light of dawn, as we await the day when the sun of your justice shines fully upon us."

■

Can it be, Lord,
   that you are fed up with us
   and are losing patience
   before the day of harvest?
Are you not our Father
   and, despite our sins,
   are we not the children of your grace?

Yes, have mercy, we pray you:
   for the honor of your name

grant us conversion
and enable us to await without fear
the day when all will be light,
because you will judge us as your heart dictates,
provided we have not ceased
to place our trust in you.

WEDNESDAY OF THE 17TH WEEK

SEDUCTION

Jeremiah 15:10, 16–21. No prophet has told us more about his interior life than Jeremiah, for he has left us his moving "confessions." The thing that strikes us most forcibly on reading these testimonies is the man's loneliness. He was unmarried and had no child; he was rejected by everyone, including his relatives. He was "a man of strife and of contention for all the land." And yet this isolation was not due to any natural disposition in the prophet's makeup; it came from outside, as it were.

An inner power took possession of him and exerted a tyrannical sway. This power was that of the word of God that forced itself upon him. He seemed like a hunted man: wherever he went, whether he was willing or not, he had to deliver his message. This was his responsibility, and he was unwilling to evade it. His only support in his loneliness was the one who compelled him to speak: God himself.

Psalm 59, an individual lament, continues Jeremiah's reflections. It expresses interior torment but also profound trust in the God who dwells within his word.

Matthew 13:44–46. Cf. p. 161.

■

On Psalm 59
God is our citadel,
a rampart against ambush;
he is our strength

against those who attack us.
His love is mightier
than a fortified wall.
Blessed be God, our Rock!

■

A man has been seduced and henceforth will have no rest. For the sake of a word that has seized hold of him, he has sold everything and naively set out on a journey from which there is no return. Everyone makes fun of him; they jeer at him and seek to make him wretched, for anyone who has found the rare pearl immediately becomes the object of envy. And anyone who gives his life to God becomes suspect, especially when he is compelled to speak words that upset everyone else. My mother, why did you give me birth? Why did I not live a quiet life, possessing no treasure, making no discoveries? Why have I been seduced if it means being rejected by everyone? An incurable wound is my burdensome solitude.

Yes, God is a loneliness and a wound at the heart of the human person. He seduces, and it is like a rape; he speaks, and soon there is constant thunder. He comes to us like a hidden treasure, but as soon as we have sold everything in order to possess him, we are shunted aside. God gives himself to us as happiness, but his is the happiness of the persecuted; he gives himself as promise, but the promise is of the cross. He demands everything and seems to give nothing. How could one fail to say: "God, let me turn back to a sheltered life in the company of my fellows."

Yet we must continue onward, constantly selling everything down to the last penny and desiring no other wealth than this presence that scorches the soul. We must let ourselves be consumed. For joy is always further on; it is not a mirage, but it does lie beyond all the adulterated happinesses, after a long wilderness has been crossed. The joy of God is our rampart, but we must start again from scratch if we are to experience it. God is not a religious pastime; he is the Wholly Other, the Inaccessible One; he is happiness in its pure state.

Happy the man or woman who, with Jeremiah and with Jesus, experiences the fire that will purify one's very soul. It is at the moment when all seems lost that we will know the joy that lies beyond all happiness—the joy of resurrection, an infinite treasure that is worth crossing the long wilderness of poverty and bearing the infinite loneliness of encounter with God.

■

We thank you,
  tenderly loving Father,
  through Jesus Christ, your Beloved.
He is the pearl that gleams in the rising sun
  and contains all the treasures
  of knowledge and wisdom.
He is the imcomparable joy
  of those who seek him without wearying
  and find him hidden in their own depths.
For those who have found him
  this world holds no other treasure,
  for he alone can fulfill their hopes.

THURSDAY OF THE 17TH WEEK

A POTTER AND SOME FISHERMEN

Jeremiah 18:1–10. Another symbolic action: Jeremiah is told by the Lord to go to the potter's house and meditate on this craftsman's work. The prophet sees that the worker is master of his product; if a vessel turns out poorly, the potter breaks it and uses the material to fashion a new one.

From this Jeremiah concludes that the peoples of the earth, and Israel in particular, are in the hand of God. If Israel refuses to be converted, Yahweh will smash it, as a potter smashes a vessel that turns out poorly. If on the contrary the people are converted, Yahweh will decorate the vessel and sell it for a good price.

Psalm 146 is a hymn comprising quite disparate elements. The verses used here include, in addition to a bit of hymn (vv. 1–2), some sayings of a sapiential kind (vv. 3–4) which recommend that we put our trust in God.

Vv. 5–9 form a Psalm of congratulation, of which the liturgy cites the opening Beatitude.

Matthew 13:47–53. Cf. p. 164.

■

On Psalm 146
Work for our God,
let his hand direct you.
Rely upon his love,
and your hearts will abide in joy.

■

A bit of clay in the Creator's hands, a deep breath from the Father's inmost being: such is man, a masterpiece in perpetual danger, today a marvel of creativity, tomorrow a poor lifeless rag. And what can we possibly say when we see a crowd of men and women gathering? A flock bleating according to the whim of the mob, or a splendid kingdom of peace and inventiveness? It depends on the day on which you see them, and there is no telling in advance. Like fishermen in the night, you cast your net into the sea and you pull out fish of every kind, delicious and worthless. It depends on the day and on the night. In the morning, human beings set out to war against one another, and in the evening they repent and talk only of peace. After all, it *is* of human beings that I am speaking. Instability reigns. Someday the angels will have to come and put things in order.

"Have you understood all this?" Jesus asks his disciples, the future Fathers of the Church. "Yes," they answer in chorus. But there are no illusions, at least on Jesus' side. As on the morning of creation, these twelve men are only a bit of clay enlivened by a mighty breath from God. Will the Spirit be victorious in them so as to bring into a being a Church that is open to everyone? Or will the weight of the flesh be so great that men will talk of the Church in the pitying tones one uses of a fossilized mammoth found in some Siberia? But as long as the Church is made up of human beings, we know for sure that we will find in it fish of every kind. Or, to put it better, the Church will perhaps always contain new and old, renewal and dead weight, sadness and grace. And every scribe who becomes a disciple of the Kingdom is warned in advance: the Church is not a dream; it is marked by the realism of God made flesh. Such realism is the only optimism that has perdured since the days of creation. Like a patient potter, God daily turns again to his work, his masterpiece: man. He daily gathers his imperilled masterpieces in his home, the Church, which he is determined not to turn into a museum of antiques. His Church is rather to be a vast body that is never in perfect health but also never completely dead. It is to be a Church made up of human beings.

Is it God's fault if on the last day there will be things "that are of no use" and that must be thrown into the sea or the furnace? But in fact is there anything really worthless to the unwearying potter who is God?

■

God the Creator, we are in your hands,
  and your Church unites in one body
  all of us poor sinners.
Do not forsake the work of your hands;
  take pity on the body of your Son
  and deign to give us new life through your Spirit.
Let the great patience you show to man, your child,
  give rise in the Church to a song of praise
  that will bear witness before the world
  to the glory of your love and your grace.

FRIDAY OF THE 17TH WEEK

TOO ORDINARY A PROPHET
Jeremiah 26:1–9a. Chapter 26 provides the historical context for Jeremiah's oracle against the Jerusalem temple (cf. v.7; see Tuesday of the 16th Week). In that indictment the prophet did not attack the temple as such but rather the false security the Jews derived from the fact that God's

temple stood on their nation's soil.

Like his predecessors, Jeremiah fought for a religion that involves the whole person. What God wants is the circumcision of the heart and a communion of love in which human beings live up to the terms of the covenant. Jesus will show the way to this goal by making of his death on the cross "a holy sacrifice, truly pleasing to God" (Rom 12:1).

But the Jews were not converted, and the prophetic oracle was fulfilled when the Babylonian armies destroyed the temple. On that day, the Jerusalem temple experienced the same fate as the sanctuary at Shiloh, which the Philistines had razed about 1050.

Psalm 69 is an individual lament. It gives admirable expression to the prophet's feelings as he thought how useless his preaching was. No one was willing to listen to him, and his enemies were even turning to threats.

Matthew 13:54–58. Cf. p. 171.

■

A prophet, a Christ, back in his country and among his own people. He upsets them; his words show no respect for accepted norms. People talk about him and even plan his destruction. Why does Jeremiah threaten the temple with destruction instead of praising it? How can Jesus work miracles, when everyone knows his mother, his brothers and sisters, his clan? Really, the astonishing astonishes only when it comes from what ought to remain part of the everyday, keeping its place, presenting no problems. When prophets come to us as unknowns, we are not surprised when they say outrageous things. But how can people from our own midst talk that way? Jeremiah, your prophecies are nothing but jeremiads. You would do better to say your prayers in the temple like everyone else. Jesus, you shock us with this Son of God business. You would do better to go back home to your mother and live like everyone else. Like everyone else: that is, without questioning everything.

But faith is precisely a calling into question. A belief in what is obvious is not faith. If a prophet sings the same song as everyone else, there is no question of believing him, and if Jesus were a scribe properly trained in the theological schools, there would be no question of putting one's trust in him. You put your trust only in

378

someone who astonishes, confuses, calls into question. That is why so many pious people are unbelievers—very pious but with little belief. You need only look at their faces when a prophet begins to call everything into question in order to give new life to a shaky faith. All the pious folk are shocked, unless, of course, the prophet comes in the form of a fakir or a brahman.

On that day, Jesus, astonished at their lack of faith, "did not work many miracles." What astonishes me is that he worked any at all. But doubtless there were in the village a few people naive enough to believe in him. And what would one not do for such people as that? Happy the simple of heart! But this means that miracles are linked to faith. That is only natural, of course, since miracles too are a calling into question. And undoubtedly there is no greater miracle than to see, even today, simple people putting their faith in Jesus, even though we are so well acquainted with his brothers, his priests, and his prophets, all of them people from among ourselves, people to whom we so often feel like saying: "Shut up, Jeremiah! How soon do you intend to stop upsetting us with your prophecies? We know you well: you're no better than anyone else."

Christ's great miracle is that his name is still blessed in his Church, where faith has long since shriveled like a wild ass' skin. That faith is still alive despite so many lugubrious souls.

■

We have silenced your prophets,
and your word sleeps under our ashes:
  O Christ, revive our faith.

We have not recognized your face,
and your Church is dying in our cold night:
  Jesus, give light to our paths.

You came to us and we scorned you;
your house is shut up and in mourning:
  Lord, open our hearts
  and heal your dormant people.

PROPHETS AND THE AUTHORITIES

Jeremiah 26:11–19. The other prophets and the temple priests attack Jeremiah because by castigating the people for their confidence in the solidity of their institutions he is undermining national unity and, in the final analysis, denying Yahweh's own choice of Mount Zion as the site of his earthly dwelling. It is also a fact that the threat from Babylon is for the time being too vague to make an impression on the rulers of the country. Nonetheless it cannot be said that the prophet's preaching finds no echo; there are those who side with him and will remain faithful to the end.

It is hard to avoid seeing a parallel between Jeremiah and Jesus. Both men pleaded for a religion of the heart; they attacked the unjustified claims of their contemporaries and were persecuted for it. Jeremiah before his judges is an anticipation of Jesus before the Sanhedrin. The word of God is on trial in both cases.

Psalm 69 is used again, this time for its trusting prayer to God who sustains those faithful to him. The Psalm ends with a promise to celebrate the praise of Yahweh.

Matthew 14:1–12. Cf. p. 174.

■

If Jesus is in fact John the Baptist risen from the dead, then he can perform miracles. That is how Herod thought. The sensational calls for the sensational. As for imagining that the Baptist had risen from the dead, it took Herod's morbid sense of guilt to accept such an idea. When Jesus is finally brought before him at the time of the passion, Herod will see in him nothing but a fool, because now this Jesus is on his way to death. An inevitable death: the death of prophets who are guilty of attacking the authorities with their stories that will not stand up to examination. Like Pilate and so many others, Herod will wash his hands of the affair, and not even the supposed resurrection of Christ will upset these men. True enough, no one brings the head of Jesus to them on a platter. The unobtrusiveness of the eucharistic table has never disturbed the authorities, except precisely when prophets appeal to the body of the Lord in proclaiming the emptiness of this world and demanding justice in the name of the poor. Then the Eucharist becomes dangerous.

Meanwhile, the Baptist shares in advance in the passion of Christ, for the servant is not greater than the master, and anyone who wishes to bear witness to the truth of God must know that he will be jeered by his fellows. An unbroken line runs from Jeremiah to Jesus, and from Jesus to the Church of our day. The passion of Christ is at the center of human history—tragically so, because today as in the past it is most often the ruling authorities who reject the message of the prophets, while the religious authorities are hardly exceptions to this rule. Herod will find support from the priests and scribes in getting rid of this Jesus, this excessively troublesome Galilean. And Pilate in his turn will have no trouble handing Christ over to the leaders of the people. A man need only prophesy against the established order, and all with one voice will decree that he deserves to die—and they will do this without even asking themselves whether the order they want to preserve may not be the worst kind of disorder in the sight of God, a God who wills righteousness and justice. Nor did Herod bother to inquire whether the promise he gave was not the worst kind of blasphemy. After all, he had Herodias. Others possess wealth, renown, religion. That is enough to justify them ridding themselves of an innocent man whose only wrong is to say aloud what really goes on.

■

Blessed be you, Lord our God,
 Father of the poor and Justice of the persecuted.
Blessed be you for Jeremiah your prophet,
 and for John the Baptist,
 a witness to truth even to martyrdom.
Blessed be you today still
 for so many men and women,
 known and unknown,
 who dare defy the order of the mighty
 in order to speak and practice
 the words of the Gospel.
Blessed be you,

and may you deign to preserve us in the faith;
may our actions bear unwavering witness
  to the word we received
  on the day when we became
  disciples and apostles of your Son Jesus
who is your Justice and Truth
  for our world.

MONDAY OF THE 18TH WEEK

WHEN GENEROSITY IS NO LONGER ENOUGH

Jeremiah 28:1–17. There has been development in the political situation. Babylon has imposed its rule on the Near East, and King Jechoniah, successor to Jehoiakim, has been sent into exile with his relatives and several thousand Judeans, among them Ezekiel. On the throne of Jerusalem Nebuchadnezzar has placed the weak Zedekiah, an uncle of Jechoniah. However, men have begun to hope, and Jerusalem has become the center of a conspiracy that includes the kings of Edom, Moab, Tyre and Sidon, as well as the Ammonite ruler. At this point we see Jeremiah again combining gestures with words and walking about the city with his neck bowed under a yoke, symbol of the enslavement that awaits the conspirators (Jer 27).

Thus the prophet has finally involved himself in politics; he has joined the pro-Babylonian party, for he wants to spare his country useless suffering, and he is convinced that Yahweh wants "not a strong and independent nation, but a people faithful to him."

Chapter 28 tells of an oratorical contest between Jeremiah and Hananiah, a false prophet who speaks of peace. Jeremiah answers him with skepticism, for Hananiah announces peace as coming immediately, whereas all the prophets until now have prophesied disaster. As soon as God's word makes itself known to him anew, Jeremiah goes over the attack and reasserts his earlier prediction: Jerusalem and the conspirators will be defeated and enslaved.

Psalm 119 continues its meditation on the divine law. While the law

382

supports the psalmist's trust, it urges a similar trust on all who profess faith in the Lord.

Matthew 14:13–21. Cf. p. 181.

■

"Give them something to eat yourselves." Nonetheless it is Jesus who takes the five loaves and gives thanks before breaking them for the crowd. Thus the Church is never abandoned to its own resources: human beings are entrusted to its care, but it is the living Christ who gives himself to them through the hands of believers.

The multiplication of the loaves is not a sensational miracle; neither is it a simple call to share. Jesus does not multiply the loaves the way a man of power might draw ceaselessly on his wealth in order to give some of it to the hungry; but neither is he content simply to urge each individual to take a share so that everything will be fine. He knows that this pitiful crowd of people is too wretched for mere generosity to be able to save the world. Neither the generosity of the rich nor the generosity of the poor would be adequate for that. He must get to the heart of the problem, to the real point of redemption, at which Christ gives his life and says: "Do the same in union with me." For the bread he breaks for the hungry is his own body. And only his body given in sacrifice can save humankind.

If the Eucharist at the Last Supper was celebrated in the recollection of the upper room, that of the multiplication of the loaves throws open the doors of the world. Jesus says the blessing, and does so in order that all the races of the world may be blessed. He breaks the bread, and does so to feed the hunger of the whole world. To this Eucharist all the poor and outcast are invited, the poorly fed and poorly clothed, the persecuted and the forgotten. How can we receive the bread that has been broken without doing all we can to effect the coming of a new world?

Let us not be deceived by the recollection of the upper room, for it is burdened with the death of the Son of Man. Jesus clearly says as much: "This bread is my body handed over for the many." In his heart that is soon to be pierced he carries the crowd in the wilderness and the limitless throng of the wretched. And though on that evening he

383

gives bread only to his disciples, his intention is that they in turn should go and give their bread to all human beings.

Every time we celebrate the Eucharist in memory of the Lord, he takes our bread and with it our bodies and our lives. He looks upon the world and he says to us: "Give them something to eat yourselves." We are not alone. Our bodies and our lives, surrendered for the many, are in the hands of him who daily first gives himself.

■

Beggars for bread, thirsty for hope,
  we stand before you, our Father.
Give us this day our daily bread,
  and open our hands that close to keep all for ourselves.

We have but a little bread,
  and the poverty of our hearts.
We pray you: through your Spirit
  make the scantiness of our offering manifest
so that in your Son's hands it may become
  a fruitful fountain in the midst of our wilderness.

TUESDAY OF THE 18TH WEEK

DIRTY HANDS AND PURE HEART

Jeremiah 30:1–2, 12–15, 18–22. Chapters 30 and 31 contain oracles depicting a wonderful future for the country; they are somewhat analogous to those in Isaiah 40—55. These prophecies appear to be ancient; they may go back to the time of King Josiah, who had taken advantage of the momentary weakness of the great powers to reoccupy Galilee, Samaria and the coastal cities, that is, the provinces lost when the kingdom of David was divided. Josiah's policy led to a rebirth of hope in a restoration, and this is echoed in the prophetic oracles of that period. But after the fall of Jerusalem these same oracles, which originally were concerned solely with the northern kingdom, were reinterpreted in favor of Judah. It was impossible for the divine word simply to lapse.

The reminder of past sufferings (vv. 12–15) stands side by side with promises of renewal (vv. 18–22). It is above all the educational aspect of the sufferings that is emphasized. As for the oracles of happiness, they describe the future state of the people: renewal of living conditions, restoration of cult, political independence, the whole culminating in a renewal of the covenant between God and his people.

Psalm 102 is an individual lament. Such poems list reasons why God should intervene in behalf of his people. Here Jerusalem is the focus of attention: let Yahweh rebuild its walls and show himself favorable to the lowly (and therefore to the psalmist). Then his glory will be great in the eyes of the nations.

Matthew 15:1–2, 10–14. Cf. p. 184.

■

(Year A. For Years B and C cf. p. 185.)

It is obvious that keeping oneself pure in God's sight is not a matter of constantly washing one's hands, any more than it is a matter of washing one's hands of various affairs. Everyone is familiar with the obsession manifested by the unfortunates who constantly feel polluted, contaminated, unclean. We cannot, of course, simply laugh at them, for religion too involves the body; on the other hand, we must be clear about the level at which the relation between our flesh and God is located. Against all tendencies to keep human beings in a hothouse, sheltered from an unclean world, the Gospel chooses to emphasize the "heart." Happy those whose hearts are pure, transparent, generous, simple, humble, for they shall see God.

But is it not necessary precisely to withdraw from the world in order to achieve this kind of purity? Is it possible to eat at the table of our fellows without losing the simplicity which Jesus likens to that of the dove? Stick your hands in the mud and sooner or later they will be dirtied. What, then, are we to do? What if the answer has to do with the gaze? The eyes, after all, are the exterior face of the heart. Happy the pure of heart, for they shall see God.

Purity is found in a gaze, in a certain way of looking at human beings and things. There are people who, when confronted with the evil of the world and with its compromises, retain an innocence of outlook; by this I mean an ability to uncover what is good and hopeful at the very moment when all are getting mired down in the mud. These people are not ignorant of what goes on in the world, but they sense God's presence even amid pollution, simply because they have heart and their eyes are able to gauge the hidden dimensions of things.

Impurity begins to stick to you on the day when you claim to wash your hands of it, to save yourselves and to find God in some germ-free oasis or other. God did not come among us into a draught-proof refuge; his table among human beings was the table of sinners and ordinary people.

When we are obsessed with the idea that our hands are dirty, let us raise our eyes to the hands of the Son of God on the cross: hands cracked and dripping with unclean blood, the hands of a man whom everyone treated like a robber. Then let us fix our gaze on his eyes. With him, let us look out on the world and murmur words of forgiveness; let us contemplate human beings in order to believe in them; let us set aside all bitterness of mind and continue struggling to our final breath. For God did not wash his hands of our wretchedness. It is precisely in this that he shows his absolute purity; he asks nothing different of us when we take our place at the table of his love.

■

Happy those with eyes wide open,
  for they shall recognize the Man.
Happy those who have heart,
  for they shall embrace the world.
Happy the hands thrust into the dough,
  for they shall receive the Lord's body.
Blessed be you, our God,
  for the bread which makes everyone live
  in Jesus, your Son and our Savior.

A STORY ABOUT A LITTLE DOG

Jeremiah 31:1–7. This oracle, which is reminiscent of the preaching of the prophet Hosea, announces the reunification of the kingdom. Vv. 2–3 refer back to the exodus when Yahweh found his people in the wilderness and, through his gift of the covenant, committed himself to love them with an everlasting love. Then, leaping across the centuries, v. 4 recalls the reign of Josiah and the recovery of the lost territories.

V. 6 contains a clear allusion to the tribal pilgrimages to Jerusalem, pilgrimages which had been stopped after the religious schism had taken place.

Jeremiah 31 supplies a canticle which consists in an oracle of happiness. Yahweh has pronounced in favor of the return of the exiles.

Matthew 15:21–28. Cf. p. 187.

■

On the Canticle of Jeremiah

Take your tambourines,
you whom God loves with an everlasting love,
and dance your joyous dance.
Let the Canaanite woman come with her faulty faith,
and the little dog from under the table;
let all those come who are hungry
and the prisoners, freed from their chains;
let young and old come,
the crippled and the lovers;
and let all enter the dance
for the God who loves them with an everlasting love.

■

Jesus is here dealing with a woman of pagan origin. Her daughter is possessed. Forms of legal uncleanness surround her, but faith makes its well-known leap forward. Yet Jesus is not tender in responding to

the woman; we are even shocked by his manner. The woman however is tremendous: a real woman with a pure heart, despite appearances. She has the faith that moves mountains, and she wins a mighty victory over the initial reluctance of the Son of God. Her faith is naive, and it touches the Lord's heart; he cannot resist her approach. For, after all, when God is the giver, what does it matter, in the end, whether the gift is crumbs from under the table or crunchy bread? The woman has recognized that God is visiting her; she does not get bogged down in details.

As for ourselves who regularly receive the eucharistic bread in our hands, would it not help to revitalize our faith if from time to time we hid under the table with the dogs as if we were nobodies? We certainly need to abandon, once and for all, the claims we make like spoiled children, and acquire a taste for the crumbs, the little trifles. Then our faith will be great, and everything will come to us in the measure of that faith.

■

Father of all life,
   keep your Church faithful
   to the mission you have given it
   to all the hungry of the world.
Let your children, who are filled with your abundance,
   spend themselves
   in the service of the poorest,
and let those who have nothing
   find themselves rich in you,
   strengthened by the love of their fellows.
Then we shall be able to praise you
   with one heart,
as your Spirit already inspires us to do
   whenever we take our place at the table
   where your Son comes to break bread
   for all the poor whom you love.

■

Son of David and Prince of Peace,
  our world is tormented by evil:
  have mercy on us.

Son of Man, Savior of the unfortunate,
  in you we place our trust:
  come to our aid.

Son of God, handed over for the many,
  your body is our bread of life:
  do for us according to our faith.

THURSDAY OF THE 18TH WEEK

STUMBLING BLOCK OR FOUNDATION STONE?

Jeremiah 31:31–34. "See, the days are coming—it is Yahweh who speaks—when I will make a new covenant with the house of Israel." Once again, the oracle seems to date from the early years of the reign of Josiah; it is addressed only to the northern tribes ("and the house of Judah" is a later addition).

In what way is this covenant new? In fact, there is nothing new about its content: the torah continues to be the focus of the covenant which Yahweh intends to make in the coming days. What is new is the way in which the covenant will be communicated. At Sinai God had spoken from the mountaintop; the people had experienced the divine will as a reality external to themselves. Henceforth, however, Yahweh will impress his will directly in the hearts of human beings. These will carry the will of God in their hearts and will wish only what God wills. Divine will and human desire will coincide. The prophet is in fact announcing the era of the Spirit, which Jesus will inaugurate on the eve of his death: "This cup is the new covenant in my blood."

Psalm 51 is entirely a call to the Spirit. It asks God to renew the human heart as announced by the prophets.

Matthew 16:13–23. Cf. p. 192.

Peter is a stumbling block to Jesus, an obstacle in his path; Jesus would risk tripping over this stumbling block if he did not order the foremost of his disciples to walk behind him. And yet Peter has said nothing outrageous; he has simply clarified the situation and tried to ward off from the Lord the dangers that threaten him if he persists in going up to Jerusalem.

Nonetheless to Jesus Peter is a "satan," an adversary; the power that opposes Jesus is incarnate in Peter—and this at the moment when the faith of the disciple has just elicited from him the decisive words: "You are the Christ, the Son of the living God." Peter's faith is real, but it is as yet unable to find expression in actions; it gets jammed up as soon as it sees what is on the horizon; it is in danger of being extinguished on the spot for lack of development. Satan, moreover, has always been in cahoots with death, and it will take the passion of the Messiah to overcome Satan and the power of nothingness; it will take a long journey on which life will seem for a time to be swallowed up in death. But at the end the stone will no longer be a stumbling block, but will have become a foundation stone. The power of death will never be able to swallow up the Church in its underworld caverns.

Peter has recognized Jesus, if only for a moment. Even if he begins to protest, let us not be too quick to cast stones. After all, Christ has first scandalized Peter, and this scandal had to come; it is necessary for our faith, with the same hidden necessity that will bring the Messiah to his death. The scandal has its source in God who cannot force faith on anyone and is unwilling to speak except to the human heart in view of an interior and freely accepted covenant. But this interior word takes time.

Jesus had said to Simon: "You will be Peter." Yes, he will be Peter, the rock, but at no less a cost than for the cornerstone to be the cornerstone. The foundation cannot be higher than the keystone of the arch. Let Peter therefore begin by walking for a long time behind the master, in faith, and allowing Christ to form his heart and his thoughts. A day will come when Peter will be able to say, less impetuously but with greater sureness: "Yes, Lord, you know I love you."

The Church stands daily at the crossroads, and Jesus daily asks it: "But you, who do you say I am?" Happy the Church if it answers, even in awkward ways: "You are the Son of God; you alone are our rock." Happy the Church that each day faces the scandal of the cross. For God continues to quarry each living stone of the Church in order to make it part of the structure that is the place of his everlasting covenant with the human race.

■

Allow us to walk behind you,
Lord,
trustingly and in faith.
Take us by the hand,
for your road is very steep
for our quickly exhausted hearts.
Teach us to discover new horizons
in your eternal Kingdom,
the Church which you founded
on the rock
whereon your Son gave his life for the world.

FRIDAY OF THE 18TH WEEK

TURN AT THE NEXT CROSSING

Nahum 2:1, 3; 3:1–3, 6–7. Jeremiah 30—31 referred to the weakness of Assyria that allowed King Josiah to reoccupy the lost provinces. The oracles of the prophet Nahum seem to suppose the same context; in language that is both realistic and highly poetic, they announce the end of Nineveh and of the yoke which that blood-stained city had imposed on the entire Near East. For the people of the covenant this oracle is a reminder of the fidelity of God who did not abandon his people during their years of suffering; at the same time it points out the ephemeral nature of earthly kingdoms, even those that are extremely powerful. In the final analysis, Yahweh remains Lord of history.

Deuteronomy 32, the canticle of Moses (dating from the exile), has the sound of a trial between God and Israel. The trial ends with a verdict of acquittal, because God's plan—one that will never be called into doubt—is to save the people. The verses used in the liturgy announce the destruction of Israel's enemies and the end of idolatry.

Matthew 16:24–28. Cf. p. 196.

■

"Listen, listen! The word of Nahum the prophet: 'Woe to the city soaked in blood! Galloping horses, countless corpses; they stumble over the dead! For God is the master of life and of death!' "

"Listen, listen again! The word of Jesus, the Son of Man: Jerusalem, the city of peace, is laid waste! The Innocent One leaves her, carrying his cross. The city has failed to recognize Life itself! For the Lord is the master of life and of death!"

Two roads intersect and God stands at the crossing. They are two roads mapped out by God. But human beings must pass from the one to the other, from revenge to forgiveness, if they are to find the master of life. Two roads cross in Jerusalem, and the road of reconquest suddenly forks, with one arm leading to the way of the cross.

They had set out to the sound of trumpet and horn, the weapons of the Most High in their hands and the cry of the prophets on their lips. They would win the battle, and the enemies of God would go down into death. Had not God himself showed the way with mighty hand and outstretched arm? For our God is the Lord of victories, the master of life and of death.

But on the side of the hill, under the walls of the city, the road of triumph suddenly crosses another road, the way of the cross, a narrow and winding path. At the crossing, God waits to put an end to victory by arms, to the too easy triumph of pride. God stands there in the form of a man, and this man is already carrying a cross. There will be no other victory save the victory of love that spends itself to the end. For God is the master of life and of death.

Peter, walk behind Jesus! Leave the triumphal road of a Messiah who is son of David, and climb the way of the cross with the true Messiah, who is Son of Man and Servant of God. Of what use would it be for you to gain the whole world while losing your life?

For the eternal Lord, almighty God, is abandoning his post as leader of the fight he has so often waged for his people. Weary of so many defeats, God now knows that he will have to pay the price for life. At the crossing of the two ways, God has made his choice. If you, the disciple, seek life, can you pay less dearly for it than the master of life and of death?

■

Master of life and of death,
  Lord our God,
    you paid a heavy price for life:
you surrendered your own Son
  on the tree of our redemption.
Do not permit us
  to seek our salvation
  by force of our own arms,
for henceforth there is
  no other fountain of life
  but the one you make flow
  from the death of your Christ on the cross.

SATURDAY OF THE 18TH WEEK

AN ATOM OF FAITH TO CURE A LUNATIC

Habakkuk 1:12—2:4. Like the prophecies of Nahum, the Book of Habakkuk is contemporaneous with the end of the Assyrian empire and the rise of Babylon. But while Nahum rejoiced at the fall of Nineveh, Habakkuk asks questions about God's action. The reason is that the new conquerors have exceeded the limits of their mission, which was to punish the pride of the Ninevites; now they in turn are trying to impose their law on the whole of the Near East. Is it possible to trace the thread of the divine action through these events? The prophet attempts a response while

393

emphasizing the fidelity of Yahweh, whose past action is a pledge to Israel despite the obscurities of the present age.

The passage cited in the liturgy describes the imperialist methods of the Babylonians. By exceeding their rights they have upset the order of creation. Human beings are no longer creatures in the image of God but are now cast in the image of fish or reptiles. Nonetheless, like a good sentinel, the prophet keeps watch; as far as Yahweh is concerned, Habakkuk can even now announce that Babylon will meet as disastrous a fate as Nineveh did. Someday this city too will be nothing but ruins.

Psalm 9 is an alphabetic Psalm; it urges praise of God's righteousness and of the concern he shows for the oppressed.

Matthew 17:14–20. Cf. p. 199.

■

Everyone knows, suspects or presupposes the good and bad influence of the moon on human behavior. This nocturnal heavenly body is supposedly responsible for the imbalance that occurs in certain individuals, who act as if possessed by some divinity. Such a "lunatic" is now brought to Jesus: not just a temperamental young man who behaves oddly, but a poor fellow who is ill, under a spell, out of joint. Is he perhaps an epileptic? But the Gospel speaks of him as a "lunatic," someone under the sway of the moon.

How did the disciples go about their unsuccessful attempt to heal the boy? Perhaps, like everyone else of that era, they tried some kind of spell or magic or divinatory exorcism. In any case, Jesus tells them that the need is for faith, an unobtrusive, seemingly minuscule faith, unaccompanied by any pomp or deceptive appearances. A faith as big as a mustard seed would cure a lunatic or even transport a mountain. Just the opposite, then, of the rites in which enchanters shout themselves out of breath trying to command the heavenly bodies and the vicissitudes of time.

Today, of course, epileptics are cared for by doctors, and mountains are moved by bulldozers. But human beings are not any the less under spells, and human relations are not any the less obstructed; each individual thrashes about in his own madness, cut off from his brothers and sisters by mountains higher than the hills that enclose our valleys. And, like the disciples, the doctors, engineers and others end by admitting that they have been able to do hardly anything to heal the world.

Yet, says Jesus, all that is needed is an atom of faith. A tiny bit of faith is all that is needed for human beings to recover balance and health, which are affected more often by despair than by germs. A tiny bit of faith to level down the mountains of division and for brethren to recover the joy of dwelling together. A tiny bit of faith for the moon, the night, to keep watch over our sleep and the privacy of our homes. All that is needed is a little bit of faith for the impossible to become real.

For what is impossible to human beings is precisely what God wants them to share: peace, love, hope, joy. An atom of faith, and you will see a new world.

■

God, Creator of the visible and invisible worlds,
  our lives are in you,
  in you our future.
Do not let the vicissitudes of this world
  cause us inward despair,
  nor the impossible dismay us.
Revive each morning our faith
  that we are building a world of peace,
  more brilliant than the moon of night
  and the sun at the center of our days.

FROM MONDAY OF THE 19TH WEEK
TO SATURDAY OF THE 20TH WEEK

Another World

The Gospel of Matthew has an undeniable ecclesial dimension. The Church of every age can find in this Gospel the norms it needs for conducting itself in accordance with the Spirit of Christ. On every page, and especially on those we shall be reading during these two weeks, concrete questions arise that make up the very web of daily life in community: the forgiveness of offenses, wealth and poverty, conjugal life, fraternal help, rivalries, saints and sinners.

At the center of these pages stands the child. Jesus offers the child as model for the Church because the child is open to grace. Children do not look upon themselves as "masters"; they know the importance of the word "father"; they feel the need of guidance. Over against the child, the Pharisee, the scribe and the rabbi, infatuated with their dignity, stand straight in their pride. Jesus often speaks against these men, shakes their poise, calls their hypocrisy by name.

This is why the Gospel also challenges—perhaps before all others—the authorities of the Church. Too often these men deserve the bitter reproaches directed by the prophet Ezekiel at the "wicked shepherds" of his day. "I myself," says God, "will go in search of the lost sheep." We know that Jesus will lose his life trying to be such a pastor according to the heart of God, for the true shepherd must even give his life. The word of which the shepherd is guardian and to which he bears witness makes its demands on him first of all, and he must consume this word so as to be one with it. The Gospel bluntly rejects those shepherds who pile on the shoulders of others burdens they are unwilling to carry themselves.

The indissolubility of marriage, the choice of poverty, humble service, the forgiveness of offenses: these requirements of the Gospel apply first of all to those who must preach them. Ezekiel had already insisted loudly on the principle of personal responsibility against all those who thought they could save themselves by invoking some privilege of caste or office. "He who has sinned is the one who shall die."

Nonetheless, the word is not given in order to condemn us. If God is demanding, this is in order that his grace may transform the human person. "I shall give you a new heart." All are called to the banquet of the Kingdom, be they good or evil; but because God pours out his grace without measure, each person must be on guard to keep his wedding garment clean, that is, to remain in the grace and love of God, like a child, who may get dirty but is quite willing to be washed. "Come," says God. "I will cleanse you, and my glory shall dwell in your hearts."

■

For the lost sheep,
  and for the immense joy in heaven
  when a shepherd devotes his life
  to seeking them out;
for the hungry sheep,
  who have returned to the fold,
  and for the joy of the entire flock,
be you blessed, O God of tenderness!

For the brethren who help one another,
  for the hands outstretched to those who were lost,
  for the soothing gaze that lifts the sinner up,
for the words of correction humbly spoken,
  and for the brethren saved
  by a forgiveness or a gesture of mercy,
be you blessed, O God of tenderness!

For the pardons given without reserve,
  for the reconciliations begun ever anew,
  for the loving hearts forgetful of the past,
and for the seventy times seven
  that you have forgiven us our debts,
be you blessed, O God of tenderness!

For the spouses who know the cost of fidelity,
  for the poor who know the burden of destitution,
  for the children who believe without thought of the future,
and for the rich who share without reflecting overmuch,
  for the divorced who still have the courage to believe in love,
be you blessed, O God of tenderness!

For the humble who recognize their limits,
  for the famous who undertake to serve
  without recompense,
  for the masters who do not impose
  the yoke of their glamorous name,
and for the unknown scholars, without awards or honors,
  for the fathers who prefer to be brothers,
be you blessed, O God of tenderness!

397

For your Church, poor and a servant,
    faithful despite its sins,
    sanctified by your grace,
    enriched by your presence,
your Church of children,
    open to those who have strayed,
    hand outstretched to the abandoned,
be you blessed, O God of tenderness!

MONDAY OF THE 19TH WEEK

FOR A CHURCH THAT IS FREE

Ezekiel 1:2–6, 24–28c. The prophets differ from one another. Jeremiah is reserved, while Ezekiel gives free rein to his imagination. He was trained as a priest and, like Isaiah, bears witness to the holiness and transcendence of God.

The first page of his book tells, in terms descriptive of an ecstasy, of the prophet's initial experience. But what was it that Ezekiel saw on the banks of the river Chebar? We must take note, first of all, of the very traditional character of the vocabulary used: a storm, lightning, the noise of waves, the purifying fire. There were the obligatory appurtenances of every theophany since the one at Sinai. Then, too, the throne that is like a sapphire recalls the throne in Isaiah's vision. It is therefore highly significant that in the midst of these traditional elements there should appear a frankly universal perspective, symbolized by the four animals that can move in all directions thanks to their four faces. And what of the location of the vision? Yahweh no longer manifests himself in the temple at Jerusalem but in the heavens and in the land of the Babylonians. The exile must certainly have been an extraordinary experience!

Psalm 148. The joyful message of this Psalm is: "Therefore let all the earth praise the Lord!"

Matthew 17:22–27. Cf. p. 202.

■

The children of the Kingdom are free. No enslavement can take away this freedom which is rooted in faith. Their Lord and Master may be put to death, but that makes no difference: the children of the Kingdom are free. Even in the persecution of death they will remain free: free to give their lives for the freedom of the world.

Why is it that the history of men's dealings with one another has so often found some enslaving others? Why this diminution of freedom that runs like a leitmotiv through the history of the human race? A single driving power is at work through the centuries: human beings reduce their brothers and sisters to slavery in order to preserve their own material goods which they protect as selfish possessions. In order to maintain their own position they believe that they must make others subject to them. In fact, each of them is afraid and holes up in his own house; then one day he breaks into the house of another in order to subject and so neutralize him.

The people of Israel were not free of this temptation. It took the exile for a glimmer of universalism to appear in their ken and for the now enslaved chosen people to discover their ecumenical vocation, that is, to discover at last their true freedom. But this was not accomplished in a day. In fact, has even Christianity, which originated in Judaism, ever fully accepted its own universal dimensions? How often will the Church fall back into selfish fear, to the point of subjecting others lest they take up too much room?

But the Church of Christ is fundamentally free; it owes tribute to no one, that is, it owes worship and submission to no power whatsoever! True enough, the children of the Kingdom pay taxes, but their spirits remain free in the face of the politics of this world's kingdoms. They are the witnesses of the living Word, of the risen Man, and through him they are the artisans of human freedom. Even if they are driven into exile on the banks of some river Chebar, the voice of God continues to tell them that no enslavement is possible for those who have faith in Christ, that is, in the Man whom no power can ever imprison.

■

God of all the living,
  we pray you

for our brothers and sisters who are persecuted
because of the human person:
grant each the strength to stand fast
against all that enslaves
the human dignity
for which your Son gave his life.
We pray for those in authority
over nations and peoples,
that they may find their glory
in serving every human being,
and may be open
to the advancement of all living creatures
as justice demands.

Grant also to your faithful
enough freedom and faith
not to find their strength
in the glories of this world.

TUESDAY OF THE 19TH WEEK

A FLIGHT TO THE TASTE OF HONEY

Ezekiel 2:8–3:4. Ezekiel tells us in a very expressive fashion about the mission God has given to him. Like a king to one of his ambassadors, Yahweh solemnly gives the prophet a scroll written on both sides. But while the message Ezekiel must proclaim is a lengthy one, it is essentially a message of misfortune, as is clear from the "lamentations, wailings and moanings" that are written in the scroll. The prophet is also bidden to eat the book, which means he must feed on the word before announcing it. But what is signified by the taste of honey in the prophet's mouth? Is it not a sign that Ezekiel is profoundly in harmony with the content of the book, despite the oracles of misfortune in it? Consequently, unlike many other prophets, Ezekiel does not protest being called.

Psalm 119, which is a long alphabetic poem, sings the praises of the law as being a true spiritual nourishment for the believer.

Matthew 18:1–5, 10, 12–14. Cf. p. 206.

■

"Open your mouth, eat . . . and keep quiet!" That is how many people treat their children, as though all that is needed is to eat and then sit humbly in one's corner, without disturbing the wise. Does the first place in the Kingdom therefore go to those who stand agape before God and, above all, do nothing to upset the divine plans? Is that how we are to understand the splendid verse in the Psalm: "I open my mouth, panting eagerly for your Commandments"? Sanctimonious wonder and wise children? But then why so much concern for the lost sheep? For it does happen that little lambs take flight.

God says to the prophet: "Open your mouth and eat what I am about to give you." What he gives him is a book of lamentations, wailings and moanings. The book is bitter to the prophet's vitals just as it is bitter to the heart of God. A book not long enough to include all the flights of Israel, God's dear child. A lament for God the Father. But then why is this book as sweet as honey in the prophet's mouth? Does this represent a bit of evangelical sadism? After all, is there anyone who does not find somewhat out of place the zeal of the shepherd who abandons the whole flock in order to scour the mountains in search of the fugitive sheep? But there is really no question of the prophet's simply opening his mouth wide and then digesting in peace. For it takes a tremendous conversion before songs of mourning can be changed into the taste of honey.

The greatest in the Kingdom is the one who becomes like a child again—but a child in the Gospel sense, and not as grownups understand "child." The child who is still prepared to challenge himself. The child who runs away but then immerses himself in the joy of the Father who has gone out and found him. The child grown older who himself spends the night searching for one who is lost. The child who does not lock up the word of God in the safety deposit box of his own securities but constantly exposes the Gospel to the dangers of little known roads. The child who becomes a prophet, devours the book and then transmits the word at his own risk and peril. The child who looks at everything through the eyes of God. The child who dares say to the heavenly Father: "What sweetness I find in

401

your Commandments! Honey is less tasty to me." Yes, such a child is the greatest in the Kingdom of God, the Kingdom in which there is great joy every time a lost sheep is found.

Brothers and sisters, grownups, do you realize how great a conversion is required in order to become like children again? Therefore open your mouths, eat the word and, above all, do not slothfully digest it in smug contentment. Be like the bee, which is constantly at work to provide the human heart with the sweetness of its honey. Traverse the hills and the secluded roads, for it is there that lost children are waiting for you in order to share with you the honey of rediscovery!

■

The law of your mouth,
  God our Father,
  is happiness to our lips.
May our hearts find their joy
  in what you ask of us,
for the words you speak
  become words of life in us,
  every time that we translate them
  into commitment to our brethren.

WEDNESDAY OF THE 19TH WEEK

YOU ARE YOUR BROTHER'S KEEPER

Ezekiel 9:1–7; 10:18–22. Chapter 8 has told of a visit to Jerusalem which Ezekiel made in spirit. What he saw there filled his priestly soul with horror: the people giving themselves to idolatry even in the temple. Punishment can be put off no longer: it will take concrete form in the departure of the divine Glory, which will abandon the city and the sanctuary.

The description of the punishment is inspired both by the accounts of the night of Passover and by the liturgies for entrance into the temple. "Who has the right to climb the mountain of Yahweh?" (Ps 24:3). Seven men commissioned by God will answer this question. The first six are each armed with a deadly weapon, and they begin to strike. The seventh is clad in linen like the priests and has orders to place a mark on the foreheads of those who have not compromised themselves with idolatry. The action of the seventh man may be an allusion to a penitential ceremony leading to the admission of the faithful to the temple liturgies.

Psalm 113 is a hymn; it urges those faithful who have escaped punishment to offer praise to God.

Matthew 18:15–20. Cf. p. 209.

■

"If your brother does something wrong, go and have it out with him alone." Your brother: those who share the same faith as you, those who partake with you at the same table. But as a matter of fact do we still have any brothers and sisters, we whose motto as Christians so often is: "Every man for himself and God for all"? Jesus founded his Church to be a vast family comprising thousands of communities in which each individual would take care of the others. Today, however, too many parishes resemble railway stations in which each individual goes his own way amid the crowd that presses upon him from all sides and knocks him about in the scuffle. Every man for himself!

"If your brother does something wrong, go and have it out with him alone." But we have reversed all values and sold the Gospel down the river. If the individual is still concerned with his neighbor, it is in order to say all sorts of evil about him, behind his back of course. To judge him, condemn him, and then bemoan his lot! We live like hunted animals. "Did you know? So-and-so . . . " Jesus, however, tells us simply: "Go, find your brother, and have it out with him alone."

"Give him your hand, speak to him, and tell him that you understand and that you are no better than he. Talk to him, reread the Gospel with him, pray at length with him. Talk to him and help him realize that because of his sin he is becoming a slave. Be to him an echo of the voice of God who calls all of us to the same holiness and has signed us all on the forehead with the same sign of the cross. Then if your brother listens to you, you have won your brother for God."

"But if he refuses to listen to these, report it to the community."
Utopianism, lack of realism, indulgence in sweet daydreams? Is that
what you see here? Do you see the community discussing in God's
presence Mr. So-and-so who is deceiving his wife, tampering with
prices, engaging in scandal-mongering, cultivating jealousy, and who
knows what else? Is that what you see here? No, the point is not to
scent sin everywhere; it is simply that black cannot be white and that
in the Church we are one another's guardians.

But in fact we are the Church in hardly any degree. "Where two or
three meet in my name," says the Lord, "I shall be there with them."
He is in our midst; he knows each of us; he entrusts us to one
another. The brother and sister who sin are fettered, chained, and
depend on us for being loosed, made happy, freed; they depend on us
for their life and even, if they remain stubborn, for help in being
converted.

Shall we then continue letting the Church die from the blows
inflicted by our individualism? Brothers and sisters, it is high time to
take the Gospel seriously.

■

You established your Church, Lord,
  as a place of freedom
  for sinful human beings.
Grant us enough concern
  for one another
that thanks to our love
  those bound by evil
  may discover the joy of a new future.

THURSDAY OF THE 19TH WEEK

A GENERAL AMNESTY?
Ezekiel 12:1–12. Ezekiel often conveys his message in the form of symbolic
actions that will stimulate the curiosity of his fellow citizens. In this

passage he is inspired to mime the shameful flight of Zedekiah, the last of the kings of Judah. The prophet hides his face so that he may no longer see his country. A prophetic gesture indeed, since Zedekiah will be carried a prisoner to the headquarters of the Babylonian army, and there, charged with treason, will see his sons slaughtered in front of him and then have his eyes put out.

When Ezekiel later on makes provisions for the new constitution of Israel, he replaces the king with a *nasi*, a prince-overseer. He does so because he has come to the conclusion that the people of the covenant may have no king but Yahweh.

Psalm 78, a lengthy Psalm, takes the form of an indictment. It recalls the many rebellions of the people in the wilderness and the supreme act of treason that was represented by the religious schism of the northern tribes; this schism was the reason why Yahweh abandoned the sanctuary at Shiloh. Once again, in the time of Ezekiel, the Glory of Yahweh has abandoned the temple in Jerusalem in order, this time, to join the people in their exile.

Matthew 18:21–19:1. Cf. p. 213.

■

How much do you love me?" "A thousand million dollars worth!" "That's not bad, but in gold it would be worth even more!" An ugly kind of calculation, but the child does not know any better, and its feelings require astronomical numbers to express them, as in the case of the ten thousand talents of the debtor in the parable. The king forgives this man's debt, but it is in fact an impossible debt, beyond imagination's power to comprehend; the point being made is that God does not calculate and that his love is of a different order of reality. God is infinite love and infinite forgiveness to us; it's useless to try to calculate them. The Gospel addresses the heart and would have us forgive with all our heart; calculations and strict justice are set aside as useless, because he who calculates, even if he calculates accurately, ends up still with a heart of stone. The servant in the parable is, after all, only acting justly toward his fellow servant who really owed him a tidy sum, the wages for a hundred days of work. This is not to be sneezed at. The injustice begins when the servant's action is put in the context of his having just been forgiven a debt

600,000 times greater. We put ourselves in the same position when we demand justice for an evil done to us. But if we are to perceive this to be the case, we must first grasp the extent to which God has forgiven us. God loves us beyond any standards—a thousand thousand million dollars' worth. He is utterly abnormal.

What is required of us is no less abnormal: to build a world on forgiveness, the remission of debts, amnesty, capitulation—really, an anti-world. As it is, people everywhere attempt to maintain a strict balance of forces and resources; justice has no choice but to weigh wrongs and responsibilities as best it can. Do you realize, then, how scandalous it is to look upon God as a judge? It is this picture of God that accounts for the hardened hearts of so many believers; they think that since God judges them, they must also judge their brothers and sisters; then just retribution will be ensured on the great day. But, says Jesus, that is how God will treat you *only* if each of you does not forgive his brother or sister with all his heart. God is in fact prepared to pardon universally on the final day; he will decree a general amnesty, but on one condition: that each of us forgives as he forgives. "As": with the same liberality. Otherwise our hash is settled: there will be strict justice.

But—some people think—what is there so serious that God must pardon us for? Well, I am not thinking of anything in particular; I think simply that God forgives us for being at each moment what we are: mean, ignorant, calculating, cheating, or even simply annoying. God forgives us all this because he wants love to triumph. If you doubt me, just look at the crucifix. You will understand at a glance. At least we hope you will.

■

Forgive as your heavenly Father forgives you.
That is the key to holiness:
  to act and think like God.

My Commandment, says Jesus,
  is that you love one another as I have loved you,
  and as the Father loves me.

Father, forgive us our sins,

as we forgive those
who have sinned against us.

MY LOVE . . . FOREVER!

Ezekiel 16:1–15, 59–60, 63 or *16:59–63.* A little girl is abandoned in the fields and discovered by a passerby. Ezekiel makes use of traditional images in describing the history of the holy city. Did not Yahweh find Israel on Sinai and make of her his beloved wife? But Jerusalem need not boast of her origins. She was only a Canaanite city and unclean. In the prophet's eyes she will always keep some mark of this pagan origin, so intense is the power that rivets evil to the human heart. Jerusalem owes her good fortune to David who made her his capital and the place of the Lord's temple. And what gratitude has she shown for this choice? She has gone looking for her old lovers by prostituting herself with idols. But what her history shows is not only the sinfulness of human beings; it also manifests the mercy of God who has never forgotten how he espoused her as a girl.

Isaiah 12. This song of thanksgiving confirms Ezekiel's promise. In the Book of Isaiah it follows upon an announcement of the return of the exiles; thus it shows that God has forgiven his people. Since it contains allusions to the Feast of Booths, it is permissible to think that the former exiles themselves will take part in the liturgy.

Matthew 19:3–12. Cf. p. 218.

■

"If that is how things are between husband and wife, it is not advisable to marry." A real cry from the heart—but what a heart! And yet it is the Apostles who are speaking. Hard hearts, stiff necks. But if we look closely, what "advisability" could there be, since people do not marry because it it advisable. A covenant is another matter entirely, and a marriage according to the mind of God is a covenant.

407

"I made a covenant with you, and you belonged to me." God has given spouses a right to use the same language: "Will you be mine? I give myself to you forever." But people in love do not give themselves to another in order to belong to that person as an object that can be rejected "on any pretext whatever" or even for a reason carefully laid down by the law. A covenant is irrevocable in God's eyes, and nothing can break it, not even the sin of the other. "I will remember the covenant that I made with you," God says, "and I will conclude a covenant with you that shall last forever." Faith does not permit any other kind of language. Anything else is a human compromise arising from hardness of heart. But when the time of grace comes in Jesus Christ the covenant can no longer be anything but a grace.

Marriage is a covenant, a sacrament, a living icon of the love of God for us. A man and a woman give themselves to one another and are now one flesh, with the same impulses, the same tenderness which God communicates to his creatures in giving himself to them. Husband and wife are the face of Christ who gives his life for his Church. This is, of course, impossible for human beings to achieve by themselves. That is why marriage is a grace, a gift of God.

Indissolubility is not based on human norms; it is a reflection of God's gift of himself. Man and woman are given to each other by Christ at the same time as they give themselves to each other out of love. This challenge—for it is a challenge—is meaningful only in the light of faith; it is impossible of fulfillment by man and woman left to themselves. But the fulfillment does exist as a divine miracle in the man and woman who live out with one another the love and forgiveness which God himself first witnessed toward them.

If the Gospel is so hard on the adulterer, is this not because it knows the wretched state into which the adulterer can fall? All grace, all beauty wither in him or her, and the heart knows only sadness— unless the heart has already hardened to that point. But the Gospel wants for human beings nothing but the joy that grace brings, and the beauty of fidelity—a beauty which is itself a challenge.

■

We pray you, Lord,
*   for N. and N.,*

and for the portion of the world
that they carry in their hands,
for love is as vast as the heavens,
as limitless as the sea.
Today they are born together:
may they remain together forever,
because their names are forever associated
in you, the God of love.
May they always know the ineffable joy
of calling, by the name they will have murmured
amid the silence of newborn life,
the children who reflect their own features
while also revealing a hitherto unknown side
of your infinite face.
And why should we not make bold
to offer you already these future children,
since they are already loved
in your smile that joins in the instant
both past and present,
today's love and its future fruit?
We offer you these children;
may they be for N. and N.
a door thrown wide
to all the children of the world.
God, you make a covenant with the human heart;
bestow your Spirit abundantly
on those whom love makes one flesh.
May their mutual tenderness
be a reflection of your ever prevenient love;
may their fidelity
bear witness before the world
to the power of your never failing presence;
may the children born of their union
grow up in the freedom
of a life that comes from you,
the God who calls us all
to the joy of a future that is daily new.

■

We pray you, Lord,
   for our brothers and sisters
   whose lives are slipping away in seeming barrenness.

We pray you, too,
   for those whom misfortune has mutilated
   and whom loneliness wounds more deeply each day.

We pray you for spouses separated
   by death, discord or human tragedy;
we entrust to you all those who remain faithful
   despite the darkness of uncertainty.

Tender Father, give your Spirit to each;
   in him may they discover the peace
   that is promised to the pure and persevering heart.

SATURDAY OF THE 19TH WEEK

DO NOT STOP THE LITTLE CHILDREN!

Ezekiel 18:1–10, 13b, 30–32. Why is the Lord so hard on our generation?
Many in Israel asked this question as they saw the deported setting out for
exile; and yet the worst was still to come. While, then, the connection
between the punishment of the national community and its sin was
becoming increasingly clear, there was nonetheless astonishment at seeing
this punishment so concentrated on a single generation. People kept
repeating: "The ways of the Lord are strange."

In answering this question, the prophet unhesitatingly draws upon tradition
in order to break new paths. What was traditional was the idea that the
individual can be apprehended only within the bonds of solidarity that
connect him with the group to which he belongs. The novelty will emerge
from the prophet's own practice of casuistry. His activity as a priest has
made him especially attentive to the behavior of individuals. Like
Jeremiah, therefore, he leads the fight against the old saw about the unripe
grapes and the teeth set on edge. Each individual, he says, is treated
according to his own behavior. This view reflected the advances in

emancipation of the individual that had been made during the period of the kings.

Psalm 51, dealing with the theme of individual responsibility, implores God's mercy.

Matthew 19:13–15. Cf. p. 220.

■

On his journey Jesus blesses the little children and proposes them as a model for all who are journeying toward the Kingdom. The grownups who are called to a total fidelity in love, to radical poverty, and to unqualified forgiveness of offenses will persevere to the end only if their hearts are as open to grace as are the hearts of children.

What is praised here is not the innocence of children, but their littleness, their unimportance, their radical poverty. Being incapable of climbing the steep road of the Gospel by their own powers, they have no alternative but to let God carry them. But how is it possible for a human being to attain to the Gospel ideal in any other way? The child is therefore proposed as a model, because he images forth the acceptance of grace.

The disciples nonetheless have the feeling that it is a waste of time to occupy oneself with children. There is still a long road ahead, and they must move on. On the other hand, why force the pace if it only means lacking energy further on? Let me be your guide, God says, and your poverty will be enriched with good things undreamed of by the man who thinks he can win all good things by force.

It is a fact that the prophet Ezekiel today issues an urgent appeal for personal responsibility. But let us not be deceived: God's grace is never a reward for human efforts; it is rather the source of these efforts. Each individual must try to climb his own path without resting on the laurels of his ancestors; yet it is equally important for the person to undertake this journey only after setting his feet in the footprints left by Christ—the way a little child would, who is too small and too poor to launch out on his own without going astray.

■

411

You treat each as a very loving father would,
  and you give your grace to each
  with your love as the sole measure.
Lord our God, grant us
  to receive you with the heart of a child,
and let our poverty be the place
  where your infinite grace manifests itself.

■

God, you will life and not death:
  put a new heart within us.
We trust too much
  in our own strength
and we have stumbled over the stones
  on the difficult road to your Kingdom.
Deign to take us by the hand,
  and let our hearts,
  swayed by your tenderness,
  trust henceforth in you
and climb with you
  the road to life.

MONDAY OF THE 20TH WEEK

THE RICH ARE SAD

Ezekiel 24:15–24. "Are you not going to explain what meaning these
actions have for us?" This is a question the people must often have had to
ask this prophet with his many symbolic actions. Look, he even refuses to
don mourning on the day his wife dies—and yet he calls her "the delight of
my eyes."

But Ezekiel has now become conscious of a special aspect of his prophetic
ministry: God has made him a "watchman" for the house of Israel; as he
sees it, then, his whole life must become a sign. He does not put on
mourning for his wife because he expects the imminent fall of Jerusalem,

and on that day there will be no one to don mourning for the dead city, since the destruction will be total.

Deuteronomy 32, the canticle of Moses, represents a typical re-reading of the events of the exodus. It takes the form of an indictment by Yahweh of his sinful people; vv. 18–25 announce punishment.

Matthew 19:16–22. Cf. p. 225.

■

Anyone who imagines the prophetic calling as pleasurable or as a beneficial form of liberation from unconscious processes would do well to think again. And anyone who dreams of giving his life to God must have no illusions: he will be totally absorbed in this gift and will experience the most complete poverty imaginable. Even the delight of his eyes and the passionate love of his heart will be taken from him, and he will not even have time to mourn their departure.

Well, then, what is this tragic demand that the Gospel makes? What is this perfection that is never reached because one must continue walking with Christ, walking ever further, and this after having left everything behind? Is there no real treasure save in heaven? To put it somewhat bluntly, if a man wishes to address God as "My treasure," is he forbidden to say the same to his wife? If so, then the evangelical counsels and evangelical "perfection" would be reserved to religious. And God grant that the latter may not continue to wear the long faces associated with their supposed indifference to "worldly passions."

An authentic experience of the Gospel refuses to entertain these poorly phrased questions. If we look more closely, we find that joy is on the side of God's poor and that it is the excessively rich young man who goes away sad. Let us understand correctly Ezekiel's strange attitude; in the morning he is busy preaching, and in the evening his wife is taken from him—and he has not even time to put on mourning. But Jesus will speak the same language: "Leave the dead to bury their dead." The fact is that the cares of the world, even the most legitimate, can so occupy the heart that there is not the slightest room left there for the urgent message of the good news. And, to put it bluntly once more, when one is a prophet one has many ways of saying to one's wife: "My treasure!" There is a good and a bad way.

413

Today, for example, millions of children die between morning and evening, and no one will put on mourning for them; thousands of adults are tortured in the night, and no one weeps for them; wretchedness spreads ever wider over the world each day, and not a single rich man will sell all that he has and join the poor. It is today as it was in the past. But today, again as in the past, from time to time prophets, whether celibates or married people, hear the voice of God and follow Christ; they follow him to the place where death reigns, and with him they sow the new seed of a hardly perceptible resurrection. Do you not think that joy is on their side even though on one or other evening the delight of their eyes is taken from them? But it is here precisely that the Gospel adds, like a refrain: "Let those understand who can!"

■

Father,
it is good to give you thanks
  when you call us to leave everything,
  though we are certain only of your grace.
Before our eyes stretches the road
  into a still uncharted future,
  an ascending journey
  on which the aridity of the cross is transformed
  into a promise of unfailing peace and freedom.
Blessed be you
  for Jesus Christ,
  for it is his way that you offer to us
  and in him you give us your joy,
  the happiness of the poor and the resurrected.
May your Spirit preserve us
  in this freedom of heart
  each day of our journey.

THE RICH ARE LOST

Ezekiel 28:1–10. In 587 the exiled prophet learned of the fall of Jerusalem. It is easy to imagine what a blow this must have been to this passionate man who had never stopped loving his country. The prophet reacted to the news. The nations have admittedly been God's instruments and have helped the chosen people to test the authenticity of their attachment to Yahweh, but now the time has come for the nations to render their own accounts. Ezekiel boldly summons them before the divine tribunal: the Ammonites, the peoples of Moab and Edom, the Philistines, the inhabitants of Tyre and Sidon—all of them convicted of idolatry, lewdness and, above all, excess.

Deuteronomy 32. The canticle of Moses pronounces the sentence passed at the tribunal of Yahweh. The nations delude themselves when they think they are the masters of history; they are in fact only instruments in the hand of God. Justice will be dealt to them in their turn.

Matthew 19:23–30. Cf. p. 227.

■

On the Canticle of Moses

Can God destroy his work,
root out the people that bears his name?
And if the pagans were to believe
in their own strength,
if they took to themselves
the glory of victory,
would it not be your name, Lord,
that suffered?
You cannot abandon us:
only make us worthy of such great love!

■

A young man has gone away saddened. In order to follow Christ, he

415

would have had to abandon the management of his affairs; for it was this forced stagnation in one situation that caused his sadness. Joy is to be found only in being adventuresome, in a future that brings renewal. Joy is not something that is possessed; it is received as a grace that comes with dawn each morning. Then, too, one must have a heart that is sufficiently ready to taste this happiness, which is as fragile as the morning dew.

Jesus is not opposed to wealth, as is claimed by attackers who are burdened by regret at not being richer. There is no element of resentment in Christ's words. He simply states a fact, and that makes the words even more terrible. He simply observes the inability of the rich to enter into the world of a faith that is lived, the world of hope and joy. The Kingdom of heaven is not a reward given to graduates in the school of meritorious deeds; it is simply the place of joy, but the joy is the joy of the Beatitudes. Try to make this understood by a rich man who is entangled in the management of his possessions! Better, instead, to pray that he may not be eternally sad!

But when Jesus—and we—speak in this manner, we are rowing against the current. "Who can be saved, then?" the disciples ask. There are many ways of understanding "salvation." There is the world's way, which identifies salvation with power and affluence. There is the way of a particular biblical tradition, which regarded wealth as a sign of God's blessing. After all, do not people still say of the poor: "Poor but honest"?

Jesus speaks against the current view. He does not say that the poor are automatically saved simply by being poor; he simply observes that faith blossoms more easily amid the detachment of poverty than amid the worry of riches. But, lest anyone seek to evade the point by a subterfuge, he explains his meaning: "It is easier for a camel to pass through the eye of a needle than for a rich man to enter the Kingdom of heaven." After that, a person may water down the Gospel and construct arguments and introduce moderation. He may, but let him not then claim that he is still talking about the Gospel! For, when all is said and done, the great danger for a rich man is to imagine that his possessions might prove useful for winning a place in the Kingdom. If the rich at least knew the real usefulness of their possessions, there might be some meeting of minds. But do you know of any wealthy man who, once he became aware of this, remained wealthy?

■

Rescue us, Lord,
from the danger of inheritances
and of this world's riches,
for no treasure lasts forever
except the one you bestow
on those who have embraced poverty
for love of your grace.

■

Father most holy, you have hidden
your Kingdom and its endless treasures
in the east, where morning is reborn,
so that we might leave the shadows of night
and, moved by the Spirit, go to discover it,
brilliant with new grace.
But you give this treasure
to those alone who have sold everything
in order to walk with your Christ,
ever onward to adventure.

Our life is hidden in him,
and we desire to know naught
but Jesus Christ, and him crucified.

Father,
because you have called us
to be your children and become your heirs,
grant us your Spirit in abundance:
may our hearts, penetrated by your grace,
seek no other riches
than the peace of the Kingdom.

Preserve your Church in true poverty:
may it live absorbed
in contemplation of this matchless pearl
it is to reveal to all of humankind.
At the table of the Kingdom
may it renounce the possessions that paralyze it

417

and, free in spirit, dedicate itself
to the body and blood of your Son,
the only bread of life for the world,
the only unclouded joy for the poor.

Then the song of hope shall be reborn
   and the dance of wonder
   and the festivity of children
   as they are led by your beloved Son
   to the country on high
   where all is grace and beauty.

WEDNESDAY OF THE 20TH WEEK

A PASTOR IS NOT A BUSINESSMAN

Ezekiel 34:1–11. Now that Jerusalem has fallen, the prophet can stand back and reflect on all the events of which he has been a privileged witness. How has Israel come to this state of affairs? Ezekiel accuses the ruling monarchy rather than the people. Siding resolutely with the opponents of the monarchy, he passes a severe judgment on the "shepherds of Israel." And while his criticisms are justified by the policies which the kings followed at the expense of the people, the chief motive of his judgment is religious. In Ezekiel's view it is not possible for the people of the covenant to have at their head a king like the kings of the nations; consequently, despite his fidelity to the house of David, when Ezekiel reflects on the status of the future prince, he sees him rather as a mediator of the covenant.

Psalm 23. Ezekiel speaks not only of judgment but of salvation as well: those who are scattered among the nations will be gathered together in good pastures, and Yahweh will lead the flock. Psalm 23 sings of the support God gives to his people; the synagogue will look upon this poem as the song of the exiles' return.

Matthew 20:1–16a. Cf. p. 230.

■

418

If bosses were to act as God does, I can assure you that the number of malingerers would increase daily. After all, if you can earn as much for a half-day's work, why toil from morning to evening? It is clear, therefore, that the Gospel is not a manual for economic productivity. Whether you bemoan the fact or are indifferent to it, social relations are based on strict justice, without any room for generosity. And that is still the least imperfect solution.

But the Kingdom of God is not a business; the vineyard of the Lord is not a wine-producing concern, and Christ was careful not to entrust his flock to salaried mercenaries. Everyone knows the difference between a mercenary and an evangelical shepherd: the first puts in his eight hours and the second gives his life.

But, to tell the truth, God has more than once been deceived in his shepherds. To understand his error, we must realize that the failing of God's heart is to put too much trust in human beings and to allow them apprenticeship periods that are long and often ineffective. What do you expect? God is God, and he is not running a business.

God was deceived, then. The kings of his people abandoned the flock. They were, however, not mercenaries but politicians—though this often comes down to the same thing. They led the people as one might manage a political venture. The result: complete failure. First, because Israel did not carry weight with the neighboring colossuses; second, because Israel had a different vocation. But how is it possible, today as in the past, to ensure the Church's vocation if its pastors persist in acting like common businessmen?

In order to correct the mistake, God decided to be the pastor himself. "I am going to look after my flock myself and keep all of it in view." Christ is the true pastor; he endured even death in order to save his flock, for a true shepherd gives his life.

Ever since then, God has been signing on workers. To simplify operations and to obey the promptings of his own heart, he gives each the same wages, that is, his grace. Some pastors hear the call almost from their cradles; others hear it later on. Some hold back for a long time; others come forward from the first hour. It matters little to God. He is well aware that if he decided matters according to the laws of social justice, his sheep would be abandoned for a long time, even if only during periods of strife.

When all is said and done, is it not better for the Church and the world to have a small number of true shepherds than a crowd of mercenaries who are always calculating whether the accounts are correct?

■

Jesus, true Shepherd,
* you do not abandon your flock,*
but lead it by right paths
* and rescue it from the valleys of death;*
to the straying you show tenderness,
* to the faithful you give grace and happiness.*
Blessed be you,
* our rest when evening comes,*
* for you show the same love to each,*
and your love is inexhaustible.

■

We shall sing to you, Lord;
* we shall dance to the rhythm of the wine-harvest,*
* intoxicated by the new wine*
* that overflows in our cup.*
On our slopes, right in our soil,
* you have planted a unique vine-stock*
* and have made us its shoots,*
* so that living in it we might bear fruit*
* in abundance.*
Until morning we shall sing to you
* with festive cries, with shouts of joy.*

We shall weep with you, Lord,
* over your ravaged vineyard,*
* where the soil is dry, broken and waterless.*
My beloved had a select vine;
* he devoted tender love and toil to it;*
* he entrusted it to his friends, his brothers and sisters.*

Weep now over this vineyard,

all you who thirst for renewing wine.
The shoots have disowned the vine-stock;
isolated, they lie there, destined for the fire,
dry and lifeless wood, like a dead tree.
I expected from it fruit a hundredfold:
on the dead wood they nailed my Son.
They shed the blood of my Child
whom I sent to begin the wine-harvest.
Weep, then, over my vineyard,
be silent at the failure of my love!

We shall sing to you, Lord,
the new song of a new vineyard,
a hymn to dawn reborn,
our joy at the life in our shoots.
You have pruned us,
your fire has cleansed us;
the blood of your Christ restores our life,
the vine of his tenderness recreates our hearts.
We shall sing to you until morning
with festive cries, with murmurs of gratitude.
My beloved had a vine on a fertile slope;
he expected fine grapes from it,
and it yielded fruit a hundredfold.
For the vine of the all-powerful Lord
is Jesus Christ, the beloved Son,
whose shoots we are
for the glory of the Father!

THURSDAY OF THE 20TH WEEK

THE WICKED ARE NOT MIGHTIER THAN THE GOOD

Ezekiel 36:23–28. While Ezekiel was quick to reveal to the people the punishments their infidelity had merited, he was equally quick to comfort them during their wretched exile. Above all, he explained God's action by stressing the point that Yahweh's honor was at stake. For in fact the nations saw the exile simply as proof that the Lord was powerless to protect his own. Thus Israel had contributed to "profaning the Lord's name among the nations." As a result, God now had to manifest his holiness by intervening in the history of the world and bringing his people back to the land of their ancestors.

Ezekiel's oracle here further specifies that of Jeremiah 31. Jeremiah had said that God would put his law in the hearts of human beings; Ezekiel advances further along this anthropological line and says in effect that God will give Israel a new life. A new people will emerge from his hands, a people with a heart of flesh and a renewed spirit; a people made unclean by idolatry will be cleansed by lustral water.

Psalm 51 quite naturally raises to God the supplication of human beings: "God, create a clean heart in me."

Matthew 22:1–14. Cf. p. 233.

■

Table of the covenant, wedding garment, marriage of the Son with the human race: everything in Scripture focuses on this unparalleled revelation that God loves human beings to the point of making them his allies, his children. A covenant of love and life, a wedding banquet, of which the Eucharist is the sacrament: such is God's dream, and this dream has become flesh in Jesus Christ.

For much too long, Israel understood this covenant as meaning a war in behalf of God, a testimony given in the face of the world, a politics of faith against wickedness, but also a certain pride in being the chosen people. It took the exile and, before that, the destruction of the holy city for faith to get back to the paths of humility, and for the covenant to regain the paths of the heart. What impression can be made on the world by a Eucharist to which the wicked as well as the good are invited, so that all may be sanctified by the body of the Beloved who surrendered to love unto the utmost? Here, everything is a matter of the heart.

Nonetheless, God values—if we may so put it—his good name among the nations. His ways are not those of a beaten dog. But the holiness, the glory and the presence of God have nothing in common with human triumphs. He does not gain the upper hand by crushing his

enemies; he manifests himself in the radiance of pure hearts which contemplate and reveal him. God's domain on our planet takes the form not of an impregnable fortress but of a shifting wilderness in which he can speak to the human heart. "I am going to gather you together," God says, "and you shall be my people," but this people will quickly set out on the roads of humanity in order to live the covenant in the hearts of the poor—right in the midst of the wilderness.

It is important to God, then, that his faithful should be endowed with a new heart, a heart of flesh and love. It is important to him that the wedding garment be kept holy, even though in contact with the dirt of the world. In order to re-establish his people God addresses himself to everyman, but this everyman must be willing to be cleansed from head to toe. The Eucharist, in which the Church finds daily renewal, welcomes the good and the wicked, in order to renew them all in the creative love that transforms hearts by giving them a share in the pierced heart of Christ.

Such is the people of the covenant, a small people in which the elect are few in number. For how can a Church that is called to reveal God's holiness carry out its mission if each member can do as he wants, under the pretext that after all he belongs to the people of God? A holy Church is a Church in which each member is willing to be daily sanctified from head to toe by the love of Christ. Unfortunately, those who are that conscious of their poverty are few in number.

■

Father, make your name holy
  on our earth today
  as you made it holy
  through your Son's love on the cross.
Put a new heart in us
  that we may reflect your presence
  despite our poverty
Make us the chosen people,
  not because of our strength or our merits
  but solely through the grace of your holiness.

A MIGHTY WIND ACROSS A CEMETERY

Ezekiel 37:1–14. A valley filled with dry bones: to the ancients, who felt the lack of burial as a great misfortune, the image was an impressive one. In any case, it shows the state of mind of those deported to Babylon. For them Israel no longer existed.

But God had said: "I shall put my spirit in you" (36:27). This was a promise of life, for the breath that enters into the bones is the same breath of life that Yahweh had breathed into the human body during the opening days of creation. The bones come alive and join together, fleshless ghosts that quickly regain sinews and skin. Men and women stand up, join hands and dash into a joyous dance; they rise up to sing the canticle of life, for love has once more proved stronger than death.

Psalm 107, which takes the form of a hymn, expresses both the disarray of the Jews, who are scattered throughout a foreign land, and the trust in Yahweh which the best of them always retained. Vv. 6–7, in particular, express the feelings of the eternal nomad who is attracted by urban civilization.

Matthew 22:34–40. Cf. p. 237.

■

Not even a cemetery:
  no bones set in order,
  no names incised in stone,
  no flowers to express hope;
  only the gray, dead dust,
  and some bones, thrown there,
  anonymous, tossed away.

Not even a cemetery,
  but only a fetid charnel-house,
  a concentration of exiles,
  children of barbed wire
  and ominous night.

424

Son of Man,
  can these bones live again?

Valley of despair,
  annihilation of a people.
The star of David is extinguished
  and the survivors of death wander aimlessly,
  without father, without home.

Son of Man,
  I am going to send my breath,
  and the dead will rise up,
for these bones
  are the house of Israel.

■

Breath,
  come from the four winds,
  breathe upon these dead and they shall live.

The breath entered into them and they lived:
  they stood upright,
  a vast army.

■

My people, I shall open your graves,
  I shall lead you back to the land of Israel.
Oracle of the Lord!

For I am the resurrection of life!

Blessed be God
  who has raised up his people:
those who sow in tears
  shall sing as they reap.

■

People of God, people of the wind,
  wild, never tamed, unpredictable;

people of prophets,
   people who carry the word of another;
people of God:
   arise like a storm-wind over the dead.
People reborn from the breath of God,
   people who are alive,
people of God:
   love to your last breath,
   love and never grow weary.

SATURDAY OF THE 20TH WEEK

THE GLORY OF GOD COMES TO US

Ezekiel 43:1–7a. Fourteen years have passed since the fall of Jerusalem. Fourteen years, that is, time enough to suggest the completion of Israel's punishment. Throughout these years the prophet has continued to preach hope to the deportees. Someday the ancient covenant formula will be revived: "You shall be my people and I will be your God" (36:28). The hearts of stone will then have given place to hearts of flesh, and all of Israel will be purified.

Then the Glory of Yahweh, which had left Jerusalem and accompanied the Jews into their exile (10:18–22; 11:22–25), will be able to return to its temple and live forever among the children of Israel. Ezekiel foresees that this glory will return by the eastern door of the temple, that is, by way of the Mount of Olives. In fact, when Jesus enters Jerusalem sitting on an ass, he will come down from Bethany, but on that day his body, soon to be handed over, will have replaced the temple of stone. He will forever be Emmanuel who came to pitch his tent among men.

Psalm 85. The oracle expresses the hope created by God's intervention in history: the hope of nothing less than the reconciliation of heaven and earth.

Matthew 23:1–12. Cf. p. 240.

■

To the east of the city, on the side toward the rising sun, the Glory of God appears. At the top of the hill, mounted on the foal of an ass, the Son of God shines with a new light. He comes; he descends to meet a people made up of the lowly, and all acclaim him. In the background, for once in almost the last place, stand the scribes and the Pharisees, the teachers and doctors in their long robes. They toss their heads. Of what glory are these ignorant folk singing, and what are these hosannas for a prophet already condemned to death?

Second act! The Glory of God has just entered the temple through the eastern gate. The crowd gathers on the square, an immense throng of the helpless and the sick. And Jesus cures them. Here is the man who expels traders and money-changers; he wants the Father's glory to receive homage from naught but the faith of the lowly and the poor. But the high priests and the scribes grind their teeth: What is this teaching that is contrary to all tradition, and this violation of the sacred place? Is it not they who are the masters and doctors of religion?

Third act! The glory of the Lord fills the entire temple, and yet the Son of Man is going off to another hill, outside the city, carrying the cross on which he is to be tormented. On his face shines the Glory of God, and yet it is the face of a leper, an outcast. They come to Golgotha. First, the rabbis and the fathers of the people; they are sneering. They have tied the burden on the shoulders of the Innocent One and are bidding the executioners do their work—the work of death.

At the moment when Jesus surrenders his breath to God, the veil of the temple will be torn from top to bottom, and the glory of God will forever leave the sacred place that is soon to be in ruins. The throne of the Eternal One will forever be a cross—a cross on which the Son, full of grace and truth, tells us: "Nor must you allow yourselves to be called teachers . . . and the greatest among you must be your servant."

For man alive is God's glory, and life consists in the love that makes all of us brothers and sisters. The temple of God is now the body of the Beloved, in which all are called to the same service. Each morning, from the East, where the sun rises, the glory of God comes to us. Look, the Master and Lord is mounted on the foal of an ass!

■

Lord and Master,
all that you say, you do;
the burden you lay on our shoulders
you carried first;
the Commandment you impose on us
you lived to the full.
Keep us faithful to your teaching;
preserve us from all pride.
And among us let there be no father
but yours,
our heavenly Father
who makes us all brothers and sisters.
May our glory be to serve,
as you served your disciples,
you who are our Lord and our God
forever and ever.

FROM MONDAY TO SATURDAY OF THE 21ST WEEK

A Different Wisdom

This week brings the somewhat abrupt end of the continuous reading of Matthew in the weekday lectionary. Only a few fragments of the final chapters are set before us. They are, however, very beautiful ones and, taken in conjunction with the texts being read from Paul (2 Thessalonians and the beginning of 1 Corinthians), present us with some pearls of Gospel wisdom.

We will doubtless find the tone adopted by Jesus toward the Pharisees to be extremely harsh. He utters violent denunciations of their hypocrisy. But the truth of religion is at issue: too many unjustified laws, too many soul-less attitudes are in danger of daily turning from God those who cannot understand such a distortion of the word. There must be ceaseless denunciation of a religion that is no longer a wisdom about life but a legalistic burden and an abominable front for important people.

In contrast to these men, "the Kingdom of heaven is like ten bridesmaids who spent the night watching in order to greet the bridegroom . . . or like faithful servants who make the grace they have received bear fruit." Truly we pass here from one world into another that is quite different, from the atmosphere of death that is cultivated by the scribes, to a hope-filled wisdom that is sung in the Gospel.

Not that the Gospel is a daydream, an escape. Jesus constantly urges his followers to be watchful and to toil, and Paul does not beat around the bush: "Let no one have any food if he refuses to do any work." But this toil, this watchfulness, this continual alertness to the return of the Master have naught to do with a nervous tension that would weigh on us like a slave's yoke: if our hearts keep watch and our hands work, it is out of love for him who has given us everything: his grace and his word.

"You are the saints of God, chosen, elected, sanctified," says the Apostle. But we are not better than others, and among us there are very few remarkable people; our glory is in God, our wisdom is rooted in the cross, and our hope comes after a long night. Each morning the dawn tells that God's future is with us. We are not Pharisees; we have doubtless but a small talent, but it is our joy to make it bear fruit—a joy all the greater because we are well aware that our very efforts are already the fruit of grace. We are like young bridesmaids who are asked only to keep their lamps lit, even if they should fall asleep when the night becomes too long.

MONDAY OF THE 21ST WEEK

AGAINST HYPOCRITICAL LAWS

2 Thessalonians 1:1–5, 11b–12. The thanksgiving of 2 Thessalonians is very like that of 1 Thessalonians; it expresses Paul's joy and gratitude at the progress of the young community. But the joy is somewhat troubled, and the Apostle speaks of persecutions and distress. Is this an allusion to difficulties that attended on the foundation of this Church? This answer is possible when we take into account the obstacles which the synagogues soon began to put in the way of the spread of the Gospel. But the contents of the Letter and the doubts raised about its authenticity also suggest that the disorders of which the Letter speaks may have been the animated discussion regarding the end of time. In any case, the thanksgiving ends with a stirring call to perseverance.

Psalm 96 bids us sing a new song to the Lord. The Thessalonians, who have just discovered the marvelous deeds of God, must have been serious about putting this advice into practice.

Matthew 23:13–22. Cf. p. 244.

■

On Psalm 96

Sing to the Lord a new song,
offer him faith-inspired thanksgiving,
bless him with all who serve him,
sing to him with all his faithful,
repeat his wonderful deeds day after day.

■

Casuistry, that is, the study of the many individual cases that can come up in moral or religious life, is not bad in itself, provided it helps people live their faith in the various vicissitudes of life. But what a mess when casuistry becomes an end in itself and especially when it begins to evade the spirit of the law and to make situations better serve those who can profit from them. Just think back to the "servile works" that are prohibited on Sunday and the pastimes that are considered legitimate: you cannot darn stockings but you can embroider a doily. Obviously, since the poor have a greater need of stockings than of doilies, casuistry here profited certain circles: the fashionable world frequented by the Pharisees.

The hyprocrisy which Jesus attacks is specifically a false judgment, a judgment that aims too low. And that is precisely the fault of the Pharisees of every age. Such people are not necessarily crafty folk; they are simply extremely bad interpreters of Scripture. They have lost the key of the Kingdom but continue to teach without rhyme or reason. There are, of course, Pharisees in every area of human and social life, but those of religion are particularly deplorable. They deal with God the way one would haggle with a tradesman, or even go so far as to attribute to God laws which our heavenly Father would be incapable of imposing. As a result we have seen piles of completely hypocritical laws attributed to God.

It all seems laughable, but Jesus bewailed it. For in the final analysis the victims in this business are the good people who know no better. In their view, if the Pharisees said it (substitute for "Pharisees" whatever title is appropriate in your situation), then it must be true. The result: these good people are entangled in chains that are as heavy as they are harmful. Need we look for any other explanation of the morbid sense of guilt that so often holds sway in religious circles? A real hell for those who no longer know where they are at, except that they imagine God to be a fickle master and perhaps even a tormentor.

Woe to you, hypocritical Pharisees! For the worst result of your hypocrisy is that too many good people have abandoned the Church, persuaded that if they are to be free they must look elsewhere.

■

God, you give life to human beings,
and you judge us by our love;
keep us from seeking our justification
in all-too-human laws,
for your Son Jesus
summed up the entire law
in love of you and of our brethren.
Teach us to love without counting the cost,
and may your salvation be ours,
in the name of your Son Jesus
who is the Christ and our Lord.

TUESDAY OF THE 21ST WEEK

AGAINST RELIGIOUS TRANCES

2 Thessalonians 2:1–3a, 14–17. "Do not get excited too soon." 2 Thessalonians gives us a glimpse of the feverish state of mind which the expectation of Christ's return caused among the first Christians. This expectation inevitably brought some disorder, since there were Christians who, convinced of the imminence of the return, cast off the constraints of everyday life and even claimed a delusory freedom from obligations.

Was the Christian community to be transformed into an "adventist" sect? Realizing the danger, Paul reacts by calling his disciples back to a more serene and balanced view of things. He urges them in particular to cling faithfully to the traditions he himself has received from the primitive Church and which he has passed on to them. It is there that the truth is to be found; it is there too that consolation is to be had.

Psalm 96 continues (cf. Monday), mingling mythological elements with a message addressed to the nations: "Yahweh is king." Note that while the Lord comes and stirs up joy on earth, the world itself abides immovably. The words contain an allusion to the Lordship of Yahweh who keeps the world safe from the primeval chaos.

Matthew 23:23–26. Cf. p. 246.

■

On Psalm 96

God has made a covenant with heaven and earth;
never again will chaos disrupt order.
Let human beings therefore respect the universe,
work it and transform it,
and so discover the hidden sign
of God the Creator.

■

No one knows the day or the hour. The coming of the Lord is not fixed to a foreseeable date; it takes place at every moment, as the hidden face of everything that comes. Jesus does not come to put an end to this world; he comes to turn our history into a different world, one in which righteousness and mercy hold sway. We are not therefore to expect any new revelation, since the entire program of his coming is written in the Gospel. It is by holding fast to the tradition of the living word that we will renew the face of the earth, not by taking flight into the future, in search of an unforeseeable end of the world. The world ends each day and begins anew each day, and even our death will be simply a revelation of what we already experience. Everything—past, present and future—has been recapitulated in Jesus Christ. The law governing the future is the one already written in his everlasting word: Love one another as I have loved you. And those who fulfill this law are already bringing human history to its completion, for in every act of justice, charity, tenderness and hope Jesus comes. There is no other coming to look forward to.

There is, however, a more subtle danger to our faith: to imagine that Christ has returned here or there, in a manner different from his daily return. People say he has returned to so-and-so or in this or that sect. Don't go running off to them, says St. Paul. For the unfortunate thing about these individuals or sects is that (according to them) the Lord returns only in order to take people away from their human tasks. The whole business is a vast exercise in hypnotizing people. This represents a serious danger to faith, since faith has meaning only in the midst of the world. Far better for the health of the world and of religion is the father of a family who toils courageously or a mother who lives her conjugal life fully, than a camp swarming with layabouts gathered around a Christ who has been emptied of his meaning. Yes, the Gospel is realistic. This is why it keeps telling us that no one knows the day or the hour; there is no other hour but the present one with its burden of human life. Everything else is a stupid dream—unless it has already reached the stage of mental derangement.

■

We give you thanks, O God,
  for you take our life seriously!
When you came among us
  it was to work with your human hands
  and to speak to ordinary people.
You did not create any universe
  apart from our history,
but instead you humbly opened a breach
  in our daily toil.
We believe
  that today as always

you come, you are present
wherever human beings carry on
their human work in faith and hope.
Grant us, then, to sing to you
the daily song of our life
and to bless you
with the simple words of our faith.

WEDNESDAY OF THE 21ST WEEK

AGAINST MORTUARY INFECTIONS

2 Thessalonians 3:6–10, 16–18. As he will do on a number of occasions, Paul puts himself forward as an example. When he preached at Thessalonica he did not want to be a burden to anyone, and therefore he worked with his hands. In so doing, he showed himself faithful to the rabbinical tradition which required future doctors of the law to apprentice themselves to a trade. The example of the Apostle was, however, a revolutionary one in the pagan world, which scorned manual work and left it to slaves.

Paul will on several occasions speak of his satisfaction at not having been a burden to others, thus emphasizing the independence of his preaching. But he does not make this practice an absolute rule. He thinks that the Gospel worker has a right to a wage, and he himself has accepted aid in special circumstances, as for example when the Philippians sent him to evangelize Thessalonica. In any case, what he wants here is a return to calm. Christians are to work: they will thus occupy their minds and quiet their imaginations.

Psalm 128 provides a way of congratulating workers. It brings together several congratulatory formulas which the priest on duty used in welcoming pilgrims. The Psalm even records, as a valuable aid to memory, the formula of blessing.

Matthew 23:27–32. Cf. p. 248.

■

On Psalm 128

May they who walk with God live happily.
May they who work with their hands experience peace.
And may a blessing be on their homes,
their place of repose.

■

They decorate the tombs of the righteous and whitewash men's
sepulchers. You'd almost think them to be cemetery-keepers.
Perhaps they are. They are constantly recalling the past, but in order
better to crush the prophets of the day. They themselves are now
nothing more than heaps of bones, real walking dead men beneath
the glitter of the uniform. Look at their heads: death-heads! In
addition, all the preparations have been made for the assassination of
Jesus the prophet: a legal death, of course, in accordance with the
laws of the past. But the body of Christ will have to be wrested from
them lest it end up in the common grave. Only later on will other
Pharisees decorate his tomb in Jerusalem. Still others will bury the
Gospel in their ossuaries, lest it begin to revive. After all, you never
know!

Obviously, in order to account for this connivance between the
Pharisees and death, we must scratch away the surface veneer. The
uniform has always been an imposing one. These are apparently
upright men. How are we to get inside them? Perhaps we must do it
by breathing in deeply their musty smell of death until it nauseates
us. Yes, they are always busy cutting away at life; their righteousness
will allow no one to live, and by "living" we mean here appreciating
life. The only words in their mouths are: "You cannot; that is not
allowed." They always oppose you with a legal text when life suggests
that you strike out on unknown paths. Above all, they do not tolerate
prophets, those who allow God to speak in them as he wishes; they
have even locked God in their mortuary chapels, with lots of flowers
to overcome the smell of the past and the deceased. For they
obviously look on themselves as sole trustees of the present, and they
will not allow themselves to be treated as mummies.

Perhaps you have met such people. If someday you meet a man, a
dignitary, a master of the type I have described, do not doubt: he is

surely a Pharisee. Then be off with you quickly, for he already has your coffin within reach.

■

O Christ, who have come forth from the tomb,
* you are forever on the side of life;*
each day your resurrection is
* the dawn of a new hope for us.*
We thank you
* and we pray you:*
let our faith never experience
* the degradation of death,*
but keep us, Lord,
* alive and creative*
in this world and for eternity.

THURSDAY OF THE 21ST WEEK

FOR A HOLINESS ON THE ALERT

1 Corinthians 1:1–9. When Paul writes to the Church of Corinth, the community there is being torn by divisions. Not only are several tendencies agitating it, but it is also being influenced by the surrounding paganism. Knowing this, we will not be surprised by the Apostle's emphasis on union with the person of Christ. For Greek philosophy does not completely liberate the human person, any more than the Jewish law did; the cross alone is the real source of salvation, and Paul can therefore tell the "saints" of Corinth that they owe their sanctification to Christ and to no one else. This communion, this sharing of life, was the object of the covenant promises; their fulfillment shows the fidelity of the God of the covenant.

Psalm 145 belongs to the category of hymns. It blesses the Lord for his greatness and splendor, his works and marvelous deeds. How thankfully the Christian, who has seen the salvation of God, should praise the Lord!

Matthew 24:42–51. Cf. p. 251.

■

The Church of God is not a rest home, and those whom Paul the Apostle addresses as "saints" do not resemble the shoddy statues from which even the neediest thief would turn away. The saints, who are enriched by all the grace they have received from the risen Christ, resemble rather the watchful and judicious servants to whom the master can unhesitatingly entrust the management of all his possessions. Yes, the Church of the saints is an active and stable house, always on the alert to make the talents received as an inheritance bear fruit.

But who are these "saints," this "holy people," these faithful whom the Apostle congratulates and for whom he gives thanks? They are simply you and I, the Christians of yesterday's Corinth and of today's countless communities. They are not always exemplary believers: a reading of the First Letter to the Corinthians makes that clear. And yet they are saints of God, for this holiness is first of all a call, a grace, a gift; only then is it a fidelity that must be constantly renewed.

To be holy does not mean resting on faded laurels; it means being vigilant in love and in conversion.

The Church of God is holy. The inheritance it has received is a vast treasure, nothing less than the body of the risen Christ. But we are not to preserve the body of Christ the way a museum curator watches over his antiquities. Holiness is not preserved in the way in which some people shelter their only too weak virtue. The Church of God is holy in the measure of the action it engages in to make the seed received bear much fruit. And no action is totally pure, especially as the centuries lengthen out and it becomes necessary to be constantly inventing a sanctity suited to today. The body of Christ is not a statue; it is a body made up of men and women in whom the Spirit dwells. That is quite a different matter.

Brothers and sisters, make sure you understand the parable of the thief. What would he find in our Church, this thief in the night who observes us so that he may break through the wall of our building? If he were to find in us only a jealously guarded holiness, then let him come and take it all away. And if he finds us sleeping, even on our good conscience, then let us give thanks for this salutary awakening.

But that image doesn't describe the real situation. It is the body of Christ that the thieves whom our faith disturbs would like to take away and hide. They prowl about trying to cut the Church off from its source and to reduce it to a museum in which an ancient religion is kept. Let us therefore be on the watch. On Golgotha no one was able to lay a hand on the beloved body. Let us keep watch night and day with Mary of Magdala. In the morning, when the Master comes, let him find us actively loving and hoping. Sanctity has no other true name except love and hope. And the Church has no other reason for its existence.

■

Lord Jesus
you make us, here, in this place,
  your holy Church;
you call us as we are
  and you sanctify us by your word.
We call upon your name
  from which ours is derived:
keep us blameless
  for the day when you will come
  to require an account of our love.
May that love be daily without limit,
  since you never cease to give us
  your grace
  which is as endless as eternity.

FRIDAY OF THE 21ST WEEK

WISDOM IS FILLED WITH LOVE

1 Corinthians 1:17–25. The Letter calls attention to the difficulties that the Christian mission encountered as soon as it came in contact with the Hellenistic milieu. Like all Greeks, the Corinthians were enamored of philosophy; in addition, the cosmopolitan character of the city had led to a multiplication of schools. The people of Corinth were thus bent on finding a doctrine that would satisfy the intellect. In this they were really not different from the Jews, who were constantly on the watch for signs that would ensure the truth of the Gospel. Essentially both groups made some form of human guarantee a necessary preliminary.

People also faulted Paul for his lack of eloquence; it seems that at Corinth his preaching cut a poor figure alongside that of Apollos, the brilliant Alexandrian orator. But Paul speaks a different language: the language of the cross. He does not scorn human studies, but neither does he think that divine wisdom will emerge at the end of a reasoning process. In his view, this wisdom is of a different order than human categories; it is a gift, and the person must receive it into the heart. This wisdom has found its perfect expression in the cross of Jesus Christ, which is the sign of a love given without reserve, a sign too that greatness is found in littleness. Can the wisdom of the world grasp this if left to its own powers?

Psalm 33, a hymn, praises the works of God. His thoughts are different from those of men; this is why he can "thwart the plans of nations, frustrate the intentions of peoples."

Matthew 25:1–13. Cf. p. 254.

■

The Jews demand signs, striking miracles, proofs. The Greeks demand a wisdom, reasoning, logic. And the Gospel refers us to ten young bridesmaids—and even then five of them are hardly to be called wise. These young women keep watch or fall asleep because the wedding party is delayed, thus holding up a dance! Really, there must be something mad about the God of the Gospel. Why should the preaching of the Gospel be burdened with a story about a bridegroom and some business or other with oil lamps? Today many serious minds once again are calling for a true wisdom and a solidly constructed catechism. But please, no stories about bridesmaids!

What does the Gospel proclaim? The cross of Christ, and nothing else, is Paul's answer. But the cross is likewise a story. I am aware that the catechisms have built a theory of redemption on it, but there is no avoiding the fact that the cross of Jesus Christ is first of all the flesh and blood story of a man who loved to the utmost and who in his

own story has revealed to us the face of God. Recall, furthermore, that it was women above all who stood at the foot of the cross. And the first proclamation of the Gospel came from Mary Magdalene, a woman and surely a loving one. Well, then? Are not the young women of the Gospel story—the ones with foresight—also loving women, capable of watching until morning for the bridegroom?

The Gospel is not a doctrine; it is a call to love, because it is the word of the God of love. Any doctrine that would claim something different would no longer be Christian. No other sign will be given to human beings than the one that was given to Mary Magdalene; no other wisdom will be set before them except that of the young bridesmaids for the wedding. For it has pleased God to reveal himself to human beings as a bridegroom; faith is a covenant, and its growth and unfolding is a feast. Exhibited on the cross, the Son of God loved the Church to the point of handing over his body for her; by means of his blood that was poured out for the many he sanctified his spouse and invited her to the everlasting covenant feast that goes by the name of the Eucharist.

The madness of God, manifested where the wise of this world saw only the pitiful story of a man condemned to death! But the young women watched throughout the night, nourishing their fidelity at the fountain of love. At dawn on Easter one of them went to the garden and there, in an encounter with love, recognized the bridegroom who was coming. The whole vocation of the Church can be seen in that moment when the Lord says to his beloved: Mary!

■

As wisdom that defies all reason
*   you reveal yourself, Lord,*
*   to the heart that keeps loving watch.*
Keep us vigilant
*   at the foot of the cross*
*   where you give yourself first in love.*
May our heart
*   be at the rendezvous each morning*
*   and hear your love speak*
*   the only word it has for us:*

our name, united to yours
  in an eternal covenant.

■

A cry has sounded in the night.
Keep watch, faithful virgins,
take your lamps
and run to meet the bridegroom.

Here he comes
aureoled with dawn, radiant in the rising sun.
He comes,
he opens the doors of the wedding feast to you.
Enter, come to the feast,
and he will clothe you in his love.

Sleepers, arise!
Was not your heart keeping watch?
Did you not know that night begets day?
Let not boredom extinguish the flame of hope in you.

Come, he knows you;
he knows your name and your longing.
Follow the bent of your heart;
fear not to leave everything for his sake.
The day will be fine
only if you walk with him
toward the light.

Let the feast come,
for God is never dull.
Be wise, be loving!
Love alone is wisdom;
the rest is only death.

Hear the cry in the night—
a cry of life as it comes to the light,
a cry of death as it is conquered on the cross,
a cry of Easter morning,
a cry of the bridegroom who is calling.
Cry out with joy to God!

Rend the night,
open the door to dawn reborn,
enter the dance of the everlasting ages;
do not let night be victorious over love.

SATURDAY OF THE 21ST WEEK

DO NOT BURY LIFE!

1 Corinthians 1:26–31. The difference between divine wisdom and the spirit of the world is illustrated by the social situation of the Corinthian Christians. Most of them were lowly folk, even slaves, and the world was contemptuous of them.

But like all lowly folk they are great in God's eyes. If they do not exist as far as the world is concerned, they exist in Jesus Christ who gave his life for them on the cross. The Corinthians could make their own what the Prologue of John says about all Christians: they are "born not out of human stock or urge of the flesh or will of man but of God himself." They are born of Love. That is their sole claim to glory, and it will not be taken from them.

Psalm 33. These further verses sing of the divine election. Daily life is a life in Christ, the sole source of salvation.

Matthew 25:14–30. Cf. p. 000.

■

Brothers and sisters, look carefully! Open your eyes to your community, your parish, your liturgical assembly. Do not be ashamed to look at one another. You who are called by God, look carefully!

What do you see? People whom the world calls intelligent? Perhaps, but if they are really religious, they will tell you that they are not so very intelligent. People whom the world considers powerful? There may be some, but we hope that they are the first to gauge correctly the weakness of their power. People of high birth? Perhaps, but we are not a club of the nobility or aristocracy, that's for certain!

Look again. What do you see? Many people of modest origins, and even some whom the world judges to be nobodies—the poor, the weak (economically or morally), sinners, people on the borderline, men and women whom fashionable society must regard as somewhat silly, and indeed they must be silly to do what we do. In short, we amount to little, and anyone coming here in the pride of his power or his wealth would be disillusioned at the door.

We will all be justified in minimizing our talents; we have only one talent, and that a very small one . . . unless—unless the Lord decides to fill us with his grace, his love, his life. These are true wealth, and by that measure we are all rich and accountable. The master has entrusted his possessions to us; he has the right to demand an account from us despite our poverty and indigence, because we do not lack his strength and his light. The Church does not conduct its business by means of human power; the Spirit lives in it, and we are responsible to him—Responsible for the fruit he wishes to produce in us.

There is no greater mistake than to lock up one's talent as one would hide a fruitless treasure. Those who do not produce fruit are nobodies, and they will be cast out into the darkness. Let them not protest that they are incapable: our strength is in God, and those who allow the Spirit to act in them will see their inheritance increase, even if at the beginning they had only a rather sorry little talent!

■

You speak to us, Lord;
  you say words of hope to us:
will they find an echo in us
  for the sake of a world in distress?

You speak to us, you fill us;
  you give us your love as our inheritance:
will it yield an abundant fruit
  and revive a barren world?

You fill us, you entrust your name to us,
  you place the future of man in our hands:
will our hands be closed tight
  for fear of losing you?

443

We pray you:
  through your Spirit stimulate us to toil
lest we be condemned
    for our inertia
    when you come to invite us
    to enter into your everlasting joy.

Short Liturgies for the Vacation Period

Do not be afraid of life;
  you were created to invent life.
Do not remain earthbound;
  Christ is leading you higher.

Do not waste your time;
  your inheritance is hidden in God.
A deep breath of fresh air
  is worth more than a strongbox.

Sing in a higher key,
  sing a hymn to life.
Christ is your future;
  he is risen.

■

You did not have time even to eat
  or time to digest . . . .
You toil and grow weary,
  you will never reach old age.

When the time for rest comes,
  will you be able to compose your soul?
To be silent
  and learn to listen . . .
to sleep in peace
  and taste the pleasures of morning . . .

to leave the crowd
  and savor the sweetness of loving . . .
and then to pray
    because a bird has sung in the sky,
    because your look has been met with a smile,
    because the silence is filled with his presence?

■

Leisure time—wasted time?

There are essentials
  and there are accidentals,
a time to work
  and a time to be re-created.

Recreation . . .
We must recover the meaning of words.
The time has come for recreation,
  that is, for re-creation.

In the morning
  may you be blessed by the eyes of a child
  as they open to a festival day
  and by the song of dawn
  as day awakens.

May you be sung and celebrated
  by the breath of wind
  that caresses your hand,
  and by the fiery sun
  that comes to consume our earth.

May the waves of the sea
  with their scintillating pearls
  and the golden stars
  in their infinite heaven
dance till they are breathless.

But above all
  may our hands and our glances,
  our lips and our silences,

445

all so fragile and clumsy,
   meet and join
to embrace this day which your favor gives us,
   in which we shall know,
   in secret and in faith,
   the weight of your tenderness
   and the intoxication of loving.

∎

Blessed be you for the parents and children
   who rediscover the joy of loving without measure,
   as one savors a loaf crisp with tenderness.

Blessed be you for the wondering eyes
   that rediscover the joy of beauty,
   as one savors a wine heady with gladness.

Blessed be you for friends, for meetings,
   for rendezvous when one is uncertain of the morrow,
   as one shares a bread
   one would like to have every day.

Blessed be you for lost paths and foggy mornings,
   for silent nights and mad dances,
   for the cups of wine that make us live again.

∎

We pray you, Lord,
   for those who have no vacation:

the sick who are dying in the cancer hospitals,
   the elderly exhausted
   by the lack of air in their hovels,
   the prisoners who long
   to find hope again through freedom,
   the abandoned, the isolated, for whom no one cares,
   the despairing, those weary of a sad and narrow life.

We pray you for them,
   and we pray you for ourselves.

May our rest give us courage to share suffering,
   may peace regained spread out from us,
   may joy flow in us
   like an abundant fountain
   where those dying of thirst may be refreshed.

■

Lourdes and Taizé,
   Saint-Tropez and Monte Carlo . . .
Whither shall we go to buy bread
   that they may have some to eat?

But why are they hungry?
The dynamics of the provisional,
   the realms of forgetfulness . . .

Give them something to eat yourselves!

■

No one, however strong,
   can, even by force,
   add a single centimeter
   to his height;
no one,
   even by taking care of himself,
   can add a single hour
   to the days of his life.
Why then are you anxious,
   O you of little faith?

For a Continuous Commentary on the Gospel of Matthew

The reader who prefers to focus his meditation on the Gospel of Matthew alone will find help in the commentaries for both the uneven and the even years.

The following table tells him where to find these commentaries. It gives the week and day, the chapter and verses, and the title of the pericope. Pericopes not indicated are those that did not stimulate us to any commentary.

THE SERMON ON THE MOUNT

10 M	5	1–12	Beatitudes
Tu		13–16	Salt of the Earth
W		17–19	Fulfilling the Law
Th		20–26	You Must Not Kill
			The New Virtue
S		33–37	It Is Useless To Swear
11 M		38–42	An Eye for an Eye?
Tu		43–48	Love Your Enemies
W	6	1–18	In Secret
Th		7–15	Our Father
F		19–23	The Treasure and the Heart
S		24–34	Seek the Kingdom
12 Th	7	21–29	Build on Rock

NARRATIVE SECTION OF MIRACLES

12 F	8	1–4	The Leper Cleansed
13 Tu		23–27	Storm on the Lake
W		28–34	The Swine in the Sea
Th	9	1–8	The Paralytic Stands Up
F		9–13	Call of the Tax Collector
S		14–17	New Wine and Fasting
14 M		18–26	Resurrection of a Young Girl
Tu		32–38	The Mute Speak

THE MISSIONARY DISCOURSE

W	10	1–7	The Twelve
Th		7–15	The Twelve on Mission
F		16–23	Servants Like Jesus
S		24–33	Do Not Be Afraid!

JESUS, A SIGN THAT IS TO BE REJECTED

15 Tu	11	20–24	Sodom and Capernaum

W		25–27	The Kingdom Revealed to Mere Children
Th		28–30	Light Burden
S	12	14–21	The Servant of God
16 M		38–42	The Sign of Jonah
Tu		46–50	The Family of Jesus

THE PARABOLIC DISCOURSE

16 W	13	1–9	The Sows
Th		10–17	Speaking in Parables
S		24–30	The Darnel
17 M		31–35	The Smallest Seed
Tu		36–43	The Final Harvest
W		44–46	The Only Treasure
Th		47–53	The Net in the Sea
F		54–58	No One Is a Prophet in His Own Country

BIRTH OF A CHURCH

17 S	14	1–12	Death of John the Baptist
18 M		13–21	Jesus and the Crowd in the Wilderness
Tu		22–36	Calming of the Storm
	15	1–14	Dirty Hands and Pure Heart
W		21–28	The Canaanite Woman
Th	16	13–23	But You, Who Do You Say I Am?
F		24–28	Walk Behind Me!
S	17	14–20	A Lunatic Cured

THE DISCOURSE ON THE CHURCH

19 Tu	18	1–14	The Greatest in the Kingdom
W		15–20	If Your Brother Has Done Wrong
Th		18:21 – 19:1	Pay Your Debt!

THE HOUR OF CHOICE

19 F	19	3–12	Conjugal Love
S		13–15	Do Not Stop the Children!

NOTES

1. J. Radermakers, *Au fil de l'évangile selon saint Matthieu* (Brussels, 1974).

2. X. Leon-Dufour, "Justice, Justification," in his *Dictionary of the New Testament*, tr. by T. Prendergast (San Francisco, 1980), 257.

3. J. Jeremias, *The Lord's Prayer*, tr. by J. Reumann (Philadelphia, 1964), 22–23.

4. J.H. Newman, *Verses on Various Occasions* XC (June 16, 1833).

5. X. Léon-Dufour, "Name," in *op. cit.* (n. 2), 300.

6. G. von Rad, *Genesis: A Commentary*, tr. by J.H. Marks (rev. ed.; Philadelphia, 1972), 325.

7. G. von Rad, *The Problem of the Hexateuch, and Other Essays*, tr. by E.W. Trueman Dicken (New York, 1966), 295.

8. *The Mishnah*, Tractate Pesahim 10, 5; cited in N. Goldberg, *Passover Haggadah* (New York, 1949), 23–24.

9. R. de Vaux, *The Early History of Israel*, tr. by D. Smith (Philadelphia, 1978), 354.

10. *Ibid.*, 355.

11. *Ibid.*, 357.

12. *Ibid.*, 370.

13. *Ibid.*, 384.

14. Goldberg, *op. cit.*, 9.

15. R. de Vaux,Yahweh *op. cit.*, 393.

16. H. Cazelles, *A la recherche de Moïse* (Paris, 1969).

17. R. de Vaux, *op. cit.*, 448–49.

18. R. Schutz, *Ta fête soit sans fin* (Taizé, 1971).

19. Compare the citation at n. 8.

20. Cf. M.-D. Chenu, "Anthropologie de la liturgie," in *La liturgie après Vaticane II* (Unam sanctam 66; Paris, 1967).

21. N. Cabasilas (fourteenth century Orthodox theologian), *A Commentary on the Divine Liturgy*, tr. by J.M. Hussey and P.A. McNulty (London, 1960), 25–26.

22. Antoine de Saint Exupéry, *The Little Prince*, tr. by K. Woods (New York, 1943), 93.

23. B.H. Levy, *The Testament of God*, tr. by G. Holsch (New York, 1980), 130.

24. This homily owes a good deal to G. Bessiere, "Le gué," *La vie spirituelle*, no. 582 (May 1971), 601–03.

25. R. de Vaux, *op. cit.*, 604.

26. This meditation is much indebted to M. Delbrel, *Joies venues de la montagne* (Paris, n.d.).

27. G. von Rad, *Old Testament Theology*, tr. by D.M.G. Stalker (2 vols.; New York, 1962–65), 1:59.

28. W.J. Harrington, *Record of the Promises: The Old Testament* (Chicago, 1965), 353.

29. G. von Rad, *op. cit.*, 2:15.

30. *Ibid.*, 2:29.

31. Concluding Prayer of Thanksgiving in the Rite of Reconciliation of Several Penitents with Individual Confession and Absolution, in *The Rites of the Catholic Church* 1 (New York, 1976), 373–74.